Medicaid Everyone Can Count On

Medicaid Everyone
Can Count On

Public Choices for Equity and Efficiency

Thomas W. Grannemann
and Mark V. Pauly

The AEI Press

Publisher for the American Enterprise Institute

WASHINGTON, D.C.

Distributed to the Trade by National Book Network, 15200 NBN Way, Blue Ridge Summit, PA 17214. To order call toll free 1-800-462-6420 or 1-717-794-3800. For all other inquiries please contact the AEI Press, 1150 Seventeenth Street, N.W., Washington, D.C. 20036 or call 1-800-862-5801.

Library of Congress Cataloging-in-Publication Data

Grannemann, Thomas W.
  Medicaid everyone can count on : public choices for equity and efficiency / Thomas W. Grannemann and Mark V. Pauly.
      p. ; cm.
  Includes bibliographical references and index.
  ISBN-13: 978-0-8447-4311-0
  ISBN-10: 0-8447-4311-9
  1. Medicaid. I. Pauly, Mark V., 1941- II. Title.
  [DNLM: 1. Medicaid—economics. 2. Medicaid. 3. Democracy—United States. 4. Health Care Reform—United States. 5. Policy Making—United States. W 250 AA1 G759m 2009]
  RA412.4.G727 2009
  368.4'200973—dc22
                                                                200904720013
14 13 12 11 10   1 2 3 4 5 6 7

Printed in the United States of America

Contents

List of Illustrations

Acknowledgments

The authors wish to thank John Holahan and Vernon K. Smith for providing detailed reviews on an early draft of this work. While we could not accommodate all of their suggestions, their insights and thoughtful comments were greatly appreciated and contributed much toward the clarity and accuracy of the final product. We thank Alice Mann for her help in editing our working drafts. And we thank the whole team at AEI that supported this book, including Robert Helms, Joseph Antos, Samuel Thernstrom, Laura Harbold, and Lisa Ferraro Parmelee.

Authors' Note

This book is being completed in the fall of 2009, while intensive public debate on national health care reform is still in progress. Medicaid has received relatively little attention in this wide-ranging debate. Nonetheless, congressional leaders now seem to be embracing certain changes in Medicaid as important components of national health care reform. Among other aims, the major proposals on the table at this time attempt to address the health insurance needs of those poor persons who have been excluded from Medicaid's categorical eligibility groups. These proposals tend to rely on existing program models, including Medicaid and the State Children's Health Insurance Program (CHIP), to expand coverage to previously excluded groups, and they recognize that states may need additional federal assistance to induce their participation in any program expansion.

Even as the current legislative process affirms the usefulness of Medicaid as a component of larger reform, it also exposes what has been missing from the Medicaid debate for a very long time: a coherent basis for making the many detailed policy decisions needed to implement policy consistent with basic program objectives. Very specific and detailed decisions such as those about provider payment methods and rates, how service use is managed, and how program costs are divided between the federal government and the states will shape the program of the future and determine its success.

Changes that will emerge from national health care reform offer an opportunity to revisit many of these detailed policy decisions of the past and to craft new solutions more consistent with meeting program goals in today's world. Such decisions—in federal and state laws, regulations, program manuals, and program policy and practices—are needed to define and fulfill the promises of the program to its many stakeholders. These stakeholders include those who receive Medicaid-funded services, those who provide the services, and those who pay for those services through their state and federal taxes.

Fundamental program objectives can get lost in the political process—or even in program implementation. What is needed is a guide to help policymakers adhere to some fundamental principles consistent with program objectives. Without such guideposts, there are risks in a program as complex as Medicaid that implementation efforts will be haphazard, misdirected, politically skewed, or poorly calibrated to bring about the intended results.

One area where providing guideposts is possible is with respect to federal–state financing provisions. In 2009, policymakers struggled to come up with some way to provide assistance to the states to take on new responsibilities, with proposals ranging to up to 100 percent federal financing for new enrollment groups. But little effort was made to precisely calibrate such assistance to compensate effectively for both the needs of the poor and state fiscal capacity. Furthermore, while policymakers understood the need to provide states with additional assistance in times of economic downturn, the process for selecting states for particular assistance was a political one, and the longer-term issue of how to make the program adjust automatically to changing economic conditions seemed to have been considered hardly at all. Federal–state financing is a core Medicaid function that can make or break the program. It deserves more careful attention.

This book provides a framework for thinking clearly about the Medicaid program at an important transitional point in the program's history—a point that offers new opportunities to get things right. This framework gives particular consideration to achieving an equitable distribution of program benefits and costs, encouraging efficient use of limited resources, and making public choices within a democratic process. It recognizes the importance of giving appropriate weight to the interests of all concerned, including program recipients, medical service providers, and taxpayers. A higher level of understanding of fundamental program issues may lead to more effective decisions as policymakers undertake deliberately to refine new plans for Medicaid throughout the process of their development and implementation. Legislation at best provides only a structure within which programs develop and evolve over time. We hope this book will help guide policymakers toward more effective solutions as part of that ongoing process. Whatever the product of this round of health care reform, the fundamental underlying problems and the approaches to finding solutions that we raise here will have continued importance for decades to come.

Introduction

As the nation's principal federal–state program for financing medical care for the poor, Medicaid has always been subject to economic and political influences. In the best of times, the economy is strong, state budgets are flush, Medicaid caseloads are steady or dropping, payment rates are increased, policymakers look to expand eligibility—and the states turn to the federal government for additional funds to help expand the program. In the worst of times, the economy is weak, state revenues are down, Medicaid caseloads are growing, provider payment rates may be cut, policymakers look to curtail eligibility—and the states, hoping to avoid major program cuts, turn to the federal government for additional funds to keep the program going. Federal policymakers, pressed with their own budget concerns, are continually frustrated that state Medicaid demands seem unending. The recurring political discontent, disequilibrium, and instability have led many of Medicaid's stakeholders to conclude that the program is not one they can always count on.

Federal and state policymakers have, over the years, engaged in nearly constant struggles over Medicaid budgets and continual debates over program specifics related to eligibility and benefits. In this environment, Medicaid has often been perceived as unstable in the sense that it cannot always be relied upon to meet fully the needs of the poor or the intentions of the voter-taxpayers to whom it must account. We can never seem to get it quite right—that is, to make all the program elements come together in a consistent and predictable way to produce the intended result. What are we missing?

In our view, perpetual dissatisfaction with Medicaid is symptomatic of a program structure that, almost by design, creates tensions among federal and state policymakers, the voter-taxpayers they represent, medical service providers of all kinds, and the low-income persons the program serves. In this book, we suggest an approach to resolving these tensions by applying

1

principles of equity, efficiency, and democracy. Refining Medicaid's structure in these ways should reduce the amplitude of expansions and retrenchments and provide a degree of political stability that will allow recipients, taxpayers, and providers alike to have a dependable, accountable program that ensures value and provides high-quality health coverage to the nation's poor.

We suggest that, with respect to the policymaking process, "how we think about Medicaid" may matter as much as "what Medicaid actually is." Medicaid is commonly thought of in programmatic terms, with reference to its authorizing legislation, federal regulations, state rules, budgets, administrative agencies and bureaus, contractors, participating providers, and recipients. This programmatic view may help us understand the program's basic elements, how it is funded, and even how it functions, but it can limit our thinking. It may not be the best conceptual framework for really understanding what Medicaid represents in our national health care system and what it reflects about our nation's underlying values and priorities, nor is it the best model for helping us discern realistic opportunities for changes that might better meet our national goals and public priorities. In this work, we want to sidestep the usual programmatic conceptual framework and propose a different model for a renewed public discussion about the future of the Medicaid program, and perhaps about health care financing more broadly.

Rather than talking about it as a set of program components, we view Medicaid in terms of its public promises and some key principles. The promises include addressing the medical care needs of the poor, to be sure, but they also include promises to the providers who deliver services, promises to the states that take responsibility for implementing the program, and, perhaps most importantly, promises to the voter-taxpayers who pay for the program, without whose support it would not exist and could not be maintained. While one might consider Medicaid in terms of any number of principles, we choose to focus on three that are central to program policy: equity, efficiency, and democracy.

Much of Medicaid policy, then, is about deciding what promises to make and how best to keep them in accordance with these widely accepted principles or public values. Promises should be made judiciously and communicated clearly; they should not be open-ended, promising more benefits to more people, ever-lower state costs, continuous fiscal gains to taxpayers, or higher and higher payments to providers. Public spending on Medicaid must balance costs and benefits. Our objective here is to help policymakers see more clearly the opportunities for making Medicaid promises consistent with voter preferences and their willingness to pay for the program.

Policymakers should be keenly aware that there must be tradeoffs among Medicaid promises. Our approach seeks a balance in meeting the needs and expectations of Medicaid's various stakeholder groups. Our inclusion of the concept of promises to taxpayers implies limits on what recipients and providers can expect. As is true with other programs, some elected representatives may find short-term political gains in overpromising to constituents. This is easy when political accountability is weak; any sanctions for broken promises must wait for the next election, and such delays make unlikely the careful comparison of promises and outcomes. We suggest instead a set of institutionalized "rules of the game" that stakeholders can count on for both support and constraint. In such a framework, each promise must have resources and incentives for fulfillment already in place. Indeed, the structure we seek meets program objectives but is self-limiting, avoiding impossible demands from any of the key constituencies. Our framework for analysis, which is based on a model of public choices, can provide a useful way for policy analysts to look at Medicaid and a foundation for principled policymaking. We hope our analysis and suggestions will help state and federal policymakers, who must deal with multiple political forces, to find compromises more consistent with the principles of equity, efficiency, and democracy.

We begin by describing how citizens may think about what the Medicaid program is—its purpose, how it is supposed to work, what it is supposed to achieve. We then observe that the ability of the program to do consistently what we want it to do has been seriously compromised from the start, despite substantial stability in its authorizing legislation. Specifically, the program has not provided a set of desirable binding assurances or commitments to Americans. It has not assured low-income people that they will have access to good-quality medical care. It has not assured the providers of care—including hospitals, doctors, and drug companies—that they will be paid in a way that makes it possible for them to continue supplying what has been promised to recipients. Finally, it has not assured taxpaying voters, who are asked to support Medicaid at both the state and the federal levels, that the program can be counted on to produce good value by providing the medical care access they want to furnish to people who are poor or needy, and by doing so at an affordable cost to taxpayers. The problem is partly temporal: What Medicaid costs and how it grows can gyrate widely over time, as a function both of the economy's business cycle and the fiscal fortunes of individual states. Less obviously, perhaps, but even more importantly, the current structure of the program and incentives is not conducive to political predictability and voter comfort. Instead, it leads to program choices that are uncertain, tentative, changeable, and ultimately unsatisfying to many, even in times of fiscal stability for the states. Fluctuations in a state's economy magnify underlying problems in its Medicaid program.

In this book, we highlight the promises of Medicaid and the importance of making and fulfilling them in a manner consistent with public values and private resources. Which promises our nation chooses to make, and the balance it strikes among them, defines the nature and scope of the program. In a chicken-and-egg relationship, Medicaid's promises to its various stakeholders both define and reflect the values of our nation and its people. Medicaid promises embody the answer to the question: What do we as a people really want for our poor, for those who provide them care, and for our taxpayers—indeed, for all Americans?

Although Medicaid's promises to recipients, taxpayers, and providers must be limited, we do not view them as static. Rather, these assurances should change in response to changing circumstances that affect needs, resources, and public preferences for what the program should do. Nonetheless, Medicaid's fundamental promises and commitments should not be compromised by the short-term whims of circumstance, whether in response to macroeconomic cycles or political agendas. Such changes, which are largely external to the social goals sought for Medicaid and the long-term resources available to meet those goals, ought not to sway the program from its fundamental purpose. These variations should be reasonably anticipated and planned for.

Medicaid needs a structure, in other words, to keep it linked to long-run goals and resources, and to change only when these deep preferences and constraints change, not when other political or economic winds shift. Indeed, if the program is best to meet its objectives, its commitments (or promises) *must* be redefined and managed effectively over time. Its current structure does not always help this to happen in ways that are true to the democratic process, that are in accordance with equity for recipients and providers, and that ensure accountability to taxpayers for resources used.

The framework we present is grounded in the theory of public choice, a field of study that spans parts of both economics and political science. Its key tenet is that choices about public spending should reflect voter-tax-payer preferences and resource constraints. We suggest these preferences are the bedrock on which Medicaid rests, and to which it ought to conform. In this regard, all decisions about Medicaid, including those pertaining to eligibility, benefits, provider payment rates, and budgets, ought to reflect voter preferences and, we would argue, the commitments or promises voters are willing to make at any given time to the poor and providers, in return for the indirect value they receive from the program as a public good. In this book we hope to help policymakers understand the significance of these promises more fully and to see the implications for key Medicaid policy choices. Our theme is that some parameters of the program have been set at levels that lead to inequities, inefficiencies, and instability. Alter these parameters, and Medicaid will be more likely to produce promises and commitments that are stable, achievable, and more consistent with the program's fundamental purposes.

Our first book on Medicaid policy was published in 1983, when the program was eighteen years old. Medicaid has grown substantially since then and now covers more people for more services at a greater cost than ever before. It is still the centerpiece of the nation's approach to financing medical care for the poor and, in many ways, quite successful at achieving its major goals. Given the changes in U.S. health care of the past twenty-six years, it is surprising how little its basic structure has changed, and how little change there has been in the major issues the program faces. *Controlling Medicaid Costs* was the title of our first book, and "controlling Medicaid costs" is perhaps still the most perplexing policy issue today. The basic federal–state partnership remains in place, and the program continues to be funded through a matching-rate formula (for federal payments to states) which, except for temporary adjustments, has remained essentially unchanged.

While state and federal policymakers continue to debate many of the same Medicaid policy issues, the health care system has seen both technological change and the development, growth, and almost continuous restructuring of the industry. The changes have led to integrated health insurance plans that employ an ever-changing variety of approaches to care management, networks of providers adept at maximizing reimbursements, and a pharmaceutical industry that is now a much more significant part of the system and its costs. All of the major players on this stage are fully cognizant of the role of public programs, especially Medicare and Medicaid, in determining their revenue, and are adept at making their voices heard in the policy process.

The Medicaid program has shown remarkable political resilience in the face of continuous public controversy. It has survived the coming and going of managed care, proposals for its replacement (such as President Bill Clinton's effort to pass a national Health Security Act), and numerous attempts to limit federal payments to the states. Only recently, in the context of the Medicare Part D drug benefit, was the program's role notably reduced—though just for drugs, and just for the dual-eligible population. It seems that Medicaid embodies a basic political bargain made at its inception that cannot easily be upset by any one interest group. But we also believe, as we did when we wrote our earlier book, that some features of that political bargain are dysfunctional, and that mutual benefit (for taxpayers, recipients, providers, and policymakers) could derive from certain changes. We think now, as we thought then, that the "rules and rewards of the game" for this program might be modified to attain substantial and general additional benefit.

Our first study provided a mixed review of the Medicaid program's structure. While we saw value in its fiscal federalism framework, we thought then, and think now, that aspects of the design and parameters of that framework ought to be changed. With this work we update our thinking and offer some new suggestions for an improved approach to Medicaid, one that can lead to better choices of key policy parameters. We believe this federal–state program can achieve its mission while better balancing the needs of recipients with the interests of taxpayers and the requirements of service providers in a complex financing and delivery system—but only if it is structured to reflect and channel underlying voter preferences (that is, public demand) for medical care for the poor. In this context we show that there are some new opportunities for Medicaid, as well as a continued need to address some old problems. There are also some imperfections in Medicaid that the country will probably have to live with, in part because public preferences for medical care for the poor (relative to other national needs) will not support better solutions at this time; in part because some changes are not worth the trouble; and in part because any change can be difficult to accomplish, as voters value a degree of stability in government programs and methods for paying for them.

We address this book to the national health policy realist. In recent years, some policy analysts have promoted elegant solutions based on a single-payer national health insurance program. Others have advocated conceptually simple solutions based on competition and market forces. They see that health care reform would be a much easier task if we could just scrap existing programs and start over with a single new national program. While we do not deny the attractions of these solutions, or their potential advantages, we do not see them as the next step in funding health care for the nation's poor and near-poor population. Rather, we see in Medicaid some fundamental unresolved problems that will need to be addressed for our system of caring for the poor to be seamlessly integrated with any more nearly universal program or system of health insurance coverage. We see the need for an intermediate step, but one that should be made with some clarity about where we want to go, and some careful thought about how to get there from here. For this reason, we assume the Medicaid program will continue for some time to involve a federal–state interaction, which virtually guarantees that it will look less simple and less elegant than either a unitary-government model or a unitary-market approach.

Our framework for considering policy choices is based on two realities: what voter-taxpayers in general are willing to support, and the persistent variation among the states in what voter-taxpayers value and are able to afford in a program. We emphasize the aim of achieving (or at least moving closer to) public objectives by taking advantage of the strengths of our federal–state financing system and by applying the theoretical model of public choice. While the specific solutions will have to be worked out through the policymaking process, we believe we have some useful guidance for policymakers that will help them avoid the frustrated expectations produced by previous efforts at reform.

It is possible, of course, that in the next few years all the various interest groups will come to agree on a single-payer, universal voucher to purchase care in a competitive market, or some other, more theoretically pure, approach to national health policy that does not include a Medicaid-like component. But for now, we proceed with our analysis of Medicaid, based on the political realities of this resilient program and the difficulties that may prevent the adoption of any ideologically pure alternative. For the near term, it is likely that the current fundamental building blocks of the health care financing system—Medicare, Medicaid, and employer-sponsored insurance, perhaps augmented with new subsidies for lower-income workers and insurance market reforms—will form the basis for reform. Financing medical care for the lower-income population, however, presents some particular issues that are not present for groups with greater ability to share in the cost of their own care. For this reason, any national health care reform plan will need to include specific provisions for the poor. Understanding Medicaid and the State Children's Health Insurance Program (SCHIP, now officially acronymed CHIP),[1] their roles in the current system, and how their roles differ from those of insurance for the working population will be important in crafting solutions that may lead to a more nearly universal and cost-effective care system.

We therefore offer this book as a guide to both federal and state policymakers who must make decisions in the context of a federal–state program of medical care for the poor. We provide a framework that builds on fundamental concepts and supports decision-making based on sound analysis and research evidence. While the Medicaid policy debate is always changing, some problems are fundamental and recurring. We hope the approach developed in these pages will help readers think more clearly about public policy choices and discover new solutions to Medicaid policy problems as they arise in coming years.

We outline this general approach to thinking in part 1, "Keys to Understanding Medicaid." This part identifies the facts about the program that we believe are essential knowledge for Medicaid policymakers and policy analysis. We outline our approach to thinking about Medicaid policy issues in the context of principles of equity, efficiency, and democracy. We introduce our approach to analysis of public choices and describe what we mean by "Medicaid promises." We identify three fundamental types of Medicaid commitments: promises to the poor and near-poor, promises to taxpayers, and promises to providers. Although determining the appropriate level of commitment in each of these areas is a problem that must be solved by the political process, we maintain that public policy can be improved by having the knowledge and tools to assess alternatives and develop program solutions.

In part 2, "Making and Meeting Promises to the Poor," we consider how state Medicaid programs meet the needs of the populations they serve. Choosing what promises to make to the poor and how to fulfill them is more complex than just picking a right level for benefits and for eligibility. Our discussion of this problem pays attention to cross-state equity in the context of widely varying state health care systems and Medicaid programs and considers in turn the choices states have in the areas of eligibility and benefits, and issues of care management for both acute and long-term care services.

Part 3 is called "Making and Meeting Promises to Voter-Taxpayers." In a discussion of public choices within our constitutional federal–state system, we critically examine Medicaid's federal matching-rate structure and the incentives it creates for state Medicaid spending. We consider Medicaid from the standpoint of taxpayers' interest in equitable sharing of program costs and in accountability that ensures resources will be used appropriately and efficiently. We suggest major changes in the way federal funds are allocated to the states. We describe a method for determining federal support that would make Medicaid more equitable among states for both program recipients and state taxpayers.

In part 4, "Promises to Providers—Payment Policies and Strategies," we discuss Medicaid's commitments to providers. Setting provider payment rates is a complicated task for reasons that include the broad range of acute and long-term care services to be covered, the need for Medicaid to procure services in local health care markets, and the diversity of Medicaid providers. We consider how states might best pursue multiple objectives through an appropriately constructed payment strategy that accounts for the incentives created for providers and reflects state priorities about cost, quality, and access to care. We consider in detail the reasons for, and implications of, Medicaid's typically low provider payment rates. We consider skeptically the argument for cost-shifting and explain what we believe really happens when Medicaid pays less than its proportionate share of provider costs. We also discuss what policymakers can do to make Medicaid providers more accountable for use of program funds.

Part 5, "Promises to the Near-Poor—CHIP and Fiscal Federalism," reviews recent issues in Medicaid's companion program, the State Children's

Health Insurance Program (CHIP). In the context of the public choice model, we consider voter-taxpayer decisions about extending publicly financed insurance to higher income levels. Understanding this program is particularly important for future policy, as CHIP starts to bridge the gap in coverage for uninsured members of the near-poor working population. What we learn from the SCHIP/CHIP experience may help guide other policy decisions on covering the uninsured.

In the conclusion of the book, we distill the results of our theoretical and empirical findings to focus the attention of policymakers on the issues that should matter most. We identify the key policy choices faced by Medicaid in the context of the nation's current health policy agenda. In a section on "things to keep and things to change," we highlight what parts of the program are working well and distinguish them from provisions that need to be improved or replaced. We apply our lessons from Medicaid to broader health care reform and identify "principles for reform" that emerge from the application of the concepts of equity, efficiency, and democracy. Finally, we note for policymakers what might be required from the political process to implement our suggestions and the results they might expect if such reforms are successful. Overall, we hope this book will provide a solid foundation for clear thinking about the Medicaid program, and perhaps also for whatever new program may someday come to replace it.

PART I

Keys to Understanding Medicaid

Before we delve into its problems and possible solutions, it is important to be clear about just what Medicaid is—and what it isn't. We use the two chapters in part 1 as an opportunity to state the key fundamental facts and to clear up some common misconceptions about the program that are often held by the public and by Medicaid policymakers themselves. We want readers to understand that Medicaid is, indeed, different from other programs and needs to be understood from multiple perspectives.

To be sure, Medicaid shares characteristics with some other federal and state programs, but it has a unique role. Comprising more than fifty different medical assistance programs, it serves several distinct population groups across the nation, covers a network of acute and long-term care providers that is more diverse than the provider network of any other program, and provides financing through a complex federal–state system. In these chapters, we highlight some of these fundamental differences and unique characteristics and identify eight keys to understanding Medicaid:

- Medicaid was made in America.

- Medicaid depends on altruism, not solidarity.

- Medicaid reflects public choices.

- Medicaid is tied to the U.S. health care system.

- Medicaid spending is unequal across states.

- Medicaid is both expenditure and revenue.

- Medicaid's role changes over time.

- Medicaid policy requires attending to an ever-changing set of implicit public promises.

These keys reflect the underlying American values that led to creation of the program and highlight some fundamental facts that reflect the program's place on the contemporary public agenda. We suggest that these "keys to understanding Medicaid" can serve as a useful framework for our discussion and for policy thinking on the Medicaid program, and on health care reform more generally.

1

Financing Care for the Poor in a Democracy

From its inception to the present, the Medicaid program has been shaped by many influences. It is a product of the democratic process in a federal–state constitutional system and of a health care delivery system that reflects the influences of other major insurance. Understanding these influences is important if one wishes to develop practical proposals for changing the program in its current environment. Here are some elements to consider.

Medicaid Was Made in America

European and even Canadian observers are often puzzled by the complexity and inconsistencies of the U.S. health care system. Medicaid is among the most complex (and sometimes inconsistent) parts of this system, yet one can argue that it represents a uniquely American solution to the problem of financing medical care for the poor, one that is particularly well suited to the economic and cultural diversity of this nation and the federal nature of its political institutions. Despite its complexity, Medicaid's structure puts each of the major players—federal and state governments and providers—in its appropriate role, puts most incentives in the right places, and allows for decentralized decision-making at levels that have the requisite information.

Medicaid takes a distinctly American approach in at least three ways. First, decentralized administration and state-level decision-making on local benefits allow for expression of local preferences that may reflect the nation's diverse cultural values, characteristics of local delivery systems, and local priorities for the use of economic resources of a diverse nation. Second, multi-tiered financing, which with federal, state, and (in some cases) local funds allows voter preferences to influence medical care for the poor, not only in voters' own states but also in others, is consistent with our federal constitutional framework. Third, the program provides for a functional mix of public- and private-sector roles in its administration. The public sector controls funding levels, payment policy, and benefits. Private-sector contractors are responsible for day-to-day claims processing and provider payment, and private-sector providers are largely responsible for the production of medical services. Individual patients and their physicians are responsible for medical care treatment decisions. All in all, the system is one of decentralized control that attempts to draw on the various strengths of public- and private-sector entities.

While Medicaid is clearly a product of the American political process, serious questions can be raised about just how well it has worked, and even whether it should be continued in its current form. We will consider its major problems (particularly in the areas of equity, efficiency, and democracy) and what might be needed to address them. Nonetheless, the fact that this rather complex federal–state system has been made to function for more than forty years should cause political decision-makers to think twice about making major changes to Medicaid's basic structure. Before changing or replacing this significant program, policymakers would do well to be sure they have a clear understanding of each part of its complex design, and the role each part has played in meeting needs of program stakeholders, including recipients, providers, and taxpayers.

Medicaid Depends on Altruism, Not Solidarity

One of the most important ways Medicaid differs from other public programs is that voters support it not because they expect to receive benefits themselves—very few average-income voters ever will—but because they care about the well-being of others. The motivation of altruism, rather than self-interest, is a characteristic Medicaid shares with public welfare programs. But this motivation differs from that of other income-security programs, such as Medicare and Social Security, where voter-taxpayers can, in fact, expect to receive benefits themselves someday. This difference shapes voter attitudes toward the program, particularly with respect to who should receive benefits and how generous those benefits should be relative to what is available to the average voter-taxpayer. Voter willingness to provide major benefits is limited to cases where the recipients are truly in need and lack the ability to obtain care on their own. This limited altruism, characteristic of the American experience, has been important in shaping the program and continues to have a profound effect on voter support for publicly subsidized health insurance in proposals for national health care reform.

Altruism versus Solidarity. Public arguments for virtually all U.S. public programs that provide care to the poor have been based on some concept of altruism. Medical care for needy persons has been provided by donors, both voluntarily, through charity, and through public programs whose services are funded with compulsory taxes. The American view of altruism differs from the approach in many European countries, where the concept of "solidarity" underlies a national commitment to provide equal health care for all. Meulen, Arts, and Muffels describe solidarity as "a moral value and social attitude regarding those in need of support" that is "associated with mutual respect, personal support and commitment to a common cause."[1] Tracing the solidarity concept back to Roman law, they highlight the emphasis on a sense of shared community obligation to a common cause. This shared obligation is reflected in various forms in continental European welfare states.[2]

The divergence of American from European views is not a recent phenomenon. Arts and Verburg point to a distinct view of altruism involving a greater degree of self-reliance in the liberal Anglo-Saxon nations.[3] This view comes with a greater skepticism about any notions of a national will or ethos to which all must subscribe. In the United Kingdom, public discourse on responsibility to provide for the poor is rooted in the strong empiricism associated with the ethical and social philosophy of Francis Hutcheson, Adam Smith, and Hume, and the utilitarianism of Bentham and Mill,[4] and stresses the view that social obligations arise from a sense of justice and benevolence toward others based on enlightened self-interest. Charity and public support for the poor, then, depend on a donor's willingness to contribute to meeting the needs of others.

This distinct tradition of social thought found its way to America and eventually into American social institutions. Until the twentieth century, providing for the (nonveteran) poor in the United States was essentially a local responsibility. At its inception in the 1930s, Social Security was focused first on providing for the needs of disabled workers and retirees and only secondarily on the poor.[5] The medical components in fuller form (Medicare and Medicaid) came later, in the 1960s, only after employer-based insurance had begun to take hold during and after World War II. Neither the favorable tax treatment of insurance nor Medicare was much based on considerations of justice for the poor. In emphasizing their needs, Medicaid was a notable exception, built upon the earlier state and local welfare efforts. A documentary narrative by Stevens and Stevens shows the development of Medicaid from a long tradition of political support for publicly funded medical care only for those categorically deserving persons who cannot afford to purchase it privately.[6]

Organized labor in the United States has largely accepted the sharp division between employer-based insurance and public health insurance systems, and has not been a particular champion of Medicaid or other programs for the non-working poor.[7] This lack of solidarity regarding public health care insurance issues has frustrated those advocates of universal single-payer health insurance who look to unite the populace in demanding that the government provide a program of uniform health insurance for all. Except in occasional periods of populist sentiment, such advocates face a public whose members—for the most part, it seems—see an obligation to provide an adequate level of care for the poor, but not to provide the same benefits they provide for themselves and their families. They find little support from U.S. labor unions, whose notions of solidarity seem to stop at the end of the union membership roll.[8]

It is important to recognize these long-established attitudes in considering the prospects for U.S. health care reform. Ideas that have evolved over the past three centuries are unlikely to change overnight. In this book, we build upon the empirical Anglo-Saxon tradition by viewing public choices about care for the poor as being determined by what voters are willing to pay in taxes to provide support for others. To the more vigorous advocates for a single-payer system, we would note that our model does not preclude adoption of a system that provides equal and uniform access to health care, if that should become the preference of a majority of voters. Nevertheless, our discussion of public choices about the provision of care to the poor is based on the assumption that, at present, most voters and policymakers still consider it an issue distinct from, though an important part of, the overall national question of medical care financing and delivery systems.

Local Altruism. It may be useful at this point to consider what motivates taxpayers to support Medicaid (and other health care programs) that may benefit others more than themselves. Underlying our thinking is a belief that people care about the well-being of others and are willing to contribute their own resources to help them. Moreover, we suggest that, while people may care to some degree about everyone worldwide, they care more or feel a greater responsibility for people living nearby. We take the view that altruism has a local dimension that produces a stronger preference to help others in one's own local community, city, or state. Motivation to pay for the care of others may also include a desire to protect one's own health from communicable disease or protect oneself and one's family in the event of a major setback; in each case, the expected benefit of the program to the taxpayer is greater for benefits applied locally than for those applied elsewhere, other factors being equal. The literature of sociobiology suggests there may even be evolutionary reasons for people to care more about the well-being of those to whom they are more closely related.[9]

While we do not have any precise ways to measure variations in the intensity of altruistic preferences with distance, unrelatedness, or political boundaries, at least some of these factors would seem to contribute to diminished willingness to pay for assistance to others; otherwise, we would be providing the same Medicaid benefits to the poor in Bangladesh that we do in Vermont. Whether this localness in preference arises from self-interest, evolutionary predisposition, or a cultural belief that charity begins at home, the idea of local altruism is important to understanding why voter-taxpayers may be more supportive of programs when they know that their dollars are going to provide services in their own states or communities.

Without a doubt, a significant element of altruism at a national level affects attitudes about medical care for the poor. Whether this national preference differs in kind or only in intensity from local or state altruism, it certainly differs in how it can be expressed and acknowledged, as it functions at such a distance that the donor voter-taxpayers can be only indirectly aware of the results of their altruistic contributions. This can affect the nature of public support for a program such as Medicaid. Feedback to Medicaid's taxpayer-donors about the results of their contributions, which may be needed to sustain altruistic behavior, just cannot be as complete at the national level.

In general, voters may be poorly informed about the details of Medicaid in other states, and they may just assume the program is about the same everywhere. This assumption may be responsible for a degree of insensitivity to Medicaid's interstate differences and the associated inequities, leading voters to express a general level of support for the program nationally but show little interest in the details of coverage or provider payment issues in states other than their own. Based on this logic, voters may perceive less altruistic value from the provision of services in other states if they exceed what is provided in their own. To the extent that the recipients themselves are easier to visualize than Medicaid service levels, national voters may have stronger preferences about who should get services (for example, pregnant women and children) and who should not (perhaps able-bodied adults) than they do about particular levels of service provided in other states. To the extent that national voters see things this way, their preference may lead federal lawmakers to focus more on questions of eligibility and leave the details of benefits to state and local decision-makers. The question for policymakers is how to design medical assistance programs that acknowledge, and if possible make use of, voter preferences that are stronger locally and more limited nationally.

It may be that Medicaid, with its delegation of details to the states, is already congruent with the split in level of specificity between local and national altruism. The limited ability of national voters to focus on the level of benefits in other states, however, has allowed Medicaid to diverge from principles of equity, which might be given more weight by national voters if they really knew what was going on with other states' programs. Voters in many lower-benefit states might not be happy to learn their tax dollars are being used to support much more generous benefits in other states.

On the other hand, perhaps voters would value such services, in their own states and elsewhere, more highly if they had better feedback about the medical effectiveness and value of the care provided. In that case, national support for Medicaid would increase if state spending were better targeted toward ensuring basic, high-value benefits and more uniform levels of eligibility across states. In this regard, comparative effectiveness research (and knowledge that it is being applied) could help engender greater public support for Medicaid among voters.

Medicaid Reflects Public Choices

The value of a nation's public goods, such as police protection, parks maintenance, and national defense, can be viewed as the sum of the value assigned to them by each of its citizens. Each citizen may receive a small benefit that, when aggregated with those received by others, justifies substantial public spending. Similarly, while the medical services purchased with Medicaid dollars are used by individuals for whom these services have a private value, the public value of the program accrues from the altruistic preferences of the voter-taxpayers who must support and pay for it. Where altruism is stronger, the program has greater value to the individual voter. This same relationship pertains to any other collectively consumed public good. Beyond this general observation, policymakers need a convenient way to conceptualize the levels of investment that strike an optimal balance between the preferences of local altruism and the social value of equity across states. To address these issues here, we employ a structured framework based on the theory of public choice.

A common public choice model asserts that policymakers in a democracy have incentives to represent the interest of the "median voter"—the voter whose preferred level of public expenditures on a program would put him or her in the middle of a line of voters placed in order by the amount they wish to see spent. Any politician who accurately represents the view of such a median voter will, according to this theory, garner more votes on the issue than any competitor. For our analysis of Medicaid, we will sometimes ask what the hypothetical median voter would want in the way of spending on medical care for the poor, and we will presume that the political process naturally finds a way to incorporate such views into public policy decisions.

Within this framework, which we will use as a policy tool in part 3, the voter-taxpayers face competing interests of several groups. Medicaid policymaking becomes a process by which policymakers (legislators and elected officials) seek to craft a set of program parameters (budgets and rules) that will induce providers to supply services to the poor in ways that will satisfy the voter-taxpayers. Hence, we focus on three distinct sets of actors—the poor who need services; the providers who are willing to supply those services but at a price; and the taxpayers who have needs and wants for private use of their incomes. The dynamic interaction among these groups provides the basis of the story we will tell about this complex, and sometimes difficult to understand, program. In effect, Medicaid has certain promises to fulfill to each of them.

If Medicaid's promises to its various stakeholder groups are to be fulfilled, the necessary public and private commitments of resources must be worked out within the structure of our federal constitutional framework. We believe the most useful policy analysis framework for this task is one that explicitly recognizes all the interests, applies some basic principles of equity, efficiency, and democracy, and deals with the practical issues of resource allocation and management in ways that account for incentives and behavioral responses. In that regard, the public choice and economic models that underlie this analysis of Medicaid should help prepare policymakers to deal directly with the complex array of interactions that determine the outcomes of the Medicaid program and of our health care system as a whole.

Medicaid Is Tied to the U.S. Health Care System

It is impossible to separate Medicaid from the health care markets in which it procures services, or from the influence of other public and private health insurers upon those markets. Today we hear constant criticism of the U.S. health care system, especially about rising costs for privately insured people and inadequate access to care for uninsured households. These broader problems have resulted from past public policy decisions that based public support for health care on four distinct funding models:

- Strong tax incentives for fairly comprehensive and open-ended employer-sponsored insurance coverage for employed individuals and their families;

- Medicare coverage for the elderly and disabled;

- Medicaid coverage for many of the poor and near-poor in certain categories; and

- limited funding of safety-net providers to help with the costs of caring for the remaining people without public or private coverage.

Public and private insurance programs have provided the financing that has enabled the growth and widespread availability of medical technology from the 1950s to the present. The widespread availability of medical insurance has also created strong incentives for biomedical research that results in better but more costly forms of medical care. The unsolved cost and access problems are products of a system that has had dramatic success in providing the majority of Americans with access to a resource-rich medical care system.

When Medicare and Medicaid began in 1965, these programs generally provided medical insurance to some (though by no means all) of those without the resources to pay in full for medical care or health insurance themselves.[10] The programs specified eligibility, insurance coverage, and the methods of financing, but few limits on the amount of care that would be financed. The open-ended nature of this insurance reflected both a trust in professionals to use resources wisely in a system of limited resources, and political compromises with provider groups, who initially accepted such government involvement only when promised that coverage and medical practice would be not be limited or otherwise constrained.

In Medicaid's early years, the most obvious financing problems (with both Medicaid and Medicare) were largely the result of the decision to provide open-ended reimbursement, in the form of payment of "reasonable costs" for hospitals and "usual and customary fees" for physicians. In time, both programs found ways to curb the open-ended commitments (at least for payment) through fee schedules for professional providers, cost limits or prospectively determined per-admission rates for hospitals, and capitated managed care programs.[11] These changes slowed the growth in spending, but only for a while. Both programs continue to face challenges to keep up with new technology and with new maneuvers of providers who are seeking ways to maximize their payments as the programs evolve over time. These challenges can be expected to multiply for both public programs over the next twenty-five years, as the aging of the U.S. population will increase the number of Medicare beneficiaries (and of Medicaid's dual-eligible recipients), while the relative size of the working taxpayer population decreases.

Beyond these challenges, many significant problems remain in health care financing that affect not only the public programs, but the entire health services sector. These include the fundamental problem of implementing politically acceptable, cost-effective cost containment methods in a heavily insured health care system while promoting high-quality care. To date, insured Americans (whether on private insurance or Medicare) have been reluctant to accept many limits on coverage; providers have been unwilling to accept many controls on their practices; and even the latest care management methods have not often produced savings that justify the additional administrative costs. We seem to cycle through generations of new care management and provider payment methods, only to see that their real constraints are unacceptable to patients and providers, who find new ways to maintain access to a growing set of services at ever-increasing costs.

The only constant in this dynamic is what we might call "the law of certain costs and uncertain savings," as each round of reforms proposed over the years entails an upfront dollar outlay for care management services or payment incentives that may be offset by presumed savings at some future date. When these do not materialize, we move on to the next generation of reforms. Today's highly touted reforms—including chronic care disease management, pay-for-performance incentives, electronic medical records, and the establishment of medical homes—do not seem much different from those of the past. While these care management–oriented reforms may well lead to improvements in quality of care, their certain costs and uncertain savings make them unlikely candidates for achieving the major cost savings needed to transform Medicaid, or to free up sufficient resources to provide insurance coverage to substantially more Americans.

Thus, Medicaid's problems must be considered as part of the overall health care financing system. Medicaid interfaces with that system in many, sometimes complex, ways. As a major payer for services, Medicaid affects the system by providing resources that support (to varying degrees among the states) a certain level of access and quality in each local health care system. As the major payer for medical services used by the poor, Medicaid defines the boundary between the covered poor and the uninsured, and thus can affect the number of uninsured. By setting payment rates that are often below the market rate, much of Medicaid functions as a large provider payment organization (PPO) with few out-of-network options, albeit one that often gives itself discounts by simply announcing what it will pay instead of negotiating with providers, as would a private PPO.

Defining the scope of Medicaid in these areas is necessary to address the broader system issues of resource allocation and the problem of the uninsured. As one looks at current issues in the overall health care system and recognizes the way Medicaid has expanded over the years, it is natural to consider the possibility that further expansion might be part of the solution, or at least a step toward a solution, to the challenge of providing insurance protection and health care to those currently uninsured. Any effort directed at resolving larger issues with the health care system faced by our nation must deal seriously with Medicaid or whatever program will replace it in providing access to health care for the poor. Likewise, any effort to deal with Medicaid must deal seriously with the issues of the larger health care system.

Medicaid Spending Is Unequal among States

The diversity of state Medicaid programs, in both income eligibility levels and in coverage, is well known. But the policy significance of this fact has been much less clear. Medicaid spending per poor person ranges widely among states. Payments per poor person differed in 2007 by a factor of 3.76, from Nevada, at $4,976, to Alaska, at $18,706. Differences existed even among adjacent states, with payments in Maryland, at $11,071, 48 percent higher than those in Virginia, at $7,474, and payments in Illinois, at $10,034, 45 percent higher than those in Indiana, at $6,919 (see figure 1-1 and table A1-2).[12] There are many reasons for this variation, and we will try to sort them out in the chapters that follow. Part of the difference in spending levels arises from geographic variations in the cost of living and medical prices, which result in real differences in need for assistance. But other aspects of the differences in payments among the states appear to be unrelated to differences in needs and raise real questions about the appropriate role of federal policy in achieving equity for the poor across the nation and equity for taxpayers across states in paying for the program.

This diversity raises some questions of equity, such as:

- Is it inequitable for a poor person in one state to receive less real access to care than a similarly situated person in another state?

- Should the level of benefits be determined by local or national standards?

FIGURE 1-1

MEDICAID PAYMENTS PER PERSON BELOW FEDERAL POVERTY LEVEL, FY 2007

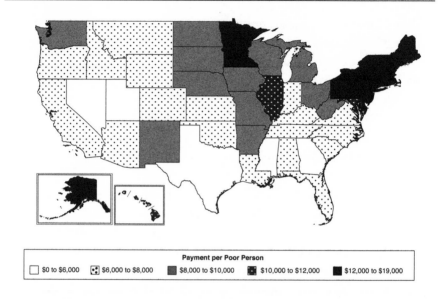

Payment per Poor Person

☐ $0 to $6,000   ▨ $6,000 to $8,000   ▨ $8,000 to $10,000   ▨ $10,000 to $12,000   ■ $12,000 to $19,000

SOURCES: Computed using data from U.S. Census Bureau (2008b) and Kaiser Family Foundation (2009, "Total Medicaid Spending FY2007," http://www.statehealthfacts.org/comparemaptable. jsp?ind=177&cat=4).
NOTE: Total federal and state medical payments include disproportionate share hospital payments, exclude administrative costs.

- Is it fair to require taxpayers in lower-income, lower-benefit states to support extensive institutional and home care programs (including personal attendant services) in the higher-income states?

- Is it fair for states that fail to control medical costs (whether due to high provider payment rates or unchecked utilization) to receive greater federal assistance to cover those higher costs?

- How much federal assistance should be available to states that want to provide above-average benefits? At what point should federal help be curtailed?

- To what extent have high-spending states found ways to supplement their general funds with federal dollars without providing additional benefits to the poor and other low-income recipients? Is this an appropriate use of federal funds?

How these questions are answered will be important for determining the equity of the program for recipients and for taxpayers. We will suggest criteria for assessing equity, and practical methods that can be used to achieve equity by some measures. We believe that better public decisions on these issues can be made by explicitly considering their effects on equity, efficiency, and accountability to voter-taxpayers in a democracy. Such a principled approach may help policymakers find common ground that balances stakeholder interests.

It is worth noting that while a few of these questions are particular to Medicaid's current structure, many of those about equity in benefits and financing are not. The same questions would need to be answered for any national program that provided health insurance or health insurance subsidies to lower-income populations. These questions would not disappear with any new program (even uniform universal national health insurance) that might substitute for Medicaid in the future. The issue of equity in having access to and paying for health care is not one that will ever be resolved once and for all; it is an issue that must be addressed on an ongoing basis by each generation.

2

Medicaid's Roles in Our Health Care System

The Medicaid program affects more than just those who receive benefits. It is an important part of our health care system that has direct impacts on health care providers. The ways in which it deals with those providers—what it pays for and how much—determines what services are delivered to whom and in what settings. Moreover, as an important source of resources, Medicaid contributes to the shape of local health care delivery systems and thereby affects all those who use services within the system. Medicaid is also an important part of state budgets; its demands on state resources and inflows of federal revenue are important in shaping state budget priorities and balancing public needs within each jurisdiction. We consider these factors as we continue to discuss keys to understanding Medicaid in this chapter.

Medicaid Is Both Expenditure and Revenue

Medicaid can be viewed in terms of either expenditures or revenue, depending on one's perspective. To the federal government, Medicaid represents a considerable expense. But to the states and providers, it can be an important source of revenue—one that can help solve problems or leave them short, depending on the circumstances.

Medicaid as Expenditure. At both the state and federal levels, the most commonly voiced concerns about Medicaid relate to the program's costs. Concerns are fourfold: the level of program costs, the rate of growth in costs, the difficulty of predicting future expenditures, and the suggestion by some that Medicaid's

26

lower payment rates "shift" cost to other payers. Especially in discussions about federal and state budgets, one often hears the cry that Medicaid costs are out of control or unsustainable. There is some evidence to support these assertions, and such warnings may help to attract attention and produce a sense of urgency needed to bring about policy change.[1] We question, however, the view that Medicaid costs are largely a product of external forces. Instead, we will offer here a more considered view of Medicaid costs as a product of basic public choices about resource allocation that can be readily changed if there is good reason and, importantly, political will.

A careful consideration of Medicaid cost problems must start with an understanding of the nature of these costs and their growth, and must be set in the context of a wider discussion of public choices about spending. Any rate of cost growth greater than the rate of growth in the gross domestic product (GDP) will, over time, consume an ever-increasing share of resources, and, in that sense, such growth is unsustainable. Any program's costs are "out of control" if the political will does not exist to control them. The question is whether Medicaid costs and cost growth are higher than needed to obtain the desired level of access to services for the program's target populations. In an economic sense, this requires an assessment of the value (relative to the costs) of services to those who are paying for them.

As a matter of national resource allocation, we should consider whether we are spending too much on medical care in general, as well as whether we are procuring the level of access to care that is desired for the poor. We share the view that our nation spends too much on some kinds of medical care. We also note that medical expense per se, except when related to medical research, is a consumption good as much as, or more than, it is an investment good. Once it is used it is gone, except for any lasting benefits of good health. Such a significant part of our national expenditures and our tax burden should not to be allowed to grow unchecked for lack of political will to align this sector with long-run resource-allocation choices and true voter preferences.

Medicaid resource allocation choices have all of the complexity of the medical cost problem in general. But they also require a way to assess how much we ought to be taxing one group of citizens to pay for the medical care of others. As this public choice dimension is central to our view of Medicaid costs and to our approach to developing Medicaid policy, let us

TABLE 2-1

MEDICAID OUTLAYS BY TYPE OF PAYMENT, FY 2007

($ BILLIONS)

Title XIX outlays	Federal share	State share	Total
Medical assistance payments			
Acute care benefits	$74.3	$54.4	$128.7
Long-term care benefits	56.1	43.9	99.9
Capitation payments and premiums	38.0	28.6	66.6
Disproportionate share hospital payments	9.0	6.8	15.8
Adjustments	1.0		
Subtotal medical assistance	1.3	1.1	2.4
Administration payments	9.5	7.8	17.3
Vaccines for children	2.7	0.0	2.7
Gross Medicaid outlays	191.0	142.6	333.6
Collections	–0.4	0.0	–0.4
Net Medicaid outlays	190.6	142.6	333.2

SOURCE: U.S. Department of Health and Human Services, Centers for Medicare and Medicaid Services, Office of the Actuary 2008.

look at some of the statistics on Medicaid costs and cost growth and consider what the numbers may mean for spending decisions and broader questions of financing.

In federal fiscal year 2007, Medicaid accounted for $333.2 billion in federal and state expenditures. The federal government paid about 57 percent, while the states paid about 43 percent of this total.[2] Program administration accounted for $17.3 billion, or about 5 percent of the total (see table 2-1). In state budgets, the state share of Medicaid in 2007 represented about 17 percent of general fund spending, and the federal share represented about 44 percent of federal assistance to the states.[3]

While levels of cost are generally high, the growth in public costs typically generates the most concern for policymakers. At the federal level, Medicaid's share of the nondefense budget grew from 2.4 percent in federal fiscal year (FFY) 1970 to 8.8 percent in FFY 2007 (see table 2-2). The

TABLE 2-2

MEDICAID GROWTH IN FEDERAL BUDGET, 1970–2007

($ BILLIONS)

	1970	1980	1990	2000	2007
Nondefense outlays	$114.0	$456.9	$953.8	$1,494.8	$2,177.7
Federal Medicaid	2.7	14.0	41.1	117.9	190.6
Federal Medicaid as percentage of the federal nondefense budget	2.4%	3.1%	4.3%	7.9%	8.8%

SOURCES: U.S. Office of Management and Budget 2008, Historical Tables, tables 3.1 and 8.5.
NOTE: State share is excluded from this table.

upward trend in Medicaid costs occurred in the context of growing health care costs for all payers. The growth rate in Medicaid expenditures—8.03 percent annually between 1995 and 2005—was slightly higher than that in private insurance spending—7.74 percent annually for the same period (see table 2-3). This difference, however, reflected benefit expansions and coverage of more individuals rather than uncontrolled growth in per-recipient spending. In this ten-year period, Medicaid enrollment grew by 58 percent, with the largest growth in coverage of children, while the growth rates on a per-person-served basis ranged from 4 percent for adults, to 5 percent for children and the elderly, to 6 percent for the disabled—all, except for the disabled, below the 5.7 percent annual rate of growth in U.S. personal health care spending per capita in the same period. Medicaid cost growth apparently has been largely a product of more general U.S. health care trends and of policy choices to expand eligibility and benefits for specific groups of recipients.

Along with other payers, Medicaid has contributed to the growing share of health care in the nation's GDP. While private insurance accounted for more than half of this growth in the 1995–2005 period, Medicaid accounted for 26 percent—more than Medicare, at 11 percent. Note that out-of-pocket payments accounted for only 1 percent of the growth in health care's share of

TABLE 2-3

HEALTH CARE EXPENDITURE GROWTH BY SECTOR, TEN-YEAR PERIODS, 1965–2005

	————Annual average growth rate————			
	1965–75	1975–85	1985–95	1995–2005
Total U.S.	12.18%	12.68%	8.75%	6.86%
Total private	9.32	12.99	7.73	6.91
Out of pocket	7.45	9.86	4.39	5.38
Insurance	11.70	15.70	9.52	7.74
Other	10.61	14.04	8.41	6.02
Total public	18.22	12.24	10.11	6.79
Medicare	N/A	15.90	9.95	6.25
Medicaid	N/A	11.78	13.47	8.03
Other	9.56	9.54	7.63	6.11

SOURCE: Computed from U.S. Department of Health and Human Services, Centers for Medicare and Medicaid Services, Office of the Actuary (2009).

the GDP in recent years, and have actually declined as a share of the GDP in all but the most recent five-year period since 1965 (see table 2-4). More importantly, out-of-pocket payments have continuously declined *as a share of medical spending*. The long-term decline in the share of out-of-pocket payments in the United States generally is indicative of a system in which consumers have ever fewer incentives to give much weight to costs in their health care decisions. Medicaid, as a participant in this system, both contributes to the situation and shares in its consequences.

Despite some expansions and contractions in eligibility and benefits over the years, Medicaid costs have been growing faster than other components of state spending. A 2008 actuarial study from the Centers for Medicare and Medicaid Services projected expenditures to grow at an average annual rate of 7.9 percent, reaching $673.7 billion annually by the year 2017.[4] CMS estimated the rate of growth in cost per enrollee in the 2000–7 period as 2.9 percent when adjusted for the mix of enrollees.[5] While total Medicaid spending growth fluctuates with changes in the number of people eligible, spending growth per person insured has not been out of line with increases

TABLE 2-4

DECOMPOSITION OF HEALTH CARE'S GROWING SHARE OF GDP

	Growth in health expenditure as a percentage of GDP			
	1965–75	1975–85	1985–95	1995–2005
Total increase in share of GDP decomposition	2.26	2.28	3.33	2.15
Total U.S.	100	100	100	100
Total private	14	65	38	56
Out of pocket	–11	–1	–8	1
Insurance	20	54	39	52
Other	4	11	7	3
Total public	86	35	62	44
Medicare	44	30	24	11
Medicaid	36	7	30	26
Other	6	–2	9	7

SOURCE: Computed from U.S. Department of Health and Human Services, Centers for Medicare and Medicaid Services, Office of the Actuary and U.S. Dept. of Commerce Gross Domestic Product.

observed in other measures of growth in health care spending per capita. For all major eligibility groups, Medicaid's annual 7.3 percent growth in spending per beneficiary from 1980 to 2003 was somewhat below the rate of increase in national health expenditure per capita of 7.7 percent and the growth in Medicare expenditures per beneficiary of 7.5 percent annually over the same period.[6]

Furthermore, there is nothing unique about the way spending for those insured by Medicaid has been growing over time. Despite differences in payment mechanisms, the extent of insurance coverage, ways of setting prices, and quite different target populations, it is striking that the long-term trend in Medicaid's growth in spending per person mirrors what has happened to other kinds of people with other kinds of insurance. Although critics often decry state Medicaid spending as excessive and lavish, expenditure growth can largely be explained by increases in the number of eligible individuals, and expenditure per beneficiary is driven by the same things that drive spending growth for all other parts of the insurance system. Another key factor is policy choices about whom to serve and what to cover—and we believe these decisions require close examination. But, as policy choices are or should be under public control, we argue that

Key Facts about Recent Medicaid Cost Growth

Statistics on Medicaid cost growth are often misunderstood and some-times misused. It is important to be clear about a few key facts.

- Fact 1: In recent years, total Medicaid costs have been grow-ing faster than general inflation and even faster than the costs of other medical payers.

- Fact 2: This *total* cost growth is due to:

  ○ Faster growth of medical care costs in general, relative to other kinds of consumption and income, so as to be increasing as a share of gross domestic product (GDP)

  ○ Medicaid's expansions in eligibility (primarily for chil-dren) and benefits (primarily for community-based, long-term care benefits and drugs for the disabled and elderly), leading to cost growth somewhat in excess of that in medical costs in the private sector, and thus in its share of national health expenditures

- Fact 3: Medicaid cost growth is *not* due to:

  ○ Faster growth rates in per-capita or per-recipient costs (which have been below those of other payers, except for those with eligibility based on disability)

  ○ Faster growth in provider payment rates (which are still low relative to other payers)

  ○ Faster growth in administrative costs (which are low rela-tive to other payers)

Medicaid spending per person served is not inherently any more out of control than spending in the rest of the health care system.

There is, then, no great mystery about Medicaid spending growth. Again, it is largely explained by growth in per-capita medical spending nationally and by expansions in eligibility to greater numbers of disabled persons, low-income children, and their parents. Solutions to the Medicaid cost problem must address the same issues of medical cost growth (such as utilization, technology, incentives, and input prices) faced by other payers, and must be considered in the context of the groups the program should serve.

Medicaid as Revenue to States. Medicaid was designed as a federal–state partnership, reflecting a common desire to improve access to health care for the nation's poor. The program has always been one of shared fiscal responsibility, with the federal government providing more than half the funding and establishing a framework in which states are allowed to craft programs in accordance with local needs, preferences, and resources. Federal assistance to the states is provided in accordance with a formula that determines the Federal Medical Assistance Percentage (FMAP), which is the federal share or federal "matching rate"—that is, the percentage share of a state's Medicaid expenditures picked up by the federal government.[7] From the perspective of the individual voter-taxpayer, Medicaid costs are paid through two separate taxing entities—federal and state governments—and are influenced by political decisions at both levels.

Despite common objectives and a shared source of support (that is, the voter-taxpayers), tensions often exist between federal policymakers and state officials. As Medicaid has grown in importance in state budgets, federal matching payments have become a major source of state funds. Tensions arise when state policymakers try to take advantage of rules that allow state expenditures to be more generously matched with federal dollars than the federal officials may have intended. The politics sometimes span party lines, as when Democratic and Republican governors join to oppose policies that would reduce federal payments to the states, and when bipartisan resistance to state fiscal creativity in matters of fiscal federalism emerges in Congress.

In a previous book, we offered a model of "fiscal federalism," in which federal matching payments would provide incentives for states to spend more than they otherwise would on medical care for the poor.[8] We suggested those incentives could be properly calibrated to cause states to choose particular levels of total spending, spending per beneficiary, and eligibility proportions among the low-income population. In this context, federal payments might be seen as representing the interest of the federal (or rest-of-country's) voters in promoting health care for specific kinds of low-income people in each state, while state payments might be seen as representing the particular local voters' interest in seeing that some of their more immediate neighbors have access to care. This mix would allow those voter-taxpayers who want to do more (or less), or to do things differently, for their states' lower-income populations to do so without having to convince people nationwide of the morality, equity, or efficiency of being more (or less) generous than average. Properly designed, such a system could help achieve a desirable, and, in an economic sense, optimal, allocation of resources to health care. Improperly designed, it could spawn inflation, inequity, inefficiency, and even political turmoil. We will have a more extensive discussion of this aspect of Medicaid in what follows.

As we pointed out in our earlier study, the federal–state Medicaid financing system has been associated with wide interstate variations in spending on medical care for poor and low-income households. We are left with the fundamental dilemma of Medicaid as a federal–state program: To what extent can the freedom of states to spend differing amounts be combined with cross-state equity for both recipients and taxpayers? Whether the establishment by Congress of a matching-rate formula was a matter of guesswork or of politics of the day, or whether it represented an awkward but appropriate short-term solution to geographic differences in state needs and resources, the formula became a fixture of Medicaid financing.[9] As states built their programs and plans around the formula, altering it without upsetting the states became increasingly difficult to consider, particularly in those that gained the greatest benefit from the system by creating extensive Medicaid programs based on the available federal dollars. While some might take this dilemma as evidence of a fundamental defect in the whole idea of federal–state partnerships (usually called "federalism") in dealing with health insurance coverage of lower-income people, in this study we take the view that federalism at its core is a sound approach, and that certain alterations in federal financial assistance to states, and other program provisions, could greatly improve the program's ability to achieve basic objectives.

Medicaid as Revenue to Providers. Medicaid is large enough to be a significant (and in some cases the dominant) payer for services in some provider markets. For example, Medicaid accounts for 43 percent of nursing home expenditures, 34 percent of home health expenditures, 17 percent of hospital expenditures, and 7 percent of physician expenditures nationally.[10] Since Medicaid payment rates are typically lower than those of other payers, the Medicaid-supported share of services delivered is somewhat larger.

The mix of Medicaid spending by service type has shifted over time, reflecting changes in modes of coverage and delivery of services. Capitated care and hospital outpatient services have increased in relative importance, while noncapitated inpatient hospital and physician services have decreased in shares of costs; nursing home care has decreased, while home-based services have increased. We will discuss these differences in more detail in part 2.

Whether a provider finds Medicaid a help or a hindrance depends on the relationship between the program's payment rates and the provider's costs. Adequate payment is the key to maintaining provider participation and access to care for Medicaid recipients. We devote much of part 4 to the issues of provider payment, as this important policy tool must support the policy balance needed to achieve the competing program goals of adequate access, reasonable costs, and incentives for provision of cost-effective care.

Many states set Medicaid payment rates for some services well below those paid by private payers and even by Medicare. While setting payment rates low is a popular means of cost control at state budget time, hospitals, physicians, and other medical providers do not typically respond to shifts in Medicaid payment by differentiating service intensity or style of practice for their Medicaid patients. As a result, buyers of other insurance often believe that costs have been "shifted" to them—that is, that providers would have charged them less if Medicaid had paid more. In chapter 11 we will discuss this issue in the context of provider payment and provide a model of the market that accounts for the differential payment rates and indicates what the real effects of low Medicaid payment may be for different types of providers. We will also indicate when and where low Medicaid payment may be a problem for access to services, for economic efficiency, for equity among providers, and for the goals states may be trying to achieve with their Medicaid programs.

Medicaid's Roles Change Over Time

Children and adults, typically in single-parent, low-income families, constitute the largest Medicaid eligibility group.[11] Eligibility rules that are less restrictive for pregnant women and infants have led to Medicaid's having a sizable share of this portion of the medical care market, with these individuals incurring significant costs related to prenatal care, deliveries, and neonatal care. Nevertheless, the per-case cost is comparatively low for these younger, nondisabled recipients when compared with the elderly and disabled recipient groups. In FY 2007, adults and children accounted for 72 percent of Medicaid recipients but just 32 percent of Medicaid payments, while the aged group accounted for 10 percent of enrollment and 24 percent of payments, and the blind/disabled groups accounted for 18 percent of enrollment and 43 percent of payments.[12]

Over the years, increasing numbers of people have become eligible for Medicaid. Medicaid growth has not, however, been uniform across its eligibility groups or its covered service types, which largely reflects changes in eligibility rules related to targeted program expansions. Table 2-5 shows Medicaid enrollment and payments by eligibility group for 1995–2005. Compared with those for the elderly and disabled, eligibility numbers for children and their parents were more closely tied to the economic cycles during this period. Children accounted for nearly half of the growth in Medicaid recipients (consistent with the proportion of recipients they represent). Nonelderly, nondisabled adults increased in relative share of recipients, with eligibility growing at an annual rate of 9 percent in the 2000–5 period. Elderly recipients, who represent a smaller overall share of the Medicaid population, accounted for less than 10 percent of the expansion in the total number eligible for the program between 1995 and 2005. The relatively slow growth among the elderly was also due to their not having been targeted for recent Medicaid expansions, and to their improving economic status. Further slowing increases in their eligibility were the relatively low birthrates that prevailed during the Depression and World War II. This effect is expected to change, however, as members of the baby boom generation pass beyond age sixty-five and become eligible for Medicare, and some become eligible for Medicaid as dual-eligibles.

Patterns of coverage and service use change over time, and they do so differently for the various eligibility groups. In recent years (2000–5), payments per recipient grew more rapidly for the disabled than for other groups. As this was also the highest cost group on a per-recipient basis, it accounted for the largest share of Medicaid cost growth. As can be computed from table 2-5, annual payments for disabled persons increased from $49 billion in 1995 to $118 billion in 2005, accounting for 44 percent of the growth in Medicaid payments in recent years, followed by children at 19 percent, elderly persons at 18 percent, and other, nondisabled adults at 14 percent. Medicaid expenditures for the disabled increased from 27 percent of all Medicaid payments in 1975 to 43 percent in 2005. The growth in noninstitutional behavioral health spending contributed to this trend, with Medicaid now accounting for more than half of public mental health spending by the states.[13] Another factor was the use of prescription drugs and home and community-based long-term care services, which have expanded greatly for the disabled, particularly those with mental disabilities.[14] The expansion reflected, in part, recent efforts among political advocacy groups representing disabled persons and their families and by providers of Medicaid-covered services, including pharmaceutical companies, home care agencies, and other community service providers. These interests, which span for-profit and nonprofit sectors, have often worked in concert to obtain expanded program eligibility and coverage for persons with disabilities.

Medicaid trends reflect changing service-use patterns in the broader health care sector; increasing use of hospital outpatient services is one recent example. They also reflect shifts in the mix of Medicaid eligibles and changes in program coverage that favor one service over another, such as home care over nursing home care. In contrast to Medicare (a program covering acute care services), Medicaid has always covered a broader set of services that includes preventive and long-term care services. But the mix of these services has changed over time. Looking only at the basic Medicaid services—excluding disproportionate share hospital (DSH) payments

TABLE 2-5

MEDICAID ENROLLMENT AND PAYMENT TRENDS BY BASIS OF ELIGIBILITY,
1995–2005

| | ————Amounts (millions)———— | | |
	1995	2000	2005
Average monthly enrollment (millions)			
Total	33.4	33.6	45.5
Elderly	3.7	3.7	4.6
Blind/Disabled	5.8	6.7	8.1
Children	16.5	16.2	22.3
Adults	6.7	6.9	10.6
CHIP	NA	2.0	4.4
Medicaid payments (millions)			
Total	$120,141	$168,307	$273,203
Elderly	36,527	44,503	62,929
Blind/Disabled	49,418	72,742	118,683
Children	17,976	26,775	46,846
Adults	13,511	17,763	32,215
Unknown	1,499	6,525	12,530
Average monthly payment per recipient			
All	$300	$417	$500
Elderly	823	1,002	1,140
Blind/Disabled	710	905	1,221
Children	91	138	175
Adults	168	215	253

SOURCE: Computed from U.S. Department of Health and Human Services, Centers for Medicare and Medicaid Services (2008).
NOTE: The adults category includes only adults not otherwise eligible based on age above sixty-five or disability.

and early periodic screening diagnosis and treatment (EPSDT) services, tar-geted case management, and Medicare premiums paid by Medicaid for dual-eligibles—we see some significant shifts in their composition between 1980 and 2006 (see table 2-6).

Percentage distribution		Annual growth rates	
1995	2005	1995–2000	2000–2005
100%	100%	0.1%	6.3%
11	10	0.0	4.5
17	18	2.9	3.9
49	49	−0.4	6.6
23	23	0.6	9.0
		17.1	
100%	100%	7.0%	10.2%
30	23	4.0	7.2
41	43	8.0	10.3
15	17	8.3	11.8
11	12	5.6	12.6
1	5	34.2	13.9
		6.8%	3.7%
		4.0	2.6
		5.0	6.2
		8.7	4.9
		5.0	3.4

First is the growth in importance since 1980 of various types of Medicaid managed care health plans paid on a per-capita (or capitated) basis for each person enrolled. Capitated services now involve more than 50 percent of Medicaid recipients, and they accounted for 21.6 percent of payments for Medicaid services in 2006.[15] The offsetting effect was a reduction in the relative importance of hospital and physician services paid for by Medicaid on a fee-for-service basis. Second is a shift in the relative importance of

TABLE 2-6

CHANGES IN THE COMPOSITION OF MEDICAID PAYMENTS, 1980–2006

Service category	1980	2006	Percentage point change
Inpatient general hospitals	26.5%	16.6%	–9.9
Inpatient mental hospitals	3.6	1.3	–2.4
Nursing facility services	33.6	18.6	–15.0
Intermediate care facility services for mentally retarded	8.4	5.0	–3.4
Community-based long-term care services	1.4	15.6	14.2
Prescribed drugs	5.6	6.5	0.9
Physician services	7.9	4.9	–3.0
Dental services	2.0	1.3	–0.7
Outpatient hospital services	4.6	4.5	–0.1
Clinic services	1.4	3.6	2.2
Laboratory and radiological services	4.9	0.5	–4.5
Capitation payments (non-Medicare)	0.0	21.6	21.6
Total	100	100	

SOURCES: HCFA Program Statistics, March 1982, as reported in Grannemann and Pauly (1983, 8), and U.S. Department of Health and Human Services, Centers for Medicare and Medicaid Services (2008, table II.6). Figures adjusted by the authors to provide consistent service categories.
NOTE: 0% indicates services not separately reported in 1980.

institutional and community-based long-term care services; nursing facility services dropped from 33.6 percent to 18.6 percent of Medicaid payments for these basic services, while community-based services increased from 1.4 percent to 15.6 percent. With the implementation of Medicare Part D, prescription drugs, which had grown to more than 10 percent of Medicaid in 2005, dropped back to 6.5 percent of these services in 2006—if one does not count the "clawback" payments states contributed to Part D for dual-eligibles.[16] This period also saw a decline in the relative importance of intermediate care facilities for the mentally retarded (ICF-MR), mental hospitals, and dental services. Clinic services, representing payments to community health centers and rural health centers, more than doubled their share of Medicaid payments.

We see, then, that the role of Medicaid changes over time, but in ways that reflect policy decisions regarding eligibility, payment, and coverage, as well as general trends in the health care sector. It is not so much a program buffeted by uncontrollable external factors as one whose composition and growth reflect the roles it is assigned by policymakers as they strive to satisfy public demand for a program that does more things for more people over time.

Medicaid Embodies a Set of Implicit Promises

Medicaid can be viewed as a set of public-sector promises or assurances to the various participants in our system for financing and delivering medical care to the poor. Governments make promises to the poor to ensure they have access to medical services; they make promises to providers to pay them fairly and adequately for services delivered; and they make promises to taxpayers to allocate resources in accordance with Medicaid's publicly stated goals and to distribute the costs of the program fairly among taxpayers. The federal government promises to reimburse the states for at least half of the program's costs; in return, the states promise the federal government they will spend in accordance with federal rules and account for the monies spent. The success of the program depends to a large degree on how well these promises are kept.

The problems of today are a product of decisions of the past. Many of today's disappointments with the Medicaid program are based on the perception that past promises have been broken. Eligibility in many states is narrower than some might have expected; provider payment rates are less than providers expect to receive for their services; the unpredictability of Medicaid budgets creates problems for legislators and for the taxpayers they represent. Each of these groups—recipients, providers, and taxpayers—might well feel that this program has failed in some significant way to solve their problems or meet their needs. They might argue that the promise of Medicaid is unfulfilled by the program as it currently exists.

Expenditure of public funds on social welfare programs, including health care programs, entails making commitments as a matter of public policy. In politics, of course, anything can be changed, but good policy requires stable commitments that make sense in themselves, and so we will postulate that such a system is desirable for Medicaid. The commitments made should be consistent with society's values, preferences, and resources. For Medicaid, several major areas of commitments are to be considered:

- Promises to state governments
- Promises to current recipients
- Promises to providers
- Promises to taxpayers
- Promises to lower-income people without health insurance

Determining what the extent and nature of these promises are today, and more importantly what they *should be*, is central to the formulation of Medicaid policy.

Promises to State Governments. With the establishment of the Medicaid program, the federal government took on a major commitment to help states provide health insurance to some categories of low-income people. The federal commitment is embodied in the administrative support it provides for the program and in the federal matching funding. While the basic formula for discharging this commitment has remained very stable, possible improvements in the extent and nature of that funding and how it is distributed among the states have been debated as central policy issues for many years. Providing some federal support for states has been an easy promise to keep, but state expectations often exceed federal promises, and states can be creative in finding ways to extract more from a federal promise than may have been intended when it was made.

Promises to Recipients. Medicaid makes a commitment to improve the access of certain populations to valued medical services. The program has long provided a fairly comprehensive package of benefits with minimal patient cost-sharing requirements, designed for recipients who have especially high needs and low ability to pay. While federal law requires states to offer specified mandatory services to persons in specified categorical eligibility groups,[17] they can limit eligibility by income level and put certain limits on services. Medicaid pays for services within the same delivery system used by private payers, but full access to that system is constrained in some states for some types of services by low payment rates. Thus, Medicaid's promises to recipients are shaped by state policies and practices. In many states, the reality is that the fulfillment of these promises is at risk in every budget cycle, depending upon the short-term performance of the local economy and the funds expected to be available in the state treasury. In subsequent chapters we will consider how states determine and manage Medicaid benefits, and explore ways to make Medicaid more predictable for recipients as well as taxpayers.

Promises to Providers. As a health care *insurance* program—not a health care *delivery* program—Medicaid relies on independent providers to deliver medical services to recipients. The commitment to providers is somewhat difficult to identify because of a divergence between stated policy and practice. There is a tacit commitment to provide fair and consistent (as opposed to biased and unpredictable) payment, but little precision as to how that is to be achieved. Federal courts have found that states have an obligation to provide payment rates that are "reasonable and adequate." Because there is no fixed definition of "adequacy," this obligation has not deterred many states from setting payment rates to some providers below those of other payers, even though doing so may reduce access of recipients to many of those lower-paid providers. Despite some court rulings that may constrain state decisions, states currently do have some degree of latitude to set payments high or low to achieve desired objectives. Some have chosen to set rates at low levels, often, in effect, limiting access or quantity below the levels that some privately insured persons have come to expect, while others pay relatively high rates to at least some of their providers. Whether these payment practices should be changed is a question we will address.

Promises to Taxpayers. Medicaid administrators and policymakers may be viewed as having an obligation to spend resources as voter-taxpayers desire, to use them wisely, and to distribute the tax burden equitably. In our current constitutional framework, no one has an inherent right to any particular level of medical coverage at public expense. As with other public programs, Medicaid is accountable to the voters through the democratic process. It must demonstrate value to voters for its requisite level of public funding.

Equity among taxpayers is also a concern. In a complex federal–state financing system with programs widely differing among states, the burden of Medicaid costs on taxpayers may likewise vary by state, and may do so for reasons other than state choices about program generosity. Every taxpayer is potentially subject to two Medicaid-related burdens: payment of state taxes that go to Medicaid and payment of federal taxes that are used for the federal share. It is the total burden (from both sources) that should matter for fairness. While the federal share of costs may be equitably borne largely through federal income taxes, the state shares can vary greatly. The required state contribution can be a barrier to the provision of benefits in lower-income states with many poor persons and comparatively few wealthy taxpayers, or in any state in times of economic downturn—a problem that, we will show, is only very inadequately addressed by the current matching-rate structure. Over the years, this dimension of the Medicaid program has remained largely below the surface in most policy analyses; that, too, is a topic we will address directly in this work.

Promises to Lower-Income People without Health Insurance. To date, Medicaid has limited its obligations by including only *some* lower-income populations in its categorical eligibility groups; a direct obligation to pay for care for all of the uninsured, or even all of the low-income uninsured, has never been assumed. Care for uninsured persons who use certain providers may be indirectly supported through Medicaid's disproportionate share hospital (DSH) payments and its comparatively generous payment rates to some safety-net providers, such as critical access hospitals and federally qualified health centers (FQHCs). The extent of Medicaid's commitment to the uninsured, however—and whether the program is the best vehicle to provide coverage as one goes up the recipient income scale—is an issue to consider as policymakers examine new ways to address the problems of the low-income uninsured population.

For each of the stakeholder groups (recipients, providers, and taxpayers), Medicaid's current promises and commitments can appear to fall short of their desires. Advocates for various segments within each class of stakeholders are always pressing policymakers to expand and extend these commitments, while limited resources may dictate cutbacks. There are bound to be tradeoffs. We believe that some policy adjustments can produce mutually beneficial changes, and that some specific commitments can be satisfied more effectively over time. Unanimity across constituencies is, however, neither to be expected nor generally desired.

Medicaid Promises as a Framework for Enlightened Policymaking

Since at least the time of Plato, or perhaps Hammurabi, policy thinkers have recognized the need for (and the difficulty of) bringing thoughtful analysis to bear on governance decisions. In modern America, a whole industry has emerged to provide public decision-makers with policy analysis. This industry includes academic researchers, research and consulting firms, and nonprofit think tanks in the Washington, D.C., area, Cambridge, and elsewhere. It also includes in-house policy analysts at government agencies such as the Congressional Budget Office, the Government Accountability Office (GAO), the Library of Congress, and various administrative agencies at the federal level and within the executive and legislative branches at the state level.

Competent analysts new to the field are often surprised at the extent to which their research is ignored or given scant attention in the policy process. The democratic process is not explicitly designed to accept such input. It is up to elected and appointed policymakers to obtain and use such information as they see fit. Analysts are, therefore, responsible for making their work relevant and presenting it in a usable form, while keeping it honest and unbiased—even at the risk of diminishing its political effectiveness.[18]

We hope our approach to Medicaid policy development will fulfill this responsibility and help other policy analysts in their work. Our approach calls for developing an understanding of fundamental societal choices, assessing the economics and political positions of key stakeholders, and only then applying research and analysis to policy decisions. We are suggesting an analytical framework and language for considering issues and interests in the context of public values, based on the level of commitment implied by promises to taxpayers, providers, and recipients. We believe this will help policymakers give due consideration to some of the complicated issues in Medicaid policy, particularly those involving resource allocation and tradeoffs. Our hope is that, by taking explicit account of the various players and the resource constraints, this approach will help produce policy that is important, relevant, and politically acceptable.

Conclusion to Part I:
Fundamental Policy Questions

What, then, are the fundamental policy issues facing Medicaid? We choose to highlight five essential questions related to the long-run fiscal sustainability of the program. None is easy to answer; each is more complex than it may at first appear. None is likely to yield any immediate consensus; each is a challenging policy problem worthy of discussion, debate, analysis, and serious consideration by policymakers at the state and federal levels. How the nation answers these questions will determine the shape of Medicaid and how well it succeeds in meeting its objectives, both as a program for today and as a stepping stone to the health care financing system of the future:

- What should be the extent of Medicaid eligibility and benefits?

- To what extent (and when) should Medicaid recipients pay for a portion of their care or their insurance?

- How should the program be managed? Are there more accountable ways to manage Medicaid's resources?

- What should be the nature and amount of federal financial support to each state for Medicaid?

- How (and how much) should Medicaid pay providers?

- What should be the role of Medicaid and CHIP in extending insurance coverage to those groups that are currently uninsured?

While other Medicaid policy questions are also important, we are highlighting these five "should" questions to draw attention to the underlying promises Medicaid makes to its various stakeholders, and to call for an assessment of the nation's values and priorities regarding medical care for the poor. Policymaking requires value judgments; we want to put these choices front and center rather than keep them in the background. We present the choices within a framework that may help policymakers find some common ground based on shared principles. Nonetheless, much hard work remains for analysts and policymakers as they sort through the costs and expected impacts of different policies for the nation. Fundamentally, these questions can only be answered, in ways that matter, through the democratic process.

Perspective matters. Federal policymakers, state administrators, state legislators, providers, recipients, and their advocates all look at Medicaid from distinct points of view. Each group has its own objectives, none of which is intrinsically or objectively "right." To some degree, the persons in these groups may hold different values about helping lower-income people or may prefer different methods of providing help. We have found over the years, however, that the positions people take on Medicaid policy are, almost invariably, shaped substantially by their distinct roles and correspond very closely with the economic self-interests of the groups they represent. For this reason, understanding these differing perspectives and the economic factors affecting each group can give policy *analysts* a much better understanding of why Medicaid policy evolves in a particular way, and a better feel for the political feasibility of policy proposals. Such understanding can also give policy*makers* a better appreciation of the forces guiding and resisting policy and a way to recognize solutions that meet the needs of all involved. In the next three parts of the book, we explore the particular perspectives and interests of recipients, taxpayers, and providers as they relate to Medicaid policy issues.

PART II

Making and Meeting Promises
to the Poor

Medicaid's promises to the population it serves have never been well defined. Even the definition of the population itself has been unclear and has shifted over time. Medicaid began in the 1960s with a promise to help states with the cost of caring for the poor. That promise did not, however, include a commitment to meet any specified standard of care. Over the years, our national commitment to serve the low-income population has evolved and grown, but it has been expressed unevenly among the states and still lacks any defined standard. We do not seek in this book to define any such standard; rather, we will try to clarify what factors ought to be considered by policymakers in assessing the public value of providing medical assistance benefits to disadvantaged populations, and the best ways to control the resources used for that purpose.

In part 2 we look at Medicaid from the perspective of its target populations, consider how the program's resources are being used to serve its recipients, and explore how those resources might be structured to use public dollars to the best advantage. States consider changes in Medicaid benefits and how they are to be managed in virtually every budget cycle. Policymaking in this area requires a clear understanding of where Medicaid dollars are going, who is supposed to benefit, and what results might actually be achieved by raising or reducing spending in a given area. Toward that end, we begin with some basic information on Medicaid spending for each of the major eligibility groups and types of services, focusing particularly on the variations in spending among states and the implications for equity and efficiency. This background provides some insight into how states have used Medicaid resources in their efforts to meet the needs of their low-income populations. We then consider the ways states have tried to stretch their dollars with care management programs, and we identify other ways they might ensure that program dollars are spent on services of greatest value to the program's beneficiaries.

3

Ensuring Access for the Poor Population

A fundamental objective of the Medicaid program is to provide access to needed medical care for those least able to pay for it themselves. But this objective has been met very unevenly in the states and territories. In this chapter we explore some of the sources of that variation in state responses to the structure and incentives created by federal law, regulations, and financing.

Disadvantaged Populations

The Medicaid program has always been defined, in part, by its categories of eligibility. Medicaid's eligibility requirements reflect a political decision that some groups are more needful or deserving than others of help in obtaining health insurance. Persons can become eligible if they demonstrate they both have sufficiently low resources and can be categorized as aged, blind, disabled, or members of low-income families with children. A Kaiser Family Foundation publication identifies seventy distinct pathways to Medicaid eligibility based on age, income, and situational criteria for the various target groups.[1] The number of these eligibility groups has grown over time, as has the complexity of the definitions. New groups have been added as federal and state policymakers have recognized additional needs, partly in response to concerns raised by various advocacy groups. To date, the largest needy groups not eligible for Medicaid include low-income adults without young children and middle-income elderly who need long-term care. While no major category has ever been withdrawn, states have altered the criteria of eligibility (such as income levels) upward and downward over time.

Medicaid is used differently by each of its eligibility groups. For those children and mothers on Temporary Assistance for Needy Families (TANF),

Medicaid is most commonly used for primary care and care related to pregnancy, including prenatal services, delivery, and neonatal care. For those dually eligible for Medicare and Medicaid (low-income elderly and disabled persons), Medicaid provides coverage to wrap around Medicare benefits, with Medicaid in most states picking up the cost of Medicare premiums and copayments. To the low-income elderly, Medicaid's most important coverage can be long-term care—a benefit of most value to those, most often women, who outlive their spouses and have meager resources. Coverage of nursing home services typically includes a requirement that the recipients spend down assets and apply any available current income toward nursing home expenses, with Medicaid paying the remainder. In federal fiscal year 2007, the elderly accounted for only about 10 percent of Medicaid recipients but about 24 percent of Medicaid provider payments, the higher payment percentage largely reflecting the cost of long-term nursing home care and drugs.[2]

The disabled population—including both disabled children and adults with physical or mental disabilities—relies on Medicaid for comprehensive medical coverage. This eligibility group contains about 18 percent of recipients, but accounts for about 43 percent of Medicaid provider payments. As with the elderly, key cost components are drugs and long-term care, and, for the disabled in particular, community-based long-term care services are increasingly a factor. Even the conventional medical costs per (older) disabled beneficiary are higher than the cost of care for TANF children—that is, children eligible as recipients in the Temporary Assistance for Needy Families program rather than as a result of a disability. State Medicaid programs often structure their eligibility rules on counting income and assets so that families not below the official poverty line can qualify for coverage for their severely disabled children. For example, the "Katie Beckett" option allows states to provide Medicaid benefits for in-home services to disabled children if it is deemed that they would meet the eligibility standard if they were institutionalized and parental income and resources were not counted.[3] This effectively extends Medicaid coverage to many middle-income families with severely disabled children.

Medicaid has had broadly defined benefit packages. Although benefits differ among the states, they build on a core set of "mandatory" services generally to cover, within limits, a full range of acute and long-term care services. In recognition of the fact that the program serves persons without the resources to contribute much to the cost of their medical care, these benefits typically come with minimal or no requirements for recipient cost-sharing. One problem often noted in the structure of Medicaid is its "all-or-nothing" eligibility: Medicaid-enrolled persons receive a full package of comprehensive benefits, while those falling outside the eligibility categories, or just above the income cutoff, receive nothing. Spend-down provisions in some states ameliorate this problem somewhat but do not eliminate a fairly dramatic drop, or "notch," in public support as a function of recipient income.

A comprehensive package of benefits with minimal cost-sharing made some sense in Medicaid's early years, when eligibility was more closely focused on the poorest of the poor—people who needed help with virtually everything and could contribute little or nothing toward the cost of their care. But this program feature has always raised questions about what to do with those who are only a little better off (or a little different in age or family status) but still do not quite meet the eligibility requirements. The social concern underlying Medicaid presumably does not fall instantly to zero for poor people in ineligible groups, so cutting them off from benefits completely can seem unreasonable as well as unfair. Moreover, this notch in benefits at the income eligibility level creates reasons for some to reject available employment to protect their Medicaid eligibility. This has been ameliorated to some degree for some elderly and disabled groups by optional program components that pay some costs, such as the Medicare Part B or Part A premium, or allow spend-down to eligibility for long-term care, or provide limited benefits to those above the usual income or when working.[4] But until the creation of the State Children's Health Insurance Program (CHIP), states had little ability to provide benefits less costly than Medicaid's comprehensive coverage, to provide anything less heavily subsidized than free insurance, or to charge the beneficiary for more than a nominal portion of the cost of the insurance or the care.

State discretion over what eligibility groups and service categories are covered has resulted in wide differences among the states, and in uneven changes over time within states. In addition, periodic spurts in Medicaid spending growth and periodic fiscal crises for different states have posed problems for accommodating Medicaid within federal and state budgets. The disparities across states and over time create a confused and contentious pattern.

Interstate Equity in Eligibility and Benefits

As a federal–state program, Medicaid lacks uniform standards for eligibility and benefits. To what degree do benefits differ among states, and do such differences constitute significant inequities in how persons are treated among states?[5] For Medicaid, with its diverse set of acute- and long-term care services, these are not simple questions to sort out, given also the wide interstate differences in incomes, cost of living, and medical care prices, and in patterns of service use. They would not be simple even for a uniform national program such as Medicare, which has a much narrower set of (acute care) services, for which the medical costs per recipient vary widely.[6]

In assessing equity, it is important to account for as many such factors as possible, and to tease out differences in benefits available to the poor and near-poor that cannot be explained by underlying cost differences. Equity depends not only on whether the dollar value of coverage is the same, or even whether those dollars could buy the same services, but also, more importantly, on the value of those services in producing better health or well-being. For this reason, we document the differences in Medicaid spending relative to the number of poor or near-poor, then consider how those differences are related to state characteristics. Finally, we make an assessment of where such differences may be viewed as inequitable for Medicaid recipients, and for low-income or disadvantaged populations more generally.

To begin, we need some convenient way to compare state Medicaid benefits. We would like to have a single measure that could be used to compare benefits provided among diverse state programs—essentially, a measure of the generosity of the benefit package that captures the effects of eligibility standards, outreach efforts, access achieved in local markets, and level of services provided.[7] A useful such measure is states' "Medicaid payments per poor person." As a simple quotient of two complex aggregates, it is imperfect, to be sure. It depends on the extent and mix of services covered and the prices paid for those services. Not all benefits go to persons actually below the poverty level, and not all persons below the poverty level receive benefits. The measure may be low in one state that restricts eligibility for children to the federally mandated minimum; it may be high in another that generously pays its hospitals or provides extensive home care services for its elderly and disabled populations. Nonetheless, as a product of all these factors across a diverse set of eligibility groups and services, "Medicaid payments per poor person" provides a reasonable and convenient indicator of the overall level of resources a state devotes annually toward meeting the needs of a typical low-income person. While recognizing its limitations, we will use Medicaid payments per poor person as a convenient measure to compare state programs. Let's look at some statistics.

We saw in chapter 1 that Medicaid payments per poor person differ widely among the states and tend to be higher in the Northeast and some midwestern states. The differences can be viewed as presenting a problem of equity. For example, a child between the ages of six and nineteen years in a family at 101 percent of the federal poverty level (FPL) would be excluded in any of twenty states, yet eligible in a family with income up to 300 percent of the FPL in four other jurisdictions.[8] We will explore how these interstate differences relate to state characteristics, particularly state income, and consider what they might mean for the health and well-being of recipients.

Differences in Benefit Levels among the States

In general, Medicaid benefits are considerably higher in higher-income states than in lower-income states, as are Medicaid payments per beneficiary, despite the much higher federal matching percentage share in lower-income states. This spending level is about 89 percent greater in the highest quintile of states by income than in the lowest (see figure 3-1). The differences exist in all the major eligibility groups and appear in both spending per Medicaid recipient (see table 3-1) and in number of recipients as a percentage of the poor population (see table A1-1). So the overall variance is due both to eligibility differences and to differences in payments per enrolled beneficiary. The differences are greater for the elderly and disabled eligibility groups. As we would expect given federal eligibility requirements for children—mandatory up to 100 percent of the FPL for children ages five to nineteen, and up to 133 percent of the FPL for children under five—the number of Medicaid-covered children exceeds the number of children below the poverty level in all states. But the ratio of Medicaid-covered children to children in poverty varies among states, from less than 1.75 (in Ala-

TABLE 3-1

MEDICAID PAYMENTS BY STATE INCOME QUINTILE

Median household income quintile	Medicaid payments by median household income quintile, FY 2006, payments per recipient		
	Children	Adults	Elderly
Top quintile	$2,419	$2,892	$14,883
Second quintile	$1,779	$2,426	$10,487
Middle quintile	$1,768	$2,868	$12,681
Third quintile	$1,907	$2,885	$11,499
Lowest quintile	$1,839	$2,302	$8,857
Ratio top to bottom quintile	1.32	1.26	1.68

SOURCE: Kaiser Family Foundation 2009, "State Health Facts. Medicaid Payments Per Enrollee, FY2006," http://www.statehealthfacts.org/comparetable.jsp?ind=183&cat=4.

FIGURE 3-1

MEDICAID PAYMENTS PER POOR PERSON, FY 2006
BY STATE MEDIAN HOUSEHOLD INCOME QUINTILE

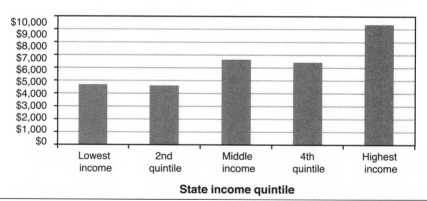

SOURCES: Computed from Kaiser Family Foundation (2009, "Federal and State Share of Medicaid Spending, FY2006," http://www.statehealthfacts.org) and U.S. Census Bureau (2008a).

		Medicaid payments by median household income quintile, FY 2006, payments per recipient		
Disabled	All	Medicaid pay per poor person	Median household income
$16,767	$6,781	$11,134	$62,729
$13,747	$4,625	$7,600	$55,848
$12,437	$4,816	$7,584	$50,584
$13,171	$4,925	$6,645	$47,503
$9,243	$4,155	$5,892	$41,035
1.81	1.63	1.89	1.53

bama, Mississippi, Texas, Kansas, Nevada, Arizona, and Oregon) to more than 2.5 (in Maryland, Hawaii, New Hampshire, Connecticut, Alaska, Minnesota, and Delaware), and over 4.0 in Vermont (see appendix 1, table A1-1). Some of the higher spending in the higher-income states is attributable to higher medical care prices there, though even many higher-income states have chosen to keep Medicaid provider payment rates low. In the past, the relationship of eligibility and spending to state income was stronger than it is now, as spending by poorer states has grown more rapidly than that by richer states, partially in response to federal mandates. But there is still a difference. The key question is whether the degree of variation in spending per poor person according to average state income is the right amount or too much. Clearly, Medicaid spending per poor person is still unequal across states. Federal assistance serves to raise spending in all states, but a large share of that assistance accrues to higher-income states to support levels of benefits (particularly for long-term care) that are not provided in states that are less able or less willing to provide such benefits.

Medicaid Benefits and State Income. What accounts for the observable differences between the higher-income and higher-benefit states and their

TABLE 3-2

STATES CLASSIFIED BY INCOME AND MEDICAID BENEFIT LEVEL GROUPS

Medicaid benefit level group	Higher-income	Mid-income	Lower-income
Higher-benefit	CT, DE, MA, MD, MN, NJ, NY, RI	AK, NH, VT	ME
Mid-benefit	CA, IL, WA, WY	HI, IN, KS, MI, MO, NC, OH, PA, TN, WI	FL, IA, KY, NE, ND, NM, SC, SD, WV
Lower-benefit	CO, VA	AL, AZ, GA, NV, OR, TX, UT	AR, ID, LA, MS, MT, OK

(Header span: ——————Taxpayer income group——————)

SOURCES: States classified using data from Kaiser Family Foundation (2009), U.S. Census Bureau (2008b), and U.S. Internal Revenue Service (2007).

lower-income and lower-benefit counterparts? To determine this, we can compare the characteristics of these states and look at the differences in patterns of Medicaid spending among the eligibility groups. We can see which states are providing higher benefits and, to some degree, what the higher-benefit states are buying with their additional spending. We can also look at the exceptions: There is at least one lower-income, higher-benefit state, and several higher-income, lower-benefit states.

For purposes of comparison, we divide the states into a three-by-three matrix of nine groups, based on overall benefit level (Medicaid spending per poor person) and taxpayer adjusted gross income (AGI) per annual federal personal income tax return.[9] Table 3-2 shows how the states are grouped on these dimensions. Higher-income, higher-benefit states (mostly in the Northeast) are Connecticut, Delaware, Massachusetts, Maryland, Minnesota, New Jersey, New York, and Rhode Island. Lower-income, lower-benefit states (in the South and West) are Arkansas, Idaho, Louisiana, Mississippi, Montana, and Oklahoma. Most other states fall in the middle in either income or benefit levels, but a few outliers appear as exceptions to the pattern of benefits related to income. Maine is a lower-income state that has high Medicaid spending.[10] Colorado and Virginia are higher-income states that have chosen to keep Medicaid spending low relative to other states.

This categorization is useful for comparing state program characteristics, both by income and by benefit levels. For the purpose of initial contrasting, we ignore the middle-income, middle-benefit group and compare higher-income to lower-income states.[11] Then we contrast the higher-benefit to lower-benefit states.[12] Finally, we compare the higher-income, higher-benefit states to the lower-income, lower-benefit states.[13] The results of these three types of comparisons are shown in table 3-3.

Let's look first at states by *level of income*, regardless of the level of benefit. In the first column of table 3-3, we see that the higher-income states in our classification have taxpayer incomes that are about 31–47 percent higher than those in the lower-income states, depending on which of our three measures of state income is used. Medicaid payments per poor person are about 43 percent higher in the higher-income states than in the lower-income states. Looking at Medicaid eligibility, we see that the ratio of recipients to the number of persons below the federal poverty level is higher in the higher-income states. The higher-income states actually have a smaller proportion of all elderly individuals covered than the lower-income states, however, presumably because comparatively fewer of the elderly in the higher-income states need assistance beyond what is already provided through Medicare. Nonetheless, the higher-income states spend more per Medicaid-covered person in all eligibility groups, ranging from only slightly more (3–5 percent higher) for children and for nonelderly, nondisabled adults, to over 25 percent more for the elderly and disabled recipients. Despite these higher benefits for their poor populations, the higher-income states' spending *per taxpayer* is about the same as in the lower-income states, but it is a smaller *share* of taxpayer income. After accounting for differences in federal financial assistance, we find the state share as a percentage of taxpayer income about 10 percent higher in the higher-income states.

We now look at the states by *level of benefit per person*, as represented in the second column of table 3-3. We see that the higher-benefit states in our classification have incomes that are about 25 percent higher than the lower-benefit states by any of our three measures of income in the state. Medicaid payments per poor person are more than two and a half times those in the lower-benefit states. These higher-benefit states cover a somewhat greater share of the elderly and disabled, and they spend more per Medicaid recipient for all of the eligibility groups, ranging from 37 percent more for

TABLE 3-3

COMPARISON OF INCOME AND BENEFIT GROUPS

| | Ratios of measures | | |
	Ratio of higher-income to lower-income states	Ratio of higher-benefit to lower-benefit states	Ratio of higher-income, higher-benefit to lower-income, lower-benefit states
Income			
Personal income per capita, 2005	136%	126%	148%
Median household income	131%	124%	142%
AGI per return 2003	147%	125%	159%
Medicaid benefits			
Payments per poor person	143%	261%	240%
Recipients per poor person	122%	157%	144%
Percentage of elderly covered by Medicaid	92%	110%	77%
Percentage of disabled covered Medicaid	105%	118%	116%
Payment per elder recipient	125%	158%	167%
Payment per disabled recipient	132%	170%	172%
Payment per child recipient	105%	170%	144%
Payment per adult recipient	103%	137%	118%
Medicaid pay per capita	104%	176%	146%
Medicaid pay per poor person	145%	266%	250%
Medicaid pay per taxpayer	97%	159%	132%
Medicaid as percentage of taxpayer income	66%	126%	84%
Medicaid state share as percentage of taxpayer income	110%	179%	155%
FMAP 2004	73%	82%	70%
Pct below FPL 2004	69%	65%	58%
Uncovered percentage of population	92%	74%	73%
Uncovered percentage of children	99%	68%	77%

Continued on the next page

Table 3-3, continued

	Ratios of measures		
	Ratio of higher-income to lower-income states	Ratio of higher-benefit to lower-benefit states	Ratio of higher-income, higher-benefit to lower-income, lower-benefit states
Physician fees			
Fees all	93%	97%	91%
Fees primary care	93%	98%	88%
Fees OB	98%	100%	105%
Fees other	86%	92%	85%
Fee all relative to Medicare	84%	89%	80%
Fee primary relative to Medicare	83%	89%	76%
Fee OB relative to Medicare	87%	93%	92%
Fee other relative to Medicare	77%	84%	74%
Physician fee all, adjusted for cost	82%	90%	79%
Physician fee primary care, adjusted for cost	82%	90%	76%
Physician fee OB, adjusted for cost	86%	93%	91%
Physician fee other, adjusted for cost	76%	85%	74%
Cost to taxpayer			
Medicaid price to state taxpayer	188%	147%	211%
Cost per taxpayer of visit for every poor person*	127%	94%	114%
Cost per taxpayer of visit for every poor person as a percentage of taxpayer income*	87%	75%	73%

SOURCE: Computations by the authors.
NOTES: See columns and rows of table 3-1 for states in these groups; * = ratio measures reflect the relative estimated average cost per state taxpayer of providing a physician office visit to every poor person in the state, adjusting for the federal matching rate and medical prices as represented by practice costs.

nonelderly, nondisabled adults to 70 percent more per child and disabled recipient. The fraction of the population without health insurance in the higher-benefit states is only about 68 percent of that in the lower-benefit states, linking the interstate differences in Medicaid to the broader problem of the nation's uninsured.

Interestingly, the higher-income, higher-benefit states do not seem to pay higher fees to physicians. In fact, their physician fee schedules have slightly lower rates; and when we account for the higher costs in these states, we find their physician fees about 15 percent lower than those of their lower-income and lower-benefit counterparts when represented as a percentage of Medicare rates. We have, therefore, little evidence that higher Medicaid spending is going to higher physician payment rates. The higher-income, higher-benefit states may, by keeping physician payments low, effectively divert more recipients to more expensive sources of care, such as federally qualified health centers (FQHCs), physicians in hospital-based practices affiliated with outpatient departments, and Medicaid managed care plans.

Perhaps the most telling finding here relates to the effective price to the taxpayer of providing Medicaid benefits to the poor, which we report in the last three rows of table 3-3. As would be expected given their lower federal matching rates, the higher-income states face a higher cost (in state funds) for each dollar of Medicaid spending. In fact, the effective price to taxpayers of providing Medicaid benefits is 88 percent higher in the higher-income states and 47 percent higher in the higher-benefit states when compared, respectively, to the lower-income and lower-benefit groups of states.

To get a true picture of what it costs the voter-taxpayer to provide higher Medicaid benefit levels, however, we can look at what it would cost to extend such benefits to all the poor in the state. We do this by estimating the relative cost (accounting for geographic differences in physician practice costs and number of persons below the poverty level) to the taxpayer of providing a physician visit to every poor person in the state. We compute such measures as *cost per taxpayer* and *cost as a share of taxpayer income*. These measures (in the last two rows of table 3-3) account for the fact that the higher-income and higher-benefit states have relatively fewer persons below the poverty level and relatively more higher-income taxpayers. We also see that, while it would cost each higher-*income* state taxpayer 27 percent more (in dollars) to provide a physician visit to every poor person (at cost-adjusted rates), taxpayers in higher-*benefit* states would actually pay about 6 percent less to provide such benefits. That is, the high-benefit states may be high-benefit in large part because the small number of poor persons relative to taxpayers in such states makes it less costly for them to provide generous benefit packages. This is not fully offset or changed by prices and the current structure of federal financial assistance. Moreover, when looked at as a share of taxpayer income, the cost (income tax rate) to provide a uniform level of such a benefit to all the poor is lower in the higher-income states than in the lower-income states (87 percent) and even lower (75 percent) in the higher-benefit states than the lower-benefit states.

What this means is that, under the current matching-rate system, it costs taxpayers in the higher-income states less as a percentage of their income to extend any specified level of benefits to their poor populations than it costs taxpayers in the lower-income states. In this sense, Medicaid, as configured with current matching rates, can be viewed as being financed with a regressive tax on state taxpayers, who are asked to support benefits for their poor through this system. It is not surprising, then, that in such a system we see the lower-income states choosing to provide lower Medicaid benefits to their poor populations.

Even though the Medicaid financing formula appears on the surface, then, to favor lower-income states, one must take into account the dual effect of relatively lower fiscal capacity (represented by lower taxpayer income) and greater need (represented by greater numbers of poor people) in the lower-income states. Overall, the current financial arrangement is regressive as measured by percentage of taxpayer income. To avoid this problem, the matching formula would need to account in a compound way for *both* taxpayer income and the number of poor people, rather than a single measure of state per-capita income.

Are the Variations Real? Some analysts question whether "Medicaid payments per poor person" is a good indicator of variations in benefits among states. They note that the federal poverty level is not adjusted for cost of living (which might lead to an undercount of poverty in higher-cost areas and an overcount in lower-cost areas). Additionally, medical care costs tend to be higher in higher-cost areas, and less care might be purchased for the Medicaid dollar there. To account for these effects, we adjust the federal

FIGURE 3-2

REAL MEDICAID PAYMENTS PER PERSON BELOW 125 PERCENT
OF COST-OF-LIVING–ADJUSTED FEDERAL POVERTY LEVEL, FY 2007

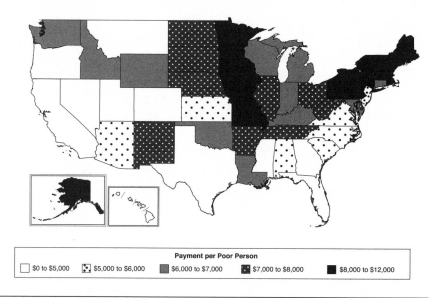

SOURCES: Computed using data from U.S. Census Bureau (2008b) and Kaiser Family Foundation (2009,
"Federal and State Share of Medicaid Spending, FY2006," http://www.statehealthfacts.org).
NOTES: Total federal and state medical payments FY 2007 include DSH, exclude administrative costs;
payments deflated by average of physician practice cost index; number of poor estimated by adjusting
125 percent of FPL by ACCRA cost-of-living index.

poverty level by a state-specific measure of cost of living and then use census data by income level to estimate the number of persons below 125 percent of the cost of living–adjusted poverty level. We also compute a *real
level of benefits* by adjusting Medicaid payments for geographic cost variations represented in the geographic adjustment factor (GAF) used by Medicare to adjust physician payment rates. The results can be seen in figure 3-2
and table A1-2.

We find that these adjustments reduce the measure of variation in
Medicaid among states—but to only a limited degree. The ratio of highest
to lowest state benefits falls to 3.11 (adjusted) from 3.77 (unadjusted), suggesting that a threefold difference in benefit levels still exists between the

highest and lowest benefit states. Also, the ratio of benefit measures at the third quartile to the first quartile falls to 1.43 (adjusted) from 1.73 (unadjusted). This indicates that a typical higher-benefit state (ranked thirteenth) would have real benefits about 43 percent higher than a typical lower-benefit state (ranked thirty-eighth; see table A1-2 for adjusted benefit measures for each state).

One might ask whether interstate differences in Medicaid payments per poor person simply reflect the differences in medical costs and intensity of care that are known to exist. We can take Medicare payments per beneficiary as a measure of the cost of providing a standard level of public medical insurance coverage to a population with common eligibility requirements. If we were to divide Medicaid payments per poor person by the state average Medicare benefit per beneficiary we would expect all states to come out about the same if Medicaid costs across states were proportional to Medicare costs. But this is clearly not the case (see table A1-3). When we compare states on this measure, we still find substantial variations, with many southern and western states spending less than half the average Medicare benefit in the state on each poor person, while other states, including several in the Midwest and the East, spend an amount per poor person that exceeds the Medicare benefit by more than 10 percent. Interstate variation in payments per person below 125 percent of the cost of living–adjusted federal poverty level divided by the average Medicare benefit per beneficiary still varies by a factor of two—from less than 50 percent to more than 100 percent for several states—and by a factor of three from lowest to highest. Again, the benefit in the state at the third quintile is about 50 percent higher than that in the state at the first quartile. This is quite consistent with the other measures that suggest real benefits per poor person vary by about a factor of three from highest to lowest and by about 50 percent from higher- to lower-benefit states. The Medicare and Medicaid benefit measures used here are not strictly comparable, of course (as the mix of services and populations differs), but they clearly indicate that Medicaid spending varies much more than Medicare—and it does so in ways consistent with the patterns we have observed for other measures.

Another question we might raise is whether the differences in Medicaid spending per poor person might be somehow counterbalanced by other forms of federal assistance for health care, such as CHIP and grants to

FIGURE 3-3

TOTAL MEDICAL ASSISTANCE (MEDICAID, CHIP, HRSA GRANTS)
PER PERSON BELOW 125 PERCENT OF COST-OF-LIVING–ADJUSTED FPL,
FY 2006

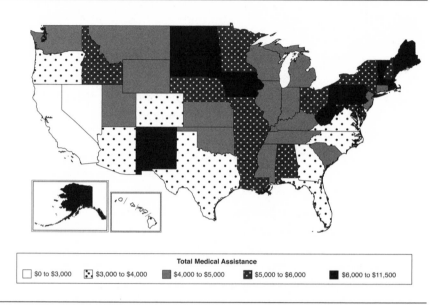

SOURCES: Computed using data from U.S. Census Bureau (2008b) and Kaiser Family Foundation (2009, "Federal and State Share of Medicaid Spending, FY2006," http://www.statehealthfacts.org).

health centers made by the Health Resources and Services Administration (HRSA) of the U.S. Department of Health and Human Services. Figure 3-3 and table A1-4 show the result of accounting for these other federal funding sources as well as cost-of-living differences. Again, it is mostly the northeastern and Mississippi Basin states, rather than the southern and western states, that have high benefits per poor person.

So, after all these checks, we conclude that there is no logical, cost-based explanation for the differences in spending among states. Medicaid benefits do differ among states, and those differences apply to all eligibility groups and all major service types. They are not fully explained by greater needs of the poor as measured by cost-of-living–adjusted poverty level, by cost of production as measured by medical practice costs, by medical use and cost patterns as represented by Medicare costs per beneficiary, or by off-setting benefits provided through other federal programs. The Medicaid spending variations do, however, appear to be, first, directly related to tax-payer income, which can be associated with willingness and ability to support the program; and, second, related to regional differences in state fiscal capacity and needs of the poor, with the highest benefits per poor person in states (many in the Northeast) with higher-income taxpayers and relatively few poor persons, which makes higher benefit levels more affordable to the taxpayers. We also observe that the current federal matching-rate structure still leaves provision of any standard benefit level more difficult to achieve (that is, more costly as a fraction of taxpayer incomes) in lower-income states burdened with relatively larger numbers of poor persons and fewer wealthy taxpayers to share the costs.

Equity, Efficiency, and Recipient Income

We have seen that Medicaid benefits for the poor differ substantially among states, even after we adjust for cost of living when determining who is poor, and adjust for the cost of medical care, and adjust for interstate differences in the resource intensity of medical practice patterns. The key policy question, then, is whether this unevenness is acceptable. Does it represent too much inequity, and does it lead to disparities in care that leave poor people who happen to live in lower-income states at unacceptably low levels of access and health?

Recall that a fundamental premise of Medicaid as a federal–state program is that different states may properly choose to do different things in their Medicaid programs, including defining eligibility more broadly, making stronger efforts to enroll eligible persons, or offering the eligible more generous benefits. As such state decisions are guaranteed to produce some variation across states in Medicaid spending per poor person, it might not be a problem that such variation is positively correlated with income levels in different states (as opposed, say, to being random). Spending also varies by region, as the highest-spending states tend to be in the Northeast, and the lowest spending in the South. The policy question is whether the variation is too much—that is, at what point do variations related to state income and geographic-related preferences impinge too much on the equitable treatment of the poor across states?

There are two ways to try to answer this question. One approach is to consider the equity dimensions of such variation from the viewpoint of recipients and try to determine whether the level of inequity is tolerable. The other is to ask whether such cross-state variations in response to matching rates reflects the interest of federal taxpayers in the welfare of poor and low-income people across states. If the impact of taxpayer income on taxpayer-desired spending (as translated through the political process) is large enough, and the response to variations in matching rates is small enough, higher spending by higher-income states could be an optimal equilibrium. The important question is what federal taxpayers think about the ultimate value of the additional funds that higher-income states spend and lower-income states do not.

We will take up the question of taxpayer promises in the next chapter; here, we consider the variation in spending from the perspective of equity for the poor, as beneficiaries or potential beneficiaries of the program. As already suggested, the higher spending buys several things which can be described by comparing spending in the highest income quintile of states with that in the lowest (with occasional consideration of the middle quintile). Many of the wealthier states make a larger fraction of their populations eligible for all the Medicaid categories: the elderly, the disabled, and children and adults. The level of spending per beneficiary in each category is also higher than in the poorest states, although the gradient is considerably steeper for the elderly and the disabled (relative to children and adults). Some of this difference might be attributable to higher prices for medical services (which might also lead to higher quality or easier access), but even after controlling for price, the differences remain.

We should also note that the higher-benefit states tend to put greater emphasis on long-term care services. In FY 2007, the ten states with the highest combined Medicaid and CHIP spending per poor person spent 41 percent of their Medicaid dollars on long-term care services, including institutional and home and community services. In contrast, the ten lowest benefit states spent only 27 percent of these funds on long-term care. The median-benefit state spent about 30 percent of total Medicaid and CHIP dollars on long-term care. In sum, much of the difference is in the eleven states with the highest benefits, which include the six New England states, New York, New Jersey, and Pennsylvania, plus Alaska and Minnesota— mostly a northeastern regional phenomenon—with a disproportionate share of the additional spending of the higher-benefit states going to long-term care services.

Of course, there are many other program differences. We can see some indications of these by comparing program characteristics in a few states representative of different income and benefit levels. In table 3-4, we see that Medicaid payments per person below the poverty level in New York are three times those in Mississippi; adjusting the poverty level, New York benefits are still more than twice those in Mississippi. Income eligibility for parents varies much more widely than for children due to federal requirements that ensure coverage of children below specified income eligibility levels that vary by child age group.

So, to consider the equity question more fully, we need to get behind our overall measure of payments per poor person. Specifically, we need to know how Medicaid spending and its effects on health and well-being differ among similarly situated persons in, respectively, states with low and high Medicaid benefits—or, to put the question another way, what does the extra spending in higher-benefit states actually buy for their lower-income populations? It seems most likely that Medicaid's impact on the poor in lower-benefit and higher-benefit states differs by eligibility group in the following ways:

- **Children under 100 percent of the FPL** and up to 133 percent of the FPL, if age five years or under, get mandatory Medicaid coverage even in the lower-benefit states, and so are likely to be little different from their counterparts in higher-benefit states, though better payment rates might provide somewhat better access in higher-benefit states.

- **Children over 100 percent of the FPL** or over 133 percent of the FPL, if age five or under, are much more likely to be insured in higher-benefit states, though Medicaid coverage may in some cases displace—or crowd out—private insurance coverage. Higher eligibility probably leads to more use of preventive care and less delay in seeking hospital and primary care for this group.

TABLE 3-4

COMPARATIVE BENEFIT MEASURES FOR REPRESENTATIVE STATES

	Representative state Higher-benefit	
	New York	Maine
Income group	High	Low
Poverty rate, 2007	14.5	10.8
Practice cost index GAF	1.078	0.950
Medicaid to Medicare physician fees	0.45	0.65
Medicaid eligibility ratios		
Recipients per poor person	1.78	1.88
Fraction of elderly covered	0.14	0.14
Fraction of disabled covered	0.29	0.21
Eligible children/children in poverty	1.89	2.85
FMAP, January 1, 2009	50.00%	64.41%
Medicaid payments per poor person (below 100% of FPL)	$16,307	$11,614
Medicaid payments per person below 125% of cost-of-living–adjusted FPL	$9,001	$8,025
Income threshold for jobless parents	150	200
Income threshold for working parents	150	206
Income eligibility for pregnant women % of FPL	200	200
Income eligibility for children 0–1	200	200
Income eligibility for children 1–5	133	150
Income eligibility for children 6–19	100	150
Net transfer per capita (Medicaid and CHIP)	$407	$657
DSH transfer per capita	$32	$55
% of population uninsured	13.6%	9.1%
% of children 0–18 uninsured	9.0%	5.6%
School-based claims, $ per eligible child	$703	$350

SOURCES: U.S. Census Bureau 2008b and Kaiser Family Foundation 2009, income thresholds (various tables), http://www.statehealthfacts.org/comparetable.jsp?ind=205&cat=4; and author calculations.

Representative state			
—————Mid-benefit—————		—————Lower-benefit—————	
Pennsylvania	Ohio	Virginia	Mississippi
Mid	Mid	High	Low
10.4	12.8	8.6	22.6
1.003	0.975	1.012	0.910
0.52	0.68	0.77	0.91
1.32	1.37	1.07	1.20
0.10	0.09	0.09	0.12
0.23	0.18	0.14	0.27
1.82	2.07	1.74	1.61
54.52%	62.14%	50.00%	75.84%
$10,674	$7,974	$6,461	$5,507
$8,545	$6,805	$4,748	$4,278
27	90	24	25
36	90	30	46
185	200	185	185
185	200	133	185
133	200	133	133
100	200	133	100
$88	$36	–$256	$657
$6	–$3	–$21	$34
9.8%	10.9%	14.2%	19.8%
7.7%	7.5%	10.7%	16.2%
$121	$66	$5	$0

- **Pregnant women under 133 percent of the FPL** get mandatory coverage, so health-effect differences among states may be more closely related to the effectiveness of available prenatal care programs than to differences in Medicaid coverage for this group. It is possible that in higher-income states this group benefits from better-funded community health centers which rely heavily on Medicaid (and are paid rates the states can't reduce). We would not, however, expect big differences between higher- and lower-benefit states here.

- **Pregnant women above 133 percent and below 185 percent of the FPL** are (like children) likely to be covered in higher-benefit states and not in lower-benefit states. Although coverage of this group is associated both with fewer premature births and with reduced problems and costs for infants of very low birth weight, evidence of benefit from coverage expansion—even in South Carolina, a lower-income state—is not strong.[14] As this is an area where we would expect to see severe consequences in a small number of cases, the higher-benefit states provide a distinct health advantage for certain recipients here.

- **Elderly persons seeking long-term care** in lower-benefit states are likely to face more restrictive asset tests and functional admission requirements. Some will remain longer in poor living situations without formal home care or nursing home care services. Most will get some of what they need from their families, and expansion of benefits will primarily reduce the family caregiver burden (rather than improve the health of the elder). Overall, the effect may be a somewhat lower quality of care and greater family caregiving burdens in the lower-income states.

- For the **mentally and physically disabled**, the higher-benefit states tend to cover a wide range of services and place greater emphasis on services in the community, including, in some states, daytime or afterschool personal attendant services for families with mentally retarded children. We expect the burden on the relatively small number of affected families to be substantially greater in lower-benefit states, but the true health effects of differences between higher- and lower-benefit states are probably minimal.

The Questionable Value of Higher Spending

What value do citizens as federal taxpayers receive when higher-income states spend more per poor person than lower-income states? Somewhat surprisingly, no formal investigation of this question appears to be in the research literature for any Medicaid population other than the long-term care population. The bulk of research on the effect of higher levels of Medicaid coverage on general medical care use has focused instead on the effects of Medicaid expansions over time. These studies deal with two topics: the effect of Medicaid coverage expansion on overall insurance coverage and associated levels of use of medical care; and (assuming the existence of effects as described in the previous section) impacts on indicators of population health.

There have been three major kinds of Medicaid coverage expansion for the nonelderly population: increases in eligibility for coverage for pregnant women and infants in the 1980s; the creation of CHIP; and selective expansions in coverage by a small number of states at various times and in response to various stimuli. The most consistent result of these expansions has been a pattern of net changes in the proportion of the target population with insurance coverage: Medicaid expansion increased the proportion with coverage of some type, but some of the coverage "crowded out" private coverage that would otherwise have been present. While empirical estimates of the magnitude of crowd-out vary, the great bulk of studies find some crowd-out, but less than 100 percent. Some evidence—less definitive because it applies to recent time periods—indicates that crowd-out was greater under the CHIP program (which extended coverage primarily to low-income but not poor households) than under earlier Medicaid expansions to poor households. When crowd-out does occur, it can happen whether the Medicaid coverage targets children only or adults and children. The net effect of a reduced proportion of uninsured is to cause an increase in use of some medical services (primarily outpatient services, some preventive and some not). As eligibility reaches further up into the income distribution, Medicaid or CHIP expansions produce smaller net increases in health insurance coverage. There is no evidence with respect to the relationship between coverage expansion and local medical care prices or other supply-side characteristics.

Studies of the effect of Medicaid expansions on health outcomes are fewer (and are made difficult) because of the insensitive nature of measured health indicators; failure to find an effect in this case definitely does not mean "no effect," but it probably does mean "no large effect." Studies of state Medicaid cutbacks in the 1970s showed important adverse impacts on the health of poor populations whose Medicaid coverage was withdrawn. In contrast, expansion for pregnant women and infants from the base level of coverage showed little or no effect on use of prenatal care, and no statistically significant effects on health outcomes such as average infant birth weight or proportion of low birth-weight babies; this small marginal effect was observed both in higher- and lower-income states.[15]

Brown and Finkelstein have conducted a set of cross-sectional and cross-state studies of Medicaid nursing home coverage and have found a large crowd-out effect, accounting for the fact that most elderly households, even the majority that are not poor, do not buy private long-term care insurance.[16] Literature on the effect of Medicaid nursing home coverage or payments on health outcomes for the nursing home population is scant, although the palliative nature of long-term nursing home care and the fact that much of the cost goes for room and board services for those near the end of life suggest that long-term survival effects are likely to be small relative to costs. Stronger effects are likely on quality of life for the patient and family caregivers where long-term home care may substitute in part for informal care, or may supplant the purchase of such services using the family assets of people, many of whom are not poor. The social value of such transfers is not zero, but their absence in the many middle- and lower-benefit states may not represent inequity for the recipients themselves as great as might first appear.

With more extensive long-term care benefits heavily favored by a few, mainly Northeastern, states, one can ask what services these dollars buy and how they are valued by the recipients, their families, in-state taxpayers, and out-of-state taxpayers in the lower-benefit states. Long-term care services involve many nonmedical costs pertaining to housing in institutional settings and personal care and support services in community settings; they may have a greater impact on general well-being than on measurable health indicators. Even if these services are highly valued by recipients and their families, taxpayers in other regions may reasonably question whether the distinct regional pattern for long-term care spending in the Northeast is something they particularly want to support with their tax dollars.

In summary, the existing literature does not contain evidence of proven and substantial health or access benefits from higher Medicaid spending in higher-income states such as might reassure a skeptical taxpayer that his or her payments for the federal share are buying substantial value in terms of health outcomes. Higher spending by richer states seems not to buy substantial improvements in beneficiary health status. The spending of resources to produce minor health effects might be viewed (particularly by those in places where such resources are not provided) as inefficient, or just wasteful.

4

Medicaid and Care Management

In Medicaid's early years, it was hard to run up a big medical bill without staying in a hospital or a nursing home. Now, with more complex procedures spreading to the outpatient and day-surgery sectors, with the price of drugs sometimes in the tens of thousands of dollars per case, and with the growing cost of community service programs, concerns about overutilization span a wider range of services. The cost trends in the medical care sector have created difficulty for Medicaid programs, which face some particular limits on tools commonly used to manage medical care costs. The limited financial resources of the people Medicaid serves, for example, make it inappropriate in many cases to limit coverage strictly or apply significant copayments to medical services. Other controls on use, such as various forms of care management, then become more necessary than in the private plans as a way to limit payments for services that are truly medically necessary. But it is not always clear just what forms of care management are most appropriate for a state or its Medicaid population. Options to states include managing the benefit package, using limited forms of cost-sharing, and developing programs to provide acute and long-term care management.

Managing Benefits

Who should be promised Medicaid benefits? What range of state commitments to the poor should be allowable from a national policy perspective? The social value of adding recipients to Medicaid (at a given premium) at higher incomes presumably declines as the income threshold increases, along with an individual's capacity to pay for services. Similarly, the value of additional Medicaid spending declines as the range of services covered increases, assuming that the most important services are covered first. If ways can be found to keep Medicaid benefits focused on the most valuable and effective services for the most needy people, then the program should engender higher levels of public support. In fact, care management initiatives aimed at just this goal have been attempted by states at various times.

While states can control *eligibility* in a straightforward way, through categorical and income criteria, Medicaid offers them less ability to control *benefits* in ways that eliminate the lower-value or less "costworthy" care among the insured.[1] This is because the patients and providers make most of the decisions about the provision of care within Medicaid, as in traditional Medicare and many private health plans. Without significant cost-sharing (copayments), controls are difficult to use in a nuanced way that would reduce only uncostworthy care. Nonetheless, states have sought to develop useful tools over the years, including contracted managed care, priority-setting, elimination of specific procedures from coverage, pharmacy benefit management, and disease management, all in an attempt to eliminate unnecessary, low-value, or uncostworthy care and reduce the cost of providing a package of Medicaid benefits to eligible recipients.

In previous research we have documented the tradeoff that states make between amount of benefits and number of recipients deemed eligible.[2] There is probably less variation across states in benefits per recipient for the Medicaid population receiving TANF (welfare) now than in previous years, at least in percentage terms. The provision of medical care has become more uniform geographically with national health and managed care plans, and benefit packages have become more standardized. More states now include the key optional services (that is, services that may be provided at the discretion of the state), such as drugs and other services that have been diminishing in relative importance as the costs of mandatory services, such as hospital outpatient care, have increased.

The most explicit (if not the most successful) effort to identify and eliminate low-value care was the priority-setting system adopted by the Oregon Medicaid program in the 1990s. Originally this priority-setting system was proposed to apply to everyone in the state, but it was actually implemented only for Medicaid. Oregon promulgated a list of covered condition–treatment pairs to rank services by priority in perceived value. Each year the state would determine how far down the list coverage would extend with the available budget. The stated intent was to ensure basic care for all and eliminate the less valuable services.

In principle, it makes sense to minimize coverage for low-value care for some recipients to ensure that basic care of higher value can be provided to a broader group of recipients. In the context of limited state spending on Medicaid, even with federal matching, this still makes sense—to put the dollars where they will do the most good. We would note, however, that federal matching encourages greater state spending by lowering the threshold for "how much good" per dollar of total spending is expected by state decision-makers. Even so, this type of subsidy should not change the *relative* value of spending on the available services, so a state would still start by offering what it considers to be the most cost-effective services; matching just allows it to go further down the list of priorities.

This kind of allocation was essentially what the Oregon priority-setting plan was attempting, though with a greater degree of specificity in control than other states had with their traditional Medicaid programs. In the process of implementation, however, Oregon added funding in recognition of the value it perceived in services upon closer examination, and to soften the edges and make priority-setting a more palatable approach. Moreover, the program was subsequently replaced by a more traditional form of managed care that achieved savings primarily through reduced eligibility rather than reduced use of low-value services.

If Oregon could not sustain even a mild form of rationing, what are we to conclude about the acceptability of limiting access to low-value care? We should not be too quick to generalize from the Oregon experience, as it involved unique policy dynamics at both the state and federal levels. Nonetheless, one can ask whether the United States is ready to address openly the question of whether some form of priority-setting is needed and, secondly, whether it would be more politically acceptable to apply such limits to all citizens or only to the poor. Oregon's choice to apply priority-setting only to Medicaid and to back away from explicit use of "the priority list" for other citizens is consistent with Medicaid experience to date nationally, wherein policymakers seem most comfortable limiting access only for the poor and, even then, only indirectly. Although it surfaced in the context of Oregon's plan in the 1990s, this country has yet to have a full, national, out-in-the-open debate about the ethics and economics of limiting medical care services based on cost-effectiveness. Such discussions are not easy; even in the United Kingdom, the National Institute for Health and Clinical Excellence (NICE) recently faced controversy over a ruling in its ethical guidelines "that saving a life cannot be justified at any cost."[3] This ruling challenged what is termed the "rule of rescue," which states that identifiable persons at risk of death should be given available medical treatment (without regard to cost) as an ethical imperative.[4] For the United States, particularly as very expensive, quasi-experimental medical procedures and drugs become possible and more widely available, the questions raised in Oregon about rationing and priority-setting remain, but usually just below the surface, in current national policy debates.

For now, it appears that policy allows states to control the costs of care (at least indirectly, through care management and payment policy) more tightly for the poor than for the general public. So, to what extent, and in what areas, should we allow Medicaid programs to limit care for the poor? How much might we be willing to let standards for the poor (say, for costly services of questionable or unproven effectiveness) diverge from those applied to the community as a whole? Should Medicaid coverage provide services that are generally covered and available to the privately insured or those who can afford to pay for generous insurance or services out of pocket? Coverage without any limits might not be considered a wise use of public funds, but one must then decide just what standard is appropriate, and a tussle between ethics and politics may result. Part of the politics comes from perceptions on the part of lower-income workers, often without coverage or with benefits less generous than Medicaid's, who may resent a program that provides better coverage than they receive themselves. Does this drive us to a single coverage standard of care somehow rationed for all, or to a system with multiple standards of coverage?

While the public choice theory may suggest multiple levels on efficiency grounds, and ethics may point toward a uniform high standard of care as an admirable goal, real practical problems and perceived ethical concerns need to be resolved in any debate about single-standard versus two-class or multiple standards of care. The effort to resolve them has never been successful, and the clash among the three perspectives (spending related to income, value for money, and equity) has usually served to confuse the debate over desirable Medicaid policies and models. Here we can only point to the logical benefit of having a social decision on these tradeoffs made in advance of more detailed analysis and evaluation of Medicaid—without expecting reconciliation anytime soon.

Contemporary medical practice constantly generates new issues about the costworthiness of care. We frequently hear of use of high-cost medical procedures and treatments, such as bone marrow transplants and anti-cancer drugs, costing tens or even hundreds of thousands of dollars; many of these treatments produce no cure, but they may extend lifespan by a few weeks or months or improve quality of life. Although they come from the cutting edge of medical innovation, where economies of scale have not yet been achieved and where drug patent protection remains in force, desperation and human optimism combine to make it difficult to withhold such care, even though significant benefits are unproven and, in many cases, unlikely. As a society, we want to encourage the development of new treatments, but from an efficiency standpoint, science can progress without trying the treatment on every candidate. In many cases, the uncertainty of effectiveness and the risks associated with side effects of an experimental treatment might not make it a reasonable choice for every potential patient, even if the treatment were free. The most difficult choices arise when new treatments have been shown to extend life or delay the onset of severe symptoms, but at a cost that seems excessively high.

More commonly, uncostworthy treatments arise when entrepreneurial providers or suppliers find they can market and get paid for a newly developed treatment, piece of equipment, or drug at rates that are two, three, ten, or more times the price of an equally effective standard treatment; overpayment causes inefficiency. Public programs with open provider participation and loose coverage rules find it particularly difficult to avoid paying for such services, as political pressure, often generated by such entrepreneurial providers, can prohibit their exclusion from public payment. Indeed, the prospect of considering cost as well as effectiveness in making coverage determinations always raises controversy.

We will never have a cost-effective system if we do not consider costs as well as effects in making treatment choices, but as a nation we have not yet agreed on reasonable criteria for defining value or for denying coverage of uncostworthy care. This fundamental problem impedes progress on a wide range of medical care policy issues, from determining Medicare and

Medicaid coverage, to acceptance of managed care in the private sector, to finding affordable ways to extend coverage to the uninsured. The solution may require a broader look from the medical community, and from society as a whole, to find a new definition of just what constitutes high-quality care—a definition that is more closely related to what patients value, with less emphasis on the rule of rescue and the technological imperative in the practice of medicine.[5] More precise methods for setting treatment criteria may be available in the future with increased attention to (and funding for) comparative-effectiveness research. Implementing such criteria will require changes to controls on coverage (for decisions at the program or health plan level) or to payment incentives (for decisions left to providers). Decoupling the physician treatment decisions from the incentives of higher payment (as with salaried or capitated payment) or by coverage decisions of an external expert panel seems necessary in some form if we are to reduce uncostworthy care significantly.

For the time being, we believe it makes sense to allow state Medicaid programs to limit, according to some reasonable standard, coverage of services deemed inappropriate, whether determined by formal comparative-effectiveness analysis or by considered professional judgment. The political process would generally prevent such a policy from producing drastic or unreasonable cuts in benefits. Even Oregon's priority-setting plan, which took on this issue directly, did not do much to limit access to care, and largely delegated the operational judgments about costworthy treatment to capitated managed care plans and providers who had flexibility to meet patient needs.[6]

For services with positive benefits but high cost relative to value, the question is whether individual states should have the power to declare medical services uncostworthy (or, in real life, "of unproven benefit but high cost"). The argument against two-class medicine seems hollow when taxpayers (through their elected representatives) have already decided to restrict access for the Medicaid population through low provider payments. It is likely that all stakeholders, including providers, taxpayers, and the poor, could benefit from a two-tier system that covers more lower-income people. Nonetheless, we recognize that the practical difficulties of identifying and eliminating less effective services for Medicaid alone (or even for all payers) have not been resolved by most of the care management schemes tested to date.

Given what we know about variance in medical practices, and about research on the effectiveness of common medical procedures, we see room for some reduction in services without adverse effects on the health of recipients. Whether this is best accomplished through care management (which we discuss below) or limits on coverage (as is practiced by most insurers, including Medicare and Medicaid) may depend on the situation. In general, some limits on coverage of high-cost, low-effect care may be desirable for Medicaid as well as for Medicare and private health plans. States should have the freedom to discourage the use of such care, whether through care management programs or limits on coverage of specific procedures and forms of treatment.

Cost-Sharing and Medicaid

A variety of market-oriented, procompetitive methods for introducing economic incentives into the U.S. health care system have been proposed in recent years. These have generally included higher levels of cost-sharing (premiums, deductibles, and copayments) than are typical now, combined with tax-advantaged health savings accounts. Some approaches developed in the context of employer-based health insurance products have been suggested for use in public programs, including Medicaid. Can they simply be transferred to this setting?

Several factors particular to Medicaid and its recipient population need to be taken into account when evaluating proposals to introduce cost-sharing. For example, most Medicaid recipients have no or very low assets and incomes (beyond usually modest government transfers); this affects their ability and willingness to pay even small cost-sharing amounts. Our view is that we cannot expect to carry over easily to the Medicaid population the success cost-sharing has had with middle-class populations. Consideration of anything more than nominal cost-sharing raises important affordability issues with respect to both premium payments and point-of-service copayments, and to health savings accounts.

Premium Payments by Medicaid Recipients. Requiring premium payments by recipients as a means of reducing Medicaid costs to taxpayers is one instance in which the tradeoff between recipient and taxpayer interest is readily apparent.[7] Premiums offer the prospect of making Medicaid more like other health insurance plans by engaging recipients in sharing the cost of their coverage. States are currently given only very limited permission to charge premiums for insurance to Medicaid recipients. Somewhat more flexibility has been extended through waiver programs. Would further increases in premium payments help or hinder fulfillment of our commitments to recipients?

We see, first of all, an administrative feasibility issue. Any program with very modest premiums suitable for lower-income recipients will have to address the efficiency of collection, both for the group under 150 percent of the FPL (where collection costs would likely exceed revenue) and the group over 150 percent of the FPL (for which collection costs could be a significant offset to revenue). With current technology, it may be more trouble than it is worth to collect small premiums. Additionally, the total amount collected would likely be less than might be expected, since some eligibles would choose not to participate or would fail to make payments.

We have fairly clear empirical evidence from a number of states that premium payments discourage Medicaid enrollment. In a review of state experiences with Medicaid premiums, Artiga and O'Malley found that half to two-thirds of affected recipients became uninsured following either premium increases or tightening of premium policies in Oregon, Rhode Island, and Utah.[8] Clear, but less substantial, and perhaps more transient, results were found in Vermont,[9] Washington, Wisconsin, and Maryland.

States that implement or increase premiums for Medicaid enrollment would incur some risks. Many of the recipients who choose not to enroll would be those with the least income and those who expect to have little or no medical expense. Refusal to enroll, particularly by low users of health care, might lead to re-enrollment retroactively when medical expenses arose. This, in turn, would lead to increases in the observed average per-member, per-month (PMPM) cost of those enrolled, since the enrollees remaining would tend to be those with higher expenses, and anyone enrolling retroactively would come with existing bills to be paid. Premiums might also increase the enrollment turnover rate, increasing administrative costs from recipients' switching in and out of Medicaid. If enrollment declined, measurable impacts might be observed in some key state health statistics. Particularly, we would expect to see a rise in the number of uninsured persons reported for the state, and possibly other health statistics associated with the uninsured. Finally, states adopting premiums would boost the burden on some providers due to an increase in the number of uninsured patients and the associated administrative costs of billing, collections, retroactive enroll-ments, and bad debt.

So the real question is whether premiums would raise enough money or reduce private insurance crowd-out enough to be worth the trouble. Most Medicaid savings from premiums come from reduced enrollment. If premiums drive beneficiaries to the ranks of the uninsured and cause an increase in charity or uncompensated care, there is no real savings, not even to the states administering the Medicaid program.

We do not believe the people driven away by premiums ought to remain uninsured. Premiums do not appear to meet the "worth-the-trou-ble" test at income levels currently used for Medicaid eligibility. The general question of premiums would, however, be more relevant should Medicaid be extended to income levels at which many families now have private insurance. Premiums paid by workers or employers should certainly be part of any financing package for program initiatives directed toward offer-ing more affordable coverage to currently uninsured lower-income workers and their families.

Copayments by Medicaid Recipients. Copayments, the other common form of cost-sharing, are also quite limited by federal regulations.[10] A behavioral response may result from even a small copayment requirement, although the research evidence on this question is mixed. Even within the Medicaid population, significant differences in income and—perhaps more importantly—other financial and family-support resources lead one to expect wide differences in response to significant cost-sharing require-ments; the "right" amount of copayment will differ greatly from recipient to recipient and service to service.

Second, it is important to note the distinct cost-sharing issues that arise in connection with Medicaid long-term care benefits for the elderly and dis-abled. In contrast to most acute medical care, long-term care can lead to a great cumulative burden of costs over time. It raises the question of who should pay and how much when Medicaid assumes the cost of housing in addition to medical services, and families have some ability to contribute to the cost of care or to support the patient with informal, family-provided care services. Such cost-sharing issues are usually handled through spend-down requirements that adjust for individual resources, rather than through a fixed copayment amount. Current federal rules are designed to protect Medicaid recipients from the sharp bite of cost-sharing, and this can sometimes frustrate state policymakers' efforts to provide strong patient incentives to be frugal and make cost-conscious choices about the use of costly institutional or community-based services.

Health Savings Accounts. Health savings accounts (HSAs) are another way to introduce the incentives of cost-sharing to Medicaid, but they present particular challenges. For one, they lack some of the attraction of such accounts in private plans because a prime motivation for having HSAs—the tax benefit—generally is not useful to Medicaid recipients. They may also lack some advantages of basic Medicaid payments, as individual payments would not generally be eligible for federal match, and purchases may not be made at Medicaid's low payment rates. Another issue to consider is the "woodwork effect," as the promise of a flexible spending benefit (or return of unspent funds in a cash-equivalent form) could attract enrollment of those eligible but not enrolled persons who expect to have very low medical expenses.[11] States might end up leaving the sick with more out-of-pocket expenses and devoting more state resources to those with few medical needs.

Acute Care Management

Acute care management in Medicaid is divided between the capitated managed care plans, where the care management functions are provided by the plan, and fee-for-service Medicaid, in which the state, often through contractors, provides care management functions (usually more limited). Our focus here is on fee-for-service Medicaid and the possible use of care management programs to control utilization and costs.

The tools available to fee-for-service Medicaid are similar to those used in the private sector. These include prior authorization, case management, and utilization review. The goals are also similar to those of other insurers—to encourage the use of appropriate, cost-effective care and to discourage unnecessary or inappropriate care. Medicaid patients face more significant access barriers, however, than those who are insured through private-sector plans. Low payment rates reduce access to providers; travel is often difficult for lower-income mothers, both urban and rural; and more limited knowledge of medical issues and the health care system can make Medicaid recipients less effective consumers of medical care. One must implement care management with caution within Medicaid if it is not to impede recipients' access to needed services further, and encouraging the use of needed preventive services may be as important as discouraging the use of costly care.

The first question to ask when considering care management initiatives is, what forms of care are we trying to encourage or discourage? We want to preserve access to needed, effective, and costworthy care and reduce the use of care that is of dubious effectiveness or does not justify its cost. Attention to the research on medical effectiveness and development of coherent practice guidelines can move Medicaid in the right direction. Policymakers should focus on services that, first, account for significant costs; second, can be identified on a prospective or retrospective basis by reviewers as overused, ineffective, or uncostworthy; and, third, can be eliminated without adverse consequences to beneficiaries. Such areas to target may be found within broad categories of services, such as emergency room utilization, inpatient hospital admissions, and disease management and preventive care services.

Emergency Department Utilization. Despite the frequency with which nonurgent emergency department services are cited as examples of Medicaid overutilization, these are among the services perhaps least amenable to achieving savings from care management. Emergency department services are obviously difficult to control at point of service, since patients present themselves as emergencies on their own initiative, and hospitals have an obligation to serve them under the Emergency Medical Treatment and Active Labor Act (EMTALA).[12] Furthermore, high rates of emergency department use by Medicaid recipients may simply reflect limited access to routine care, particularly from primary care physicians, resulting from low physician payment rates. There is little evidence that Medicaid patients use emergency departments for unneeded care.[13]

Furthermore, reports of differences in payment rates between emergency room visits and physician visits greatly overstate the true differences in resource costs. The actual marginal cost to the provider of treating an earache may be no greater in an emergency room than in a physician's office, especially if the treatment is administered during slack time between more urgent cases. The off-peak marginal cost of an emergency department visit is a small fraction of the *average* cost of visits in such settings, which of necessity includes the costs of staff and facilities required to meet serious emergencies.[14] Emergency department visits for routine care do cost Medicaid more, but largely because of the way in which services are paid for—not how they are delivered. The fact that Medicaid in many states pays hospital ERs two, three, or four times as much for services that could be delivered in physicians' offices virtually ensures that much of the care will be delivered in the setting more expensive to the program. If Medicaid were to pay hospitals and physicians the same amount for equivalent services— paying by the service, rather than the setting—overuse of emergency department visits would greatly diminish, because other providers could be more adequately compensated for routine care and so would accept more Medicaid patients in their offices.[15] The real problems with overuse of emergency rooms concern quality, as it results in long waits for visits that might have been scheduled if provided in another setting, and lack of continuity of care. These, too, would be corrected with changes in access that would be brought about by an equalization of payment by setting. Paying providers by service rather than by setting is a topic we will discuss in chapter 13.

Policymaking to reduce excessive ER use would probably be most productive if, rather than focusing on care management, it concentrated on paying for the true resource cost of needed care and on creating payment incentives for care to be provided in the most cost-effective settings. This means paying hospitals for trauma emergencies at a rate high enough to more than cover the costs of staffing to provide such care, but not paying them more for routine ambulatory care in the emergency room than the cost of providing such care in the most efficient setting, such as a physician's office. Some premium could be allowed for differentiated services, such as urgent care units with extended hours, or for enhanced intensity or continuity of care, such as may come from application of new care models (for example, the "medical home" model) or systems with improved coordination through sharing of electronic medical records. Such payment advantages should be available equally, based on documented quality, to all types of providers, whether hospital outpatient departments, FQHCs, large group physician practices, or even drugstore-based clinics.

Inpatient Hospital Admissions. A more appropriate goal of Medicaid care management than reducing emergency room use would be to reduce inpatient hospital admissions. For example, a 2005 study reviewed admissions that were classified on claims as potentially avoidable based on diagnoses. It attributed more than half of the avoidable Medicaid hospital costs in New Hampshire to inpatient treatment of low birth-weight infants.[16] It follows that the best way to reduce unnecessary admissions may be to implement more aggressive outreach for prenatal care, and possibly for family planning services. Other diagnoses that may lead to unnecessary hospital admissions for Medicaid patients include pneumonia, congestive heart failure (CHF), chronic obstructive pulmonary disorder (COPD), diabetes, and asthma. These would be high-priority areas to address in any Medicaid disease management or chronic care management program. The focus should be on prior intervention to prevent the onset of illness or of circumstances that lead to admissions.

Disease Management and Preventive Care. Chronic illness is clearly a major cost factor for Medicaid, as it is for Medicare and private insurance. Persons with multiple chronic conditions are among the most costly beneficiaries for all payers. Logically, care management resources should be focused on conditions associated with high use and cost, particularly when preventive practices of proven effectiveness are available. Yet the empirical results produced to date on the cost-effectiveness of disease management programs for Medicaid—at least those from independent sources—show few clear and consistent effects.[17] A number of factors limit the cost-effectiveness of disease management from the perspective of state Medicaid programs:

- Preventive care management programs have an inherent and prevalent problem: To achieve savings, care management costs for a broad set of enrollees must be recouped through savings on a small number of cases for which the program effectively prevents adverse outcomes. Great attention must be devoted to targeting those most likely to benefit, encouraging behavioral change, and keeping the cost of the preventive care intervention under control. For many chronic conditions, the intervention is some form of preventive drug therapy—for example, drugs to control blood pressure, cholesterol, or asthma attacks. Cost-effectiveness requires that each individual receive the lowest-cost treatment that is effective and be brought into compliance with the required regimen without too much expended on program operations and overhead.

- A large share of the costs for chronic care arise from the dual-eligible population of elderly and disabled persons, for which Medicaid pays only a minority of the costs for acute care. States do not have much incentive to invest in preventive care for this population. Since much of any savings for dual-eligibles will accrue to Medicare, perhaps it would make sense for the federal government to provide enhanced federal matching for states to provide care management, including disease management, to dual-eligibles not enrolled in Medicare managed care (Medicare Advantage) plans.

- Savings opportunities from disease management are smaller for the TANF (welfare) population, which is composed mostly of children and their mothers. Chronic conditions are less prevalent in this group, although the targeting of the more common ones (such as asthma and diabetes) may still be productive. Also, since turnover is more frequent among these Medicaid recipients, states may have more difficulty recouping costs spent on care management as an investment, as part of any savings may accrue to other insurers after Medicaid eligibility has ended.

- Disease is more difficult to manage in a population with very low incomes and low levels of education—factors that characterize much of the Medicaid population. This presents challenges, as private-sector methods of care management may need to be adapted to take better account of cultural differences.

States should be cautious when considering adoption of disease management or any other care management programs with the expectation of saving money, rather than just improving care for those with chronic conditions. It is important to start by making a realistic estimate of costs and savings:

- They should, at a minimum, look hard at the plausibility of any vendor-projected cost savings, and obtain an independent assessment of the expected effects of care management on specific types of services for the specific groups that will be managed, as they relate to the history of aggregate costs associated with those services for those specific groups.

- They should determine if the expected savings computed from current expenditures on the services likely to be affected are, when multiplied by the expected effects on those services for the targeted groups, sufficient to cover both the full costs of the care management program and additional costs that may be incurred for greater use of drugs and other preventive services. Conversely, they should ask what percentage changes in the use of key services would be required to cover the costs of care management.

- They should be skeptical of cost-savings estimates provided by disease management or other care management organizations; results of a careful, fully independent evaluation of a similar program applied to a similar population will provide more reliable predictions.

- They should be especially vigilant to ensure that all costs have been accounted for, and that touted savings estimates do not apply the percentage of savings previously achieved for a small targeted group to a proposed broader population group. Appropriate targeting is needed to ensure cost-effectiveness. Per-person fees paid for managing a large, broad-based group may seem small but will need to be offset with savings achieved from more intensive management of a much smaller group of persons at risk.

Acute care management is probably best approached as a means of enhancing quality of care rather than of achieving cost savings. Once one accounts for program administration and offsetting increases in service use from better access to care, there is little evidence of substantial net savings from disease management, preventive care programs, or other such acute care management programs. This should not, however, deter states from pursuing these activities (without high savings expectations) where favorable health and quality impacts can be demonstrated.

Medicaid Managed Care

Managed care, provided through capitated managed care plans or primary care case management programs, is a key part of the Medicaid program. About half of all Medicaid recipients use some form of managed care. We have chosen to devote relatively limited space to the important topic of Medicaid managed care in this work. This is in part because we have more to say on other topics, and in part because many of the issues we would address on it are already well covered in other sources. In particular, we would refer the reader to the Hurley and Zuckerman article, "Medicaid Managed Care: State Flexibility in Action" (2003); the Brown et al. report, *Reforming Medicaid: The Experiences of Five Pioneering States with Mandatory Managed Care and Eligibility Expansions* (2001); and the Kaye paper, "Medicaid Managed Care: Looking Forward, Looking Backward" (2005).

State Experiences with Managed Care. Historically, it is worth noting that Medicaid began without a managed care component, and there has never been a consistent and uniform federal effort to shape state Medicaid managed care programs.[18] Consequently, the Medicaid managed care experience comprises a diverse mixture of state efforts pursued under waivers that allow states to provide services on less than a statewide basis through managed care programs that may limit the beneficiary's choice of provider and/or pay providers through arrangements outside of Medicaid's fee-for-service rules.[19]

Medicaid managed care programs have included comprehensive mandatory statewide efforts, such as the Arizona Health Care Cost Containment System (AHCCCS),[20] as well as various efforts to contract with managed care plans to serve specific geographic areas. In some programs, recipients are automatically enrolled in managed care; in others, enrollment is voluntary for the recipient, who may have an option to continue under the basic fee-for-service program. Some programs make contracts with existing HMOs using the same provider network and fee schedules as private-sector managed care; some are Medicaid-only managed care programs, sometimes created by safety-net providers who become Medicaid contractors to ensure access to a Medicaid funding stream. Some Medicaid managed care contractors (particularly in more rural areas) are primary care case management (PCCM) programs that provide care coordination and continue to pay providers on a fee-for-service basis under existing Medicaid fee schedules.

The greatest growth in Medicaid managed care occurred in the 1990s. While recent years have seen consolidation and declines in enrollment in commercial plans, plans that have primarily public enrollment have continued to grow.[21] As of 2002, 14.9 million, or about 37 percent, of all Medicaid recipients were estimated to be enrolled in comprehensive managed care organization (MCO) plans. An additional 8.3 million, or about 21 percent of all, were enrolled in more limited forms of managed care, such as preferred health plans (PHPs) for limited services or PCCM programs.[22] As a share of Medicaid acute care spending, managed care ranges from essentially zero in several states to more than 50 percent in several others. Arizona, a latecomer to Medicaid, based its acute care program from the start solely on contracted managed care and spends more than 80 percent of its Medicaid budget on it (see figure 4-1 and table A1-5). State Medicaid managed care spending typically follows the state's overall HMO penetration rate.[23] But twelve state Medicaid programs have managed care shares that exceed twice the share of managed care in the state health care marketplace (see table A1-5). In these states—Alabama, Arizona, Delaware, Georgia, Kentucky, Minnesota, Nebraska, New Mexico, Ohio, Pennsylvania, Tennessee, and Virginia—Medicaid has utilized managed care much more extensively than has the private market. It is worth noting that most of these are lower-benefit states.

In terms of quality of care or health outcomes, we do not have conclusive evidence that Medicaid managed care is inherently any better or any worse than fee-for-service Medicaid. Hurley and Zuckerman cite two studies showing that HMOs "improved health care utilization" for adults and children compared with traditional Medicaid, but Zuckerman and others note little evidence that HMOs reduce hospitalization.[24] Nor is there much evidence that particular forms of managed care produce distinct recipient outcomes. No strong and clear differences are apparent in satisfaction or

FIGURE 4-1

MANAGED CARE AND HEALTH PLANS AS A SHARE OF
MEDICAID ACUTE CARE PAYMENTS BY STATE, FY 2007

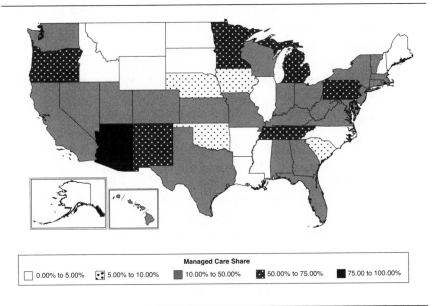

Managed Care Share

☐ 0.00% to 5.00%   ▦ 5.00% to 10.00%   ▦ 10.00% to 50.00%   ▦ 50.00% to 75.00%   ■ 75.00 to 100.00%

SOURCE: Kaiser Family Foundation 2009, "Distribution of Medicaid Spending on Acute Care, FY2007," http://www.statehealthfacts.org/comparetable.jsp?ind=179&cat=4.

perceptions of access among enrollees in the various types of Medicaid HMO plans. Brown and colleagues report that few indicators of satisfaction or access differ by plan characteristics (such as prior enrollment or extent of Medicaid enrollment; prior use of safety-net providers; whether the HMO is for-profit; whether services are provided statewide; and whether many primary care providers (PCPs) are paid on a capitated basis).[25] The mixed experiences in the states suggest that most choosing to take on managed care are able to engage successfully in managed care contracting and eventually find a form that fits the local health care system environment and changing budget constraints.[26]

Medicaid's ongoing struggle to make capitated managed care work as a method to provide high-quality care in a cost-effective way reflects the similar difficulties the nation has had in reconciling the promise of the original

HMO concept with the economic and political influence of various stake-holders in the health care system. The health maintenance organization origi-nally was designed to provide incentives to achieve high-quality, cost-effective care by means of a limited budget allocated and controlled by a staff or group model, in which doctors working together would develop patient-centered practice styles that emphasized preventive care. The keys to making the HMO work are, first, for the physicians to save enough in patient care costs to pro-vide high-quality care with minimal out-of-pocket cost-sharing to attract patients; second, competitive professional salaries or incomes and perhaps a less demanding working environment to attract participating physicians; and, third, low premiums to attract employers who would offer the product.

This model is one that makes particular sense for Medicaid, with its potentially captive set of patients and strong public interest in controlling costs and maintaining quality without frills. But, as in the private sector, things can go wrong. Principally, problems arise from the difficulty of devel-oping and maintaining the culture of a staff- or group-model HMO in a system that bends toward the best revenue possibilities and does not do much either to limit resources or reward cost savings. The same market forces that have led to backlash against managed care, the replacement of HMOs by PPOs, and consolidation in the health-plan industry have moved the market away from the traditional HMO. While Medicaid-only managed care plans might logically be thought to have the capability to overcome some of these barriers, they also might not achieve low costs, as such plans are often based in public hospitals serving as academic medical centers with high cost structures, or rely on community health centers with their feder-ally mandated payment rate floors.

Medicaid Managed Care Effects. Medicaid has had a somewhat mixed experience with managed care up to now. In general, states have been suc-cessful in awarding and administering contracts for managed care that have ranged widely in form and scope. They include contracting out essentially the entire Medicaid program (as in the AHCCCS); capitated programs involving mandatory participation for some populations (usually the TANF groups); voluntary participation programs in which the recipient has a choice between a managed care and fee-for-service plan; primary care case management (PCCM) programs; disease management programs targeted to specific groups and medical conditions; and, finally, pharmacy benefit programs limited to managing the drug benefit.

While programs have generally worked well administratively, success in demonstrating cost savings has been more mixed. Pharmacy benefit management programs appear to have been quite successful in achieving savings by compelling substitution of generics or lower-cost brand-name drugs for more expensive brand-name drugs. But the cost to Medicaid of recipient enrollment in a capitated managed care plan for acute care can be higher than that of a comparable fee-for-service plan, even when it includes more effective use controls. This is due to higher administrative and care management costs and, more importantly, the fact that managed care plans must pay competitive rates to providers and return expected profits to their shareholders. The lesson seems to be that while Medicaid can successfully contract with outside care management providers, savings will depend on the situation. They are unlikely to exist for programs that pay providers at private-sector rates, as care management is unlikely to save as much as Medicaid does through its typically low fee schedules.

The challenge, then, is to find a way to obtain the utilization controls of managed care with the low payment rates Medicaid programs maintain. This type of solution calls upon states to keep payment based on Medicaid fee-for-service rates but add care management services, either provided by the states themselves or obtained through one or more managed care contracts of some form. This may not be possible, because providers only accept Medicaid fee levels if they are permitted to determine the volumes of care they will furnish.

While Medicaid normally creates capitated managed care programs for acute care by purchasing care management services from existing health plans or managed care organizations (MCOs), states have a choice in some cases of producing these services in-house rather than contracting to an external source. Some operate care management programs for prior authorization and long-term home care administered by state employees. This can make sense if the state agency has the expertise to administer programs that require detailed understanding of local program and delivery systems to be successful. For some types of care management, however, specialized expertise unrelated to the locality may be needed. For example, pharmacy benefit management and disease management require specialized expertise that is more often possessed by experienced national care management providers and may be more difficult for the state to develop locally.

Government organizations are not often the best choice for taking on more of the production process of either care delivery or management than is necessary. Government's key role in Medicaid is to ensure financing of services for those who need them and to create and provide effective oversight to an accountable care management and service delivery system, with incentives for cost-effective delivery of care. This is not an easy task for the states. The question is to what degree the intended care management outcomes can be described and measured so they can be included in contracts, as opposed to what state employees can be expected to do. State and local governments generally produce services themselves when there are quality dimensions that cannot be prespecified and monitored in a contract setting. Low state salary structures resulting from tight budgets can make it difficult to hire and retain qualified clinicians for case management activities.

In general, states are often best advised to contract for care management services, but there can be difficulties with contracting, as well. Although national private-sector firms may lack the necessary understanding of local programs and delivery systems, and local not-for-profit agencies may lack capabilities, this situation can reverse with time as they develop expertise and local connections. Once established in a key care management role with such expertise and connections, either type of contractor can be difficult to replace. The care management administrative functions can be effectively captured by outside organizations, making the state dependent on contractors. So there are dangers on either road.

State Medicaid programs have pursued a variety of care management programs, in both PCCM and capitated managed care (MCO) forms. Programs are often not statewide, do not include all eligibility groups, and are not comprehensive in services included. Even with managed care, most states continue wraparound coverage and carve out services for separate management.

Some Medicaid programs have reported modest savings from managed care. Vernon Smith reviews six PCCM programs and reports savings of 5–15 percent; a Lewin study of Medicaid managed care reports savings of 2–19 percent.[27] Altogether, state reported savings seem to average (with wide variation) about 10 percent, at least for the PCCM programs, which can maintain Medicaid's low fee structure. Hurley and Zuckerman, however, cite evidence that cost growth in Medicaid managed care is at or near the national average. They are less certain that initial savings will be maintained over time, and they recommend long-term studies.[28] States will need to design and manage their managed care initiatives carefully to ensure savings.

The areas in which we are likely to see savings depend on just what form of managed care is implemented, who is included, and how well and how intensively the care is managed. Programs must achieve reductions in service utilization large enough to cover administrative and care management costs before any true savings are realized. State experience varies. Some studies have reported savings from PCCM in emergency room utilization and inpatient admissions, with some evidence from Florida that effects are greatest for the Aid to Families with Dependent Children (AFDC)/TANF population. Presumably this comes from reducing unnecessary ER visits (for preventable conditions and/or conditions that can be treated with primary care) and avoiding unnecessary hospitalizations. For capitated MCO plans, savings may come from reduced inpatient and ER use, but pharmacy and outpatient costs may be higher. A number of states have reported that savings were less in the early years of their programs, so states should not expect large savings initially. Achieving Medicaid budget savings with management programs oriented toward preventive care, such as disease management, can be difficult, as Medicaid's high turnover rate, particularly in the TANF population, may lead to some of the savings accruing to other payers.

The results from more rigorous independent analysis look less promising. In their review of five states' experiences with mandatory managed care HMO plans, Brown and others find little evidence that costs are reduced and conclude that "any savings relative to prior fee-for-service costs or relative to other states' experiences are likely to be fairly small." They caution states not to assume "they will generate large savings in the short run by switching to mandatory managed care." They also note the difficulties states encountered in setting rates "that are sufficient to attract enough good HMOs, but are sustainable for the state." They recommend states invest in efforts to risk-adjust rates based on plan enrollment to minimize adverse selection and compensate plans that serve the less healthy enrollees.[29]

Also important is that states building managed care not double-count savings from multiple programs. Each dollar of current costs can only be eliminated once, if that, and opportunities in a specific state may not allow even this level of savings through a traditional managed care contract. Attainable results will depend on the degree of competition in the managed care market and the ability or inability of MCOs to contract with providers for services at Medicaid rates. For reasons noted above, such savings (relative to Medicaid fee-for-service) are unlikely from a fully capitated system, particularly if it must pay providers at higher private-sector rates.

Of course, if a state's primary purpose is not to attain cost savings but rather to improve access while providing a means to control utilization somewhat, then managed care may be the best vehicle. Higher payment rates offered by the managed care plan to individual providers will ensure access, and utilization control will probably be no better or worse than in the private sector (though results with Medicaid-only managed care plans may differ). It only remains to be seen whether the state legislature will support the necessary level of funding. In the end, managed care can be a good option, but only for states interested in ensuring good access to care for their recipient populations and willing to spend a bit more to achieve this goal.

The results we have seen from existing programs are generally consistent with the idea that some types of Medicaid managed care programs can save about 8 percent over fee-for-service payment. But this estimate may understate the savings potential of a program that manages care like an MCO but pays providers at or near current Medicaid fee-for-service rates. State MCO savings estimates include plans that pay providers at private-sector rates. Indeed, some physicians support Medicaid managed care, expecting that it provides higher physician payment rates. Ultimately, the competition and prices in local markets for health plans' services will largely determine the end costs of MCO plans, and states must, on a case-by-case basis, assess whether the budget will support them.

In sum, a potentially viable strategy to attain savings is to combine the wide array of care management methods of MCOs with access to low Medicaid fees. We use the term "PCCM partnerships" to refer to partnering with existing Medicaid providers to provide PCCM services while maintaining the ability to pay the providers at Medicaid's lower-than-market fee schedules and rates. Such a program could be implemented in a variety of ways, depending on which functions are contracted out and which are retained and developed. One such approach could involve one large care management contract encompassing PCCM, disease management, pharmacy benefit management, and prior authorization functions; another might utilize separate, but coordinated, contracts with existing providers, including federally qualified health centers (FQHCs) for PCCM services, with one or more external sources for disease management, high-cost case management, and prior authorization services. Network development, provider profiling and selection, and payment for performance could be incorporated into the plan.

Among the determining factors that would affect savings achievable by any care management program for a state are the following:

- Scope of care management (what services, diseases, or conditions are managed?)

- Expected payment rates for services (low Medicaid fee schedule rates versus competitive rates in competitive markets versus private-sector rates in noncompetitive markets)

- Intensity of care management (care management functions expected of the primary care provider [PCP]; extent of over-the-phone versus in-person care)

- Training and implementation (for example, of PCPs and care managers)

- Geographic coverage of service areas (how well are all areas covered?)

- Timing of phase-in plan for care management functions and geographic areas (when will all areas be served?)

- How the program will affect PCP behavior (will it change practices or just improve willingness to accept Medicaid recipients as regular patients?)

We do not have definitive evidence from well-designed studies of Medicaid managed care in all its many forms in the various states. Evidence suggests that managed care can save on costs, but results vary widely. Success requires a concerted effort to manage care actively, careful program design, coordination of diverse care management functions, attention to contract definition and rates paid for care management activities, active provider network development, and effective implementation within the local health care delivery system. This is a major commitment for a state.

Long-Term Care Management

Long-term care presents to Medicaid a combination of care management challenges not faced by other insurers and programs. These include meeting the care needs of elderly and disabled recipients with distinct functional disabilities and widely varying financial and family caregiver resources and working with institutional providers highly dependent on Medicaid payment, as well as a diverse array of not-for-profit and for-profit community service providers.

Nursing Home Care. Nursing home care is Medicaid's largest cost element. State policies for controlling costs of nursing facilities have included controlling payment rates, controlling access to Medicaid-covered nursing services, and seeking savings through efficiencies thought to result from substituting community-based services for institutional services. While Medicaid covers services of skilled-nursing facilities (SNFs), usually for post-acute recovery and atypical care, most Medicaid nursing home services for long-term care are for a lower level of care at intermediate care facilities (ICFs). Provider payment policy in this area has long been based largely on controlling nursing home reimbursement rates, usually keeping the Medicaid rate below private-sector rates for similar services.

One means of controlling who uses the nursing home benefit is limiting admissions based on functional needs. Another is restricting financial eligibility through asset limits. Asset tests for nursing home benefits have encouraged an industry of Medicaid financial planning for families of modest means. Although we do not have well-documented evidence of the extent of Medicaid estate planning or its effects on Medicaid long-term care spending, it has been a growth area for legal services and financial planning advice. The practice often entails transferring assets to categories not counted by Medicaid—for example, transferring ownership of the family home to children, or setting up an annuity for the spouse still living in the community.[30] This is typically done in advance of needing a nursing home (Medicaid now looks-back five years prior to admission to count assets).[31] In such cases, Medicaid benefits are effectively used to protect assets for the use of spouses or other family members. Some states have been more aggressive than others in limiting the use of such techniques.

Elusive Savings from Community-Based Long-Term Care. Numerous federally funded demonstration projects have attempted to show how programs to promote community-based long-term care can reduce nursing home use and bring down spending on long-term care. The evaluations of these projects have, however, consistently shown that case management and community service programs have little or no impact on nursing home use and do not generate institutional savings sufficient to cover the extra cost of community-based care.

In a review of early projects, William Weissert identified "Seven Reasons Why It Is So Difficult to Make Community-Based Long-Term Care Cost-Effective."[32] Among the reasons are these:

- For most patients, home and community services are additional services, not a substitute for institutional care.

- Few of the elderly are at high risk for institutionalization.

- Community care has not been effective at reducing short institutional stays, while relatively small numbers of community care users are truly at risk for long institutional stays.

- Community care has a limited effect on health status.

Results of demonstration projects have tended to confirm these findings. Consider this paragraph by Kemper and others summarizing the findings of several community care demonstrations:

> What the demonstrations have shown is that expanding publicly funded case management and community care does not reduce aggregate costs, and is likely to increase them—at least in the current long-term care service environment, which already provides some community care under Medicare, Medicaid, and other

public programs. Small reductions in nursing home costs for some are more than offset by the increased costs of providing expanded community services to others who, even without expanded services, would not enter nursing homes. Program eligibility criteria can only imperfectly identify in advance those who would enter nursing homes without expanded services. Expanded community services can therefore not be limited to *only* those bound for more expensive nursing home care. Services also have to be provided to many who would live in the community in any case, but without the expanded services. Although costs are lower in the community, *aggregate* costs increase because many in the community receive more services as a result of the expanded coverage.[33]

The largest and most rigorous federal evaluation of community-based alternatives to nursing care was the National Long Term Care Demonstration (channeling),[34] a federally funded demonstration of case management and community services in ten states. This major national demonstration did have a small impact on reducing nursing home use. Nonetheless, its evaluators wrote that although channeling

benefited clients and the families and friends who cared for them in several ways . . . contrary to its original intent, [it] increased costs. The costs of the additional case management and community services were not offset by reductions in the cost of nursing home use.[35]

In conclusion [the evaluators wrote elsewhere], adding channeling services to the preexisting service systems in ten demonstration sites increased costs. The increased cost of case management and expanded community services exceeded the cost savings from reduced nursing home costs. Overall costs increased by about 6 percent in the basic [case management only] sites and by 18 percent in the financial control model [case management and services] sites.[36]

Similar results were found in the Medicare Alzheimer's Disease Demonstration, a multisite, national demonstration focused on providing community-based support for patients with Alzheimer's disease. Fox, Newcomer, Yordi, and Arnsberger reported that

> reduction in regular Medicare expenditures was not enough to offset the added demonstration costs. It did not reduce the rate of nursing home placement. Informal care networks . . . were generally able to function effectively, regardless of . . . whether a long-term care benefit was available.[37]

More recently, the Cash and Counseling Demonstration in three states tested a program model that gave Medicaid recipients needing home and community-based services greater flexibility in the use of funds to pay formal and informal caregivers. Although the program had significant positive effects on well-being, total costs to Medicaid were higher.[38] David Grabowski provides a review of evidence on the cost-effectiveness of the more recent care models of noninstitutional long-term care services, including Medicaid waiver programs, consumer-directed care, capitated acute/long-term care models, and subsidized services. He concludes that "generally these new care models were found to be associated with increased costs, but greater client and caregiver welfare."[39]

In short, the major national demonstrations with scientific evaluations have consistently shown that while community-based long-term care programs provide services that are valued by patients and family caregivers, they do not have large impacts on nursing home use and do not typically reduce costs overall. Based on these findings, some basic guidelines emerge for states considering long-term care reform:

- **Focus on the elderly.** Savings opportunities for increasing home care alternatives to nursing home care are probably greatest among the elderly rather than the disabled, since home care systems for the disabled often add in-home services and can be more costly to Medicaid.

- **Be skeptical of projected cost savings.** Over the past twenty years, many ideas for community-based case management and service programs have been touted as cost saving. No credible research evidence supports claims of significant cost savings from such programs, and the few studies that have shown cost neutrality generally involve narrowly defined populations and interventions.

- **Be sure of your target.** The effects of community care alternative programs are highly dependent on exactly who is enrolled, what case management services are provided, and what services are authorized. A program that focuses on highly impaired persons may find that they cost more to serve in the community than in an institution. A program that focuses on the moderately impaired may find it is providing extra services to those not likely to enter a nursing home in any case. Previous studies have found it extremely difficult to target only those likely to enter nursing homes. Any new intervention should have a well-defined and identifiable target population with well-understood service needs.

- **Be sure of your program model.** Given the poor cost-saving performance of nearly all community care interventions, it would be wise to avoid statewide implementation of any program model that is not well tested and well evaluated. Pilot or demonstration projects might be used to show what effects are achievable for the target population with the proposed care management tools and program resources.

Perhaps even more than with other types of care management interventions, community-based long-term care services provide recognized value—at least, to recipients served and their families, who find the services very helpful. Policymakers, however, have a more difficult task than just pleasing these families; they must judge the public value of providing such services as perceived by the taxpayers. Based on experiences to date, they cannot justify such programs based on any realistic expectation of net cost savings to come from reduced nursing home use.

Concluding Note on Care Management

It is tempting for states, when considering proposals for new care management programs, to be guided by hopes or promises for cost savings. Offers from care management contractors to save the state more than their services cost, and presumably enable it to reduce its Medicaid budget, can be very attractive, but we suggest caution for a number of reasons. One is the often questionable data presented on potential cost savings. Another is the difficulty of ever accurately measuring what the true cost savings are and holding contractors accountable.

We also suggest that a considerable margin be allowed for any improvement in value or costs saved over expenses of the program. When one weighs the social value of paying care management staff to curtail service use against that of allowing the use of services with low, but limited, value accruing to Medicaid recipients, it may make sense to err on the side of allowing benefits for the poor. A program that saves $1,000,000 by reducing services but costs $800,000 to implement may save the state $200,000, but if those $1 million in services were worth even $300,000 to the recipients or to the community, it may not be a good social bargain. In this sense, a social cost-effectiveness test should be applied to any care management program proposal. In short, states should have a very clear understanding of the effects any proposed care management program will have on service use and costs—and the value to recipients of any expected reductions to those services.

5

Achieving High-Value Care for the Poor

What have been Medicaid's promises to the poor? What should the priorities be for making future commitments? In the current system, poor persons below the federal poverty level who meet Medicaid eligibility requirements probably get adequate (though sometimes inconvenient) services in all states. The story is less clear for those who fall outside Medicaid's categorical eligibility groups. These uninsured have some access through safety-net providers, such as community health centers and hospitals, since these providers receive funding through various federal and state sources that include grants and DSH payments; access, however, is not guaranteed, and it can vary widely among locations.

For those above the poverty line, Medicaid has made very different promises, depending on the state. The scope of a state's promise—in terms of eligibility, benefits, and access—tends to correlate with the state's average income.[1] A person in the lower-income population is more likely to be covered in a higher-income state and also to receive higher benefits. For these persons, there is little evidence that the additional services have substantial positive effects on health. This ambiguity reflects the same pattern that has been shown in Medicare: Payments that are much higher in some states than in others do not seem to be associated with demonstrably better outcomes.

Evidence also suggests that some of the largest dollar-value benefits—in long-term care, for the elderly and disabled persons, for example—accrue to families in the form of reduced caregiver time and lower private financial outlays. If taxpayers overall are mainly concerned about the elderly and disabled (rather than their families), one can question whether the marginal value of the additional coverage of long-term care services provided by higher-benefit states is worth the cost to taxpayers in other, often lower-income, states. Especially, to the extent that the benefits accrue to family members with incomes above Medicaid eligibility levels, one can also question whether such spending ought to be supported by taxpayers in other states at the same level as other Medicaid spending. Later, we will propose an adjustment to reduce the incentives higher-income states have to spend more.

As policymakers seek to balance the interests of the poor, providers, and taxpayers, there are some principles to keep in mind. We propose certain priorities, starting with those services that seem most likely to affect health for persons who might not otherwise be able to obtain services, and ending with those services that have little or no proven impact on health or might simply provide a financial benefit to nonrecipients, such as family members or other heirs.

Priorities for Care

From the perspective of the public choice model, the highest-value Medicaid services may be the mandatory ones provided to mandatory eligibility groups.[2] In a sense, Medicaid has already recognized these priorities in its benefit structure by requiring all states to cover specific services for specific groups; these mandates seem to match fairly well with the groups least able to provide for themselves and the service categories most likely to produce significant health benefits. Some add-on program components (such as the breast and cervical cancer program) may also provide high-value services to some who would not otherwise be eligible for Medicaid. Even for persons not categorically eligible, such services might be regarded as high-value because the persons might not receive needed, effective medical care without public assistance. Generally speaking, however, Medicaid's promises seem to be clear and well-fulfilled for the mandatory eligibility groups. The needs of those not eligible for Medicaid may be met, if sometimes inconsistently, by safety-net providers such as public hospitals. Where such services are known to be effective and appropriate, most would agree that the federal government and the states should find ways to make sure they are delivered and include them through Medicaid or something like it.

A second tier would include services for categorically eligible persons with incomes somewhat above the mandatory eligibility levels, along with certain services that are optional for states to provide.[3] These are the services and eligibility groups that tend to be more fully covered in higher-income, higher-benefit states and not as well covered in lower-income, lower-benefit states. They are also the services and groups that states consider cutting or reducing when state budgets are tight. A parallel group of noncategorically eligible persons with less access to care may have its needs met to varying degrees by safety-net providers. Coverage has varied widely for all these groups and services—both across states and over time within individual states—making for varied promises and inconsistency in fulfilling them for those affected. For this tier, expansion and stabilization of services to make them more equally available among the states is desirable, to the extent that a balance can be struck between the competing needs of providers and tax-payer willingness to provide funding.

A third tier might include services benefiting those who might otherwise have the ability to pay for them themselves, such as persons with access to employer-based insurance; elderly persons who engage in Medicaid financial planning to transfer assets that could be used for long-term care expenses; and disabled children or adults in higher-income families that might have the ability to provide or pay for care without assistance. These services may have some public value, as well as private value to recipients and their families. Services that crowd out or substitute for expenses that would be paid by others might properly be discounted when valued as a public good.[4] As with the second tier, this raises questions: What is the right level of subsidy for such services? Are taxpayers and families sharing in costs appropriately, based on value and family obligations? And what should be the obligation of one state to support such benefits in another? The services in this tier may be valuable to users; they may even be appropriate for the more wealthy states to provide (with state funds) as protection to the relatively small numbers of persons and families in the state who experience catastrophic long-term care costs. But questions can be raised as to the appropriateness of using federal funds obtained from western and southern states, where such benefits are typically not provided, to support the more extensive long-term care benefits provided to families in the higher-income states in the Northeast.

In a fourth tier we would put services that do not meet our standard for costworthy care—that is, care that is known to be valued, for those affected, at least as highly as its cost. These may include treatments whose effectiveness has not been proven, services that are of known effectiveness but more costly than accepted alternatives, or costly services with known, but small or unlikely, effects on health. When services are provided for free without meaningful limits, overuse can occur to the point where some are valued at less than cost, even by the recipients and their families, and even for some that are highly valuable for other people in other settings. These services can be hard to identify and may include low-value care of various forms, such as extra diagnostic imaging with a low probability of changing treatment, use of brand-name rather than generic drugs, unnecessary emergency room use, or transplants with low probability of success. Moreover, there are very few services that do not provide high-value benefit to someone, though for many treatments the odds of success are very low, and the expected benefits not sufficiently high for many potential patients. Policymakers would be well justified in finding ways to set limits based on effectiveness research and/or to provide payment incentives to discourage care in circumstances where the combination of low probability of positive effects, limited benefit, and high cost suggest that the care is not cost-effective. The all-or-nothing metric of Medicaid coverage can be viewed as part of the problem, in that those in the program may be covered for many services of low benefit or value, while those out of it, even with pressing medical needs, are denied coverage for basic, effective, and important high-value care.

Recommendations for Managing Eligibility and Benefits

Medicaid policy would be more coherent if promises to the poor were made and kept according to a set of priorities, such as those described above. Deciding how far down the list the Medicaid program will extend coverage requires policymakers to balance the needs of the poor with the resources taxpayers are willing and able to provide and the payments providers need to supply the care. The following are our principal suggestions for managing eligibility, benefits, and the resulting service use:

- Any care management tool ought to **recognize that Medicaid populations are different** and take into account the specific economic situation of each lower-income group actually or potentially eligible for Medicaid.

- In recognition of the fact that Medicaid shares the health services delivery system with other payers, policymakers should **work with other payers** to promote common, cost-effective standards of care and to reduce the use of services that are worth less than their cost.

- New program models should be well tested by **pursuing demonstration programs** with rigorous evaluations, and not accepted or rejected on the basis of cheerleading by advocates or self-interested criticisms by negatively affected stakeholders.

- Medicaid eligibility should be made to **interface better with the private insurance market.** We suggest more continuity across income groups in the public subsidies made available through public programs, tax credits, and other means. Also, Medicaid and CHIP eligibility and benefits should be administratively integrated seamlessly with the insurance coverage provided by employers.

- There should be **more uniformity in eligibility and benefits** across states for purposes of interstate equity for the low-income population.

Recognize that Medicaid Populations Are Different. Medicaid's current categorical eligibility groups are situated differently from the rest of the population: They have lower incomes and other special circumstances that limit access to highly beneficial medical care, particularly when it entails unexpected, significant costs. This means these groups may be more sensitive to cost-sharing than the bulk of the population; and while modest premiums or copayments might discourage their use of low-value care, care that most people would consider necessary or costworthy might likewise be discouraged, even by small charges. Although we might like to use the same types of cost-sharing mechanisms for Medicaid as are commonly used in other settings, we must recognize the need for a different architecture for cost-sharing (though not necessarily its elimination). The choice of some recipients in some circumstances not to seek care at all, rather than make a very modest copayment, may be the right one in some cases and not in others. Since even middle-class people are known to fail to fill prescriptions because of a $5 copayment,[5] the poor might be expected to respond even more strongly. Requiring Medicaid recipients to pay premiums when care needs are not apparent will lead some to remain uninsured until their needs are serious. They may view insurance as an investment they should only make when they are sure it will pay off.

Generally, it would be better to have everyone covered by some insurance—rather than having some with generous coverage and others with none at all, as is currently the case with Medicaid for poor people—and to promote efficient use by careful calibration of cost-sharing at the point of use. The lower-income population does present distinct economic and social circumstances and often heightened medical needs. Given the sorry state of medical knowledge about the clinical benefits and value of many treatment protocols, however, we cannot assign with confidence to each Medicaid recipient a cost-sharing amount that would discourage use of low-value care and still provide access to costworthy care.[6] In fact, we cannot do this very precisely for higher-income groups either, but social concern about cost-sharing is obviously greater when we are discussing those with greater needs. While it may be useful for some current Medicaid patients to pay something for their care when possible, additional cost-sharing beyond current levels is probably not a solution to Medicaid's care management problem for the poor. Cost-sharing might be more useful if Medicaid, or some program similar to it, were extended to income levels above the poverty line. As we have discussed, other financial incentives (such as health savings accounts, which may work for higher-income groups) would also present problems if applied to Medicaid without modification, in part because some providers may find it impractical to collect deductibles and copayments from poor recipients; noticing the lack of collection, some recipients might then choose to ignore the deductibles and copayments they are asked to pay.

We have also raised some cautions for states seeking to control costs through care management programs of various forms, including capitated acute care, community-based long-term care, pharmacy benefit management, and disease management. Given current low provider-payment levels, large across-the-board savings (compared to current levels of spending) in Medicaid are going to be hard to find. The chances of reducing *additions* to spending for new technology may be greater, but even this will be a challenge.

Savings are most likely to be found for care management programs under the following circumstances:

- The particular form of program has been tested and carefully evaluated in other settings, including well-documented measures of costs and outcomes. Claims about reductions in spending associated with expansion of benefits should especially be viewed with skepticism.

- The program is able to secure beneficiary access to services at rates paid under existing Medicaid fee schedules rather than competitive market rates.

- Pharmacy benefit management has been included in the program. Although the prospects for savings are good here, nothing is guaranteed. Cost offsets that seem so plausible in the abstract often fail to materialize in practice. And, in some cases, more services will be used by people who would not have generated other costs to offset.

- Decision-makers avoid poorly or inadequately targeted care management programs that incur costs for a broad population that will have to be offset by savings from a smaller group.

Work with Other Payers. When it comes to controlling the use of low-value care (relative to its cost), Medicaid is usually a small player in a larger system; long-term care is an exception. Community practice patterns in a given area develop around available resources. Most providers do not maintain two standards of care, so the patterns of care for Medicaid patients tend to reflect local practice, at least as practiced by those providers who see Medicaid patients. Controlling practice patterns while maintaining availability of the needed services is not a problem Medicaid can successfully tackle alone.

Even so, while Medicaid care is influenced by the actions of, and the resources provided by, other payers, it is also true that Medicaid can influence the care they provide to their non-Medicaid patients. One study has shown that Medicaid drug formularies change doctor prescribing patterns for all patients, though the change is larger in practices with a larger share of Medicaid patients.[7] Furthermore, when Medicaid contracts with a private managed care plan to cover its recipients, it effectively taps into an existing provider network and adds its enrollment to the plan's, which may give the plan additional bargaining power with providers, in turn allowing Medicaid to use the plan's care management apparatus.

The most important other payer, of course, is Medicare, which will be growing in importance over the next twenty years as the population ages and baby boomers exceed age sixty-five. State Medicaid programs may find it useful to monitor closely and support Medicare's efforts in utilizing electronic health records and e-prescribing. These innovations in information technology may provide tools for better care management that is more easily coordinated across care delivery settings. Additionally, states may choose to be guided by Medicare's national and local coverage determinations, which set standards for coverage. National quality standards exist in many areas, especially for managed care, and the Agency for Healthcare Research and Quality (AHRQ) in the U.S. Department of Health and Human Services provides quality initiatives that state programs may participate in or follow.

Cutler has noted the temporary slowing of aggregate medical cost that occurred as the "managed care era" phased in.[8] Changes in care practices may be made with less controversy when they come system-wide rather than differentially among the payers. Ways need to be found at the system level, whether through care management or reduced payment, to slow the increase in the flow of funds into the health care system.

Pursuing Demonstration Programs. Medicaid demonstration projects can be valuable in allowing states to experiment with new care management methods. Current law requires that any waiver project be designed to achieve cost neutrality—that is, that it not result in Medicaid spending that would exceed the projected amount. This sets up a situation in which states have an incentive to overestimate future cost growth and then seek federally matched dollars up to the inflated projected amount. Without significant external review based on research evidence of the effects of similar programs, the waiver project may incorrectly be deemed cost-neutral based on the state's own estimates. As a result, state waiver projects may be accepted without enough attention paid to the true likelihood of success. The larger waiver projects become vehicles for states to obtain significantly greater amounts of federal funding based on very thin promises of future cost savings and can go on apparently forever (as in the case, for instance, of Arizona's AHCCCS). The U.S. Government Accountability Office has looked skeptically at such demonstration waivers and has raised concerns that projects in several states have not adequately demonstrated budget neutrality.[9]

In our view, it is important to continue giving states the ability to experiment with innovative programs, but much more attention should be paid both to preapproval of plans and postapproval results. The focus should be more clearly on what is being learned from the projects, and sufficient resources should be invested in careful evaluation at every stage—design, implementation, administration, and operations. Formal, independent program evaluation methods should be used to measure outcomes and assess cost-effectiveness. We are not as concerned with the strict cost neutrality the current law requires as we are with ensuring both that the most sensible and promising approaches are tested, and that we really learn what works and what doesn't from such potentially important state experiments. Given the measurement difficulties and the politics involved in setting baselines and trends, waiver cost neutrality is not a precise concept, in any case. Perhaps a panel of experts should be used to assess the costs and effects of these programs and whether there is national value in continuing such state experiments. A state would be given time and options to reform its waiver program toward another, more promising, model if the first one were to fail this test.

Interface Better with the Private Insurance Market. To reduce the gaps in coverage and pockets of uninsurance in the population, Medicaid eligibility should be made to interface better with private health insurance. Doing this in a way that maintains public support will require at least two types of changes: fundamental changes in the level of public subsidies provided by income and employment status, and new administrative forms of subsidy for private insurance.

Public support for Medicaid depends on whether the typical voter-taxpayer sees program funds being put to good use. Perceptions that Medicaid benefits are overly generous in comparison to what is available to lower-income workers can damage public support for the program. This problem of perceived inequity can arise when lower-income workers, particularly those who have difficulty obtaining or affording their own coverage, perceive Medicaid recipients as getting a full package of services for free. Addressing these voters' concerns may be done in part by providing better information to the public on the program and the real needs of those it serves, and in part by providing information on the benefits of the program in promoting health and avoiding costly adverse health outcomes, such as premature births.

The problem, however, may sometimes be that Medicaid recipients are getting too much help (beyond the point of cost-effectiveness), and sometimes that those lower-income workers ineligible for public assistance are getting too little, in that they are not benefiting from the subsidy provided to others through employer-based coverage. Closing this gap in continuity of public subsidy across the income distribution may engender better public support for Medicaid in some segments of the lower-income working population.

Administrative means to address this issue may include developing new forms of insurance products with income-conditioned subsidies. These might be offered in the private sector or as a public plan, perhaps coordinated by some type of insurance exchange, as has been much discussed in the debate on national health care reform. The key will be to ensure that any such plan meshes with Medicaid to provide continuity in the public subsidy and to ensure that it interfaces with Medicaid eligibility without leaving gaps or any group (regardless of income or employment status) without access to a means of obtaining affordable coverage. We have provided some thoughts on this in a separate monograph.[10]

Medicaid itself is probably not the best administrative vehicle for subsidies to employer-based insurance, and employer-based insurance is probably not the best long-run vehicle for coverage for workers in small and low-wage firms. Most state Medicaid programs have no experience with such methods or with dealing directly with employer-sponsored insurance plans. Even Massachusetts's new administrative entity, Commonwealth Connector, does not directly support employee participation in employer plans, but rather facilitates an arrangement for employers who do not offer other insurance to contribute to the costs of a Connector-sponsored plan for their employees.[11] Increasing the coverage for this group may require working to ensure better access to care for those workers for whom employer-based coverage is unavailable or not reasonably affordable (due to its high cost or limited subsidy). Such access may come from some combination of subsidy and the development of more affordable, limited-benefit health insurance products.

Bring about More Uniformity in Eligibility and Benefits. While we are generally supportive of considerable flexibility for the states in the area of benefits (to which more evidence-based limits should apply) and of provider payment (to allow states to adjust payment to minimize the costs of achieving the desired degree of access to care in local delivery systems), we are nonetheless open to greater federal constraints and requirements on eligibility, provided—as we suggest in part 3, below—that this is supported by more appropriate federal funding to prevent the undue burdening of taxpayers in lower-income states.

Federal eligibility rules are linked directly to equity for the poor, and greater clarity from the federal government and more uniform requirements for cross-state consistency in eligibility may be effective in three ways.

First, they may help address interstate differences in health care for the poor. Current requirements for the coverage of children to specified higher levels of income reflect this interest and, as we have shown above, have resulted in more uniform eligibility for children across states as compared with other eligibility groups. If greater equity for recipients across states is a high-priority goal for reform, consideration should be given to extending the mandatory coverage groups, or perhaps even to setting most Medicaid eligibility criteria uniformly at the federal level, leaving decisions pertaining to benefit levels and payment rates to the states. The underlying rationale for this is the federal voter-taxpayer's interest in coverage for everyone in Medicaid's categorical groups.[12] Federal requirements should include both minimums and maximums to ensure not only that those most in need are covered, but also that some higher-income states do not use the program to obtain generous federal funding to cover persons whom lower-income states could never afford to cover.

Second, making Medicaid eligibility more uniform would simplify the task of any new national program to extend insurance coverage to more persons—whatever form it may take. With the current wide interstate differences in income eligibility, any such program would have to provide for Medicaid expansions or reach down unevenly to fill Medicaid gaps in the various states, posing difficulties for program design and implementation.[13] More uniform federal eligibility criteria would make it much easier to craft new coverage initiatives at the federal level that would apply in like ways in all the states. Medicaid could, for example, cover everyone up to some specified percentage of the federal poverty level, while the new program covered everyone above that level or outside Medicaid's categorical groups. We have suggested this elsewhere.[14] Greater uniformity might be phased in over time by gradually extending Medicaid mandatory coverage groups somewhat further up the income and asset scales, making more consistent what is counted and how categorical eligibility rules are applied. Such an approach has been proposed in Congress and may well emerge as part of health reform legislation. If so, it will be important to provide additional federal funding in a way that enables all states to implement this without undue taxpayer burden, an issue we address in chapter 8.

Third, federal encouragement and financial support are needed for a program component that would provide help to the growing numbers of average-income persons who, at some time in their lives, incur medical bills during a period of unemployment, or when they are otherwise uninsured or underinsured. While accomplishing this may require some combination of provisions that may include tax credits or long-term repayment schemes, consideration should be given to adapting Medicaid's medically needy provisions to help protect persons of moderate incomes from catastrophic medical expenses. Some whose incomes are above the eligibility level fall below it if one subtracts their medical expenses. Provisions for such persons commonly apply for long-term care, especially for those in nursing homes who have long-term predictable expenses in excess of limited incomes.

But Medicaid's medically needy logic might also be applied to extending coverage to lower-income children and working adults, and temporary coverage to persons with high, one-time medical expenses, to reduce burdensome debts for the individuals and uncompensated care for their providers. This would be a form of income- or resource-conditioned catastrophic coverage. Formulas would need to be devised to provide a public subsidy toward payment of accumulated medical bills, allowing the individuals under specified conditions to repay high bills over time on a spend-down basis as their income allows. Retroactive Medicaid eligibility would allow Medicaid coverage for accumulated bills in certain circumstances. Medicaid rates would apply, effectively reducing the obligation to the provider to a level of payment that would have applied had the individual been Medicaid-eligible from the start. In this way, an extension of Medicaid's existing spend-down provisions could address one of the most vexing problems of our current financing system that occurs when uninsured families incur high medical expenses at private rates that most others would not be required to pay.

With respect to benefits, we suggest most detailed coverage decisions be left to the states or to the health plans that provide Medicaid managed care services. Some broad parameters should be specified at the federal level, however, to curb wide variations in overall state spending. If federal financial incentives (embodied in matching rates) are set correctly, this will be less of a problem, as we discuss in chapter 8. Nonetheless, to ensure greater consistency across states, as well as clarify the scope of the Medicaid program, it would be useful to review carefully all services covered in every state and to exclude or set reduced matching rates for services determined to be beyond what federal taxpayers are willing to support.

For example, all nonacute care or nonmedical residential services provided outside of hospitals and nursing homes, including school-based Medicaid spending, should be reviewed to determine what portion should be eligible for match as a medical service and what portion might be more appropriately funded by other state or federal programs covering residential services. The idea here would be to clean up areas where some states may have stepped over the bounds to obtain federal matching on services that go beyond what is nationally accepted as the intended scope of the Medicaid program, and thus put all states on an equal basis so service options would be clear, and available to all or none of the states equally.

Consistent policy on eligibility and benefits is important for ensuring that Medicaid makes realistic promises and meets them consistently. A stronger federal role in ensuring greater interstate uniformity will only work, however, if it is supported by changes in federal funding, which we address in part 3, below.

Conclusion to Part II:
Achieving Access, Control, and Value

We have seen inconsistencies across states in how Medicaid makes and fulfills promises to the poor and other lower-income individuals and families. We do not call for complete elimination of such differences, as to some degree they represent differences in local needs and underlying preferences. We do, however, suggest that policymakers look at the evidence and determine whether such wide differences really reflect national and state values. They may then consider the necessity of using Medicaid and CHIP as tools to reduce the differences and improve access of the poor to the medical services most needed and most effective in improving health outcomes.

Setting policy toward Medicaid recipients entails pursuing competing objectives. The primary objective of ensuring access to needed care confronts the reality of limited budgets. Controls and limits, of some kind, are needed to ensure that limited resources are used wisely to meet the needs of as many lower-income people as possible. We suggest that policymakers focus on maximizing the value of services to make sure Medicaid dollars go toward those that are most important for protecting and improving health. Pursuing this objective will require changes in financing, as well as judicious use of care management and coverage policy.

Perhaps the greatest impediments to access under Medicaid are the more limited eligibility and coverage in the lower-benefit states—mostly, lower-income states in the South and West. Solving this aspect of the access problem will require changes to the federal–state financing relationship. We address this issue in detail in chapter 8. In short, care management controls on service use or limits on coverage should be designed to promote use of high-value services, discourage use of low-value services, and not spend inordinate amounts on the care management process itself.

PART III

Making and Meeting Promises to Voter-Taxpayers

Medicaid's commitments to taxpayers do not usually constitute an explicit topic of detailed policy analysis. Much has been written on Medicaid eligibility, benefits, providers, and services. While taxpayer interests underlie the perennial budget debates, it is unusual for policy analysts to discuss in a serious way just what those interests are and how they can best be met. This is somewhat surprising, as taxpayer needs and interests are fundamental to the budget and program decisions made by legislators on a regular basis. Voter-taxpayers are critical to providing the political support and resources needed to keep the program going, and their issues are no less interesting or complex than those of patients or providers. Taxpayers are rightly concerned about the overall level of Medicaid spending; about how those costs are shared between the federal government and the states; about the value delivered by the program; and about how well the monies spent are accounted for. We need to be thinking seriously about these issues, and about an even more fundamental question: What promises has Medicaid made and what promises should it be making to taxpayers?

In part 3 we consider Medicaid's obligations and commitments to the voter-taxpayers who pay for the program. We focus on the financing of the program in the federal–state context and consider how best to determine the amount to be spent and the distribution of those costs among federal and state taxpayers. More specifically, we ask how much of the cost of a given state's Medicaid program (or of changes to that program) should be borne by the state's own taxpayers, and how much should be paid by taxpayers in other states through federal matching payments. We consider the financing of Medicaid benefits for mandatory and optional medical services within the traditional eligibility groups (the elderly, the disabled, and families with dependent children), and also of certain common supplements and expansions in the Medicaid program. These include supplemental payments to providers, such as disproportionate share hospital payments (DSH), which extend Medicaid matching to safety-net providers, and the CHIP program, which extends Medicaid-like federal matching assistance to somewhat higher-income families with children.

Our goal here is to provide policymakers with guidance on how to make the program more efficient and equitable for taxpayers. We do not assume that "the state government" and "the federal government" can be adequately represented as single, distinct entities with preferences of their own. Rather, each comprises an array of legislative, executive, and judicial actors.[1] We do presume that, at each level, government is largely responsive to the legislative bodies that make the laws and provide the budget needed to finance the program. Within these entities, different sets of politicians may represent citizens in different ways and different settings; we take the fundamental public choice view that those politicians should be (and usually are) expressing voter-taxpayer interests. Our model allows for the fact that politicians sometimes do things that voters do not prefer, but this will be the exception rather than the rule. And, even in those cases, we suggest ways to improve political transparency so that voters can more easily perceive what their representatives are doing and communicate to them what they ought to do.

In this public choice framework, if the policy process is working properly, taxpayers in every state should feel they are paying through their federal taxes an appropriate amount and share of costs to support the program nationally, and through their state taxes an appropriate level of support for their state's program. Taxpayers should also feel that the overall program they are paying for is one they support; they should not be frustrated by a strong desire (given the taxes they pay) to expand it or to cut it. The taxes needed to finance both the federal and state shares of Medicaid should be collected in ways that do not distort economic activity and that do reinforce taxpayers' support for a workable political resolution of choices about the program's scope and generosity. But determining what is efficient and what is fair in this federal–state relationship can be difficult.

The next four chapters examine the Medicaid program from the perspective of voter-taxpayers. They explore the role of taxpayer preferences in shaping the program through the democratic process, suggest ways in which Medicaid's tax burden might be more equitably shared among the various states, and consider how Medicaid spending might be made more accountable to those who pay for the program.

6

Medicaid Financing as a Product of Democracy

Medicaid was set up as a joint federal–state program in 1965, building on smaller federal–state programs for poor children and the elderly that had existed in many states before its enactment. The program has retained that structure to a surprising degree for the past forty years (although one might view CHIP, with its modified block grant–like capped funding, as a modest change).

While governments at both levels are involved in Medicaid, each state has considerable discretion about how it administers its own program. Medicaid state plans, which are filed with the Centers for Medicare and Medicaid Services (CMS) by the state administering agency, define the elements of each state's program. Medicaid policy changes are usually accomplished through changes in the Medicaid state plan. Because state plan changes can affect eligibility, benefits, and spending, such administrative practices or rules require either the explicit or tacit approval of the state legislature. These changes are normally accepted at the federal level if the proposed state plan amendment (SPA) is consistent with federal laws and regulations. Similarly, Medicaid waivers also must meet federal requirements and are typically approved if they fall within the scope of the authorizing federal law. State waiver requests typically become controversial only when they push the envelope of what is allowed, or if the state is unable to document adequately its ability to meet the criterion of cost neutrality.

In contrast, changes in federal Medicaid policy can be more difficult. Significant changes in Medicaid normally require Congress to pass an amendment to Title XIX of the Social Security Act and may require federal budget changes, as well. Legislative changes are then translated into regulations by the U.S. Department of Health and Human Services. While Congress is free to change the Medicaid program at any time, it has been very reluctant to make changes to the basic structure of the program, and even adjustments in the level of federal financing are hotly debated and only infrequently approved.

As a consequence, within some rather broad limits, states possess the authority to decide on the number of eligibles and on the generosity of spending per eligible person, while the federal government's role has largely been limited to raising tax revenues to pay for a program over which it has asserted little direct control. Federal legislation could change this, but the durability of this arrangement suggests that it is more than a historical accident. What, then, is the rationale for the form the Medicaid program has taken? Is that rationale as relevant for the future as it has been in the past?

A useful way to think about this question is to use our "public choice" framework, in which governmental actions are viewed as reflecting the preferences of a decisive voter or set of voters. While real-world politics involve many more state-specific and strategic considerations than this model can take into account, the framework has the virtues of both simplicity and predictive ability; and when the dust clears, the public choice model does a serviceable job of predicting generally what will happen in many situations. This model asks us to imagine that the actions of policymakers in a democratic governmental system will generally reflect the preferences of the "median voter." As mentioned earlier, if one imagines all voters lined up according to preferred level of public expenditure on Medicaid, the "median voter" would be the one standing exactly in the middle. Hence, the median voter's preferred spending on Medicaid (and its implied fraction of the population made eligible and level of benefits) is at the midpoint of preferred spending in the whole voter population.[1] It will be in the interest of those seeking election in a democracy to represent such median preferences, as anyone politically positioned to the left or the right of the median will attract less support. In the simplified case of a two-candidate race without complex coalition building, any elected representative taking the median position prevents anyone with a position to the right or left from achieving a majority; it is in this sense that the median voter is "decisive" on the issue. We explain this in a more technical way in the following section.

The Median Voter Model of Public Spending

To apply the idea of public choices reflecting the median voter to federal–state Medicaid arrangements, let us begin by considering one state's choice of some single, key policy parameter for its Medicaid program—say, the expense per eligible citizen for a defined group of lower-income eligible citizens. If the state had to finance health insurance for this population entirely on its own, the key consideration would be taxpayer willingness to pay higher state taxes in exchange for raising the level of benefits. We assume that most taxpayers are willing to pay something for insurance for lower-income people, based on consideration of external benefits to the taxpayer, such as the prevention of contagious disease, altruistic preferences for medical care for people who on their own cannot afford it, and possible spillover benefits in terms of a higher quality standard for all in the community.

We also assume, however, that taxpayer willingness to pay diminishes as the fraction of the cost borne by the state (and, hence, by the median voter in the state) increases; the lower the state taxpayer's share of the cost per unit or dollar of increase in benefits or eligibility, the higher the level of benefit the median voter will prefer. While positive marginal benefits proceed from increased generosity, the value of an additional dollar of benefits diminishes as the amount of spending increases. The voter most prefers the level of spending at which the additional taxes owed would just equal the money value placed on increasing benefits for Medicaid recipients. The level of benefits per eligible person that this voter would choose if there were no federal assistance would be smaller than the level chosen if the federal government were to bear most of any additional cost. Federal matching reduces the marginal cost to the state voter-taxpayer of favoring the provision of higher benefits.

So, compared to a lump sum or block grant of an equal dollar amount, federal matching will lead state voters to prefer more generous benefits. In fact, the level of benefits with a block grant should be only modestly higher than what the state would do on its own, as long as the block grant amount is not larger than what the state would have spent on its own. It is important to recognize the role of matching (at the margin) compared with other financing arrangements, such as block grants that provide no incentive (at the margin) for additional state spending. This incentive has been key to sustaining the level of Medicaid spending we have observed.

There is another key actor in this drama: the national median taxpayer for federal decisions (which we assume to be the person with the median preferences for Medicaid generosity per beneficiary among all voters in the country). The "national demand curve," or national marginal evaluation curve, would plot levels of benefits desired by national taxpayers as a function of the federal (versus state) share. If the state were to pay nothing toward the cost, a certain level of benefit would be selected; if the state were to contribute a larger percentage, the level of benefit desired by national taxpayers would rise (other things being equal), because the state would be picking up some of the cost. As we have noted earlier, it would be reasonable to assume that a given voter would be willing to pay more to expand the benefits of someone in his or her own state rather than for a similar person in another state; charity begins at home, but does not stop there. Nonetheless, the curve slopes downward, as we posit the marginal value of any state's spending to out-of-state taxpayers declines as the benefit level in that state increases.

Figure 6-1 illustrates how the ideal level of spending can be specified. Since the median state voter and the median national voter both attach positive values to the prospective beneficiary's use of medical care, it is appropriate to add the marginal valuation curves (or valuation lines, in this case) vertically. The optimal quantity, Q^*, is where the sum of these marginal evaluations (MEs), the vertical sum of the national and in-state demand, equals the marginal cost (or price, P). (If the beneficiary were willing to pay something toward Medicaid coverage, that marginal evaluation should also be included in the summation; but we will assume that poverty makes that willingness to pay negligible, though it may be a different story for CHIP.) The diagram used for this example implies that, in this case, the state should pay the largest share, and the federal share should make up the difference. Note that any quantity smaller than the optimum, financed in a way that covers the cost, would be associated with a desire for at least one, and possibly both, of these actors to want to do more. Note also that if (given the consumer's share) the state and federal shares were set at some level other than this ideal, conflict between governments would be inevitable. If the state share were set too low, for example, national voters and the policymakers who represent them would be complaining about excessive generosity in the Medicaid program, while state policymakers would be talking about how much more they needed and how little they

FIGURE 6-1

NATIONAL AND STATE DEMAND FOR MEDICAID

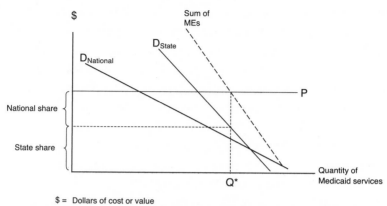

$ = Dollars of cost or value
$D_{National}$ = Demand or marginal evaluation curve of national taxpayers (other than in state)
D_{State} = Demand or marginal evaluation curve of state taxpayers
Sum of MEs = Vertical sum of $D_{National}$ and D_{State}
Q^* = Optimal quantity of Medicaid services
P = Price per unit for Medicaid services
National share = Optimal share of Medicaid spending paid by national taxpayers
State share = Optimal share of Medicaid spending paid by state taxpayers

SOURCE: Authors' diagram.

were able to do, all because of the unresponsiveness of the national government. Neither claim (of overspending or underspending) would be cosmically true; federal officials, according to this model, might be happy with more spending if the state were to pick up a larger share of any additional spending, while state policymakers might find reason to be content with less spending if they were to find they had to pay most of the cost with state funds.

The variable that is usually identified as a major shifter of all of these marginal benefit curves is taxpayer income. A nonpoor voter-taxpayer with a relatively low income might be unwilling (whether or not unable) to support generous amounts of charity care, and the clear implication of empirical work in this area is that charity is a normal (perhaps even a luxury) good for voter-taxpayers. Figure 6-2 shows a single national voter demand curve, and individual state voter-taxpayer demand curves from a lower-income state (D_L) and a higher-income state (D_H). The summed demand curves

FIGURE 6-2

MEDICAID DEMAND IN HIGH- AND LOW-INCOME STATES

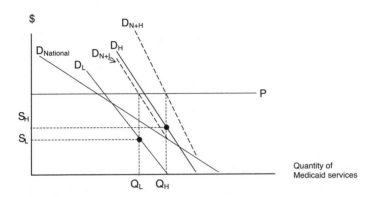

$\$$ = Dollars of cost or value
$D_{National}$ = Demand or marginal evaluation curve of national taxpayers
D_L = Demand or marginal evaluation curve of state taxpayers in low-income state
D_H = Demand or marginal evaluation curve of state taxpayers in high-income state
D_{N+L} = Vertical sum of $D_{National}$ and D_L
D_{N+H} = Vertical sum of $D_{National}$ and D_H
P = Price per unit for Medicaid services
Q_L = Optimal quantity of Medicaid services in low-income state
Q_H = Optimal quantity of Medicaid services in high-income state
S_H = Optimal share of Medicaid spending paid by high-income state taxpayers
S_L = Optimal share of Medicaid spending paid by low-income state taxpayers

SOURCE: Authors' diagram.

D_{N+L} and D_{N+H} reflect the combined national and state demand curves. The optimal and equilibrium state shares would then be S_L and S_H, and the associated quantities would be Q_L and Q_H. The implication is that, at the optimum, the needed state share should be higher for the higher-income state. The efficient quantities of care or spending per beneficiary (of a given income) should not, however, be identical across states. As in the diagram, optimal spending should vary positively with median voter-taxpayer income, but it should not vary as much as it would were there no federal presence. And it probably should be larger in all states than any state would choose in isolation. The key determinants of how much final choices of Medicaid generosity vary with income depends on the distribution of income, the price-responsiveness of taxpayers' federal demand curve, and the price-responsiveness of their state demand curves. In summary, considering a set of states with differing state-level demands for Medicaid generosity, federal shares should vary inversely with state median income; total program spending (perhaps a measure of effective generosity) should be greater than if there were no federal program, whereas program generosity should vary with income to some extent.

So, it is surely possible that the ideal or efficient Medicaid spending level in a given lower-income state is higher under fiscal federalism than if the state were to go it alone, but lower than in the higher-income states or in states where state voters may choose to be more generous, even potentially at a higher state share. With this model (as already noted), it is also clear that, under fiscal federalism, Medicaid spending is higher in every state than would be chosen if national voters were going it alone without state participation. This is an important insight into the implications of federal–state financing of Medicaid. But it is also an important insight into public demand for national health insurance coverage for the poor. A purely federally financed program with uniform national benefits would likely lead taxpayer-voters to prefer and choose lower levels of spending than if they could direct some of their dollars locally with state participation, as is currently the case in Medicaid.

Medicaid's federal structure would make sense even if voters cared equally about their fellow Americans regardless of where they lived, because the intensity of those preferences almost surely varies across geography. That is, even if I care about lower-income children in South Dakota just as much as those in Pennsylvania, if I live in Pennsylvania I may be able to do much more about children in my state than elsewhere. Especially if I have a higher level of concern than the national median, and if the other taxpayers in my state likewise have relatively greater concern, the existence of a federal program allows me to favor a program that, at least in my state, better reflects my preferences than what is politically feasible nationwide. Put slightly differently, a uniform national program would leave about half of taxpayers frustrated by levels of generosity lower than they preferred, while a federal–state program allows some of that frustration to be diminished. We can see, then, that there is reason for a federal–state program if regional preferences are strong or the intensity of preferences for medical care for the poor differs geographically.

Medicaid Budgets

Medicaid budgets define Medicaid's relationship to taxpayers. Budgets embody policy objectives, choices about resource allocation, and, often, hopes or desires that needs can be met with the funds available. Medicaid budgets have direct implications for taxpayers, who must pay the necessary taxes or give up other public services to support the budgeted Medicaid expenditures.

Federal Budget Issues. At the federal level, the Medicaid budget is over $200 billion, making it the third largest of the mandatory human resource programs after Social Security and Medicare. Federal Medicaid budgeting is largely a matter of estimation and projection of what the states will do in the future, because the federal government has little direct control over Medicaid spending. Federal policymakers in Congress and the executive branch debate alternative ways to induce states to make changes in their Medicaid programs but cannot always produce the desired changes at the state level.

The Deficit Reduction Act of 2005 (DRA) is a useful example. That act provided for a number of significant program changes that were expected to produce $43 billion in federal savings over ten years.[2] It called for premium and cost-sharing changes and modifications in the way Medicaid pays for drugs. States have not made many changes in response to the DRA provisions, however. Coughlin and Zuckerman report, "With a few important exceptions, these changes have been fairly circumscribed, but despite their expressed interest, states have not yet fully used this flexibility for their Medicaid programs."[3] And in November 2007, the National Association of State Medicaid Directors reported that over 75 percent of states had indicated they were not actively considering a change in drug payment policy, and only twelve had said they might increase drug dispensing fees as allowed by the DRA.[4] The states, apparently, are not on track to produce the level of DRA savings estimated by federal policymakers. The lesson here is that states will not respond to federal policy changes unless they are mandatory or coincident with state interests, or come with strong and favorable financial incentives.

As this example illustrates, federal policymakers are in the unenviable position of trying to guess what types and sizes of (politically feasible) incentives might induce states to make desired Medicaid program changes.

With too little incentive, the changes just won't occur; with too large an incentive, the responses may be greater than intended. This makes it very difficult to use federal policy to achieve any specific change, whether a savings goal or a desired program expansion. Since the federal government does not have the instruments to micromanage state Medicaid policy or to compel states to take actions that will save money, perhaps it should stop trying. Instead, it might rely on the broad-based incentive inherent in the matching rate (which it can control), while at the same time putting more effort into research and analysis of the question of which state actions are likely to follow from which kinds of matching-rate changes.

The most direct tool to adjust the budget is the schedule of federal medical assistance percentages (FMAP) and federal policies specifying what costs will be allowed for federal matching. While FMAP changes in a pre-specified way from year to year (for states above the 50 percent minimum), adjustments to the FMAP formula have only occasionally been made, and only for broad policy purposes rather than precisely defined program goals. The latter can be affected by changing rules about either the eligible populations or the eligible services. In tight years, federal budget proposals often include additional limits on what states can claim as Medicaid costs for matching, and provisions that would shift a greater share of costs to the states without allowing them to reduce Medicaid spending (since service reductions are politically unpopular). So, aside from any plan to cut either eligibility or benefits, there is a push-and-pull at budget time between the federal government and the states over the division of costs.

State Budget Issues. Medicaid budgeting at the state level is a challenge. The budgets proposed by governors and passed by the state legislatures determine total Medicaid spending targets. But a target is just that. To affect costs, state program administrators must actually make the adjustments in eligibility, benefits, and payment rates necessary to achieve the targets. Even these are loose controls, since Medicaid spending depends on enrollment, utilization, and, in some cases, prices that the state does not tightly control. Fluctuations in the state economy can create uncertainty and swings in enrollment and, even more importantly, in the state revenue needed to support the program. This makes it difficult for states to predict accurately what Medicaid spending will be, and they are frequently surprised by spikes in spending, such as when their economies slow down, or drug prices increase sharply.

Medicaid budgeting processes vary widely among the states. Budgeting is the context in which most decisions are made about levels of eligibility, benefits allowed, and provider payments the state will support. Budget dynamics often reflect very state-specific political factors.[5] In some states, there is general agreement to keep eligibility limited: Benefit commitments are stable, and provider payment rates are indexed to inflation. As a result, the basic Medicaid budget is largely predetermined, and varies only as the needy population varies. In many other states, managed care contract rates determine large parts of the costs, which depend significantly on the local market for managed health plans. In still other states, eligibility, benefits, and payment rates are essentially up for grabs in every budget cycle. Payments to providers and to the managed care insurers usually absorb the impact of economic and political fluctuations; budgets are often frozen or reduced in periods of state fiscal stress (usually, though not always, related to an economic slowdown or recession), and are relaxed when overall state tax collections are rising (because of economic growth and resultant decreases in the number of poor residents without insurance coverage). This kind of state behavior—cutting the budget when the economy turns down, increasing it when it grows—obviously does not help to dampen macroeconomic fluctuations and does not produce stable promises.

Periodic surveys of state Medicaid program budgets and activities illustrate the wide diversity among the states in the types and extent of program changes. Vernon Smith and others, for example, show differences in the use of provisions for flexibility available under the Deficit Reduction Act.[6] Their survey also shows some states expanding and some imposing new limits on benefits; it reports sixteen states engaged in changing their managed care policies and another, distinct set of sixteen states developing new disease management or case management initiatives; and it reports wide variation in the use of pharmacy cost containment methods. This all contributes to distinct patterns of cost growth among the states, with some being early adopters of new program opportunities and others lagging behind or pursuing different program priorities. While there are general demographic trends and sensitivity to economic conditions, Medicaid spending changes reflect, to a large degree, state policymaker decisions—and these decisions differ among the states.

The main point here is that, in large part because of its mixed federal–state financing structure, Medicaid never moves entirely and consistently in any one specific direction. States are continually adapting their programs to local needs, political pressures, and economic conditions. At any given time, Medicaid budgets and spending growth (even after adjustment for local price changes) will differ among states, among eligibility groups, and among service categories.

Desirable Characteristics of Federal–State Financing

Many variations are possible for the structure of federal–state financing. But, although changes around the edges have been noted, no major change has occurred in the basic federal–state financing arrangement since the Medicaid program began in 1965. The current matching arrangement has demonstrated resilience that may reflect widespread acceptance, but it may also reflect the political power of states in general and higher-income states in particular. It may also reflect the lack of a clear path toward better-achieving program goals—when you do not know where you want to go, you might as well keep to the path you are on. We suggest below an approach to providing federal financial assistance based on matching rates that will improve efficiency while also providing a higher degree of equity for taxpayers and recipients.

At this point, however, let's begin by considering the characteristics we would like to see in Medicaid's method of providing federal financial assistance to states. Such a system should do the following:

- **Reflect voter preferences.** First, and perhaps most important, we would like this system to reflect both local and national preferences about care for the poor. An all-federal or all-state program might lead to inefficiently low levels of Medicaid spending. In our public choice model, it is the combined demand for Medicaid among federal and state voters that counts. While preferences for local benefits are more intense at the local level, the widespread, but diffuse, demand of large numbers of voters at the national level contributes to total demand for, and willingness to support financially, publicly funded medical care for the poor. In the ideal equilibrium described at the beginning of this chapter, the median voters at both levels of government would have their preferences exactly satisfied—while any other matching rates would leave one or the other actor seeking more or wanting less.

- **Adapt to local delivery systems.** Federal financing should provide for considerable state flexibility in benefits and payment policy (with accountability) to allow state-level administration that permits adaptation to local health care delivery systems. The key issue here is which characteristics of local systems are most relevant. Some obvious technical differences, like the types of provider organizations appropriate for rural versus urban areas, should be taken into account, and states are arguably better at determining this than the federal government. This adaptation problem is illustrated by struggles to make Medicare (both fee-for-service and the Medicare Advantage plans) work as well in rural as it does in urban settings. Other distinguishing characteristics, such as potentially lower real resource costs in rural areas and potentially greater shortages of specialized providers in such areas, are harder to adjust for in ways that produce some semblance of uniformity in the final quality of care. For example, some rural areas with few doctors use independent nurse practitioners to provide services; there may be less reason for such, however, in urban areas.

- **Promote equity for recipients.** If reduction in the wide interstate variation in Medicaid benefits per beneficiary is desired, the matching-rate structure could be changed to promote more equal distribution of benefits among the nation's poor. We discuss this in more detail below.

- **Promote more equity for taxpayers.** To the extent that states differ in their preferences for Medicaid program generosity, state taxes on households at given income levels will vary across states—but they should not be inherently inequitable. If higher program expectations arise in part from taxpayers with higher incomes, then higher total taxes (even if not higher marginal tax rates) may even be thought to improve equity. Still, a higher-income state could choose to "split the difference," using part of its higher income to provide more generous benefits and part of it to lower tax rates. States with a disproportionately large lower-income population face a different choice—either to expend a higher share of taxpayer income (than other states) to support the state share of costs or to provide a lower-than-average benefit level. Most such states choose the latter. We will discuss below whether variation in matching rates can address these incentive-equity problems.

- **Reflect priorities for covering the most vulnerable and resource-poor population groups.** Federal matching should provide greater incentives for covering the most vulnerable populations as a top priority for use of additional resources. This could be accomplished through higher federal matching for state coverage of poor children and a lower match for nonpoor (though lower-income) adults with some resources and/or earning ability. The George W. Bush administration's proposal that states be required to seek out and cover nearly all of the lowest-income children before being allowed to use CHIP funds to help children from less-poor families was one example of this approach; the solution suggested by this model is to reduce the matching for covering easy-to-find, nonpoor children, but increase it for efforts to find the truly poor children who have fallen through the safety net.

- **Provide for adjustment to changing situations.** Federal medical assistance to states should be structured so that it automatically responds to economic conditions and can be adjusted to reflect policy preferences better over time. The most obvious improvement here would be an automatic increase in federal support that occurs when the economy goes into recession, since then state tax collections fall at the same time program enrollment rises, and the federal government has a greater capacity for deficit spending. Any program of adjustments should apply on equal terms to all states and be based in a predetermined way on objective measures of state economic conditions. This would be considerably fairer than the current process, in which politically powerful states have room to argue that their "changed economic situation" is more severe than that of others.

• **Avoid inefficient or untargeted spending by higher-income states.** As noted earlier, much of the higher spending by higher-income states does not seem to flow into basic medical services for Medicaid's target population. Even poor states appear able and willing to provide basic services, so additional spending by a higher-income state is unlikely to provide much social benefit from the point of view of the federal taxpayer. Part of this additional spending seems to be transferred to the families, relatives, and heirs of nursing home and home health patients, a result that might be desirable but is not consistent with the characterization of Medicaid as a program to meet the medical needs of poor people.

Conclusion

Medicaid exists in the world of public programs and budgets. It faces many of the same challenges as other programs in reconciling valued objectives with the realities of budget limitations. Medicaid's distinct financing issues arise from the interactions of a federal government with more ready access to funds but few direct controls on state spending, and state governments often facing acute needs for services in the population and unceasing demands for payment by providers. Policymakers are left to try to discern public preferences for the program with very limited information on the marginal value of spending. Still, states operate with a clear effective price of services (discounted by the federal share) and can make reasonable choices, at least for themselves, within the framework of federal financing. The broader question is whether all these parameters have been set up correctly, and in particular whether the federal matching rates, which do much to determine state spending, have been set to reflect truly national voter support for the spending in each of the states.

So we see that our goals for financing include reflecting public values about spending levels, providing some flexibility to the states in how funds are used, providing greater equity for the poor by promoting more equal spending across states, and providing equitable sharing of the burden among taxpayers. These are, in many ways, competing goals. Achieving the right balance will require an approach that is theoretically well founded, technically correct, and ably implemented. Leaving implementation to others, we offer in the next two chapters a theoretical and technical approach to determining federal financing—one that is built upon objective equity criteria and is flexible enough to be scaled and adapted to reflect changing public preferences for the level of Medicaid spending.

7

Medicaid Financing for Taxpayer Equity

"Equity" can have many meanings. The simplest and least controversial is horizontal equity—the principle that, in an equitable system, people who are similar will be treated in the same way by government, both as it levies taxes and as it distributes benefits. In general, Medicaid can be viewed as more horizontally equitable in the imposition of state taxes on taxpayers than in its distribution of benefits among the states. The state share of Medicaid payments averages about 1.5 percent of taxpayer income. Though there are regional differences in willingness to support the program from taxpayer income (lower in the West; higher in the Northeast), these differences, as figure 7-1 shows, do not follow income differences among states. At this level of aggregation, taxpayers in higher- and lower-income states pay (in state taxes) about the same share of their incomes toward Medicaid—much closer to equity for them than we observed for recipients in our measures of Medicaid payments per person below the federal poverty level.

Redistribution Effects of Medicaid and CHIP

One major purpose of a national program is to make resources available for services—in this case, for health care for the poor—where they are most needed. The program is financed through the federal tax system with its mildly progressive income tax based on ability to pay (to the extent that Congress can define, and the Internal Revenue Service can measure it). We might then expect the Medicaid program to redistribute resources from higher-income states with relatively wealthy taxpayers toward lower-income states that have fewer well-off taxpayers and are burdened with a greater share of poor residents. We can measure the extent to which this is

FIGURE 7-1

STATE SHARE OF MEDICAID PAYMENTS, FY 2006, AS A PERCENTAGE OF
TAXPAYER INCOME, BY STATE-MEDIAN-HOUSEHOLD INCOME QUINTILE

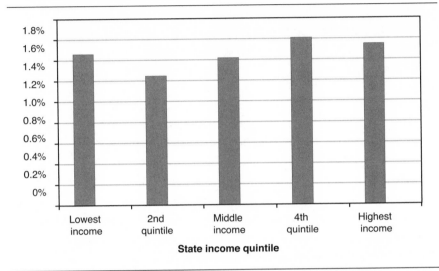

SOURCES: Computed using data from Kaiser Family Foundation (2009, "Federal and State Share of Medicaid Spending, FY2006," http://www.statehealthfacts.org); Kaiser Family Foundation (2009, "Federal
Matching Rate [FMAP] for Medicaid and Multiplier," http://www.statehealthfacts.org/comparetable.
jsp?ind=184&cat=4); U.S. Internal Revenue Service (2007); and U.S. Census Bureau (2007).

the case with Medicaid and associated program components using data on
Medicaid and CHIP payments and federal taxes.

Thus, we compute for each state a measure of the "redistribution effect"
of Medicaid as an estimate of the extent to which the state gets back more
(or less) than it puts into the program. We look at what each state receives
in federal Medicaid medical assistance payments, then calculate its contribution to the federal funding by assuming its share is proportional to its
share of aggregate federal personal income taxes. In this way, a higher-
income state is given credit for its more-than-proportional share of federal
income taxes. We do not count other federal taxes (such as corporate
income taxes), as they are less clearly attributable as a contribution of the
state's residents. We subtract the imputed contribution toward Medicaid
paid in federal taxes from the federal Medicaid payments provided to the
state. The resulting measure is, then, an estimate of what the state receives

FIGURE 7-2

DONOR, RECEIVER, AND "ABOUT-EVEN" STATES BASED ON
AGGREGATE DOLLAR AMOUNTS OF FEDERAL MEDICAID PAYMENTS NET
OF PROPORTIONAL SHARE OF FEDERAL TAXES, FY 2006

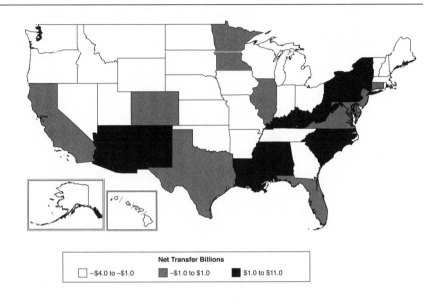

SOURCES: Computed using data from Kaiser Family Foundation (2009, "Federal and State Share of Medicaid Spending, FY2006," http://www.statehealthfacts.org/comparemaptable.jsp?ind=636&cat=4) and Internal Revenue Service (2007).

in federal Medicaid dollars, net of what its residents contribute to the federal share of program costs nationally. This will be positive for some states (net receivers) and negative for others (net donors).

Figure 7-2 indicates geographically which states are net donors, which are net receivers, and which come out about even (within $1 billion, plus or minus, in net transfers in FY 2006). Table 7-1 shows the overall redistribution of aggregate funds from Medicaid and CHIP among states by income quintile. Overall, the programs serve to redistribute about $10 billion to the states in the lowest quintile. This amounts to about 5 percent of total program funds nationally. So we can say that the net redistributive effect of Medicaid in aiding the poorest ten states is a relatively modest

TABLE 7-1

REDISTRIBUTION EFFECT OF MEDICAID,
MEDICAID PROVIDER PAYMENTS, DSH, AND CHIP, 2006
(Millions net of proportional share of federal personal income taxes paid)

	Net transfer due to Medicaid, DSH, and CHIP	Net transfer due to Medicaid	Net transfer due to DSH	Net transfer due to CHIP
Redistribution by median household income quintiles				
Top ten	−$9,464	$8,964	$359	−$141
Second ten	−$2,761	$2,716	$136	$90
Third ten	$3,455	$3,521	$166	$100
Fourth ten	−$905	−$765	$63	−$202
Bottom ten	$10,107	$9,299	$618	$189
District of Columbia	−$432	−$376	−$20	−$37
To bottom ten as percentage of national total	5%	5%	6%	3%
Redistribution by region				
Northeast	$6,290	$5,498	$1,041	−$249
Midwest	−$3,967	$3,402	−$530	−$35
South	$1,350	$1,151	$131	$69
West	−$3,673	$3,246	−$643	$216

SOURCES: Computed using data from Kaiser Family Foundation (2009) and U.S. Internal Revenue Service (2007).

5 percent of national Medicaid spending. The second-lowest quintile, however, actually sends funds to other states as a result of these programs, suggesting that these relatively lower-income states do not receive a net benefit from outside resources under the current system. Tables A1-6 and A1-7 show the redistribution effect of Medicaid, DSH, and CHIP on an aggregate and a per-capita basis for each state. States with the largest gains in net transfers ($400 or more per capita) are Mississippi, Maine, West Virginia,

FIGURE 7-3

**INTERREGIONAL TRANSFERS DUE TO MEDICAID AND CHIP
NET OF FEDERAL INCOME TAX BURDEN BY CENSUS REGION, 2006**

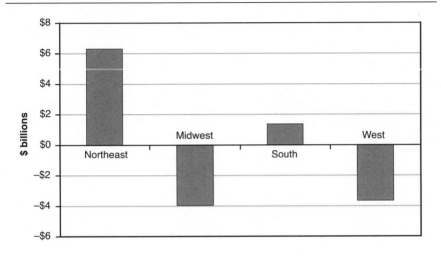

SOURCES: Computed using data from Kaiser Family Foundation (2009) and U.S. Internal Revenue Service (2007).

Vermont, and New York—a list that includes some of the lowest-income states, but also some middle- and higher-income states. Jurisdictions with the largest negative transfers per capita (indicating they paid $400 or more per capita to support other states) include the District of Columbia, Delaware, and Minnesota.

On an aggregate basis, the states with the largest populations account for the greatest redistribution effects. New York received a net transfer due to Medicaid of more than $7 billion in 2006. Part of this can be viewed as a transfer within the New York–New Jersey–Connecticut tristate area, as New Jersey's net transfer is a negative $2.5 billion; and Connecticut's is a negative $1.2 billion. But, even subtracting that suburban-to-urban transfer, New York still comes out with more than $3 billion in Medicaid-related transfers from out-of-area states in excess of taxes paid to support the program. For CHIP, California captures the largest net transfer, receiving more than $260 million in 2006 net of its tax share. With these large-state effects dominating the aggregate numbers, the net redistribution effect of the program regionally is that the Northeast is the primary beneficiary of Medicaid and DSH net transfers, with the funds coming from the Midwest and West. The West is the primary beneficiary of CHIP, with the funds coming from the Northeast. The South is a modest net beneficiary of all these program components (see table 7-1 and figures 7-2 and 7-3).

Although we have not conducted a comprehensive study of the issue, we have observed that some states with redistribution effects more favorable than might be suggested by their income rank are those with broad-based or extensive Medicaid waiver programs. That is, some states have made the effort to develop and receive approval for program extensions outside usual Medicaid eligibility and benefit criteria, and this seems to have enhanced their receipt of federal funds. Obviously, the higher-income states are better positioned to contribute the state shares needed to participate in such program extensions, while some lower-income states with high matching rates may also find it advantageous to participate in Medicaid more fully than their neighbors.

So we see that Medicaid's redistributive effect toward the lower-income states is a modest one, that it does not consistently benefit all lower-income states among the income groups, and that it varies widely among the states individually on a per-capita basis. These results tend to suggest that the redistributive effect of these programs depends more on the program, decisions, waivers, and financing schemes in the states than on a strict ordering by need as reflected in median household income.

Adjusting Federal Matching to Achieve Medicaid Equilibrium

Despite its fairly stable administrative structure, the Medicaid program seems never to be in equilibrium when it comes to satisfying voters and policymakers at both state and federal levels. The premise that state voters should get what they want has not been satisfied; a kind of disequilibrium pervades political economy. In one sense, this is no surprise, as states should prefer additional federal funds if the money would pay more for new programs of positive (though more modest) marginal benefit that lie just beyond the current cutoff. If it thinks it might be effective, a state could be expected to seek to increase its federal matching rate. We will consider this proposition in explaining the CHIP program below.

A second consideration may be even more crucial and is central to our critique of today's Medicaid program and our proposals for its reform. At the current matching rate for higher-income states and the level of spending they choose because of that rate, the marginal evaluation by *federal* taxpayers of that spending may well be low. It is at least lower than the fifty cents per dollar of spending implied by the federal matching rate, and probably lower than the marginal value those dollars would have if they were spent on Medicaid benefits in lower-income states. Federal voters may attach lower value to state spending than is consistent with the share they are paying, and therefore desire lower spending in higher-income states. The key implication, then, is that *federal matching rates should be lowered in higher-income states, and raised in some lower-income states.* Doing so would lead to more equalized spending per poor person and—what is equally if not more important—to spending levels on which federal and state taxpayers would tend more nearly to agree.

The evidence suggestive of low marginal value in the additional state spending of higher-income states relative to lower-income states has already been documented: small differences in the use of basic services, the addition of people higher up the income stream, and general discomfort with the high spending and federal costs in the higher-income states. In addition, we imagine that federal taxpayers might not attach such a high value to a Medicaid program that effectively makes transfers to extended families and heirs—even those not participating in caregiving.

We saw, above, empirical evidence suggesting that a significant part of the additional benefits provided in higher-income (particularly Eastern) states goes to provide more extensive Medicaid coverage of long-term care services for the elderly and disabled—services that are less closely related to acute medical needs, but do reflect regional differences in patterns of care in the mixture of formal services and informal family caregiving. Such patterns could reflect simple regional cultural differences, or perhaps long-term care services being treated as a luxury good—an affordable choice only in the higher-income states. In either case, federal taxpayers in the lower-benefit states may see little real value in supporting for other states the higher benefits that are not available in their own, particularly when such benefits are extended to higher-income families. The rich states apparently are now spending in ways that provide little marginal benefit to federal taxpayers located elsewhere. While this argument may never be conclusively proved, a good case can be made for lowering the out-of-state subsidy through reductions in federal matching rates for such high benefits in the higher-income states. We expect this would lead to greater equality of spending per poor person across states.

The argument here is not just based on equity for recipients, but also on equity for taxpayers and on economic efficiency. This is because, as we noted, variation may actually be less in the real value of benefits across states than spending differentials would suggest because the additional spending in higher-income states may not pay for higher-value benefits. Rather, the inequality in spending reflects variation in efficiency, with marginal benefits in higher-income states being less cost-effective in health effects and—what may be even more important in our public choice framework—of lower value to federal taxpayers. Policy development for any such change would need to consider the nature and value and distribution of the benefits that would be lost in such a cutback.

This model assumes that what states furnish (and voters at both the state and federal levels care about) are the quantity and quality of care for (eligible) lower-income people. States pay less than half the cost precisely because they need to be encouraged to spend more than they would choose to do on their own. The general economic rule that decisions are more efficient when decision-makers face the full cost of their actions will not apply in this context, because state decision-makers cannot be expected to take the interests of people elsewhere in the nation into account.

Indeed, state policymakers are expected to pursue the interests of the state's citizens (including taxpayers, recipients, and providers) and, particularly, voters. They have no reason to represent the interests of those out of state unless those interests are expressed through federal financial incentives or regulatory requirements. Similarly, federal policymakers (except for the representatives of those states) have no obligation to commit federal funds to support unusually high local preferences for medical benefits for people who might contribute to the cost of their care.

Neither federal nor state policymakers alone, it seems, have reason to reflect fully the preferences of all taxpayers. Our federal system of government allows for this possibility and presents opportunities for a solution in which public spending can reflect preferences of both federal and state citizens. It allows for policymakers at both federal and state levels to make independent decisions on the program parameters they control, each entity accounting in its own decisions for the contribution to costs paid by the other. Federal policymakers can afford a more comprehensive program because they know states will share in the costs; states can spend more freely knowing they pay only a share of the costs. This is as intended; Medicaid financing allows for decisions that express voter preferences for the program at both national and state levels. One just needs to get the program parameters set to reflect these preferences accurately.

Federal–State Financing Options

In our previous book, we provided a "Catalogue of Policy Options" for federal–state Medicaid financing arrangements, focusing on various suggestions that have been made to modify the way the federal and the state governments share costs of the program.[1] In abbreviated form we review here the types of arrangements and their expected effects on Medicaid spending and equity issues. We will pursue variants of some of them at greater length when we discuss policy directions for the future. A major motivation for our discussion of these options is our earlier conclusion that current arrangements lead to higher spending on lower-value services in higher-income states; effectiveness in correcting this inefficiency (and associated inequities) will therefore be a part of the evaluation of each option.

Current Matching Rates. The basic formula determining federal financial participation in state Medicaid programs has not changed since the start of the program. As of this writing, the standard federal share currently ranges from 50 percent in seventeen higher-income states to 76 percent in Mississippi, with enhanced matching rates for CHIP ranging from 65 percent to 82 percent. Federal matching is higher for lower-income states and depends on state per-capita income, according to a formula.[2] The American Recovery and Reinvestment Act (ARRA) of 2009 provided a temporary increase in the standard rates of 6.2 percentage points, with somewhat greater increases in federal matching for states that have experienced increased unemployment rates.

Block Grants. Converting federal Medicaid funding to block grants for the states is often suggested as a means of predetermining federal Medicaid costs, at least for some new program components. In such proposals, states are usually given greater flexibility in how they may use those funds.

Block grants fundamentally differ from matching funds in the incentives they create for state spending. Incentives can differ dramatically, even when the block grant and the matching funds end up having the same monetary value to the state. A block grant at the level of current federal matching funds would reduce the incentive for keeping a Medicaid program at current levels of eligibility and benefits provided, while the marginal (state taxpayer) cost to maintain or extend benefits would greatly increase. If Medicaid were changed to provide the same level of federal support but in a block grant, a higher-income state with a 50 percent matching rate would see the "price" of providing a dollar's worth of Medicaid benefits double at the margin. A lower-income state with a 75 percent federal matching rate would see the "price" of Medicaid quadruple. So, even though a state would be getting the same amount of federal money as it did previously, and would have the same ability to pay for Medicaid, it would receive no additional federal subsidy by spending more. Without a subsidy at the margin, we would expect states to reduce Medicaid spending greatly and transfer their savings to other programs— or perhaps lower taxes.

Our research and that of others show that the state response to such variations in price would be significant. We would expect a conversion to block grants to result in very substantial and widespread reductions in Medicaid benefits. If state taxpayers in different states had Medicaid demand curves of similar price responsiveness, we might expect larger cuts in lower-income states with higher matching rates because a conversion to block grants from the current formula would raise the effective price to the state of providing Medicaid benefits by more in the lower-income states. For example, a higher-income state with a matching rate of 50 percent would see the effective price increase by 100 percent (to $1 from $.50 on every dollar spent); but a lower-income state with a matching rate of 75 percent would see the marginal price of Medicaid spending increase by 300 percent (to $1 from the current $.25 on every dollar spent). These are both very substantial increases that could result in major Medicaid spending cuts in both lower- and higher-income states, but the effects of a conversion to block grants could be much greater in the lower-income states.

Of course, a block grant proposal could require state contributions to continue at existing levels (so-called "maintenance of effort" rules), but the block grants would still inherently carry strong incentives for states to cut back on the scope of Medicaid programs. This would almost certainly lead eventually to substantial reductions in Medicaid spending, unless a particular level of services were required as a condition of the block grant or spending were propped up by a very large federal block grant. A Medicaid financing system based entirely on block grants thus makes sense only if the federal government imposes specific requirements that states maintain higher spending levels than they otherwise would choose. If one thinks that spending in higher-income states is too high, however, converting to block grants in only those states might be a way to curb spending without imposing higher costs on their taxpayers. Block grants are better suited to providing general fiscal relief than to encouraging states to spend money on specific purposes, such as health care.

Medicaid Coverage of Dual-Eligibles. An important exception to the application of matching incentives arises in connection with acute care for dual-eligibles (persons eligible for both Medicare and Medicaid). For these people, the federal government provides standard Medicare coverage. This leaves Medicaid (with federal matching at FMAP rates) to pick up the costs of Medicare Part B and Medicare Advantage plan premiums, deductibles, copayments, and services not covered by Medicare—and the states make "clawback" contributions to Part D drug coverage.[3] This arrangement creates intergovernmental inefficiency and tensions. The inefficiency comes from claims that have to be processed twice, first by Medicare as a primary payer, then crossing over to Medicaid as secondary payer. The tensions arise from how costs are divided and controlled (or not controlled).

The arrangement has two important effects on state incentives. First, the states, as secondary payers on claims for dual-eligibles, have very little administrative control over the use or costs of Medicare-covered services, since coverage and payment rates are determined by Medicare for the duals. Even states with Medicaid managed care find most of their duals in fee-for-service Medicare. The Medicaid share of these costs depends on federal policies that set Medicare copayments and Part B premiums and copayments. Second, since the federal government is paying most of the acute care costs (through both Medicare and Medicaid) and all costs at the margin for some services, it insists on primary control, and states are more concerned about Medicare cost-sharing contributions than efficiency in service use and costs for this segment of the Medicaid population. As a result, dual-eligibles are generally exempted from any state Medicaid cost control programs such as care management, payment rate reductions, or cost-sharing requirements.

The recent initiation of Medicare Part D coverage of outpatient drugs (in place of Medicaid coverage) has further eroded state control over medical costs of its lower-income seniors and disabled persons.[4] With the implementation of Part D, Medicare picked up the drug costs for those who are dually eligible for Medicaid and Medicare. States continue to contribute to these costs through phased-down state contributions or "clawback" payments to the federal government for the dual-eligibles.[5]

Partitioning of Federal and State Responsibilities. Although federal–state cooperation in Medicaid has been stable over the years, proposals have at times been made to divide responsibilities differently. While sounding rather innocuous, such proposals threaten the underlying basis of this federal–state program. For example, it has been suggested that states assume greater responsibility for long-term care (reflecting closer state and local regulation and financing of nursing homes), and that the federal government assume greater responsibility for acute care. In seeking more equal benefits among states, there may be reason to reduce matching—even to zero—for some services for some (higher-income) recipients in higher-income states; partitioning responsibilities, however, effectively reduces the match to zero for all states, and would create great incentives for them to cut back on those services for which they are made responsible.

On the acute care side, some have proposed full federal funding of certain parts of the program, with continued state administration. This would take advantage of federal taxing capacity and allow for state-level administration that may be more closely adapted to local needs and delivery systems. On the long-term care side, such an arrangement would sever federal support and make states responsible for all costs and administration. Partitioning of fiscal responsibility in this way would, like a block grant, eliminate the incentives for additional state spending that exist with federal matching, and could lead to sharp program cuts to low levels that do not reflect the interests of voters in supporting care for the poor.

Should one be skeptical, in general, of proposals that would partition federal and state responsibilities by service type or eligibility group? Such proposals fly in the face of Medicaid's broad role for the states and often seem to be arbitrarily assigning responsibilities without due consideration for how changes would affect incentives for provision of services. Although that broad role may not be carried out well at present, restructuring of state incentives may be a better solution than heavy-handed partitioning, especially as proposals about the allocation of responsibility by politicians at one level of government sometimes seem motivated more by a desire to shift the more rapidly growing parts of the program to the other level of government than by a desire to improve program administration.

Mandatory Lump-Sum Intergovernmental Transfers. For some purposes, such as achieving an equitable distribution of costs, additional financing tools may be needed. One such tool for balancing the federal–state split of costs without changing incentives (the way matching-rate adjustments do) is to provide for a lump-sum federal transfer—or a reverse transfer to the federal government from the states. Already a reality for drug coverage for dual-eligibles under Medicare Part D, this entails continued state funding through a phased-down state contribution or "clawback" payment.

Ad Hoc Matching-Rate Proposals. At various points over the years, proposals have been put forth to alter Medicaid matching rates to meet some short-term objective. Usually this is in response to a perceived need, either to reduce federal expenditures by reducing federal matching or to provide short-term relief to the states by increasing federal matching. Somewhat surprisingly, the idea of paying higher federal matching rates for more valuable medical services or more vulnerable populations has almost never been put into practice. (We will outline below how such a system might work.) The changes we see proposed in Medicaid matching are often somewhat arbitrary on the federal government's part. Proposals for new rates often focus on the most direct cost impacts, with little consideration for how rates may create incentives that affect state decisions on eligibility and benefits, or how states may respond to these changed incentives. The one case of higher matching rates for a large population—that of CHIP—implemented higher federal matching rates for a *less* vulnerable population. We will discuss, in part 5, how this led to the need to cap the program payments for each state.

A number of proposals have been suggested, discussed, and, in some cases, implemented as temporary adjustments to federal matching, though never as a permanent change to the FMAP formula. The first such option is an across-the-board, uniform percentage-point reduction in federal matching rates for all states. On the surface, this would seem to be a fair way to spread the effect of reduced federal matching among all states. Such a uniform reduction, however, can affect lower-income states more than higher-income states. A reduction of five percentage points in federal match would raise the state share by 10 percent (from 50 percent to 55 percent of provider payments) in a higher-income state, but by 50 percent (from 20 percent to 30 percent of provider payments) in a lower-income state. This is effectively a 25 percent price increase in the cost of Medicaid for the lower-income state in our public choice model. Such a change in the cost to the state taxpayer of providing Medicaid benefits could greatly affect the budgets and willingness of affected states to continue providing their current level of benefits. The effect would fall disproportionately on lower-income states and, rather than close the spending-per-poor-person gap, would exacerbate it.

Another federal cost-saving option is to reduce the minimum federal matching *percentage* from 50 percent to some lower proportion for the higher-income states. Given the differences in Medicaid benefit levels we have observed, this might move states in the direction of more equality. This is a rather crude approach that would leave in place the existing formula, which is without scientific or computational justification. Politicians in the higher-income states could be expected to oppose this change. It might, however, move in the direction of reduced inefficiency and improved beneficiary and taxpayer equity.

Program-Specific Matching. While most federal funds for Medicaid are provided through the share specified by FMAP percentages, some specific program elements are eligible for enhanced federal matching. Family planning services, for example, are matched at a 90 percent federal share for all states, with the intention of promoting such services to a greater extent than states would choose to do if the matching were at the usual level. Higher federal matching is also available for implementing and operating Medicaid management information systems (MMIS), used to process and pay medical claims and report on expenses. Costs to develop, implement, upgrade, or replace Medicaid management information systems are matched at 90 percent, with MMIS operations funded at 75 percent matching. This encourages states to invest more in the data systems needed to account accurately for Medicaid spending and meet federal data-reporting requirements.

Finally, the CHIP program has enhanced rates seven to fifteen percentage points higher than Medicaid matching rates, with no explicit rationale. (We discuss this case in more detail below.) What is important to note here is that these efforts, which deviate from the standard matching formula, have been politically acceptable and apparently successful in encouraging specific state activities (though there have been no studies to establish how much lower state spending on the specific activities would have been at uniform matching rates). These exceptions to the usual matching formula demonstrate the feasibility of a matching-rate structure more closely tailored to specific program objectives, and they document state responsiveness to specific matching incentives. But these examples do not provide a framework to determine which state activities should be encouraged more than others.

To illustrate the difficulty of using the political process to set matching rates, we need only consider some of the forms of federal Medicaid matching rates proposed in connection with the health care reform debate in 2009. As Congress realized that additional federal financial assistance would be needed to induce states to participate in planned Medicaid expansions, various methods were developed to provide higher federal matching rates. These were to be applied only to newly covered individuals and only for a limited period of time, usually several years.

Among the proposals considered and adopted by committee were the following:

- A provision for 100 percent federal matching, with the federal government assuming the full cost of the newly covered, non-traditional eligibles for all states for a limited period, dropping to 91 percent in later periods

- A provision for new matching rates 27.3 percentage points higher than current rates for expansion states (those currently with high benefits) and 37.3 percentage points higher than current rates for other states (those with lower benefits); some limits would apply.

- A provision for full federal financing to "high need" states with total Medicaid enrollment below the national average as a percentage of state population and a seasonally adjusted unemployment rate of at least 12 percent for August 2009—a generous provision that appeared to apply to only three states, all represented on the Senate Finance Committee where the proposal originated.

Some good intentions were represented in these ideas: to help states most in need, to conserve federal funds, to do more to address needs in the lower-benefit states. But where was the logic in, or the basis for, relating each state's funding precisely to the needs of its poor, its economic conditions, and its ability to contribute to costs? There is just too much at stake here for this to be a sensible way to set matching rates. A one-percentage-point difference in the matching rate for New York alone would swing more than four billion dollars annually either to state or to federal taxpayers. Small differences in matching percentages in more than fifty jurisdictions can add up to real money over time. We see the need for a more precise technical solution to the problem—one that allows political factors to be considered in setting overall budgets, but uses mathematical calculations to determine how funds will be distributed to meet objective criteria for allocating federal funds among states equitably, for both the poor and for taxpayers.

Conclusion

For Medicaid, CHIP, and any other jointly financed federal–state program, it is important to pay attention to the incentives created for state spending by the structure of the financing arrangement. Block grants reduce incentives for additional spending, while matching payments increase them. Which is best in any given situation depends on the intended outcome. The way in which matching rates are set determines the distribution of federal dollars. The rates directly affect the ability of states to provide modest or generous benefits without undue burdens on their taxpayers.

To date, surprisingly little effort has been made to craft matching rates to meet specific equity criteria. Matching rates represent the most powerful and underutilized federal Medicaid policy tool. Matching is a strong but loose form of federal control that does not preempt a large number of state decisions on program details. Plenty of room remains to tailor matching incentives to meet policy objectives better without undermining the advantages of the federal–state structure—once someone determines what those policy objectives are. The equal-burden-for-equal-benefit matching rates, which will be discussed in the next chapter, might serve as a useful tool or as a benchmark for equity in any such discussion.

8

Recommendations for Revising Federal Financing

We have noted the inequality among states in Medicaid spending per poor person, and the lack of evidence that the additional benefits provided in the higher-spending, higher-income states buy much in the way of additional health. Our most fundamental recommendations are twofold: first, to increase the "tilt" of the formula that determines federal matching rates so that the rate increases for lower-income states and falls for higher-income states, and, second, to make the federal matching rate fall for benefits in excess of the national average. Consideration of these general readjustments opens the broader question of tailoring matching rates more closely to program goals, not only across states but also across different lower-income groups within states.

Rationale for Changing the Matching-Rate Structure

First we consider explicitly the design of matching-rate variation across states. We want to outline arguments for modification of the federal matching formula, beginning with the case for simple modifications of the current, relatively simple, structure: Would there be gains from altering the level of matching rates, and especially the way they vary across states? Then we consider more complex formulae that might be appropriate for a Medicaid program with multiple and nuanced goals and promises.

The level of Medicaid spending per poor person varies substantially across states but is highly correlated with state income per capita. This statistic picks up two effects: When it is high, the proportion of poor people in the state's population is low, and the income of taxpayers is high. The combination of higher incomes and smaller poor populations leads taxpayers in higher-income states to want to be generous to the poor people in their states. In principle, a matching formula with the state share positively correlated with income per capita will make state-chosen spending levels per poor person larger but closer together than if each state were to go it alone. In practice, the matching formula in Medicaid has not resulted in anything close to equality. Lower-income states still provide much lower benefits to their poor.

What accounts for this wide variation? One factor that contributes a small part of the answer is that prices for medical services tend to be higher in higher-income states. The cost of living is higher there, which leads to higher labor costs and higher costs of locally produced goods and services, including medical care. In the face of higher prices, more people at a given nominal level of money income may be judged in need of help. Another factor is that promoting use of medical care (through subsidized insurance to people who would otherwise use too little) is probably a normal good to voter-taxpayers; the absolute amount of charity demanded rises as taxpayer income rises.

Optimal Matching Rates

The main policy question is how to set matching rates that reflect voter willingness to pay to provide Medicaid benefits to the poor and other low-income persons. A little economics is needed to explain. Figure 8-1 describes what would be needed for current policy to be optimal. D_H and D_L are the (median-voter) demand curves for Medicaid benefits per poor person in representative high- and low-income states. Representing the recent matching-rate structure, S_H is drawn as the 50 percent matching share in high-income states; S_L is the 24 percent rate that would prevail in the lowest-income state. These rates could be optimal, and will be if they are the rates that represent the relative state and rest-of-country demands or willingness to contribute to Medicaid benefits in both the high- and low-income states. Consider the "rest-of-country" demand curve D_C passing through both the corresponding 50 percent and 76 percent federal matching rates for higher- and lower-income states, respectively, at the same quantities as the states would choose. The quantities of medical services, provided as benefits Q^*_H and Q^*_L, that each type of state would choose at

FIGURE 8-1

OPTIMAL MATCHING IN HIGHER- AND LOWER-INCOME STATES

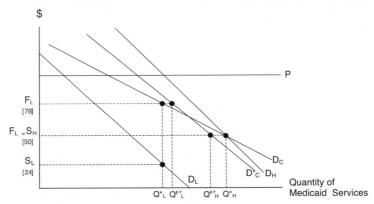

$ =   Dollars of cost or value
P =   Price per unit for Medicaid services
D_C =   Demand or marginal evaluation curve of national "community"
D'_C =   Alternative demand or marginal evaluation curve of national "community"
D_H =   Demand or marginal evaluation curve of state taxpayers in high-income state
D_L =   Demand or marginal evaluation curve of state taxpayers in low-income state
Q^*_L =   Optimal quantity of Medicaid services for low-income state when national community demand is D_C
Q^*_H =   Optimal quantity of Medicaid services for high-income state when national community demand is D_C
$Q^{F'}_L$ =   Quantity of Medicaid services demanded by national community when national demand curve is D'_C
$Q^{F'}_H$ =   Quantity of Medicaid services demanded by national community when national demand curve is D'_C
$FL_{[76]}$ =   Federal or national share of low-income-state Medicaid spending at 76%.
$F_H = S_{H\ [50]}$ =   Federal or national share of high-income-state Medicaid spending and high-income state share at 50%
$S_{L\ [24]}$ =   Low-income-state share of Medicaid spending of low-income state at 24%

SOURCE: Authors' diagram.

these matching rates would be optimal, which can be seen by noting that at these quantities both state and rest-of-country demands are satisfied at the specified matching rates, and the matching shares together cover the full cost of care. This would be both an optimal and an equilibrium point, since the state and federal governments would then agree that the level of benefits states chose to provide at these matching rates were the ideal level.

If, in contrast, the rest-of-country demand curve were like D'_C, then federal taxpayers would be dissatisfied with what states do. At the 24 percent matching rate, for example, the low-income state would still prefer Q^*_L. But federal taxpayers would want benefits to be higher (at $Q^{F'}_L$); they would also want benefits to be less generous than before in the higher-income states (at $Q^{F'}_H$). Our perception is that federal preferences seem frustrated in precisely the pattern described by the D_C demand curve. It seems quite unlikely that Medicaid is in an optimal equilibrium, and quite plausible that matching rates should be altered to fit better with a federal demand curve like D'_C. It seems quite unlikely that the current Medicaid shares lead to an optimal equilibrium, and quite plausible that matching rates should be altered to fit better with the federal demand curve. In particular, this would mean raising the federal matching rates (FMAP) in lower-income (low-demand) states and lowering them in higher-income (high-demand) states.

It is important to pay attention to the distributional effects of changing matching rates. Would such a strategy of raising the federal matching rate in lower-income states and lowering it in higher-income states improve or worsen taxpayer equity? Recall that state tax burden as a percentage of taxpayer income is not particularly related to state income; in all income quintiles, the average state contribution is near 1.5 percent of taxpayer income (see figure 7-1). But this arrangement supports only relatively low benefits in the lower-income states. It would, therefore, be a step toward both fairness to the poor and fairness to taxpayers to raise the federal matching rates in the lowest income states to allow them to provide higher benefits without spending a greater share of their income than is required in other states. If states continue to be willing to devote about the same share of taxpayer income to the state share of Medicaid, we would expect this type of adjustment (higher federal matching in the lower-income states and lower federal matching in the higher-income states) to lead to adjustments in Medicaid spending (up and down) that would produce more interstate equality in benefit levels. Thus, at least over some of the range, both equitable treatment of the poor and equitable treatment of state taxpayers would move in the same direction if federal matching rates were raised for poor states and reduced for rich ones.

Categorical Matching Rates

One approach to such changes in the matching-rate structure would use multiple matching rates for the various categories of recipients—matching for each recipient group depending on its needs and ability to contribute to the cost of care. This would be especially important for CHIP and any higher-income groups that might be included. Greater federal support reflected in a higher matching rate would be provided for those groups of persons that tend to have significant medical costs but the most limited ability to obtain funds to pay for services. The traditional Medicaid eligibility categories (children, the elderly, and disabled persons below the poverty level) would receive the highest matching, as they have greater needs and limited ability to obtain the resources needed to purchase their own medical care or insurance. Efficiency in the public choice model requires that the extent of this additional subsidy depend on how much value federal voter-taxpayers place on access to care for these groups, and on the marginal benefit of additional care for each group that would result from a higher level of subsidy. There should be some matching (perhaps at a lower rate) for childless poor adults who are now largely excluded from Medicaid entirely.

Reduced matching would be available for those above the federal poverty level, though the match for children could be higher than the match for their parents. To the extent that federal taxpayers are less willing to contribute to the cost of care for persons outside the traditional Medicaid eligibility categories, lower federal matching rates should apply to these groups—to include them would require greater recipient cost-sharing and/or a greater state share.

The categorical eligibility requirements reflect such thinking by those who developed the program in the past; renewed consideration could refine matching rates to support public preferences better in the future. Political leadership could correct misperceptions of the value of such federal matching, based on presumptions that it supports care that is more effective than it really is or on a lack of appreciation of what access to care is needed and what effective care such coverage provides for covered individuals in each eligibility group. In the end, the decision rests in public debate about the true effects and value of the program—something that can be improved with better information, including the results of program evaluation and a better understanding of programs by policymakers.

All this suggests that matching should be set higher for those types of recipients whose additional use of services has the highest value to national taxpayers at the margin. The goal is to set rates so that the value per federal dollar is the same (at the margin in equilibrium) across all categories of recipients and types of care. Federal matching would be lower for the more financially able eligibility groups.[1] These distinct matching rates by group would be overlayered with a structure related to state fiscal capacity or tax-payer income, as provided by the current formula. Additionally, the formula would be set to adjust automatically for state economic cycles that affect state revenue. We might also allow for differential rates for long-term care and acute care—to interface better with spend-down, although we will not develop this feature here.

Finally, at the higher recipient income levels, the federal subsidy rate should mesh with the employer-based insurance subsidy rate for the working poor. The logic here is based on continuity of preferences, as taxpayer willingness to pay for a subsidy declines as recipient income rises. For the lowest-income groups—Medicaid recipients—the federal subsidy is 50 to 76 percent federal matching. For workers with employer-sponsored insurance, the federal subsidy from tax exclusion may be something like 30 percent. The continuity (really monotonicity) of subsidy principle would imply that lower-income workers without access to employer-sponsored health insurance ought to receive a subsidy somewhere above 30 percent but below the Medicaid matching rate. The enhanced match for CHIP for those above the poverty level may be explained as special preference for children. But it seems inconsistent to provide no subsidy at all to lower-income workers without access to employer-based coverage who clearly have needs for assistance at least as great as those receiving the benefit of the federal subsidy on employer-based insurance [2]

The continuity in preferences should suggest continuity in the federal subsidy spanning all these groups. One advantage of federal subsidies that decline in a continuous way as beneficiary income levels increase is that they reduce the incentive for crowd-out. That is, if minimum-wage workers with access to employer-based insurance were to receive a subsidy, somewhere between, for example, CHIP's 65+ percent and the average employer-based 30 percent, there would be less to gain from dropping employer coverage in favor of CHIP. And, for some Medicaid recipients not eligible for CHIP and expecting significant medical expenses, such a subsidy might encourage a return to employment.

The logic of providing federal subsidies for populations and services where they will do the most good might also suggest a means of financing any additional subsidy for this group: to cap the tax exclusion of medical insurance at some multiple of the cost of a typical plan—say, 100 or 120

Notable Quotes on the Difficulty of Changing the FMAP Formula

So we were trying to tweak the formula so that it didn't hurt any state. But there was no way you could create a new formula that didn't— didn't wind up hurting at least one state.

—Stuart Altman
Sol C. Chaikin Professor of National Health Policy, Brandeis University

And so Representative Pelosi said, "Oh, we're going to look into this." Good luck. I would say it's a great issue to look into as long as you don't try to actually change anything.

—Joseph Antos
Wilson H. Taylor Scholar in Health Care and Retirement Policy,
American Enterprise Institute

Source: Smith and Moore 2006.

---

percent—so that persons who choose coverage much more costly than average for their risk groups would not have taxpayers sharing the cost of their more expensive coverage. Our intent in raising this problem, which goes beyond Medicaid issues, is to point out the importance of thinking about Medicaid and CHIP in the context of the system we have for providing federal subsidies for differentially situated lower-income persons and families.

Equal-Burden-for-Equal-Benefit Matching

The need for Medicaid matching-rate reform has long been recognized on equity grounds.[3] But suggested alternatives to the current matching formula have never offered a logic sufficiently compelling to overcome the political barriers to changing the method on which states have come to depend for allocating billions of dollars every year. Here we suggest a new approach to setting federal Medicaid matching rates—one that is relatively easy to understand and has some obvious properties for interstate equity.

We are trying to accomplish two primary goals. The first is to ensure that every state has the ability to provide a specified standard level of Medicaid benefits for each poor person without having to spend more than a specified, typical share of state taxpayer income on the state share of benefits. This is accomplished by defining what we call "equal-burden-for-equal-benefit" (EBEB) matching rates, which would help direct more Medicaid resources to states where poor people are more numerous, and taxpayers have more limited incomes.

The second goal is to curb the extent to which taxpayers in lower-benefit states subsidize the more generous benefit packages in higher-benefit (often higher-income) states. We want to provide some federal subsidy to encourage provision of benefits, but only up to a point. This is accomplished by gradually stepping down matching rates for aggregate Medicaid payments in states where benefits exceed a specified standard, such as the amount needed to provide the U.S. average benefits per poor person.

Here are the elements of such a matching-rate reform plan:

- The current FMAP structure would be replaced.

- New federal matching rates would allow all states to achieve a specified standard (such as U.S. average benefits per poor person adjusted to inflation over time) by spending a specified standard (such as the current U.S. average) percentage of taxpayer incomes on the state share of Medicaid (EBEB matching).

- State spending above this amount would receive federal matching, but at a reduced rate, according to a tiered structure.

- The top tier would use EBEB matching for all state spending up to a specified state-specific dollar amount, determined as 100 percent of the specified U.S. standard benefit level per poor person, multiplied by that state's number of poor persons.

- The lower tiers would each use a specified fraction of the top-tier rate; the tiers would provide for federal matching that would step down as the state spending per poor person increased above the U.S. average levels.

- Federal matching would drop to zero for additional spending in states with benefits above a specified multiple of the standard benefit level.

- Provision could be made to allow for enhanced matching for specific favored services or eligibility groups.

- Transparent formula parameters would help Congress to understand better the implications of matching and to set rates consistent with policy objectives.

- Parameters would be adjusted quickly and regularly to reflect current economic conditions.

- A countercyclical adjustment for economic conditions would be implemented on a timely basis.

As is currently done, states would be notified in advance of the applicable matching rates and the levels of spending to which they apply. This way, they would know that if their spending exceeded some aggregate level, federal matching on the amount over that level would be at a lower rate—and even lower on the amount over that specified for the next tier.

With this matching-rate structure, states would have the freedom to continue operating their Medicaid programs as they currently do, but would also have incentives to move benefits toward the specified standard, which could be set to represent the current U.S. average. This would be expected to lead over time to much greater equality in benefits across states, with cuts in higher-benefit states, unless resources were added, and expansions in lower-benefit states. While the policy parameters in the formula would give Congress levers with which to adjust the target benefit level and the division of costs between federal and state payers, the inherent equity relationships would be maintained.

It is not too difficult to translate this concept into a workable form—at least, to calculate the matching rates needed to equalize both benefits and tax burdens across states—though political acceptance may be harder to come by. So how does one compute such matching rates? Another way to put the question might be to ask what matching rates would be needed to provide each state with the ability to achieve the U.S. average level of benefits per poor person while spending a uniform average percentage of state taxpayer income on the state share of Medicaid. We call these equal-burden-for-equal-benefit, or EBEB (pronounced "Eee-Bee-Eee-Bee"), matching rates.[4]

The EBEB Matching-Rate Formula. The federal rate for EBEB matching can be computed for a state i as:

$$EBEBFMAP_i = 1 - (AggFiscal\ Cap_i * FixedPct) / (Npoor_i * StdBenPPP * MedPrice_i)$$

Where:

- **EBEBFMAP$_i$** is the equal-burden-for-equal-benefit matching rate

- **AggFiscalCap$_i$** is the measure of the state's aggregate fiscal capacity (such as adjusted gross income reported in individual tax returns)

- **FixedPct** is the fixed percentage of the fiscal capacity measure (for instance, state taxpayer income) to be devoted to achieving the standard benefit level (in the United States, by our estimates, 1.625 percent of state taxpayer income in 2006)

- **Npoor$_i$** is the number of persons below the federal poverty level in the state

- **StdBenPPP** is the standard dollar Medicaid benefit per poor person (here the U.S. average, by our estimates $7,692 in 2006)

- **MedPrice$_i$** is a state medical care relative cost index based so the U.S. level is 1.00 (our examples use the physician practice cost index)

We provide an example of EBEB matching rates computed using data from 2006 and compared to matching under the current standard FMAP formula for 2009. Table 8-1 gives a general description of the resulting matching rates, with the uniform benefit level set at the U.S. average and at 130 percent of the U.S. average (which is roughly equivalent to Pennsylvania's benefit level).[5] The table reports on four variations of EBEB rates: a benchmark level EBEB, in both proportional and progressive forms, and enhanced EBEB, in both proportional and progressive forms. All are computed with an adjustment for cost differences among states.[6] While we provide results of a simple computation here, if such rates are ever to be used

TABLE 8-1

EQUAL-BURDEN-FOR-EQUAL-BENEFIT MATCHING,
ILLUSTRATIVE COST-OF-LIVING–ADJUSTED EBEB MATCHING RATES

	Current matching	
	FMAP	Enhanced FMAP
Aggregate state fiscal capacity	N/A	N/A
Fiscal burden multiplier	N/A	N/A
Benefit level benchmark	U.S. average	U.S. average
Top matching rate	76%	83%
Minimum matching rate for standard benefits	50%	65%
Minimum matching rate for high benefits (with step-down)	50%	65%
Overall generosity of benefits	Same as U.S. present	Same as U.S. present
Progressivity of financing, state share	Regressive	Regressive

SOURCE: Authors' computations based on cost-of-living–adjusted EBEB matching rates.

in practice, it will be important to consider carefully the measures of medical prices (perhaps a weighted average of regions within the states). Other measures of state fiscal capacity might be considered, but we see public choice advantages to using taxpayer income over some broader measures (such as the U.S. Treasury Department's total taxable resources), simply

EBEB U.S. benchmark level (Current U.S. average burden and benefit)		EBEB enhanced level (Current U.S. average burden, 130% of U.S. average benefit level)	
Proportional EBEB	**Progressive EBEB**	**Proportional EBEB**	**Progressive EBEB**
Adjusted gross income	Federal personal income tax	Adjusted gross income	Federal personal income tax
U.S. average percentage of state income devoted to state Medicaid	U.S. average percentage of federal tax devoted to state Medicaid	U.S. average percentage of state income devoted to state Medicaid	U.S. average percentage of federal tax devoted to state Medicaid
U.S. average	U.S. average	130% of U.S. average (Pennsylvania)	130% of U.S. average (Pennsylvania)
80%	84%	85%	88%
20%	20%	39%	39%
0	0	0	0
Same as U.S. present	Same as U.S. present	Same as Pennsylvania	Same as Pennsylvania
Neutral as percentage of taxpayer income	Progressive equivalent to U.S. income taxes	Neutral as percentage of taxpayer income	Progressive equivalent to U.S. income taxes

NOTE: Pennsylvania selected as representative state with benefits at 130 percent of U.S. average.

because it is more meaningful as a concept for policymakers who need to understand the nature of the burden they are imposing on state taxpayers.

The example calculations show how the current rate structure deviates from the rates needed to equalize benefits and burdens. In general, using the EBEB method to set rates, the higher-income states would see reductions in federal matching, and lower-income states would see increases. But as the formula accounts for both number of poor and taxpayer income, the greatest increases in federal matching are in states with many poor persons and lower-income taxpayers; the greatest decreases are in states with few poor persons and higher-income taxpayers. New York could receive an increase in federal matching for basic benefits, while neighboring commuter states Connecticut and New Jersey could see reduced federal assistance—in this case, the formula would be doing a better job of spreading costs over the higher-income suburbs in the New York–New Jersey–Connecticut tristate area. Note, however, that while New York matching for basic benefits might be increased under the proportional version of EBEB rates, this state could see lower rates at the margin under the progressive scenario due to its higher-income taxpayers, and lower matching for much of its higher-benefit program due to the step-down provision. California and Texas would tend to benefit under this system, in part due to the large numbers of poor persons reflected in their higher-than-average poverty rates.

In a few states with relatively small numbers of persons below the federal poverty level, the federal matching would be very low, as those states could achieve an average benefit for their poor without spending more than the specified average percentage of state taxpayer income on benefits—even without much federal assistance. While it might not be politically feasible to reduce federal assistance for any state to zero, this analysis raises the question of what standard should be used for a matching formula. Clearly, the present formula deviates greatly from a standard based on the criterion of "equal burden for equal benefits." In fact, the current formula would be much closer to this standard if, at the program's origins, Congress had not set (presumably for practical political purposes) a floor of 50 percent on the federal matching rates. So this question of a standard for matching goes back to the fundamental purpose of the program. Is it to equalize the benefits and burdens of caring for the poor? Or is it to give some politically acceptable level of federal assistance to every state?

These example rates reflect current levels of benefits and taxpayer burdens. Over the longer term, these parameters could be adjusted to reflect changes in cost, taxpayer income, the desired standard benefit level, and the share of taxpayer income that policymakers are willing to devote to the program. For instance, suppose a goal were to make Massachusetts-level benefits affordable to all states willing to spend 10 percent more than the current U.S. average state share of taxpayer income. Computing rates with the Massachusetts value of benefits per poor person used for **StdBenPPP** in the formula and 1.1 times the current value of **FixedPct** would provide the higher federal matching rates that would make such a benefit level attainable to those states.[7] Thus, the formula provides a framework for making long-term adjustments to federal matching to reflect current policy and/or meet budget requirements, while maintaining a structure that promotes some degree of equity among taxpayers and among the poor in different states.

Some may suggest that an approach based on states contributing equal proportions of state taxpayer income does not go far enough to support lower-income states—that some degree of progressivity ought to be built into the structure. This can be accommodated through an adjustment involving the aggregate income variable. Using aggregate adjusted gross income in the EBEB computation essentially employs taxpayer income as the measure of fiscal capacity. The rates that emerge reflect a burden that is proportional to income rather than regressive or progressive. If, instead, we were to replace **AggFiscalCap** by federal income taxes paid in the state and **FixedPct** with the fraction of such an amount we think states should contribute toward Medicaid, then the resulting rates would reflect a progressive structure for the state share, with higher-income states devoting a somewhat greater share of income to pay their portion of Medicaid. Medicaid financing would then be made progressive to the same extent as the federal income tax structure.

These rates can be further adjusted for differences in cost of living among the states by making the measure of the number of poor a count of the number of persons below some multiple of the federal poverty level (FPL), adjusted for the cost of living. As there is no suitable published federal measure of this concept, we use the ACCRA cost-of-living index as a proxy for a state cost-of-living index and compute with interpolation an estimate based on U.S. Census figures for the number of persons below multiples of the FPL. We use these figures in our cost-of-living–adjusted EBEB matching rates. We would suggest that the federal government establish a program to produce such an index on a regular basis, as it would be needed not only for these matching rates but for any federal program requiring income-adjusted eligibility criteria—an adjustment that is needed to provide for greater equity in any such program.

A word of caution is in order here, however, as these rates will not guarantee equal benefits or burdens among the states. States willing to spend more than the average share of taxpayer income could still choose to provide higher-than-average benefits, or they could choose to spend less than average and provide lower than average benefits.[8] But the step-down in rates for higher-spending states, and our observation that the share of income spent on Medicaid tends to vary less among states than benefits, suggests that both taxpayer burdens and benefits to the poor would be much closer to equal under this arrangement than we currently observe.

The politics of such a change could be interesting. We cannot realistically expect states that have received Medicaid matching at the 50 percent floor for more than forty years—and built relatively generous Medicaid programs based on this federal financing floor—to give up such advantages willingly. The interest of higher-benefit states in maintaining their high federal subsidies will make it difficult to move policy toward directing more federal Medicaid resources to states with greater numbers of poor and uninsured. Will policymakers be able to support the view that the higher-income, higher-benefit states have no inherent right to continue receiving the windfall they have enjoyed for many years from the current matching arrangement?[9] We expect the situation can only be changed in a politically acceptable way if it is done gradually over a period of many years—perhaps a decade or more—with some form of hold-harmless provision in effect in the short run, but only for a year or two.

Enhanced Matching Rates. One way to minimize this problem would be simply to provide higher matching rates for most or all states. Again the equity criteria require that the EBEB formula be used to calculate these higher rates, which we call "enhanced matching." We illustrate the possibility of enhanced matching rates using this formula in table 8-1. Enhanced matching rates could be used to provide greater incentives for services, or groups may be identified as important for meeting program goals—much as children are under the CHIP program. As noted above, we question the value of enhanced rates set so high that a cap or allotment is needed to keep federal costs under control; but within the context of the enhanced-rate formula suggested here, incentives could be offered for states to make greater efforts to provide benefits to children, to provide better access to primary care, or to meet whatever goals Congress determines are particularly important. Determining these rates by augmenting the **StdBenPPP** parameter in the formula ensures that the taxpayer and recipient equity characteristics of the original formula are maintained in setting the enhanced matching rates.

Step-Down Rates. The EBEB rates have their desirable equity properties only for states that choose to set benefits at the benchmark level, and we expect states will have incentives to move their benefit levels toward the national average. Nonetheless, some states may still choose to provide higher-than-average benefits. While a state that so chooses will receive additional federal assistance, we want the amount of federal subsidy for the benefits in excess of the benchmark to reflect what taxpayers in other states are willing to spend to support that state's higher benefits. As noted, we think this willingness declines as the benefit level rises, and so the matching rate for benefits in excess of the benchmark should decline the farther above that benchmark the state goes. The match could continue for some higher-than-benchmark benefits but ought to decline to zero at some point (perhaps when the state benefits are twice the benchmark). Again, this is a policy parameter; the match could decline slowly or quickly, and the match could stop at 20 percent above or 50 percent above or 100 percent above the benchmark. (For purposes of our examples, we will assume a match that declines in steps and stops at 75 percent above the benchmark. This would allow some degree of federal matching for states that choose to provide benefits up to 175 percent of the benchmark, which could cushion effects in high-benefit states in a transition period.)

Phase-In Schedule. What is proposed here is a fundamental restructuring of the financial foundations of the Medicaid program. This is not something that can easily be accomplished overnight. We would suggest phasing in the matching rates over a period of (perhaps five) years. In the first year, matching rates would be a weighted average (80 percent old, 20 percent new), with the proportions shifting toward the new rates each year. This would give states time to find any additional state financing they may need, respond to the new incentives, and reshape their programs, if desired. We would anticipate these adjustments to include expansions in eligibility and benefits in some lower-income, lower-benefit states that would see increased federal matching, and the finding of additional state funds to support programs in some higher-income, higher-benefit states that would see lower federal matching. The latter would also need time to take a hard look at their more expansive program elements (particularly in long-term care, where their benefits are typically higher than in other states) to see if they find all of them important enough to support with a greater share of state funding. A phase-in period would also give Congress time to observe emerging state response and refine formula parameters, if necessary. For example, if higher-benefit states were to cut back substantially, that could provide room in the federal budget to increase the matching by using a somewhat higher standard benefit for all states.

Adjustments. Rates would be adjusted as new state spending patterns became established. The intent is that this would not be a static set of matching rates, as was the case with the previous matching formula. Rather, rates would be reviewed and adjusted periodically to reflect more accurately federal voter preferences for supporting the state-administered Medicaid program, which could expand over time if sufficient federal matching were provided by federal policymakers.

Countercyclical Adjustments

As we noted in our introduction to this work, one of the main reasons Medicaid is viewed as potentially unreliable is the tendency for states to expand eligibility and coverage in good times and the necessity to reduce eligibility and benefits when times are hard, just when need is greatest. This can create problems for recipients in optional eligibility groups—that is, groups that states are not required to cover—who cannot be certain benefits will be available when needed; for providers, who often face frozen or reduced payment rates; and for taxpayers, who are threatened with the burden of additional costs just when many are experiencing difficulties themselves. Medicaid at present lacks an automatic adjustment mechanism to ensure states have timely access to the additional financial resources they need in economic downturns. This is one critical element needed to make Medicaid a program everyone can count on—to do what it is supposed to do, in both good times and bad.

This problem is not unique to Medicaid or even to the United States. In other countries with universal coverage, overall government budgetary problems often lead to fairly dramatic cuts in payment and benefit generosity levels for reasons unrelated to medical care benefits and costs. It surely is difficult to find ways to advise the government to save itself from its own budgetary problems. But some things could be done.

Problem. Let's consider, to start, the need to adjust medical assistance resources to cyclical economic activity.[10] Several factors are to be considered in designing a method for dealing with this situation. For one, states have less ability than the federal government to borrow or otherwise obtain funds to cover deficits in hard times. Also, it is important to understand that state needs in economic downturns are related to at least two distinct components that may differ among states, though they will be correlated with national economic conditions. These are that, first, on the demand side, downturns generate greater numbers of eligible Medicaid recipients; second, on the supply side, state fiscal capacity diminishes with reduced revenue, particularly from the traditional state funding sources of income taxes and sales taxes. While closely correlated, these two factors will play out differently in the individual states, in part due to differences in local economic conditions, in part due to differences in the poor populations, and in part due to differences in the states' tax structures.

On the demand (or need) side, state economies differ in average severity of economic cycles. States with cyclical industries, such as the automotive industry, will be prone to larger swings in economic activity than others. It may also matter who is affected by the cycles. Changes in the financial services industry that affect relatively well-paid workers may have proportionately less of an impact on Medicaid eligibility than changes in small manufacturing operations with lower-skilled workers. Whatever the sources, any plan for cyclical corrections should be designed to deal fairly and effectively with these differences among states in the resulting need for medical assistance.

Next, we consider the state revenue side. Virtually all tax sources are, to some degree, cyclical, but individual and corporate income taxes and general sales taxes are perhaps more so. The share of state taxes that comes from these three sources varies from more than 80 percent in ten states to less than

40 percent in four other states.[11] Clearly, states without income or general sales taxes, like Alaska and New Hampshire, will see less-pronounced fluctuations in revenue than states such as Georgia, Massachusetts, or California that heavily rely on such sources, especially state individual income taxes.

Now consider sectorial trends such as industry decline and longer-term displacement of workers. These may be relatively unrelated to the economic cycle, though the associated problems may be aggravated by a downturn. Medicaid can play a useful role in ensuring access to medical coverage—particularly for children—while readjustment takes place, whether that comes from eventual relocation of the families or growth of replacement industries in the local areas. From the recipients' side, this situation may not be much different, but in planning for any countercyclical reform, these one-time or irregular events may enter differently into the calculation of financial resources that need to be set aside to handle the associated changes in Medicaid eligibility.

Solution. We suggest a multipart approach to implementing countercyclical Medicaid matching rates that would provide for automatic adjustments in federal assistance. The first part of the solution is to use the EBEB matching rates we have proposed. The EBEB matching rates are an improvement over current matching rates from the countercyclical standpoint because they account not just for the one income measure in the current formula (state per-capita income), but for both the number of poor, which rises in recessions, and taxpayer income, which falls in such periods. They would thus be more responsive to economic conditions and, because of the EBEB equity properties, would provide a formal method for computing just how much adjustment is needed in response to changing conditions.

The difficulty is that matching-rate changes are at present implemented with a lag, using data on income that are several years old by the time they affect matching rates. To be timely and effective in meeting its countercyclical objectives, a matching-rate system would need to be adjusted more often and based upon the most recent data, or even projections using leading indicators of economic conditions. For this reason, the second part of this solution is to provide for more timely updates to the matching formula. We suggest developing projection models for the fiscal-capacity (**AggFiscalCap**) and number-of-poor (**NPoor**) variables in the EBEB matching formula. The

> Doing something that coordinates a state's FMAP more with the current fiscal reality, than with what happened two years ago in the economy, would make sense.
>
> —Diane Rowland
> Executive vice president of the Kaiser Family Foundation
>
> Source: Smith and Moore 2006.

projected estimates of these variables would be used to compute interim matching rates and to make initial federal payments based on prospective estimates of the formula parameters. Later, when all the economic data were in, the final amount due to the state for a specified period would be reconciled with the previous interim payments and adjustments, plus or minus, made to add to or offset part of the current payments to the state. This would allow states to start receiving higher federal matching as soon as an economic downturn is recognized, with federal assistance to increase by design in a timely manner as Medicaid enrollment rises with unemployment.

As a third part to this solution, we suggest the establishment of Medicaid trust funds by both the federal and state governments to help fund such cyclical swings in payments. The federal government's "Medicaid Countercyclical Trust Fund" could stabilize budgets as Medicaid spending fluctuates with the economy. The fund would retain some of the federal budget allocated for matching funds in good economic years when federal matching rates are relatively low and disburse additional funds to the states in poor economic years when federal matching rates are higher.

Similarly, states could be required to contribute in good times a corresponding amount based on their FMAP shares, perhaps as a withholding from federal Medicaid payments. The state portion of the trust could be maintained at the federal or state level. As this contribution would increase in good economic times, it would provide a counterweight to the state's tendency to overexpand eligibility and benefits when its budget is flush and cut eligibility and benefits in more difficult times.

These trust funds, which would allow both federal and state Medicaid budgets to be more stable and predictable over time, would have a purpose related to, but distinct from, the Medicare trust fund. The Medicare trust fund is intended to ensure that funds will be available with long-term changes in population demographics. The fund for Medicaid would ensure that funds are available through cyclical changes in state fiscal capacity and to meet the needs of the greater number of otherwise uninsured poor who appear in economic hard times. Research would be needed to determine the appropriate parameters for such a countercyclical adjustment and to establish the criteria for accumulating and releasing funds from a counter-cyclical trust.

Finally, an increase in the state share for the higher-income states that have most extended coverage in good times might perhaps itself furnish a kind of cushion as program expansions are chosen by states with a closer eye to the benefits relative to the spending. We cannot guarantee that this intui-tion will prove correct; short-term fluctuations in tax collections may desta-bilize well-chosen and high-value programs as much as those more at the margin. But some automatic improvement does seem possible, and we can at least be sure that states will take more seriously the possibility of the need to protect against bad times when they are putting up more of their own money.

Expected Effects and Advantages of the Proposed Structure

The proposed matching-rate structure would represent an improvement over the current FMAP system in supporting more equal treatment for both recipients and taxpayers across states. Additional work remains to specify the parameters of a new matching formula, simulate expected impacts, and adjust the parameters to reflect the level of commitment in the current political environment. In any case, we believe the approach outlined here provides a framework for a serious discussion about how, with some key changes, Medicaid could better meet the needs of the poor, provide for a more equitable distribution of its costs, and play a significant role in help-ing states address the problems of the uninsured—all within a context that better represents voter–taxpayer preferences for public resources that should be allocated to medical care for disadvantaged groups.

9

Medicaid Financing for Accountability

Medicaid spends billions of dollars every year. Federal money flows to the states, who report on its use in broad categories. State and federal money flows to providers, who report on its use on medical claims or on cost reports. While documentation is required at every stage, there is sometimes room—even within the law—for the states and/or providers to overstep the bounds of planned uses and claim payment for services that may not have been strictly intended by voter-taxpayers or by the entities responsible for ensuring the appropriate use of funds. Such behavior threatens accountability and program integrity, not just in terms of budgets, but because it can damage the confidence of voter-taxpayers in the program and, hence, threaten the very foundations of support for the program and the priority of its claims on public funds.

Supplemental Payments and State Financing Arrangements

Supplemental payments have been an important and growing component of Medicaid spending in recent years.[1] Such payments to hospitals and nursing homes were originally permitted to encourage higher state reimbursements to safety-net providers serving the uninsured and Medicaid patients. That is, particularly deserving providers would get supplemental payments on top of what the state chose to pay to all providers, to help them address the needs of uninsured patients not on or eligible for Medicaid.

On logical grounds, such a patch seems less sensible than trying to get the states to raise payment levels and to broaden eligibility directly. The significant and uneven growth of this part of Medicaid spending has led to wide criticism of many states that have employed questionable mechanisms for raising the state funds needed to meet matching requirements. Compared to traditional Medicaid provider payments, supplemental payment funds are less closely tied to specific services for persons eligible for Medicaid, and that has led to questions about whether funds are being used by states to achieve general fiscal relief rather than support medical care for the poor, or about whether these additional payments represent concessions to the safety-net providers and their lobbyists.

Our view is that many of the perceived problems with Medicaid supplemental payments arise from incentives inherent in the program and from a lack of clear guidance from federal policymakers, who seem not to understand fully the incentives and their implications. States are taking advantage of loopholes and inconsistencies that ideally should not have been present in the first place. The solution lies not in blaming the states and providers, who are in any case responding to strong, if misdirected, financial incentives. Rather, it is important to identify problem areas and to assess the need for revised financial arrangements—ones with different incentives, clear limits, and stronger controls.

Questionable Financing Arrangements

In a recent report, the U.S. Government Accountability Office identified five types of Medicaid financing schemes used to generate federal payments viewed by the GAO as inappropriate:[2]

- Excessive payments to state health facilities

- Provider taxes and donations

- Excessive disproportionate share hospital (DSH) payments

- Excessive DSH payments to state mental hospitals

- Exceeding of upper payment limits (UPLs) for local government health facilities

Many of these financing schemes have been limited or eliminated in recent years. Others continue in various forms. Coughlin and colleagues report on state use of supplemental payments made using provider taxes, intergovernmental transfers (IGTs), DSH payments, and UPL payments.[3]

These schemes typically have involved Medicaid payments to providers (using matched federal and state funds) that have then been returned to the state treasury in whole or in part, resulting in the state's paying less than the share specified in the FMAP formula. In effect, additional federal funds have been claimed to match ghost services (or ghost prices) rather than real services or prices actually paid. Some of these arrangements still exist in various forms, with some uncertainty at the state level as to just what is allowed. This uncertainty is reflected in the differing extent to which states (all presumably trying to get all the federal funds to which they are entitled) have taken advantage of such provisions.

The GAO concluded that steps taken by the U.S. Centers for Medicare and Medicaid Services to end inappropriate use of state financing arrangements "lacked transparency," in that CMS had "not issued written guidance about the specific approval standards for state financing arrangements."[4] These types of financing schemes have been a source of contention between federal policymakers and the states.[5] The U.S. Department of Health and Human Services has tried to curtail their use, while states have pushed for flexibility to implement schemes of various forms and have opposed federal limits. Congress has responded with a series of efforts to limit the use and scope of these programs but has not eliminated them, and states continue to find ways to use such methods to obtain federal funds. Coughlin, Zuckerman, and McFeeters document continued growth from 2001 to 2005 in both state and federal dollars devoted to the DSH and other supplemental payment programs,[6] though the trend has subsequently changed for DSH.

Although evidence that funds are transferred back to the state general fund may indicate inappropriate use of FMAP, we suggest that the criteria for distinguishing appropriate and inappropriate financing methods should not be based on the use or source of funds. Rather, they should depend on whether the arrangement fundamentally alters the effective federal matching rate and its application to cover the cost of services actually delivered. That is, such arrangements should not be allowed if they serve to reduce the share of costs (limited to reasonable costs) paid by the state below what is required by the FMAP formula. Failure in these respects would fundamentally alter the cost-sharing structure and the state incentives for wise use of funds. A problem exists if the arrangement goes beyond taking advantage of federal matching as specified in the FMAP formula and so reduces the state's obligation to contribute its required share. We will consider in turn each type of state financing scheme identified by the GAO—including the five in the list above, plus three others—to see whether it violates the fundamental federal–state sharing requirement of the Medicaid program.

Excessive Payments to State Health Facilities. If a state makes Medicaid payments to state-owned hospitals or nursing homes in excess of cost, it receives federal matching payments on the profits or surplus revenue in excess of actual costs—that is, it receives payment for medical care services overpriced beyond the resource costs used to produce them. Of course, such excess payments could also result from payments to private providers whose Medicaid reimbursement rate exceeds their costs (unlikely as that may be). The difference is that federal payments in excess of costs to a state-owned facility channel more money back to the state itself, which creates an incentive for the state to overprice services and receive additional payment without any obvious limit. This violates the logic and intent of the Medicaid matching share and results in a transfer of federal funds to the state without any real state contribution. It is possible that these facilities would use the additional payments to upgrade the quality of care, but such improvements are unlikely to be confined to the Medicaid population, and are not especially desired by federal taxpayers. To the extent that Medicaid payments to state-owned facilities are allowed to exceed the costs of caring for Medicaid eligibles, the state is contributing less than its required share. In such cases, the state obtains an advantage relative to other states and effectively tricks federal taxpayers into making an extra transfer of resources outside the intended framework of Medicaid matching. This practice increases federal expenditures and magnifies inequities among states in access to federal funds.

Provider Taxes and Donations. A 1991 amendment to Title XIX of the Social Security Act prohibits provider contributions to states and limits provider-specific taxes as a means of generating revenue for the state share of funds for Medicaid matching. General taxes on a broad group of like providers, such as hospitals or nursing homes, are permitted and are used by some states to raise funds for Medicaid from within the health care sector. These taxes do not alter the share of Medicaid costs borne by the state as a whole, as long as they are not linked to a change in what Medicaid pays to providers (for example, offsetting the tax by raising provider payments). Taxes do not, in themselves, alter the incentives inherent in federal matching. They simply have an effect similar to paying Medicaid rates below average cost, which we discuss in part 4. If the provider taxes reduce the resources available to the state's health care sector, they may result in lower service quality or fewer amenities. So long as they do not affect the size of federal matching payments, however, provider taxes are neither more nor less pernicious than low Medicaid payment rates *as a way to balance state budgets.*

An exception is when they are imposed on providers that can obtain reimbursement for the taxes. This occurs, for example, when such taxes are included as an allowable cost on Medicare cost reports that are used to establish disproportionate share hospital (DSH) payments, to set upper payment limits (UPLs) on payment rates, or to set cost-based payment for hospitals exempt from Medicare's inpatient prospective payment system (for example, critical access and children's hospitals). These hospitals are typically reimbursed for costs (subject to limits) and can recover all, or most, of these costs. Cost-based reimbursement, whether for DSH, UPLs, or PPS-exempt hospitals, is based on the assumption that the measured costs reflect the actual cost of producing the service. But provider taxes are unlike conventional state and local taxes, which are uniformly imposed on businesses and can be viewed as representing the hospital's fair share of the cost of police and fire protection and education of a trained workforce. Provider taxes, which come without such benefits to the hospital, do not represent a real cost of producing the service. Allowing provider taxes to be treated as cost for cost-based payment purposes leads the federal government to pay more than true cost for Medicare services and to pay more than its share of cost for Medicaid services. Allowance of provider taxes as a cost permits the state effectively to avoid entirely or pay less than its share of Medicaid costs and (in some cases) to capture the excess Medicare payments for the state treasury.

Since allowable provider taxes are applied without regard to the provider's involvement in Medicaid, they may serve to engage nonparticipating providers in paying some costs for Medicaid. Why medical providers (and their customers) should be singled out (compared to other firms selling other products) is not clear. Some have suggested instituting pay-or-play provider taxes—such as taxes on physicians who choose not to participate in Medicaid—with the intent of distributing more equally among providers the burden of caring for the poor at low Medicaid rates. This, however, would be contrary to current federal law requiring that provider taxes be applied equally to all providers, and it presumes a provider responsibility contrary to Medicaid's traditions of voluntary provider participation and taxpayer (rather than provider) responsibility to fund care for the poor.

In general, if the federal goal is to pay no more than its share of reasonable cost, we do not see a problem with provider taxes per se; they are only a problem when combined with one or more Medicare or Medicaid payment provisions that allow providers to escape accountability for delivering specific services at reasonable cost to covered individuals. These provisions for reduced accountability include cost reimbursement, payments in excess of the Medicare-based upper payment limit (UPL), and payments not related to specific services provided to Medicaid eligibles (such as with DSH). As long as Congress permits these exemptions from provider accountability as part of the Medicare and Medicaid payment systems, they can be used by states acting in concert with providers to extract federal payments in excess of the percentages allowed by the FMAP formula. Provider taxes can facilitate and amplify the effects of these activities but would not be a problem without them.

The major goal of federal health financing programs, however, is to put more, not fewer, resources into the hands of medical providers serving federal beneficiaries. Given the difficulty of monitoring state behavior, it may make sense to find new ways to discourage or disallow states from offsetting the effects of federal financial assistance with provider taxes. Excluding them all as allowable costs is a start. It would not be unreasonable for the federal government to make state participation in Medicaid conditional on their not imposing taxes that fall disproportionately on providers, on the grounds that such taxes serve to reverse or offset program payments that are designed and intended to assist providers.

Tightening federal rules around cost reimbursement and DSH could discourage such taxes by removing the ability of, and temptation, for states to use this as a means to substitute federal funds for state dollars. Federal policy, however, cannot dictate how states choose to raise revenue. There may be some states, particularly those with constitutional or political limits on other types of taxes, that will continue to see provider taxes as an attractive revenue option that reduces resources to the health care sector. Where the extent of employer-based insurance and market conditions permit, these costs may be passed along to employers and workers, where they may constitute a hidden "tax" that takes the form of higher private health insurance rates and is likely to be regressive as a proportion of worker income. Overall, we see taxes that fall totally or disproportionately on the health care sector (which public policy is trying to support) as reflecting a poor choice among revenue sources for states. Federal policymakers should question what support they are willing to provide to states that choose to undo with tax policy what the Medicaid program is attempting to accomplish with payment policy.

Excessive Disproportionate Share Hospital (DSH) Payments. DSH payments are intended for hospitals that provide services to a disproportionate number of lower-income patients. In contrast to Medicare, which bases DSH payment solely on Medicaid, Medicaid DSH counts charity care in its payment calculation.[7] The Omnibus Budget Reconciliation Act of 1993 (OBRA '93) limited the amount of such payments to no more than the amount hospitals can document as lost on Medicaid and the uninsured, and it required hospitals eligible for DSH to have at least 1 percent Medicaid patients. Federal matching percentages of FMAP apply. Again, it is the combination of DSH with other elements, such as intergovernmental transfers (IGTs) and provider taxes, that raises concerns.

For example, even with the OBRA '93 changes, if the state sets the provider taxes in a way that fully offsets DSH payments to hospitals, it can return the full amount of the DSH funds (federal and state) to the state treasury. Under such arrangements, the state treasury effectively captures the federal share as a net gain in general revenue, leaving the hospitals to recover any uncompensated care and Medicaid shortfall by keeping costs below what they are able to obtain from private payers. In the end, the federal government pays its share, and the state share is effectively paid as a hidden "tax" by those with private insurance (perhaps in the form of reduced value from quality or amenities in care, as we discuss in chapter 11 in the section on cost-shifting). It may be a preferred strategy by states with limited public support for tax revenue. States that play this game have every reason to make DSH as high as is allowed. Only federal limits and provider willingness to provide services for funds retained keep costs in check. OBRA '93 reduced the amounts involved, but the OBRA limits are inadequate to prevent states from reducing the state government share below FMAP percentages if they use such a technique.

Excessive DSH Payments to State Mental Hospitals. Prior to the imposition of limits by the Balanced Budget Act of 1997, a large share of DSH payments were made to state mental hospitals.[8] By making payments in excess of reasonable cost, states were able to get federal matching beyond the FMAP percentage of the cost of producing the services. This allowed them to add federal funds to their hospital budgets that could be used for non-Medicaid purposes, such as to support the care of patients in such facilities who were not eligible for Medicaid. To meet the federal–state sharing intent of the program, federal matching should be limited to apply only to the reasonable cost of such services for persons eligible for Medicaid. Although now limited, we mention this as an example of the danger of abuse that exists when states do not have the arm's-length relationship with Medicaid providers that was presumed when the federal matching arrangement was established.

Exceeding the Upper Payment Limit (UPL) for Local Government Health Facilities. Similarly, excessive payments above the Medicare-equivalent rate have been used by states to obtain Medicaid funds for local government health care facilities that often serve as safety-net providers. DSH payments may appropriately be used to support government facilities where applicable. Our view is that it is not the government status of facilities that matters; any payment in excess of reasonable cost should be disallowed for federal matching, whether for a government or private facility. While states have obvious incentives to use such overpayment to support government-owned facilities, the same concern arises with other providers, especially those with strong local political influence. States should be prohibited from using Medicaid funds, including DSH funds, to pay any facility more than reasonable cost. Current rules that set upper payment limits by class still allow states to pay some providers more than others, and this leaves open the possibility for abuse of state flexibility. These UPLs warrant attention to tightening up criteria for use and ensuring close monitoring of state actions in this area.

Upper Payment Limit (UPL) Programs. Federal Medicaid rules apply Medicare upper payment limits at an aggregate (rather than at a provider) level to different classes of facilities—that is, so long as payment for a class of facilities is below Medicare payment levels, payments to an individual facility can exceed what would be allowed at Medicare rates. States have been allowed to make supplemental payments to designated facilities (such as publicly owned hospitals and nursing homes) that may exceed individual facility costs. The game here is to put a highly paid, favored facility in a class with lower-paid facilities so that the average for the class is still below the UPL. Formerly, when the categories for UPL were "all hospitals" and "all nursing homes," states were able to provide favorable rates to state-owned or dependent facilities. In 2001, federal rules were changed to apply UPLs separately to state, local public and private hospitals, nursing homes, and intermediate care facilities for the mentally retarded (ICF-MRs). This limited the extent to which lower payments for private facilities could be used to justify higher-than-cost payments to public facilities. Nonetheless, many states continue to have UPL programs that facilitate additional payments to government-owned or other favored providers.[9]

Intergovernmental Transfers (IGTs). Medicaid has long allowed for other government entities, such as cities and counties, to contribute toward the state share of Medicaid costs for matching purposes. Recent criticisms have arisen from intergovernmental transfers from public-sector providers, such as city or state hospitals, especially when combined with excessive payment rates that allow the provider entity to return excess funds to the state treasury. Again, we suggest it is the payment in excess of cost, rather than the transfers of funds among entities, that should be the focus of federal concern.

Criteria for Judging State Financing Arrangements. Many of the financing schemes described above are used to give the state effectively a higher matching payment. While the matching-rate formula is far from sacrosanct, any changes should be made in a transparent legislative process at the federal level, not implicitly by gaming of the system by individual states. Arguments that a state needs the additional federal money to avoid cuts in its programs for the poor or to finance new and praiseworthy programs are irrelevant to the extent that they are considered only for one or a few states. Federal funding should be available equally to all states and determined in an open and equitable process. It is worth noting that state arguments for using questionable means for unquestionably desirable ends has never been made strongly. The integrity of the Medicaid matching-rate process requires that states not be able to obtain federal matching without making real payments for the full state share of cost of services actually delivered, at the rate actually paid to the provider and no greater than cost. We argue, however, that whether those funds come from general revenue, county or local contributions, or general provider taxes is immaterial (at least to federal policy), so long as some combination of entities within the state pays the state share.

DSH payments, which cannot be directly tied to specific services delivered or to specific Medicaid-eligible recipients, are not appropriate for federal matching unless strictly limited to a predetermined amount based on equitable criteria for distribution among states. Any open-ended use could allow for federal matching without a real state contribution. If DSH payments are to be continued, it would be helpful for federal policymakers to review, define, and consistently apply rules regarding which services and costs are allowable for DSH payments. In states willing to exploit the possibilities, DSH payments can currently be used to cover all uncompensated care costs—that is, all hospital direct care costs not covered by other payers. Depending on state allocation methods, some hospitals can receive DSH payments that regularly cover virtually all costs of uncompensated care, including any shortfall in Medicaid payments relative to costs. This raises questions about just what charity care and bad debts might be covered by Medicaid DSH payments, and whether this effective cost reimbursement provides any incentive for efficiency. The lack of accountability for DSH spending is a problem.

DSH payments may be an effective mechanism for financing safety-net providers for costs of serving uninsured persons not eligible for Medicaid who cannot afford to pay for their care. However, the wide interstate variation in use of DSH payments (with a handful of states receiving disproportionate benefit) suggests that a few states may have used DSH payments to tap additional federal funds to cover their expenses beyond costs of persons

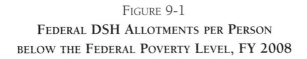

FIGURE 9-1

**FEDERAL DSH ALLOTMENTS PER PERSON
BELOW THE FEDERAL POVERTY LEVEL, FY 2008**

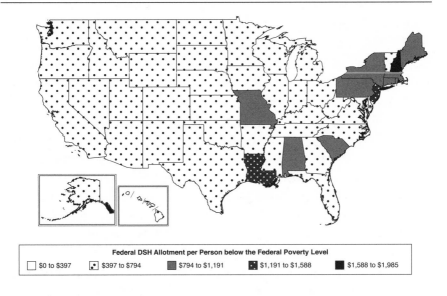

Federal DSH Allotment per Person below the Federal Poverty Level

| ☐ $0 to $397 | ⟍ $397 to $794 | ▨ $794 to $1,191 | ▓ $1,191 to $1,588 | ■ $1,588 to $1,985 |

SOURCE: Computed from Kaiser Family Foundation (2009, "Disproportionate Share Hospital Allotments under the American Recovery and Reinvestment Act, FY2009," http://www.statehealthfacts.org/comparetable.jsp?ind=678&cat=4&sub=154&yr=90&typ=4) and U.S. Census Bureau (2008b).

eligible to enroll in Medicaid. In some cases, funds may have been directed to purposes other than medical care.

Evidence that the distribution of federal DSH payments among states corresponds with needs of the poor is scant, though high DSH payments may, in some states, be related to low Medicaid hospital payment rates. Ku and Coughlin found that only a small share of DSH and related special financing funds were available to cover the cost of uncompensated care.[10] As shown in figure 9-1, the states with the highest 2008 federal DSH payments per poor person were New Hampshire ($1,984), Louisiana ($1,087), New Jersey ($817), Maine ($696), and Connecticut ($610).[11] Of these, only Louisiana was among the twenty lowest income states by median household income, and New Hampshire, which is a higher-income state, received a federal DSH allotment per poor person of more than ten times that of the median state.

Variation in DSH spending across states apparently is unrelated to indicators of need for such funds and reflects, rather, differences in state propensity, willingness, or ability to take advantage of this financing mechanism.

This counterintuitive situation raises the question of whether the DSH program is the most appropriate means of distributing federal funds to meet the medical care needs of the lower-income population. DSH payments effectively extend Medicaid financing to an area where federal regulations and controls over how funds are used are few. In the ideal case, federal payments to facilities providing large proportions of their services to needy people might better flow through a separate program specifically constructed for this purpose, rather than being piggybacked on Medicaid (and Medicare). Such a program could be designed with its own more accountable procedures to provide better assurance that federal funds are used for their intended purposes. Any national program that reduces the number of lower-income uninsured would, of course, reduce uncompensated care and the needs of institutions designated to receive DSH payments.

In contrast, provider taxes—which, as currently allowed, often play a role in such schemes—will not generally in themselves violate these criteria, should not be precluded at the federal level, and may be useful to help limit net resources flowing into the state health care system—if such constraints are desired. The incidence of such taxes (who really pays for them) is, however, unclear; the burden will probably not fall entirely on provider net income but may result in providers' choosing less costly styles of care as, we argue in chapter 11, they cannot readily be shifted forward to other insurers. Taxes on broader bases (such as income or retail sales) may have a less distorting effect on the local health care system and will better reflect taxpayer responsibility and choices about the appropriate level of funding for care for the poor.

Again, our view is that less attention needs be paid to source of the state share, whether state general funds, provider taxes, or IGTs, since all real payments from within the state should be applicable to the state share. Rather, policymakers should reduce use of DSH payments in order to increase the accountability for use of federal Medicaid funds. Standard Medicaid requires states to report on claims paid for specific services for Medicaid-eligible individuals at rates that are no more than what Medicare would pay. DSH payments allow states to circumvent these requirements and can allow selected hospitals effectively to be reimbursed with federal funds for costs higher than what Medicare would allow for similar services and for persons who would not meet Medicaid's eligibility requirements. Federal matching for Medicaid payments, including DSH, should not be made for amounts that exceed the cost of producing services at an appropriate quality level. (Medicare UPL represents such a limit.) This rule should apply to all types of providers, both government-owned and private. National health care reform could be an impetus for eliminating DSH if it involves reducing the number of uninsured. Expanding coverage to more people would reduce uncompensated care at hospitals and demand at safety-net facilities once poor people had insurance that would pay for them if they were to go somewhere else.[12] Once alternate sources of payment for those persons were in place, uncompensated care would decline, and DSH could be phased out. This might be done simply by reducing the federal matching rate that applies to DSH, setting it, for example, ten percentage points below the state's current FMAP the first year, twenty points below FMAP the second year, and so on, until it disappears after five to eight years, giving the lower-income states a bit longer to adjust.

In sum, attention should be paid to ensuring that Medicaid DSH payments are limited to costs actually incurred and not otherwise covered by Medicaid, Medicare DSH, other federal programs, or other payers, and that all states are given clear instructions on exactly what is permitted. Replacing DSH payments with broader Medicaid eligibility and other subsidies for those now uninsured would introduce a much greater degree of accountability for use of funds.

Program Integrity

Another important promise to taxpayers is that program funds will be used for intended purposes and not wasted through fraud and abuse. This is a particular challenge for Medicaid, in part because any health plan without copayments lacks the best fraud protection there is: the incentive for beneficiaries to report misuse of funds. We have noted the very valid reasons for Medicaid to avoid use of copayments for low-income recipients, but one needs to recognize that, as a consequence, fraud will be worse in Medicaid than in Medicare or private insurance. The alternative, of course, is for Medicaid to make greater efforts and spend a greater share of resources on program integrity efforts.

Medicaid provider fraud has long been a problem, reflecting the difficulty of monitoring the activities of providers, particularly those who operate largely out of public view. In the 1970s, we began to hear of Medicaid "mills" in which doctors generated large numbers of bills for questionable services for Medicaid-eligible patients One of the earliest-documented reports appeared in 1973 in a twelve-part series in the New York Daily News by William Sherman, who won a Pulitzer Prize for his efforts.[13]

Similar scams continue to this day. A few examples will illustrate the wide range of fraudulent activities that have been reported. In 2003 in Brooklyn, New York, a two-dentist practice offered free CD players to anyone with a Medicaid card and then used the recipients' numbers to bill more than $5.4 million in Medicaid payments, with daily billings for procedures in excess of services that could possibly have been provided.[14] Abuses in billing for transportation have included ambulances "upcoding" claims from basic life support to more costly advanced life support, and the submission of claims for reimbursement for personal transportation that are difficult to monitor due to the large number of small transactions. Pain-control centers have been cited for inappropriately dispensing controlled substances without proper medical documentation of the need for prescriptions.[15] These types of fraudulent operations are small in dollar terms, however, when compared with the indiscretions of major providers and suppliers. Florida reported receiving $32.8 million as part of two separate global settlements totaling $649 million with pharmaceutical firm Merck and Co. Inc. and $9.8 million from a $35 million multistate settlement with the Walgreen Company.[16]

School-based services have also been a source of inappropriate billings.[17] In a review of one year of claims for school-based clinics in Minnesota, the U.S. Department of Health and Human Services' Office of Inspector General found that of the $26.8 million in Medicaid claims for the sixty school districts reviewed, only $7.3 million (or 27 percent) was allowable. States, of course, seeking greater federal support for their publicly funded activities may find it advantageous to allow school districts to overstate claims for school-based clinic services, so this is an area that deserves particular federal scrutiny.

Program integrity efforts need constantly to keep up with technology. Expanding use of Internet linkages for electronic medical claims processing systems can give access to Medicaid funds even to international small-scale or organized crime organizations if they are able to obtain recipient identity information, a provider number, and a billing manual. Medicaid programs need to know who their providers really are and to be able to verify that services billed were actually delivered to eligible recipients. While large-scale computer scans of claims for irregularities can detect some problems, criminals can construct bogus claims that go under the radar to meet individual claims criteria and may vanish from the scene before a pattern of irregularity is detected.

Program integrity efforts need to deal with a great many manifestations of fraud and abuse. These range from the professional criminals who submit entirely bogus claims, to the fraudulent providers who go through the motions of providing services that may be unneeded—sometimes paying Medicaid eligibles to participate in their scams—to abuse by legitimate providers, who overstep bounds through upcoding in efforts to maximize payments or simply fail to return excess payments to the state when inadvertent errors are discovered. Although provider organizations often complain about stepped-up efforts in program integrity, it is an area in which investment of additional public funds can produce net savings, as well as ensure that public funds go for their intended purpose.

As with so many aspects of Medicaid, the extent of fraud and abuse differs greatly among the states.[18] Many reports of concern have come from larger states. Although the California Attorney General's Office of Medi-Cal Fraud and Elder Abuse reported $16 million in criminal restitution and $145 million in civil monetary recoveries for the 2007–8 fiscal period, this is only about one-half of 1 percent of the $34 billion Medi-Cal program's provider payments—far less than many common, but unreliable, estimates of the extent of Medicaid fraud. One wonders what fraudulent payments might have been recovered or prevented but were not. Medicaid programs in the smaller states are perhaps better able to keep tabs on their providers and provider activities, but they sustain many abuses as well.

Another opening for fraud is the general requirement that the fee-for-service side of Medicaid be open to any provider willing to participate. While this open-door policy may help achieve better acceptance of the program in the provider community, it does create difficulties in controlling the provider network. States can exclude providers for cause, such as submitting false claims, providing excessive services, or unacceptable recordkeeping, but some states, such as New York, have been much more willing than other states (and Medicare) to exclude providers where evidence of wrongdoing exists.[19] Provider exclusion is an underused tool that could be applied more broadly. Clearer federal guidance in law, regulation, and policy regarding the criteria for excluding providers for cause (based on preponderance of evidence of wrongdoing, short of a conviction) could encourage states to undertake more aggressive enforcement activities in this area.

Other approaches to developing a network of trustworthy providers might also be tried, such as a probationary period of close monitoring to include onsite inspections of all new providers. One advantage of closed-panel HMOs and competitive-bidding payment methods is the ability to limit participation to known and verifiable providers. It might be useful for states to obtain waivers to experiment with some forms of closed-panel provider networks that exert greater effort to establish provider credentials prior to participation, more intensive monitoring of quality and compliance during participation, and greater ability to terminate provider participation when problems arise and are not resolved.

States would further benefit in the area of program integrity from a strong federal technical assistance program to help their agencies and claims-processing contractors do a better job. In the Deficit Reduction Act (DRA) of 2005, Congress provided CMS with resources to establish the Medicaid Integrity Program to review the activities of Medicaid providers and support the states in efforts to combat fraud, waste, and abuse.[20] The report on the first full year of this program shows progress in developing an organizational and programmatic foundation for this work.[21] Another recent report puts forth plans to develop "one-stop shopping" for provider enrollment, develop a national integrated data repository, establish a fraud-and-abuse research team, conduct data-mining, develop an information management system, and develop an audit tracking system.[22]

Despite all the recurring press attention and new program integrity efforts, we still do not have a good understanding of the full extent and nature of Medicaid fraud. A comprehensive national research study is needed to measure scientifically its extent by tracking a random sample of all claims all the way back to the recipients—that is, the study should not stop with electronic claims review, but should verify eligibility and contact recipients to determine what services were actually provided and to whom. With a sufficiently large sample, even a one-time study could do much to gauge the full scope of fraudulent activity and help guide future program integrity work to target all the areas of abuse more efficiently. This would be an expensive undertaking to do well, but very worthwhile.

Conclusion

Accountability for Medicaid funds is not a problem that will ever be solved once and for all. It is an issue that requires constant vigilance. Program accountability is its own specialized area for policy analysis and policymaking—one that requires thinking about Medicaid from a bottom-up perspective. As it pertains to states, one must ask, from the states' point of view: How can one maximize federal reimbursement? One must then determine whether such state behavior is consistent with the intended use of the funds. With respect to providers and program integrity, one must ask, from the fraudster's perspective: In what ways might one as a provider or pseudo-provider get access to Medicaid payments? One must then determine what can be done to prevent such unauthorized access. Public program integrity efforts teamed with private provider compliance programs should be an important and growing part of Medicaid program efforts in the coming years. It will be important for federal and state policymakers to ensure that these activities are given suitable priority for funding and staffing.

Conclusion to Part III:
A Basic Promise: Protecting
Taxpayer Interests in Medicaid

In part III, we have shown that the logic of Medicaid's basic financing structure fits well in our federal–state governmental system and provides a means
for adjusting Medicaid spending to underlying voter preferences. Importantly,
this basic program structure has the capacity to meet voter preferences better
than other financing methods, such as full federalization, block grants, or
state funding alone. In particular, it allows voters to express preferences for
public funding of medical care for the poor at both a local and a national level.
We believe that such preferences are in part local and in part more general,
so both aspects ought to be accounted for in public spending decisions. If one
is willing to manipulate parameters, the program can also be adjusted to
reflect preferences for the level and distribution of benefits.

The incentives for states to respond to federal matching work effectively
when the state actually pays its specified share and uses the funds to purchase in the market valuable services used by poor persons, within groups
designated to be eligible for Medicaid. Problems arise, however, when states
are allowed to manipulate the system to obtain federal payments beyond the
lesser of actual or reasonable cost of producing services or for services delivered to persons not eligible for the program. Accountability and cost-sharing
according to the FMAP formula break down whenever payments are not tied
to particular covered services for specific eligible individuals. This happens
whenever Medicaid payments are made outside the claims-processing
system, as they are with DSH and other supplemental payments. It also
happens whenever Medicaid payments exceed the cost of producing the
service, as has been reported when state or local government (or "captive"

194

state-dependent) entities become Medicaid providers, as with school-based or nonmedical residential services. Medicaid is then reduced to a mechanism for transferring funds to states, particularly those creative enough to use the rules to their advantage. While federal agencies have indicated their awareness of these issues and have attempted to address them in some ways, more fundamental changes are needed in law and regulations.

Taxpayers have two administrative "friends": the claims-based payment system and the upper payment limits. These mechanisms are key to ensuring that funds go to pay for covered services of eligible individuals, and that they are paid at rates that are no more than reasonable cost. Where either of these protections is not effectively applied—most often with DSH, other supplemental payments, captive state-dependent providers, or services with enforced cost limits—accountability is at risk. Eliminating all payments that are not based on claims and establishing and enforcing upper payment limits for all Medicaid services would be one solution. But these alternative financing mechanisms now serve a legitimate and needed function in maintaining the safety net. Until everyone has access to claims-based payment, and Medicaid payment rates are high enough to induce provision of service without supplements, these payment methods will be needed, and special attention will be required to ensure their accountability.

Beyond this, taxpayers have legitimate interests in ensuring that they pay a fair share of program costs and that their costs are, to some degree, expected and predictable. The principles of vertical equity (among higher- and lower-income taxpayers), horizontal equity (across states), and cyclical equity (across varying economic conditions) apply for taxpayers as well as for recipients. Attention should be paid periodically to how the burden of Medicaid falls on taxpayers across states, making sure that the share of income going to the program, as well as the transfer effects, are in line with program objectives and basic equity criteria.

PART IV

Promises to Providers—
Payment Policies and Strategies

Provider payment has deep and widespread implications for a state's Medicaid program. Payment policy helps set the substance and tone of relationships with the providers needed to deliver Medicaid-covered services. Each state's Medicaid commitment to providers is largely defined by the level and structure of its provider payment rates. Its decisions on provider payment methods and rates will, over time, do much to shape its Medicaid program. Such decisions have implications for the availability, quality, and quantity of services; how easily adjustments can be made to accommodate changes in demand for services, program requirements, or state finances; and how cost-effectively public resources are employed to meet program objectives.

Providers complain—sometimes about Medicaid administrative requirements, sometimes about Medicaid patients, but, most of all, about low Medicaid payment rates. What is it about the way Medicaid sets its payment rates that sets the program apart from other payers and evokes such wrath from the provider community?

In part 4, we consider the issue of Medicaid provider payment in some detail and from multiple perspectives: from that of the providers who want to be paid adequately; of the recipients who want provider payment levels that will give them access to needed care; of the taxpayers who want good value for their tax dollars; and of the state and federal administrators and policymakers who, caught among these competing demands, face a complex set of issues in setting payment policies and rates for a wide array of services in diverse local markets. With Medicaid's broad coverage of many services, its importance in the state budget, its diverse array of provider types, its mandate to serve all geographic areas in each state, and its sometimes politically charged price-setting environments, provider payment issues can present significant challenges to state programs.

While federal policy specifies the framework, most provider payment decisions are made by states. Our primary goal in part 4, therefore, is to provide some guidance to the states on how best to develop a provider payment strategy that reflects their desired levels of commitment to providers, taxpayers, and recipients. We offer some criteria that should help states evaluate provider payment methods and payment levels but, more importantly, should serve to guide development of provider payment strategies that can be applied over time to help the states achieve longer-run objectives for adequacy, accuracy, equity, and efficiency.

A second goal is to suggest how the federal government can better structure the framework for this state decision-making. We note the authorization for a new federal entity to oversee Medicaid payment and access issues: The Medicaid and CHIP Payment and Access Commission (MAC-PAC) was authorized by Congress in early 2009 and initial appointments were made in December 2009. The commission is to review the payment policies of Medicaid and CHIP and make recommendations to Congress on policies affecting access to care. It is unclear at this point to what extent this new commission may bring added federal oversight or technical assistance to the states, or whether it will lead Congress to take a more active federal role in issues of provider payment for the Medicaid and CHIP programs.[1]

However the state and federal dynamics may play out, the result will be a product of the democratic process. In the end, voter-taxpayers will get what they are willing to pay for in terms of access to care for their lower-income populations. Payment levels will, in turn, reflect these choices, and what voter-taxpayers are willing to fund may provide less in access than the poor may desire. Our objective in this part, then, is to provide policymakers with a framework for making better decisions and some tools for implementing provider payment policy in ways that are equitable and promote efficient use of resources.

10

Provider Payment in a Democracy

The key insight from the public choice view we have adopted is that Medicaid policy tends to reflect the tradeoffs voter-taxpayers are willing to make between Medicaid and other spending priorities. In this context, provider payment is merely a tool for policymakers to use to achieve what voters want in terms of access to care for the poor. But the democratic process will not always achieve everything its citizens want. Fiscal constraints often conflict with lofty program goals and special-interest aspirations. A program that maximizes access for recipients and minimizes provider discontent is almost guaranteed to be one that a state cannot finance and taxpayers will not support. Too often, the process for setting and maintaining appropriate provider payment is neglected, reduced to a debate between state officials and provider lobbyists, treated as a purely administrative matter, captured to some degree by provider interests, or left to be resolved politically at budget time. Too often, payment policy fails to be based on a well-defined, explicit plan that ties payment to state or taxpayer program goals, either implicitly or explicitly. The mixed results are reflected among states in the diversity of payment methodologies, in the widely differing levels of payment, in the irregularity in updating payment rates, and in the varying extent of provider participation in the program.

Medicaid is a health insurance program, not a health services program. As an insurer, it relies on the participating medical providers and managed care plans to deliver medical care to recipients. An essential task for Medicaid managers, therefore, is to promote and maintain the willingness of appropriate numbers of providers to accept Medicaid patients and supply them with appropriate services. Because of the size and political character of the program, however, Medicaid rarely chooses to be a price-taker in the market.[1] With limited ability to use patient cost-sharing as a tool, provider payment has come to be one of the main choice variables for Medicaid programs. This is a change from the passive reimbursement of costs or charges characterizing the old Blue Cross and Blue Shield programs that were the norm when Medicaid was started. Developing and maintaining appropriate payment methods and adequate payment rates are essential to meeting the goals of any Medicaid program.

States have chosen to pursue a wide variety of payment methods and to set rates in varying ways that reflect local political influences and health care delivery systems, as well as the resources made available by state legislatures and, ultimately, taxpayers. Medicaid differs from Medicare and from private fee-for-service insurers in its role as a purchaser of health care services. Because Medicare generally is responsible for a much larger share of the revenue of typical acute care providers, it cannot set rates too low and rely on the cross-subsidy of other payers. Still, it has usually been able to get most providers to accept its payment rates, which are somewhat higher than Medicaid's. Medicaid also can set, rather than accept, rates, but many state programs have been unable or unwilling to set rates high enough to get all, or even most, providers to accept its payments and its patients. Because Medicaid rates are lower than other payers, including Medicare, states are often frustrated in their efforts to cajole or compel all providers to participate in the Medicaid program. They end up facing tradeoffs between low spending on provider payments and better access for Medicaid recipients.

Developing a State Medicaid Provider Payment Strategy

Having a rational, realistic, and well-thought-out provider payment strategy is a central part of any well-formulated state Medicaid plan. State Medicaid budgets and provider payment rates are determined through political processes that can be considerably influenced by providers and beneficiary interest groups. In this environment, having a payment strategy based on defined criteria can help the budget process meet provider needs and interests appropriately. It can help policymakers resist undue pressure from particular provider interests and allow the allocation of payments based on the objectives the state is trying to achieve.

The structure of provider payments is interdependent and should be consistent with other state policy priorities and decisions. This includes political choices on the eligibility and access of Medicaid recipients and treatment of providers; budget choices on resources to devote to provider payments; and administrative choices on investments in the staff and data systems needed to implement and manage the payment policies.

A basic economic model of this problem would posit a supply function for providers (indicating both the number of Medicaid patients they will accept and the quantity and quality of services per eligible Medicaid patient they will furnish at various payment rates) and a voter-taxpayer demand function for eligibility and care per beneficiary. The state could then be advised to choose the point on this supply function that corresponds to the level of access, quantity, and quality of care that voters desire for their states' Medicaid populations, given the cost at that point. This approach rules out the notion of some immutable and fixed level of provider "cost" that can be discovered, measured, and paid for. Instead, the concept here is that different levels of payment will bring forth different levels of access, quality, and quantity. The existence of a supply curve implies that some providers have lower costs (opportunity costs, for the most part) than others, so there is no such thing as "the" cost. States set payment rates to achieve a politically acceptable level of access for their Medicaid recipients.

There are some exceptions, of course: a payment level so low that almost no providers can cover their costs even at minimum acceptable quality levels, or a payment level so lavish that providers seek out Medicaid beneficiaries, reward them or their referring physicians with high-quality processes, and face the temptation to induce yet more demand because Medicaid services are so profitable. Between these two extremes are many options. Historically, Medicaid programs have selected relatively low-priced ones, but exactly at what level any given program should set its payment rates is a choice, not a necessity. In states with Medicaid managed care programs, the issues take a different form at an aggregate health plan level, but the same principles still apply.

Payment Requirements and Objectives

Medicaid payments are set by states as authorized by federal laws and regulations. Within this framework, which specifies general requirements, states vary considerably in how they set payment rate levels and make year-to-year adjustments.

Legal Obligations: Federal Laws and Regulations, State Law, State Plans. States have considerable freedom to set provider rates and methods, provided such methods are uniformly applied, and rates are reasonable and adequate. The methods of payment must be specified in each state's Medicaid state plan, which is subject to federal approval. The federal role in Medicaid payment has been mainly limited, however, to ensuring that payments are not excessive; it has not involved prescribing payment methods or levels of payment rates (provided they are generally not higher than Medicare levels).

Within this framework, the methods and rates used to pay providers differ widely among states. Decisions of state legislatures underlie all state rate structures, but the level of active involvement of legislatures in rate-setting varies. In some states, legislatures take an active role in specifying rates or rate increases for specific types of Medicaid providers and services as part of the budget process. In others, the structure of rates is well established, and increases are applied proportionally to the available budget. In still other states, the rate-setting process is structured to provide for automatic increases indexed to costs or prices or Medicare rates. Many states pursue multiple, mixed approaches that vary with the types of services. In rate-setting, as in eligibility and benefits, Medicaid state plans filed with the U.S. Centers for Medicare and Medicaid Services (CMS) generally reflect policy decisions, rather than prescribe or precede them.

Legal Requirements for Adequate Payment Rates. Federal regulations require state Medicaid programs to pay providers at rates that are generally "consistent with efficiency, economy, and quality of care," without specifying exactly what these terms mean.[2] There are some specific constraints and areas of flexibility, but, in general, specifying payment rates and methods is a state responsibility. States are expected to pay amounts for Medicaid services that adequately compensate providers, but not more than reasonably needed to ensure adequate provision of services. Hospitals and long-term care facilities, for example, are to be paid "rates that are reasonable and adequate to meet the costs that must be incurred by efficiently and economically operated providers to provide services in conformity with applicable State and Federal laws, regulations, and quality and safety standards."[3] For some services, there are specific limits on payment, such as upper payment limits based on Medicare payment rates. As a result, we normally see Medicaid rates below, and in many cases substantially below, Medicare rates. Even when these Medicare-based upper payment limits apply, they apply to the average for a class of providers. States may set rates to meet payment-level targets on average so long as all providers in a class are treated equally. By thus specifying classes of providers and payment rules within each class, states can tailor payment to meet specific goals.

On many occasions, state Medicaid payment rates have been challenged in court. Providers, often represented by trade associations, have sued for adequate rates under federal law, but generally they can challenge only rate levels, not rate-setting methods. Recipients, often represented by advocacy groups, have sued on the grounds of rates being inadequate to ensure access to care. The Supreme Court found in *Wilder v. Virginia Hospital Association* that states have an obligation to provide reasonable and adequate rates,[4] and some courts have found that Medicare rates define a reasonable level. Nonetheless, states have latitude in how rates are set (for example, statewide or by facility), with recent federal laws providing more flexibility in some areas;[5] and, in the absence of legal action, enforcement of any "reasonable and adequate" standard is not uniform.

Since states have to certify reasonableness to CMS only when rates change, the federal government does not get involved in constant monitoring of specific rates that may apply under an approved state plan. And how to specify what "reasonable and adequate" means is still up in the air, although courts sometimes allege they know it (or know its absence) when they see it. In short, case law and regulation provide an ambiguous and uncertain basis for setting or challenging payment levels, methods, or payment rate increases.

When a state contracts with a private managed care plan as part of its Medicaid program, the managed care organization (MCO) rates are required to meet a test of actuarial soundness.[6] This should allow for adequate resources, and MCO plans may use an existing provider network and its payment rates. But each managed care plan is responsible for setting rates for its individual providers, and the plan, rather than the state Medicaid program, usually becomes the first point of contact for provider dissatisfaction. Any challenges are more likely to come in negotiations with potential network providers rather than in court.

There is, in fact, evidence of push-back from providers in Medicaid MCOs, as well as reports that Medicaid health plans "are finding it increasingly difficult to negotiate favorable terms with health care providers, particularly hospitals."[7] Medicaid-only MCOs may be better able or more willing to accept the limited network that lower payments may support.[8] Medicaid-dependent nonprofit and public providers, such as public hospitals, may be more willing to accept lower payments from Medicaid managed care plans.[9] Nevertheless, Medicaid managed care plans are not exempt from court oversight. As one example, a federal district court ordered the District of Columbia Medicaid program to increase DSH payments to hospitals based on services delivered to Medicaid recipients in a managed care plan.[10]

Medicaid's Relationships with Providers

Medicaid payment rates cannot be set in a vacuum. Rate-setting for providers must reflect realities of the medical services marketplace (especially the prices paid by other insurers) and the political environment. The market and political power of Medicaid providers vary widely among the many types of services and types of providers.

State Medicaid programs have never been obligated to provide a rigorous or transparent justification for the prices they pay providers for medical services, or to pay prices high enough that Medicaid patients can go anywhere for care. Originally, in the 1960s, Medicaid followed Medicare (which itself followed Blue Cross and Blue Shield) in reimbursing hospitals for whatever costs they incurred and paying physicians whatever they billed as reasonable and customary charges. But states soon chose to limit Medicaid physician payments for budgetary reasons, and, in the 1980s, many followed Medicare in adopting some form of prospective per-case payment to hospitals for inpatient services. Medicaid managed care programs, while competitively bid, distanced state officials from the rate-setting function for at least a portion of the acute care providers. Nonetheless, many state Medicaid programs continue to specify payment rates for a significant share, if not most, of their acute care services, and most long-term care services.[11]

Provider Interests. State policymakers tend to be acutely aware of the interests of Medicaid providers, who must be heard as part of the rate-setting process to ensure that local needs are met. But this responsiveness to provider interests must be balanced with a healthy skepticism and concern for spending. Provider needs and interests should be part, but only part, of the policymakers' concerns in developing policy on Medicaid provider payment.

Providers and their advocates in the policy process typically represent their economic interests very well. Provider lobbyists can be fairly creative in presenting plausible rationales for higher payment rates, sometimes pointing to their shared interests with recipients who desire the better access that higher rates may produce. Providers rarely present a balanced picture to state policymakers, however. Lobbyists will tend to omit facts that may be suggestive of lower rates, such as the possibility that the providers are doing quite well on some services despite coming up short on others. The other side of the story needs to come from administrators prepared with benchmarks and analysis of rates, or from legislators voicing concerns for state budgets—and state programs vary in how well they perform this important function.

Provider Market Power. Medicaid obtains medical services for its beneficiaries in local health care markets. Its freedom to set prices depends on the relative market power of Medicaid as a major purchaser and of providers as sellers. Each side may have some degree of market power: Medicaid as a large, monopsonistic purchaser, and providers as sellers with the ability to fill their offices and beds with privately insured patients for whom they may receive higher payments.

Factors associated with high seller's market power include the following:

- A larger seller's market share (relative to the share of any single buyer) for specific services—for instance, a single hospital in a town facing a dozen insurers

- A small number or capacity of competing providers of a service or substitutes for the service

- A strong and growing private-sector demand for services

- The ability to withdraw from participation without adverse consequences to the seller's community image

- The ability to price-discriminate across different categories of buyers (for example, to charge more for patients covered by private insurance than what Medicaid pays)

All of these factors make more credible a provider's threat to withdraw from Medicaid participation or reduce service provision if payment is perceived as unsatisfactory.

Provider Political Power. Medicaid payment rates are set in a political environment and driven in the short run largely by the budget allocated to provider payments by the state legislature. In many cases, the budget may specify amounts at the line-item level earmarked for specific types of providers or services. The ability to influence legislators to spend more on specific budget lines can be an important determinant of how well the various types of providers, and even specific providers, do in obtaining higher rates.

One might think that providers and recipients would compete for Medicaid resources—payment rates versus benefits. But this is not always the case. In many instances, political support for preferential rates for specific services comes from a coalition of recipient and provider interest groups. Advocacy groups for the disabled or elderly, for example, may support the providers of the services their recipients use, such as home care services for the disabled, in the interest of improving access to such services. And providers may speak out in support of greater eligibility and coverage for the types of recipients they serve, in expectation of higher demand for their services. Advocacy groups and providers may then align themselves behind common interests for funding of specific types of recipients and services. Conversely, they may perceive their interests to be more competitive with other types of medical recipients or providers of other types of services. The politics of state Medicaid budgets (and provider payment

PROVIDER PAYMENT IN A DEMOCRACY 207

rates) may depend, for example, on the relative political influence of advocates for disabled persons compared to those of the Temporary Assistance for Needy Families (TANF) and elderly recipient populations.

As a result, state policymakers face the question of whether limited state funds should be allocated to favor particular (or particularly vocal) eligibility groups rather than to support more adequate payment rates for the providers of the services they use. When payment rates are linked to populations served, rather than services delivered, however, states can find themselves paying different rates to the same or similar providers for the same or similar services, depending on the eligibility status of the Medicaid beneficiary.

State legislators have three basic choices in the rate-setting process, ranked in decreasing order of how much direct control the legislature chooses to exercise. They can play an active role in specifying rates for every service and even specific providers; they can turn that job over to administrators; or they can focus on developing policies, methodologies, and structures that permit rate levels to be set and adjusted over time to reflect changes in costs, considerations of equity across providers, or benchmarks that are not under political control. The choice is not very predictable, as it depends on how legislators choose to deal with local political (often provider) influences. So, in fact, we see much variation among the states.

Market power underlies political power (and vice versa), but provider influence is enhanced through political factors, such as

- strong provider trade association advocacy;

- strong support of recipient advocacy groups;

- positive public perception of providers in the community; and

- political connections and influence with state political leaders.

All of these can contribute to the willingness of legislators and other policymakers to respond to provider interests rather than interests of state taxpayers (or, in some cases, Medicaid beneficiaries).

We might characterize providers in their approaches to Medicaid rate-setting as falling into four groups. The classification illustrated in table 10-1 has two dimensions that represent how vocal providers are in presenting demands and how influential they are relative to other providers

TABLE 10-1
PROVIDER CLASSIFICATION MATRIX WITH ILLUSTRATIVE PROVIDER TYPES
(DETAILS WILL VARY BY STATE)

	Influential	Not influential
Vocal	**Type I:** For example, hospitals and nursing facilities with special rates	**Type II:** For example, large physician groups or providers represented by trade associations
Not vocal	**Type III:** For example, CAHs, FQHCs, provider-based primary care	**Type IV:** For example, professional providers

of similar services. The clearest distinctions are between the vocal influential providers, who may already receive favorable treatment (in the upper left corner of the table) and the quiet, less influential providers in the bottom right corner. Type I providers are important providers (such as large teaching hospitals) whose services would be hard to replace, and they often have the political clout to influence Medicaid budget allocations. Type II providers can be vocal but, because alternative providers are readily available, they may not command the immediate attention of state policymakers; this group may include freestanding ambulatory surgery or imaging centers.

Type III providers typically do significant Medicaid business but may not need to press their cases aggressively to receive special treatment. They include nonprofit organizations with special relationships to state Medicaid programs or supported by requirements in federal law. Often these providers are in a mutually dependent relationship with Medicaid in that, while they may be highly reliant on public funding, they also supply services to populations the state has a responsibility to serve. When they serve significant numbers of persons who require state support but are not all Medicaid-eligible (such as the mentally ill, or disabled persons, or the lower-income uninsured), the state has an incentive to maintain generous

Medicaid payment rates to support their budgets and thus minimize the need for supplemental funding with 100 percent state dollars. These providers can be less publicly vocal, in part because Medicaid policymakers (federal and state) appreciate their role in dealing with vulnerable populations and have learned how to anticipate their payment needs and desires; federally qualified health centers (FQHCs), critical access hospitals (CAHs), and community mental health centers, for example, are often designated to receive favorable rates. They can also become quietly insistent and still receive their favored share of resources. Finally, type IV providers are generally under-represented in the payment rate debates; they attend to their business of providing services without a lot of complaint but may withdraw their services if their needs are not met. Various types of professional providers with small Medicaid shares fall into this category.

These groups are all-important Medicaid providers. Our point here is to characterize the distinct types of Medicaid relationships with the provider groups in discussions of payment rates.

Medicaid Provider Payment Strategies

States approach provider payment in different ways, reflecting local political processes and influences. Here we try to classify the basic payment strategies, recognizing that a state may employ more than one approach, as well as a variety of specific payment methods in implementation. The state may also, however, wish to adopt an explicit overall approach to rate-setting that reflects its primary objectives and apply it more or less consistently across service categories.

Low-Payment Strategies. Low-payment strategies may be favored by states with strong fiscal constraints, such as constitutional or political limitations on the ability to raise taxes, or by states with less influential providers or greater willingness to use regulatory means to reduce public costs. With this approach, virtually no "slack" is built in to cushion ebbs and flows of provider wages, device prices, or fluctuations in malpractice premiums. This creates risks that access to needed services will be impaired for some recipients at least some of the time.

- **Strategy 1: Set payment rates at the minimum necessary to induce an acceptable level of access to services.** This approach exercises monopsony (sole-purchaser) market power to set low rates and minimizes state spending subject to an access constraint; it accepts that Medicaid may pay less than its proportionate share of costs; it forgoes federal revenue opportunities but keeps state spending down; and it uses low Medicaid payment rates to exert some downward pressure on the overall costs of the local health care delivery system. In one version of this approach, the state only raises rates when pressed by providers through lobbyists or by threats of lawsuits or withdrawals of participation. In the long run, this may be cost-minimizing, but it runs the risk of creating inadequate access when providers find it easier to withdraw rather than raise the rate issue with policymakers, or when provider costs increase unexpectedly.

- **Strategy 2: Minimize the state Medicaid budget.** Many states appear to follow a strategy of Medicaid budget minimization, subject to political constraints that result from provider pressure. With such a strategy, rate increases are avoided or deferred when possible. Then Medicaid rates fail to keep up with inflation in medical costs and, over time, drift downward relative to other benchmarks. Periodically, some providers will gain enough influence with the legislature or the courts to force upon administrators a major upward adjustment. Others, without such influence, will see rates in real terms decline, which could eventually lead to their reduced participation. This is quite similar to strategy 1, but with less-intensive monitoring of access (or with the determination of "acceptable" access tasked to the political arena).

Mid-Payment Strategies. Mid-payment strategies may be favored by states that wish to provide a reasonable level of access to many, if not all, providers and wish to moderate the level of conflict with providers over payment rate issues.

- **Strategy 3: Set rates at some percentage of Medicare or other benchmark rate.** This approach accepts that the state budgeting process will lead to a budget that will not, for whatever reason, support payment at average market prices or Medicare rates. The benchmarks provide a guide to finding acceptable rates and a distribution of payments that are in line, at least proportionately, with those of other payers. This may serve either as a method to find rates to implement strategy 1, or a commitment to meet some politically acceptable target percentage of Medicare or private payment rates. It incorporates Medicare decisions about relative prices for different services or different kinds of providers, and so shields the Medicaid program from having to referee that kind of argument.

- **Strategy 4: Set rates at estimated marginal cost.** This approach tries to ensure access by covering provider marginal cost. It may not be entirely practical, as it requires figuring out the marginal costs for a wide range of services at widely varying potential levels of quality. Here, as elsewhere in health care, trying to assemble all the information needed to base payment on cost—even some notion of marginal cost—is a fool's errand. It may, nonetheless, be useful, if only as a general concept, for some states seeking to maintain provider participation and access to care at modest spending levels.

- **Strategy 5: Mete out pain proportionately in segmented markets.** With this approach, Medicaid assesses provider ability to absorb payment below average cost. Provider types such as hospitals and physicians that tend to serve a greater share of private payers are paid lower rates relative to private-sector rates and average costs. Provider types that serve proportionately more Medicaid patients, such as nursing homes and community health centers, are paid higher rates relative to private rates for similar services and average costs, as they have proportionately fewer private paying patients able to pay more than average cost and make up for any shortfall.

Higher-Payment Strategies. Higher-payment strategies may be favored in states where providers have considerable political influence or where voters support access for Medicaid recipients to mainstream providers.

- **Strategy 6: Set rates at or near Medicare levels.** Like strategy 3, this approach builds on the considerable research, political bargaining, and effort that have gone into determining relative payments for Medicare services. But it further accepts the federal budgeting political process as a basis for determining overall payment levels. This may not be a problem for states, as provider types that have been successful in achieving favorable rates at the federal level might tend to be equally influential at the state level. The strategy accepts the results of Medicare's process for setting urban and rural hospital classifications and rates—a process that is currently subject to considerable gaming by providers in some states. It also accepts Medicare's approach to physician payment, which has been criticized for underpaying primary care services. Since Medicare rates generally represent the federal upper payment limit (UPL), this approach effectively allows states to maximize federal matching payments.

- **Strategy 7: Set rates at local average or market rates.** This approach allows the other payers to determine the level of Medicaid payment. Whatever level of payment is determined by other payers, Medicaid pays its proportionate share of rates typical in the community. States could use other-payer benchmarks to set rates but would still be bound by Medicare upper payment limits, so any amount over the UPL would not be eligible for federal matching. Such market rates are more likely within Medicaid managed care plans, and, indeed, the ability of providers to get higher rates through managed care plans may be a motivation for providers to support adoption of managed care within Medicaid.

States can choose among these payment strategies depending on what their voter-taxpayers prefer. While budget minimization has some appeal to states in the short run, in the longer run such a low-cost approach to rate-setting can damage a state's Medicaid program more than taxpayers are willing to accept. States that follow such an approach for a number of years are likely to see provider rates well below those of Medicare and other payers. They are likely to hear complaints about "cost-shifting" from other providers who have the ability to sustain differential prices. The viability of providers unable to make such adjustments could be impaired, federal matching funds could be below what might otherwise be achieved, and the access of Medicaid patients to private medical providers could be reduced. The result might be increased pressure on safety-net providers, hospital emergency rooms, and state-funded health care programs.

But who really wins from low payment? From the whole-state point of view, it would seem that low payment misses an opportunity for obtaining additional federal revenue. Imposing taxes to enhance the Medicaid budget, then, might be better than following a low-payment strategy, unless the state is using lower payment rates to control access or limit health system resources. From a federal point of view, however, lower Medicaid provider payment rates clearly help keep costs low. With federal dollars accounting for 50 percent or more of Medicaid payments in every state, and 57 percent nationally, the federal government is the primary beneficiary of state Medicaid low-payment strategies, at least from a Medicaid-spending standpoint. State budgets are a secondary beneficiary.

Conclusion

With state legislatures playing the key role, states' Medicaid payment structures for various types of providers reflect a variety of influences within the democratic process. They reflect underlying voter preferences for approaching mainstream access for Medicaid recipients at the expense of higher public budgets. They reflect choices made in the tradeoff (within a given Medicaid budget) between improved access from higher payment rates versus using such funds to extend eligibility or provide greater coverage for recipients. They reflect the relative influence of providers of specific types in the state's political process. They also reflect how each state's policymakers have chosen to deal with necessarily limited information and state resources to devote to the rate-setting process. Finally, they reflect legislative and administrative choices in responding to needs as presented by those engaged in influencing the public decision process. In the end, how all this plays out in the democratic process reflects unique characteristics of each state, its voters, and its providers.

11

Medicaid Payment for Provider Equity

Medicaid providers regularly complain that Medicaid per-service rates are too low; business groups offering health insurance to their workers complain that when Medicaid pays less than its share of costs, costs are "shifted" to private payers. Evidence supports the contention that, for many types of providers, Medicaid programs often pay less than other payers. But is this a problem? Does it lead to higher private-sector prices and total expenses, and, if so, is that unfair or inefficient? Who benefits, and who loses when Medicaid pays less than other payers?

In this chapter we consider the general questions of setting Medicaid payment rates. Three types of criteria may be used for rate-setting:

- **Political criteria**—satisfying demands expressed by constituents (including taxpayers, beneficiaries, and providers)

- **Cost-based criteria**—basing rates on some measure of the estimated average or marginal cost of producing the services

- **Market-based criteria**—basing rates on observed market rates or the amount needed to induce the desired supply

Each of these approaches has some desirable characteristics. Each has some flexibility that would allow rates to be set high or low, depending on the specific criteria selected. In many states, one can find these approaches variously used to set rates for different types and groups of providers. We try to provide some guidance to states on the implications of alternative rate-setting strategies and some guidance to federal policymakers on how best to understand state payment strategies and support more rational rate-setting approaches. In the end, rate-setting decisions boil down to two components:

level and *distribution*. That is, first, how high or low to set rates, which affects the total resource or budget requirements; and, second, how to assign rates to services so as to compensate providers equitably for the services they deliver, which affects how those resources are distributed among providers.

Why States Can Set Medicaid Payment Rates Low

Health care markets can be viewed as "payer-segmented." That is, each segment of the market—defined by the payers Medicare, Medicaid, managed health care plans, and other private insurance, as well as self-payers—often arranges its own payment rates independently. For various reasons, medical care providers often accept different rates for similar services from distinct payer segments. Such differential prices for identical products are common in many industries. They occur in markets in which goods or, more commonly, services, cannot be resold, and in which buyers differ in market power or price sensitivity. Differential pricing in health care is common, and it exists in both the private and public sectors. In such a market, if a health plan lowers its payment rate, it does not lose access to all providers; some are likely to continue to supply some amount of care to some patients. Medicaid programs are able to pay lower rates than other payers in this segmented market and may choose to do so for several reasons:

- **Monopsony.** First, as a significant purchaser, Medicaid has some monopsony (buyer) power when it faces a large number of providers. It may, therefore, rationally choose to set rates low and accept some reduced supply and access to services (if the forgone services for a few recipients are viewed as worth less than savings on all). To keep the unit price low, Medicaid may refrain from raising the price it pays for additional quantity or quality—even if some providers might be willing to provide these increases at costs less than what Medicaid might pay—because it would have to pay the increased price to those providers who would have already been willing to take less. As economic theory says, monopsonist purchasers tend to pay lower prices and obtain fewer services than would occur in a fully competitive market. In this regard, value-seeking states may adopt a long-run policy of low provider payment, provided they are willing to accept what may be a two-quality care system, with Medicaid recipients having fewer choices of providers.

- **Temporary imbalance in financing.** At times, states facing the need to balance their budgets may find cuts in provider payment rates (and associated reductions in beneficiary access and quality) more politically palatable than explicitly cutting eligibility or benefits, making cuts in other state programs, or increasing tax rates. Providers cannot be blamed for not accepting lower prices, even if the major beneficiaries of the lower Medicaid prices are state taxpayers or those who benefit from other state programs. Of course, if Medicaid funding were on a more stable basis, this would not need to occur.

- **General medical cost control.** States may rationally choose to set rates low if they are unwilling to allow the Medicaid program to consume a large fraction of state resources, public and private, flowing into the local health care market. Setting Medicaid rates low to reduce the flow of funds to providers (particularly hospitals) can be viewed as constraining providers' abilities to invest in costly technology or provision of costly care.

Medicaid policymakers often want to know what will happen if they change payment rates. Will providers withdraw services if rates are cut? Will they provide more access or more services if they are increased? Provider responses to changes in Medicaid payment levels depend on several factors:

- The initial level of Medicaid payment, and how low or how high the changes in payment rates are

- The nature of local market competition for the service

- The provider's market setting and the share of Medicaid in the provider's business

- The provider's goals or objectives

- The relative importance of fixed versus marginal (variable) costs

Some providers, for their part, may choose to accept low Medicaid payment rates. Those with excess capacity and some fixed costs may willingly accept Medicaid rates if those rates cover marginal costs (but they will stop doing so if they reach capacity). Those altruistic providers who are willing to sacrifice their own or their employees' net money incomes in the interest of doing good may take less than if they pursued profit maximization or even sought to break even. Some providers who serve privately insured patients may find ways to differentiate the amenities and services they provide to Medicaid recipients, such as offering them the less desirable appointment times, so that Medicaid patients do not displace their more lucrative private patients. Some in lower-income markets will find ways to adopt lower-cost practice patterns, with shorter visits and greater use of nonphysician clinical staff, perhaps lowering marginal costs enough that Medicaid services contribute to net income. Public or community hospitals with defined public missions may simply accept the low rates as part of doing business, seek subsidies from local taxpayers or philanthropists, and adjust services and staffing patterns to meet available budget from all sources, including Medicaid, Medicare, private insurance, self-pay, and uncompensated care.

Can Medicaid Shift Costs?

A common claim is that when Medicaid payments are cut, providers, particularly hospitals, shift their costs to other payers. Many economists are doubtful of such claims, as they seem to contradict some basic economic models. Between these two extremes, we have our own view of what kind of "cost-shifting" might be going on in connection with Medicaid.

Models of Medicaid Provider Payment. In an article in *Health Affairs*, Al Dobson and others provide an analysis of hospital revenue by payer source and argue that "hospital cost shifting is alive and well," and that the sustainability of low public-sector hospital payment rates depends on the "private payers' willingness to accept a rising cost-shift burden."[1] They note that public payers (Medicare and Medicaid) tend to pay hospitals less than average costs, and that private payers (mostly with private insurance) pay them more than average cost. Their model, unfortunately and inaccurately termed (by them) a "hydraulic" model, seems to imply that pushing down on public-sector hospital payment rates automatically pushes up private insurance rates—that costs are shifted from one payer to another.

But a hydraulic system only works when it is a closed system with no leakages or other places for the hydraulic fluid (in this case, hospital resources) to go. This model does not account for the great flexibility in hospital costs due to production decisions on staffing levels, services offered, and intensity of use, nor does it allow hospitals to suffer losses in the short run, which they may offset with philanthropy or other sources of net revenue in the longer run. The wide variation we see in hospital costs even within market areas tells us there is no such thing as "the cost," which must either be covered or cause losses and shutdown if payment is reduced below some absolute threshold. A hospital day or admission is not a precisely defined measure of output with a unique cost; rather, the content of services in a day or a stay can vary substantially. The model also does not account for the possibility that the hospital may have already set a private price so high that further increases will drive away patients, to the extent that less, rather than more, net revenue is collected in the private segment of the market. For this reason, a closed-system, fixed-production hydraulic model is clearly not appropriately applied to production of hospital services.

Medicaid Cost-Shifting. Dobson and colleagues base their assertion that cost-shifting exists in hospitals on empirical grounds: Hospitals are observed to receive different amounts from different payers for the same services.[2] In what sense do different payment rates constitute "cost-shifting"? In the limited sense in which Dobson uses the term, cost-shifting exists because some pay more than others, so those who pay more are subsidizing those who pay less. This cross-subsidization is termed "cost-shifting" by Dobson and some others who focus on low Medicaid payment, rather than market forces, as a cause of high private-sector medical costs.

Is differential pricing really cost-shifting? Most economists would probably say no. An economic definition of cost-shifting would involve the ability of firms faced with a lower price from one buyer to raise the price for another without reducing profit, with everything else held constant. Under this definition, economic cost-shifting may not exist in the simple case of price discrimination, where two customers pay different amounts for the same service. Two adjacent airline seats sold at different prices may not represent cost-shifting even if one is sold below average cost, since the airline is constrained in each market segment. The airline may be maximizing what it can get for each seat sold in different submarkets. If it maximized profit in each submarket, would the airline lower the price of the business-priced seat simply because it discovered it could sell the tourist seat for more? In this case, most economists would argue, the airline is not in a position to shift costs in an operational sense, even though it maximizes profits by charging different fares for adjacent seats. This story can even apply to changes over time. If tourist demand becomes more price-elastic at about the same time as business demand becomes less price-elastic, business fares will rise and tourist fares will fall, but the one will in no sense be the cause of the other.

Similarly, most economists would not take observed differences in hospital payment rates as conclusive evidence that hospitals have the ability to shift costs. In the alternative model, hospitals may set or negotiate payment rates with private payers to maximize profit or surplus and be price-takers in the Medicare and Medicaid markets. So long as the public payers pay more than marginal cost, the hospital may find it advantageous to serve them and receive rates below those it receives from private payers. This may well be profitable in the sense that the hospital can generate more than it spends with this strategy.

A nonprofit community hospital may, however, choose to plow any surplus into salaries, high-tech equipment that makes its doctors more productive and reduces waits for patients, and amenities in its facilities for patients and staff. Particularly in the long run, the hospital very likely has more flexibility in raising or lowering its costs than it does in influencing the rates it is able to obtain from private payers, and certainly from Medicare or Medicaid. The hospital is already maximizing what it can get from the private market, so any Medicaid rate reduction is likely to lead to a reduction in some aspect of service intensity (and cost) rather than higher rates for private payers.

In the alternative, hospitals might respond to a shortfall in government-payer revenue by reducing quality, intensity, or amenities in service for all users. Hospitals would do this because lower Medicaid margins reduce the revenue available to support higher quality and because, if they are already maximizing profit in the private market, shaving quality perhaps imperceptibly may be preferable to raising private prices above the profit-maximizing level and risking loss of business. Costs are not shifted in the sense of the economists' definition above, in that private payer prices do not go up; rather, all patients are affected by reduced quality or intensity of services.

Such an alternative is consistent with the empirical evidence. Not-for-profit hospitals operate at stable low margins by spending their full revenue streams to produce services at the best level the multipayer revenue stream allows. We observe private payers' payment rates as a percentage of hospital cost to be higher where Medicaid payment rates are lower. But this is entirely consistent with our model. What happens to the payment-to-cost ratio when hospital Medicaid payments are lowered? Lower public payment rates lead to a reduced revenue stream; that leads to reduced costs. This reduces the denominators of both public and private payment-to-cost ratios. But the numerator only changes for the public ratio; the numerator (price) in the private submarket can (and would in our model) remain unchanged. Thus, the private price-to-cost ratio changes without changing the true price for the private payers.[3] Lower Medicaid payment need not lead to higher private payment, and we still see the private-sector payment-to-cost ratio going up. But this is due to comparatively lower costs, not higher private prices.

One can ask whether the technology of hospital production would allow for such adjustments in quality and cost. We think this is quite plausible. Hospitals paid prospectively per admission—for instance, by diagnosis-related groups (DRGs), or even on a per-diem basis—can change quality on many dimensions without affecting payment. To save costs, they can reduce nurse staffing ratios, delay acquisition of new technology, get by with fewer MRI units (imposing longer waits), reduce amenities in waiting areas, or cut the cafeteria or parking subsidy. Some hospitals that might not have already fully exploited the possibilities might also reduce wages by exercising previously unused monopsony power in the market for nurses and medical technologists; those with research and teaching programs might reduce their programs.

In this alternative model, the hospital maximizes profit in the private market but takes the prices set in the public sector and then adjusts quality to break even. The hospital thus imposes a cost on the private payers, not in terms of prices paid, which are already set to maximize profit, but in the form of reduced quality. This is cost-shifting in a sense, perhaps, but not by the economists' definition, and not in a form that can be measured by price–cost markup or even actual prices paid. Rather, it is manifest in the reduced quality, access, and amenities in care borne by all hospital patients and, perhaps to some degree, by the staff as well.

Here or elsewhere, we see support for what we might call "burden-shifting" rather than cost-shifting. Burden-shifting can be viewed as a change in the amount of cross-subsidy inherent in differential prices that could be due to price discrimination. This does not require the price response required by the "hydraulic" definition. Public debate usually focuses on the perceived inequities of the obvious price differential. Policymakers only go awry when they occasionally try to infer behaviorally that higher public payments will reduce private prices, or, conversely, that lower public prices will lead to higher private prices.

Policymakers can stay on solid ground identifying Medicaid as contributing to differential pricing and perhaps constraining resources in the system. They should not assert that Medicaid can make private insurers pay more than what the hospital has already obtained from them under current market conditions. Rather, they might acknowledge the possibility of burden-shifting, which can be viewed as sharing the burden of lower quality and fewer amenities in the standard of care that may occur for all users as a result of low public payment. This definition focuses on the quality-related behavioral response to resource constraints that is more consistent with theory, hospital behavior, and hospital production technology than is a price response.

All of this is consistent with the so-called evidence of cost-shifting in differential payment rates offered by Dobson and others. Some may prefer to call it cost-shifting either because of the differential payments or because the hospital cuts service for all. Some may prefer to say the hospital responded by reducing costs rather than shifting them (and held private payments constant). But, in either case, we see no evidence that lower Medicaid payment rates are likely to lead to higher private payment rates, or that higher Medicaid payment rates will result in reduced costs for the private payers. Moreover, careful econometric analysis of cost-shifting in the period of the 1990s and beyond has found very little evidence of substantial cost-shifting in the short run, with estimates ranging from 4 to 17 percent of the reduction in public plan payment levels.[4] We see no sense in which existing costs are shifted to private payers; in fact, the consequence of lower payment is that system costs are lower, though if private payments are the same, the private insurers will end up paying a larger share of the reduced total.

Effect of Medicaid Payment Rates on Private Payers. The cost-shifting question is also interesting to pose in reverse: What would hospitals do with additional revenues if public payers, specifically Medicaid, were to pay at more generous rates? Would they automatically use them to reduce charges to private insurers?

The answers may rest on hospital incentives and management behavior. There is no reason to believe that a hospital would necessarily devote all these new funds to reducing the prices charged to private payers. Whether that would happen at all depends on how it fits with hospital goals. Economic models of the not-for-profit hospital have variously suggested that managers might seek to maximize hospital importance as reflected in bed size, volume of services, or total revenue, or that hospitals might seek prestige from adopting the latest technology (such as technology for diagnostic imaging, cardiac surgery, cancer treatment, or electronic medical records). In a manager- or physician-controlled institution, the hospital might seek to maximize resources, providing more adequately staffed and equipped facilities to minimize burden on managers and provide more revenue opportunities for physicians.

Each of these plausible goals has implications for how not-for-profit hospitals would spend additional revenue. None, however, includes an immediate rationale for returning revenue to private payers. If reducing private prices might bring in a large number of new customers, that might please a hospital that cared about the volume of output in general or the volume provided to taxpaying citizens of the community. Some hospitals claim they owe allegiance to middle-class people in their communities who would benefit from lower insurance premiums resulting from lower hospital charges. We would not expect for-profit hospitals to reduce private payer payments in response to an increase in Medicaid rates, unless there were a strong desire to curry good will on the parts of local movers and shakers who would notice this action.

As we have suggested in our alternative view to the Dobson hydraulic model—one more realistic and better founded in economic theory—

224 MEDICAID EVERYONE CAN COUNT ON

hospitals operate in a payer-segmented market. The rates paid by one payer segment are largely determined independently of other payers. Hospitals do the best they can to maximize revenue in each segment, then provide the services that can be supported by the revenue obtainable—that is, the services that can be delivered for the average payment rate obtained from all payers. Any extra revenue the hospital may obtain from the private sector is used to support enhanced services, and any decline in revenue from Medicaid and Medicare will most likely be reflected in future service levels and quality, not in a return of revenue to private payers or reduced private-sector prices for hospital services. Services and technology (cost, quality, accessibility), not the prices of other payers, are adapted to the available resources, including Medicaid payments as part of the mix. In this payer-segmented, service-integrated market model, private-sector prices depend on the nature of competition in local provider markets, local use patterns, and the extent of care management to control use—not, to any appreciable degree, on Medicaid payment levels.

These competitive factors are crucial, particularly in explaining differences in the effects of low Medicaid payment levels on the hospital services markets, as opposed to the professional services markets. Hospitals have enough market power to shave quality to meet budgets affected by low Medicaid payments, and some have a community expectation that they will serve Medicaid patients even at substandard payment rates. Professional providers, however, can and do more readily turn down Medicaid participation or limit the number of Medicaid patients they serve.[5] They may also be better able to provide distinctly different levels in some dimensions of quality—by giving Medicaid patients less favorable appointment times and, in larger practices, seeing them in separate office locations with shorter visits. Some with many lower-income patients may develop a distinctly lower-cost style of practice.

The point is that professional providers will tend to respond to lower public prices in ways that differ from hospitals. They may refuse to see Medicaid patients, which reduces access. Other professional providers may choose to differentiate service levels by contact time, by location, or by the extent of other services, such as lab tests—that is, some providers may be able to develop lower-cost, and perhaps lower-quality, Medicaid-friendly practice styles. So for professional providers, but not usually for hospitals, state Medicaid policymakers need to be more cognizant of the resulting limits on access and quality when considering low payment rates. The effect on quality may also be greater among physicians and dentists, as we are suggesting service-integrated hospitals provide essentially the same quality to everyone, and the effect of low Medicaid payment is diluted among all users. But professional providers have more opportunity to segment services and reduce at least some dimensions of quality or amenities for the Medicaid segment of the market. It is really these factors that need to be considered in determining how low Medicaid rates should be set.

How Low Can You Go? How low can, or should, Medicaid rates be set? If Medicaid costs could really be shifted, the answer to both parts of this question would have to be "very low," because any Medicaid payment cut could always be accommodated by cost-shifting; neither access nor quality need suffer. But that proposition would be absurd for a provider with few privately insured customers and is not consistent with the view that many physicians avoid Medicaid patients, since they could just take them and then cost-shift.[6]

A more realistic answer may depend on circumstances and vary greatly among types of providers, based on the providers' reliance on Medicaid as a revenue source and the availability of other potential sources of payment. Some types of providers will be more capable of sustaining underpayment by Medicaid programs than others. Some nursing homes, for example, are highly dependent on Medicaid as a source of payment, with Medicaid (and resident Medicaid spend-down payments) accounting for up to perhaps 90 percent of revenue in some intermediate care facilities. Hospitals and physicians, on the other hand, typically have a mix of patients; their Medicaid business typically accounts for less than 20 percent of patients and an even lower percentage of revenue. In times of budget necessity, therefore, states interested in preserving access to care for Medicaid recipients may find hospitals and physicians better able to absorb payment reductions than nursing homes and other Medicaid-dependent providers. The ability of states to set payments low (relative to market prices or costs) for specified types of providers depends on the share of Medicaid in their payment mix and the elasticity supply in that market. Table 11-1 provides our subjective assessment of how these factors may affect the potential for low payment for some common types of Medicaid providers.

TABLE 11-1

POTENTIAL FOR LOW PAYMENT FOR MEDICAID SERVICES
FOR SELECTED PROVIDER TYPES

Service type	Medicaid share	Supply elasticity	Low-payment potential
Inpatient hospital	Low	Low	Great
Outpatient hospital	Low	Medium	Moderate
Physician services	Medium	High	Moderate
Nursing home	Very high	Low	Small
Home and community services	High	High	Small
Ambulance services	Low	Low	Great

The main point here is that state Medicaid programs choosing a low-payment strategy for rate-setting should be cognizant (in the various provider markets) of both Medicaid market shares and supply elasticity and adjust Medicaid payments accordingly. A state that chooses a simple rule, such as "pay 80 percent of Medicare," may seem to equalize the percentage burden of Medicaid low payment, but it is likely to impose the greatest burdens of quality and amenity inefficiency on providers that participate most heavily in Medicaid, and risk losing needed providers in the more supply-elastic markets. In contrast, a state that wishes to avoid such problems will need to develop rates that account for Medicaid market shares and supply elasticity along the lines we have suggested.

In fact, we observe states following such strategies to preserve access to doctors who provide some of the services most commonly used in Medicaid. For example, many states choose to pay a higher percentage of Medicare payment rates for prenatal and obstetrical care and delivery and for the "evaluation and management" codes (used on claims for primary care office visits) than they do for specialist physician services. This may be due in part to the importance for Medicaid of ensuring access to primary care providers and in part to a Medicare rate structure that, some have claimed, underpays for primary care services. In any case, ensuring access to primary care is a priority for Medicaid payment policy, particularly for the non–dually eligible recipients for whom services are paid at Medicaid, not Medicare, rates. Medicaid should not blindly follow Medicare in the rate-setting process.

Providers Sharing the Burden of Medicaid. Can we then provide guidance to states on how any impact of low Medicaid payment rates might be shared among providers? How might they want the burden to be shared, assuming their horizon goes beyond the Medicaid program and extends to payments and incomes in the private sector? Some combination of fairness and political judgment is called for.

Let's assume that Medicare payment rates represent an approximation of the average cost of services efficiently provided at a quality level acceptable to Medicaid.[7] In that case, a provider of average efficiency would be able to break even at Medicare rates, and community standards of care would develop around Medicare payment levels. (Indeed, even if Medicare's rates were initially set above cost, competition among providers might increase standards of care and associated cost by enough so that, in equilibrium, providers would break even.) Many acute care providers are able to obtain higher payments from private insurers than from Medicare and Medicaid. Taking Medicare as an approximation for break-even rates, Medicaid payment rates—for hospitals, for example—can be below average cost for most providers of service at community standards of quality.

Provider response will depend to a large degree on the level of competition in the private-sector market and on the flexibility in the long run to adjust production methods that may affect cost and standards of care quality (access waiting times, facility amenities, and wages). A not-for-profit hospital in a less competitive market will have the greatest flexibility here. With local monopoly (dominant provider) power and some monopsony (dominant purchaser as employer) power in its local specialized labor markets (such as nursing), such a hospital, even if it is already optimizing in its private segment, can adjust to changes in Medicaid pricing. Higher Medicaid payment will raise revenue and give the hospital resources that could be used, for example, to

- acquire new diagnostic imaging equipment, perhaps reducing waiting times for use and encouraging more frequent use of such diagnostic tests;

- develop new programs in specialized care, such as cancer care or cardiac surgery; or

- provide more amenities in public and staff spaces.

Whatever these may be, what is important here is that, in the long run, standards and expectations for hospital services can vary greatly and depend on the resources made available. In noncompetitive, not-for-profit hospital markets, the production and cost of care depends on resources made available by Medicare, by Medicaid, and by what can be obtained from the private payers. In more competitive markets, the level of resources may depend on demand and how it is supported locally by the proportion of the population with employer-sponsored insurance and public entities.

So, in conclusion on this particular issue, Medicaid cannot be much to blame for high private-sector costs, though it may bear just a bit of the responsibility (with relationship to its market share) for the volume, intensity, quality, and amenities of care offered by providers to all their patients.

Achieving an Equitable Distribution of Payments

Up to this point, we have been discussing the overall level of provider payments. An overall strategy for payments provides a framework for such decisions. Next, we turn to the question of how to set relative payment rates that are fair to different providers. We outline key considerations and comment on what might be desirable, or at least acceptable, policy.

Provider Motivations for Medicaid Participation. The effect of low Medicaid payment rates on provider participation may differ among providers, particularly professional providers, depending on how willing or committed a provider or practice is to serving the poor or meeting the needs of its service area. From one viewpoint, discriminating among providers to identify those willing to work for less supports the objective of holding down Medicaid spending, but, from another viewpoint, discrimination here as elsewhere in economic markets will appear unfair to those who would have gotten more under a uniform payment policy. Still, a high-priced provider's claim of discrimination from a Medicaid program's unwillingness to pay that high price may not evoke a great deal of sympathy. Providers vary in their level of commitment to the program, and this is important to keep in mind in developing payment policy. We identify four distinct groups of providers:

- **Committed providers** are those who may be particularly committed to serving the poor, and who may locate in underserved areas with this intent and develop a practice style that can be supported by Medicaid and other programs for the lower-income population. These providers may adapt to available Medicaid payment and continue to serve Medicaid clients. For providers serving lower-income populations, Medicaid may pay more than can be obtained from many patients, particularly the uninsured. This committed group can be "exploited" up to a point, as they will continue to participate at low payment rates. Perhaps their satisfaction in serving Medicaid patients is its own reward.

- **Willing providers** are those who may be willing to serve what they perceive as their fair or target share of Medicaid patients. They may limit the number of Medicaid patients and voice concerns about inadequate participation of other providers and inadequate payment rates. These are the marginal Medicaid providers, whose participation depends critically on adequate payment and the perceived burden of serving Medicaid patients.

- **Reluctant providers** may not see any particular obligation to participate in Medicaid. They may be willing to service Medicaid patients only if the program pays rates that cover costs—say, Medicare-equivalent rates. These reluctant providers may not participate if they are offered rates significantly below Medicare or the average cost of providing services at community standards.

- **Unwilling providers** may see serving Medicaid patients as inconsistent with their professional or business objectives. They have adopted a private market strategy, and they are not willing to serve Medicaid even if rates are at the Medicare upper payment limit, and even if they serve some Medicare patients at those rates. These unwilling providers' style of practice may not be compatible with having Medicaid families in their waiting rooms, or with the higher rates of broken appointments common in the Medicaid population. In most cases, these providers will not see more than the occasional Medicaid patient.

Policymakers need to be aware of all these groups. Even the unwilling providers are important to Medicaid payment policy, as their existence can create perceptions of inequity in the provider community. Willing providers and even committed providers may question their own willingness to participate if they perceive themselves to be taking on an unfair share of Medicaid patients, and this perceived burden will be directly related to low Medicaid payment rates. Some argue that provider participation is voluntary and, therefore, Medicaid should not be particularly concerned about such arguments. Others seeking to address a perceived inequity suggest policymakers take seriously proposals by participating providers to prescribe by law or licensing requirements that all providers must serve a minimum share of Medicaid recipients. We do not see such a regulated system as practical or consistent with Medicaid's tradition of voluntary provider participation. Nonetheless, policymakers should take note that perceived equity may be important to at least some providers, and that adequate payment rates may affect provider perceptions of equity, provider participation, and access to care for some Medicaid recipients.

Provider Response Factors to Consider. As we have discussed, the effect of low Medicaid rates is likely to depend on the provider's type and situation. Nonfavored low-volume Medicaid providers, such as physician practices, may simply withdraw from Medicaid participation; hospitals with some local monopoly power may respond to lower rates by reducing service intensity, effectively adjusting costs to meet available revenue from all payment sources. In this situation, many states have chosen to keep costs low and accept some reduced access in the professional provider market, provide rates above the Medicaid average to Medicaid-affected providers such as federally qualified health centers (FQHCs) and community mental health centers with significant Medicaid shares, and allow hospitals to adjust the quality of care for all to adapt to low Medicaid payments, using DSH payments to ameliorate their impact only for those hospitals with significant Medicaid shares.

The effects of low rates depend on the type of provider, and they call for careful consideration by the states that set them. Low inpatient hospital payment rates will likely lead to a diminished flow of funds to hospitals and may result in marginally lower quality and amenities for all hospital users.

Low rates for physicians (and other professional providers) will likely reduce provider participation and access to services, which can, in turn, lead to less use of preventive services and greater use of more expensive care settings, such as emergency rooms and other hospital outpatient services. Low nursing home payment rates may lead to lower levels of staffing and quality in Medicaid-dependent facilities.

In all cases, we expect providers to respond to low rates by shifting patient mix and services where possible to maximize net reimbursement. Especially when some rates for some providers are low and others are not, this can lead to distortion in the patterns of care, possibly diverting patients from the most cost-effective providers. For example, paying independent physicians less than is paid for similar services in hospital outpatient departments of FQHCs may lead to higher costs than necessary. States should take all these factors into consideration and ensure that the rate structure of the Medicaid program reflects their choice as to the degrees of access, quality, and efficiency they desire.

Finally, it is worth noting that there may be a tradeoff between care management and low rates as a means of controlling service use. States with managed care programs must purchase such services in the market and, hence, typically pay higher per-service rates to providers; but they may with managed care have better control over utilization. Thus, we seem to have linked the cost and access control issues: Medicaid programs based on fee for service may be more prone to rely on low rates to control access, while states with managed care can afford to pay a limited subset of providers more competitive rates per unit, and perhaps even in total. The issues of provider payment rates, revenue sources (taxes), utilization control, and provider equity are interlinked and call for a single, consistent payment and care management strategy.

Conclusion

Provider payment levels are a key Medicaid policy issue—important in determining provider participation and access to care, as well as levels of state (and federal) spending. We are unconvinced by arguments that Medicaid is responsible for shifting costs, at least in a way that makes private payers pay substantially more than providers are already able to charge them in what are often fairly uncompetitive local markets for health services. In our model, low Medicaid payment leads some providers (for example, physicians) to refrain from participating in the program and others (such as hospitals) to find ways to produce services for all at lower costs; rather than shifting costs, low payment leads to less extensive care for all patients. We prefer, therefore, the term "burden-sharing" to "cost-shifting" when referring to this phenomenon.

As to how high or low rates should be set, we suggest policymakers seek to pay what is needed to obtain the level of access to care desired by voter-taxpayers for Medicaid patients. There is no one right answer in a democracy—some will be willing to pay taxes to support access equal to that of fully insured private patients; others will have different priorities for public spending or lower taxes.

12

Implementing Payment Policy

Having discussed payment strategy and payment levels, we are now ready to consider how to achieve these objectives through the rate-setting process. We are mainly talking about fee-for-service Medicaid here, but some of the principles will apply in Medicaid managed care contracting as well.

Rate-Setting Methods

The considerable freedom that states have with rate-setting comes with a responsibility to use justifiable methods to arrive at equitable payment rates for all providers. Many different prospective and retrospective rate-setting methods have been developed over the years since Medicaid was established. These might be generally classified as

- benchmarking;
- competitive bidding;
- rate adjustments;
- evidence-based methods; and
- pay for performance.

Benchmarking Methods. Benchmarking involves setting rates by making comparisons with what other payers are paying for the same services. Medicare and private-sector rates, as well as Medicaid rates in nearby or similar states, can provide useful benchmarks for state Medicaid rate-setting functions.

233

Medicare Rates. Medicare rates provide convenient and logical benchmarks for Medicaid, but with some caveats. Medicare employs some useful measures of the relative costliness of many services which have been developed based on objective research into the cost of producing them. Diagnosis-related groups (DRGs) for hospitals and resource-based relative value scale (RBRVS) units for professional services are examples. But the rates Medicare pays do not always correspond to such measures. Medicare payment levels across providers and types of providers can reflect the political influence of provider groups in Washington in setting rates overall for categories of providers. Moreover, rates paid depend on how providers are classified, and Congress has established many intricate rules for provider classification— sometimes designed to favor providers in specific legislators' districts. Additionally, providers working within these classification rules may have the ability to reclassify themselves to maximize payment. This is particularly true with respect to Medicare hospital payment rates, which in recent years have become subject to provider manipulation to such a degree that in some states the integrity of the rate structure has been effectively destroyed for both inpatient and some outpatient services in some areas.

Two distinct issues relate to provider classification. One is the classification of a hospital for payment purposes as an urban or rural hospital, a rural referral center, a sole-community hospital, or a critical access hospital. Each status has distinct implications for payment purposes under Medicare, and this classification can affect Medicaid as well. The second issue is classification of providers that affiliate with a hospital as "provider-based." Each of these is part of a diverse array of special provider payment preferences that Congress has added over the years.

First, for inpatient hospital classification, the main point is not that differential rates shouldn't be made at all, but that they ought to be made for well-justified purposes. Rural hospitals, for example, have a legitimate case for higher rates only if they can be justified on economic grounds. To ensure the availability of hospitals in rural areas, higher rates may be appropriate to compensate for these hospitals' greater tendency to have unfilled beds and excess capacity than urban hospitals, which can capture larger economies of scale. We suspect that much of the perceived need for higher payments in rural areas is not cost-related at all, however, but rather arises from the lower proportion of the population privately insured there, which limits the ability of providers to cross-subsidize and sustain services at low Medicaid (and, to a lesser degree, Medicare) payment rates.

Whatever the source or justifiable need for higher payments, the size of any rate differential ought to be grounded in some objective criteria and the calculations of cost accountants or economists or actuaries—not the political influence of particular hospitals' Congress members to provide loopholes for classification or other access to more favorable rates than are available to other providers. Significant problems can occur when a Congress member can be persuaded to argue even for an urban hospital to be classified as rural (for some contrived or trumped-up reason) to get the higher rates.

We are so far now from the original purposes of provider classification that a case can be made for just starting over and insisting hospitals meet real, objective criteria and be placed in the most appropriate payment categories. We suggest, for instance, that teaching hospitals and research programs in children's hospitals be paid separately for educational and research-related services through an accountable system that looks at performance based on their accomplishments in those areas. The present system for tacking on teaching differentials or payments to Medicare and Medicaid rates may be convenient, but it does not relate payment to the content or value of services delivered. If the costs of medical education are to be publicly supported, they should be covered in a way that better ensures the return of the value of such expenses to the taxpayers—by offering loans to medical students with generous forgiveness provisions for subsequent community or public health service, for example. Simply tacking graduate medical education expenses onto Medicare and Medicaid provides extra money without extra accountability to a select few providers and may do little to improve access to care for Medicaid recipients more generally.

The ratcheting effect of such detailed, legislative-granted favors in rate classification can, in the end, be pointless and inequitable. Specific urban providers are given special rates to compensate for their higher costs. Then specific rural providers are given special rates to account for the need to ensure access and compensate for low service volumes. Providers in in-between areas then seek legislative permission to reclassify in one of the favored categories. After a time, in relative terms, everyone is back where they started with only a few unlucky (or poorly represented) providers left without the favored rates. It may make more sense just to pay everyone the same rates for identical services, regardless of where they are delivered.

The second problem with Medicare as a benchmark is provider-based status. Provider-based status is granted by Medicare to providers who choose to operate (or at least submit bills through) a hospital. This arrangement has advantages for the provider under Medicare, and often Medicaid, as professional services can be billed as higher-paid hospital outpatient services even if they are simply office visits provided off the hospital campus. This is permitted by Medicare regulations, which allow providers to obtain provider-based status with a hospital by attesting to meeting rather minimal requirements of integration and control by the main entity.[1] Paying a set percentage of Medicare in this situation might lead a state to overpay for professional services of providers with provider-based status and perhaps underpay similar providers without such a hospital affiliation.

We don't really want to prohibit hospital affiliations if providers choose to organize that way, but they should do so because the hospital provides the best administrative or facility services, not because it is the ticket to higher Medicare and Medicaid rates. If Medicare and Medicaid were to pay the same regardless of affiliation as represented by provider-based status, thus ending the payment incentive of hospital affiliation, professional practices would likely soon find that their billing services could be provided as efficiently by data system firms as by their local hospitals.

Private-Sector Rates. Private-sector rates are generally much higher than Medicaid rates and reflect more local market effects than Medicare benchmarks. Measures of private-sector rates can be more difficult to come by, as they are generally less available publicly, and when available may emerge only with some delay. Because private rates are higher than what Medicaid typically pays, they may be less directly useful as benchmarks. But again, it is the relative rates that are important here, and they may nonetheless be useful as a guide to rates that may reflect (better than Medicare does) local market influences. States may choose some percentage less than 100 percent of private rates as a policy target, and this target percentage may be appropriately lower where the market power of providers and health plans relative to employers is strong and private prices are greater.

Other States' Medicaid Rates. Other states' Medicaid rates can serve as useful benchmarks for state rate-setting. They may, however, reflect deviations that depend on state-specific policy and budgeting issues. Rate levels in adjacent states can indicate what is possible within a geographic area, while more distant states with similar demographic, economic, and/or health system characteristics may also provide useful comparisons for rate levels and payment methods.

Competitive Bidding Methods. Although competitive bidding methods have long been used in Medicaid on a limited basis—for capitated managed care such as Arizona's ACCESS program and for hospital services in California, for example[2]—Medicaid programs have traditionally set payment rates for their fee-for-service medical services either through fixed fee schedules or cost-based reimbursement.[3] A number of issues must be considered to apply competitive bidding concepts to fee-for-service programs. The key issue is how to preserve adequate access to services while limiting the provider network to those with contracts. We offer a few suggestions to states contemplating competitive bidding for fee-for-service Medicaid services:

- **Identify competitive markets.** Services put out to bid must be ones for which competition or potential competition is adequate in the local market to which the bidding applies. There have to be enough legitimate bidders beforehand and enough winning bidders selected to serve the Medicaid share of the market adequately.

- **Exclude emergency services.** For obvious reasons, states will not want to limit the choice of providers for emergency care. This makes emergency services unlikely candidates for competitive bidding.

- **Exclude dual-eligibles.** For Medicare-covered services, states pay Medicaid's share (usually part B premiums, deductibles, and copayments), while the price of the service is determined by Medicare. Consequently, states will not wish to include dual-eligibles for Medicare-covered services in competitive bidding.

- **Include costly services.** Operating a competitive bidding process will entail some administrative costs for bid solicitation and contracting and for directing patients to contracted providers. From a cost containment standpoint, competitive bidding will only make sense if it applies to services that entail significant costs, either with respect to high cost-per-unit services (such as cardiac surgery) or high-volume services (such as outpatient radiology or outpatient surgery).

- **Include less costly settings.** Competitive bidding, coupled with prior authorization to direct patients to contracted providers, can help encourage use of lower-priced care settings, such as ambulatory surgery centers (versus inpatient or outpatient hospital care) or rehabilitation hospitals (versus acute care hospitals).

- **Be prepared to pay competitive prices.** If prices in a market are already at competitive levels, bidding will lead to prices at about the same levels. Consequently, states with fee schedules well below competitive levels will not see savings from competitive bidding unless it entails substantial substitution of less costly for more costly forms of care. If the state is interested in rock-bottom costs, or cost savings alone, fee schedule adjustments may achieve lower rates than competitive bidding.

- **Use bidding when prices are not known to be competitive or costs are not known.** Bidding will elicit a price that just covers cost when the buyer does not know what the cost is or, by extension, does not know whether prevailing market prices just cover cost. Putting forth the expense and effort of implementing a competitive bidding system is unnecessary if the state already knows the rates it wants to pay and can set rates at that level.

- **Use competitive bidding to increase control over quality.** Another reason to consider competitive bidding is to obtain better control over the quality of services delivered. Medicaid's traditional requirement of open provider participation in its fee-for-service system gives states little leverage over the quality of services delivered by licensed providers. Competitive bidding can give Medicaid the choice of contracting with providers who meet specified quality standards, and contracted providers may be more attentive to Medicaid needs and more responsive in solving problems when they arise.

- **Ensure transportation for access.** If the number of providers is limited by contracts, the state should ensure the availability of Medicaid-reimbursed transportation to get patients to contracted providers.

Competitive bidding as a provider payment strategy is best pursued by states interested in using a process to help determine competitive payment rates, and to encourage provision of services in less costly settings and adoption of less costly forms of care. Since a state taking a competitive bidding approach gives up its ability to set rates below prevailing competitive levels, pursuing competitive bidding for some services as part of a Medicaid fee-for-service payment strategy entails—as it does for capitated managed care—giving up control over prices paid to rely on the market processes. The competitive bidding approach may not be suitable for every state or every service. It is not appropriate if the state desires to pay providers at rates below those prevailing in competitive markets and is willing to accept the lower quality and/or limited access that presumably accompany the lower prices.

Rate Adjustment Approaches. As a practical matter, many states seem to change provider payment rates only when they have to—that is, when compelled by previous agreement, law, market forces, or political pressure. Other states tend routinely to apply specified percentage adjustments to all providers based on the available budget. In either case, existing rates are then taken as a starting point for any negotiated changes, and the rate-setting process becomes one of finding adjustments to existing rates.

A more refined approach to finding such adjustments would be to allow rates to be sensitive to market conditions. In the private sector we see that payment rates for medical services tend to depend somewhat on supply, as reflected in the number of available providers and the extent of competition in local markets, and on demand, as reflected in the extent of insurance coverage. In contrast, federally set Medicare payment rates tend to be uniform, designed to approximate average costs, with variations arising only from a limited number of parameters, such as local wage rates. Should state Medicaid programs try to follow Medicare, or should states set rates that more strongly reflect local market conditions? Medicare-like rates might better reflect the cost of delivering the greater degree of access usually offered to Medicare beneficiaries and be more equitable by objective measures. But market-oriented rates, in theory, obtain adequate (though not maximal) access at lower costs, at least in some of the more competitive markets.

A common Medicaid payment strategy in many states, it seems, is simply not to change rates until shortages develop and/or providers complain particularly loudly, especially to their state legislators. Providers often have a case for higher payment, as Medicaid rates are usually below those of other payers. Legislators, for their part, want to conserve budget funds for other purposes and will try to resist such complaints. With some providers complaining more than others—and not always based on need or real justification—the outcome of the debate may depend on a balance of interests and influence, as well as the state's short-term fiscal situation and real provider needs to alleviate real shortages.

But "fixing the squeaky wheel" can fall short of being an effective payment strategy. One reason is that only some providers will have figured out how to play this game. Those who do significant Medicaid business, are well connected politically, and have effective lobbyists are usually the ones who realize that rates aren't going up unless they make them into an issue. Others, not as well organized and with Medicaid as only a minor part of their business, may simply drop from provider participation. For this reason, as well as out of concern for equity and efficiency, we do not recommend response to the "squeaky wheel" providers as a sound basis for Medicaid rate-setting.

Evidence-Based Payment Rates. The fundamental struggle of the U.S. health care system has been how to reduce financial barriers to access for individuals while still having some mechanism to keep costs under control. The moral hazard problem of insurance's leading to economically inefficient overuse of services has not yet been solved in any practical sense by any of the major payers, public or private. Medicaid is intended to create some moral hazard to push rates of use for low-income people up to levels taxpayers regard as adequate. But with zero patient cost-sharing and high provider prices, there is a danger of overshooting. Low-value care may be the result.

We have known for many years now that something needs to be done. With studies of economic incentives in the 1970s, small-area studies of medical practice variations in the 1980s, and research on quality and effectiveness in the 1990s, almost all the evidence points toward the need to counteract the behavioral effects of insurance coverage and reduce use of care that is not worth its cost. The problem is translating research into practice, as evidenced by the fact that the data on regional variation have so far not led much beyond calls for more studies and a plea for evidence-based medicine. Finding a politically acceptable mechanism to ration care of positive, but low, value has been difficult; Oregon Medicaid came closest, but then pulled back.[4] Managed care met with push-back from patients and providers happy with a system that did not require them to make hard choices at the time and point of service. Yet this must somehow be done if we are to reduce the use of uncostworthy care.

In general, such mechanisms as prospective rates and fee schedules used by preferred provider organizations (PPOs) and public payers have met with somewhat less resistance from patients and providers than care management methods. Perhaps it is time to put more effort into using the incentives of provider payment rates to shape care patterns. We have enough evidence to identify some medical treatments that are associated with improved outcomes and some that have been studied and have shown no substantial effects. While there are many in between, with unknown or mixed evidence of effectiveness, and while we would not want to prescribe or proscribe specific procedures, that need not deter us from establishing payment rates that reflect the general or specific evidence available. Oregon tried to consider evidence of effectiveness in developing its priority list of condition–treatment pairs, but such an approach can result in an all-or-nothing coverage decision, at least in the fee-for-service sector.[5] In contrast, evidence-based rates would simply provide a little boost in payment for treatments supported with solid evidence of cost-effectiveness, and a little reduction in payment for services of questionable effectiveness.[6] Then we could see what happened and decide if it were an improvement. If so, we could continue to adjust provider payments for treatments until frequency of use better matches frequency of effectiveness.

A federal agency such as the Agency for Health Care Research and Quality (AHRQ), or perhaps a federal health board as has been suggested in various reform proposals, could be designated to develop lists of services whose effectiveness has been proved to be targeted by states for payment, say, 20 percent over standard Medicaid rates, and a list of services without such evidence to be targeted for rates, say, 5 percent below standard Medicaid rates; services associated with research suggesting ineffectiveness might get rates 20 percent below the standard. Efforts by the AHRQ's predecessor to set standards based on outcomes data ended without much success, so perhaps alternative models (competing entities offering lists used by competing insurers, for example) might be considered. Under this approach, payment for physician-authorized services would never be completely denied, but lower payment for services identified as less cost-effective would be a general disincentive for their use. Payment should not, however, be set so low as to lead providers not to provide services in cases where they may by exception be important to patient health and safety.

Perhaps we would not see much change in provider behavior with such an approach to setting rates, but, in any case, a smaller share of Medicaid payments would be going to support less effective care, and a larger percentage would be going to support provision of services of proven effectiveness. This might be viewed as a lean-against-the-wind strategy that, if demonstrated to be workable and joined by other payers for wide application, could help bring about the provision of more effective and cost-effective health care.

Pay for Performance (P4P). States are pursuing a wide variety of approaches to paying providers incentives to achieve specified quality, utilization, or participation objectives. Kuhmerker and Hartman report that in 2006, more than half the states had pay-for-performance plans of some form in operation.[7] Many of these were connected with capitated managed care plans or primary care case management (PCCM) programs. But P4P programs range widely and include

- rewards for managed care plans that meet Healthcare Effectiveness Data and Information Standards (HEDIS);

- bonuses for hospitals that meet specific goals, such as including discharge instructions or smoking-cessation counseling in inpatient stays; and

- incentives to make use of electronic health records or e-prescribing.

Some states also make the automatic assignment of enrollment in managed care organizations dependent on performance, adjusting the percentage of cases sent to each plan on that basis.

While many such programs have been operating for several years, many are still in early stages or under development, and some are known to have failed. Questions remain about just how much provider behavior changes, how well quality can be measured, and whether the most appropriate measures are being used. While we do not yet have much in the way of solid evaluation of effects, states do seem to have taken the initiative in this area to experiment with a variety of methods and may, over time, find useful and worthwhile ways to encourage better provider performance, particularly for those providers with Medicaid managed care contracts.

Provider Payment Issues by Type of Provider

Perhaps more than any other payer, public or private, Medicaid has to deal with widely diverse types of providers. These include providers of acute and long-term care, institutional, professional, and home- and community-based services, mental health facilities, drugs, medical equipment and supplies, school-based clinics, dental services, and emergency and nonemergency transportation. Each type presents its own set of issues for provider payment. We highlight some of the key issues for some important types of Medicaid providers.

Hospitals. Hospital payment methods can be among the most complex in Medicaid. A variety of methods are used across the states, differing for both inpatient and outpatient services. For inpatient services, some states follow a DRG-based system, while some have hospital-specific per-diem rates linked to recent or historical costs, and some base rates on some measure of case-mix. Medicaid pays only part of the cost of inpatient services for dual-eligibles, normally picking up the deductible and copayment not covered by Medicare. As such, Medicaid is not involved in pricing inpatient services for dual-eligibles. Still, inpatient services (mostly for non-duals) account for about 14 percent of Medicaid provider payments. As we suggest in our discussion of cost-shifting and cross-subsidization in hospitals, states may use low hospital payment rates to control the flow of resources and keep hospital spending in check, at the cost of limiting some aspects of quality to some small degree for all hospital users.

Hospital representatives are quick to provide state policymakers with many reasons Medicaid rates should be increased. Among the most common are low hospital operating margins, which are often cited to suggest that hospitals are just getting by this year and will certainly need more funds next year. In our model, discussed in chapter 11, above, in connection with cost-shifting, hospitals tend to adjust the production of the services they provide to fit the resources available. Not-for-profit hospitals, with no need to provide a return to shareholders, will, as a matter of regular business, tend to operate with little or no operating margin by incurring only those expenses that are supported by expected revenue. A margin that averages 1 or 2 percent, even if negative in some years, is usually sufficient to maintain operations. As hospitals can generally manage to meet available resources, low margins per se are not a valid rationale for raising or even maintaining hospital payment rates. In contrast to physicians, hospitals, for a large number of reasons, have been unwilling to refuse Medicaid patients; this reduces their bargaining power.

Prescription Drugs. The direct state role in Medicaid payment for prescription drugs was greatly reduced in January 2006 with the start of Medicare Part D drug benefits for Medicare beneficiaries, which shifted about $10 billion in prescription drug costs for dual-eligibles from Medicaid to Medicare. Prior to that, prescription drugs were a significant and growing component of Medicaid provider payments, and in 2005 Medicaid accounted for more than 10 percent of the U.S. prescription drug market.[8] As mentioned in previous chapters, now that Medicare has assumed control of pharmacy payment for dual-eligibles, states make a phased-down contribution or "clawback" payments to the federal government to defray drug expenses they otherwise would have had to pay.[9] This change reduced the pharmacy benefits that states directly manage to less than 5 percent of the national market in 2007.[10]

Aside from the clawback, most state Medicaid pharmacy payments now go for non-dual adults, particularly for treatment of mental illness, and for low-income families—adults and children. Many states have shown success in reducing the growth in pharmacy payments with negotiated discounts through multistate purchasing pools, sometimes in conjunction with a contract for pharmacy benefit management (PBM) services.[11] While their bargaining power may have been reduced, this benefit has in any case become less important as a policy issue for states. PBM will remain an important cost control tool for states if political factors (such as legislative response to industry lobbying) allow it to be used to advantage.

Nursing Homes. Payments to nursing facilities account for the largest share of Medicaid payments by provider type—about 17 percent. Medicaid covers stays in skilled nursing facilities (SNFs) and intermediate care facilities (ICFs). SNF care is typically for short-term post-acute and rehabilitative care, while ICF services are typically for long-term placements. Some states have distinct rates for ICF-MRs—facilities for the mentally retarded—and for atypical nursing facilities that may serve specialized types of patients. Payments to all types of facilities are subject to Medicare upper payment limits (UPLs) to ensure that state rates are no higher than what Medicare would pay for the services. The ICFs and ICF-MRs often have a large share of their patients in the Medicaid program, and many are highly dependent on Medicaid as a funding source. Therefore, state payment rates must cover very nearly the full cost of care for these facilities to be viable, and Medicaid payment rates may, in fact, do much to determine the staffing levels and intensity (and quality) of care these facilities can provide.

Physicians. Many Medicaid programs have traditionally kept physician payment rates well below rates in the private market. This can be useful in controlling physician payments through both reduced unit costs and utilization effect when access is reduced. But low physician rates can be self-defeating in several respects. When physician participation and access are reduced, alternative sources of care can be more expensive. These include hospital outpatient departments, hospital emergency rooms, community health centers, and provider-based physician practices, all of which may be paid more than independent physician practices for the same services.

States should look closely at the rates they pay for similar services in different settings—the cost to treat a routine earache, for example—to see whether their rate structure is encouraging use of more costly settings for routine care. Payments made directly to physicians account for only about 4 percent of Medicaid payments, but physicians are instrumental in authorizing the use of many other Medicaid services. States may be better off paying independent physicians a bit more and enlisting their help in ensuring that patients are served in cost-effective settings.

Dental Services. Dental services represent a small part of Medicaid, accounting for only about 1 percent of provider payments nationwide. As an optional Medicaid service, dental coverage for adults varies widely among states. Dental services, in general, are mandatory only for children, and for adults when services are provided by a hospital. Such cases are often seen in emergency rooms when patients have severe problems, and treatment does not include routine preventive care. Some states provide orthodontia services to Medicaid-eligible children, but usually only if they have severe problems that require correction for functional rather than cosmetic purposes.

Medicaid rate-setting for dental services can be challenging, as demand for them is high and dentists are currently doing quite well in the private market. This market has been bolstered by growth in private dental insurance, with provider supply reduced by past closings of dental schools and by rising private demand for cosmetic dentistry with high profit margins. As a result, it can be difficult to get dentists, many of whom work quite independently in their individual practices, to treat Medicaid patients, who tend to have more complex dental problems and are often in need of restorative procedures. In some instances, advocacy groups have sued states to raise dental payment rates needed to ensure access to services for Medicaid recipients. All this means that, to achieve real access to dental services, Medicaid payment rates for dentists may need to approximate private-sector rates more closely than those for other providers.

Community-Based Providers. Medicaid programs typically make use of an extensive array of community-based service providers, primarily to meet the needs of the elderly and disabled living in the community. These services include home health services, which are often provided by skilled nurses on a short-term basis to assist patients following an acute care hospital stay, and personal care services, which are provided, often through Medicaid home- and community-based waiver programs, on a long-term basis as an alternative to nursing home placement. The skill level of the caregiver and level of cost on a per-hour basis for the two types of services are quite different. Payment rates should reflect, respectively, the higher skill level and shorter visits typical of skilled nursing home health visits, and the longer, lower-skilled visits of personal care services. Managing utilization, including visit length, number of visits per week, and duration of services in weeks, can be important to effective cost control of personal care.

Also not to be overlooked is the cost-effectiveness of adult day health services for a significant subset of the elderly and disabled recipients in need of community-based care. Where families are available to provide services at night, adult day health care can provide ready access to a wide range of long-term services for persons who might otherwise require nursing home care. By saving on room and board and twenty-four-hour monitoring services, this can be a cost-effective alternative, even if transportation costs are included.

Freestanding Facilities. In many areas, ambulatory care services are available through freestanding facilities such as ambulatory surgical centers (ASCs), and MRIs and other radiology services through diagnostic imaging centers. These facilities can offer cost-effective alternatives to hospital out-patient departments. Community hospitals often take a dim view of such competing facilities and may argue that their payment rates should be kept low. We would suggest that this is an instance in which Medicaid payment rates should be set to reflect equivalent payment for equivalent services regardless of the setting. Payments should differentiate between the complexity and severity of patients' conditions where possible, but should be more comparable to rates paid to hospitals for similar services so as not to preclude access for Medicaid recipients in less costly settings.

Medicaid and Safety-Net Providers. Safety-net providers predominantly serve the poor and uninsured with free or nominally priced care as part of their missions. They typically provide services without regard to ability to pay, often on a sliding fee scale for the uninsured, and they include public hospitals, community health centers, rural health centers, community mental health centers, and school-based clinics.[12]

Federally qualified health centers (FQHCs), which may include community health centers (CHCs) and rural health clinics (RHCs), range from large public inner-city entities in major urban areas, to hospital-based centers, to small physician practices in rural areas that have found it advantageous to assume RHC status to obtain the RHC's higher Medicaid payment rates. Medicaid programs were required by federal law and regulations to pay FQHCs at a single fee per visit (encounter rates) based on costs until recently, when they were converted to prospective rates guaranteed to be at least as high (to begin with) as the former cost-based rates. There are two questionable payment issues here. One is whether such entities should be paid the same fixed fee for every visit regardless of type, duration, credentials of provider, or services provided in the course of the visit. The second is whether it makes sense to require states to pay these organizations at rates that are substantially higher than what most states pay for similar services in private physicians' offices. Similarly, in many states, community mental health centers also have special arrangements for funding by state agencies that can include Medicaid payment at comparatively generous rates.

We mention these arrangements to take note of Medicaid's existing role in supporting safety-net providers who care for the uninsured. Such providers piece together funding from various sources, including federal grants, state and local programs, Medicare, and Medicaid. They almost always accept what Medicaid pays (including DSH payments for hospitals), since that is typically more than they get for many of their non-Medicaid patients, and it is preferable to depending on a sliding scale and uncertain collection. While Medicaid is often disparaged by many private-market providers as having low payment rates compared to those of insurance companies, in fact, it often pays safety-net providers more generously than it pays others. Medicaid is a major source of funds for many safety-net providers, who serve patients without regard to ability to pay, including many uninsured persons without the ability to pay rates close to costs. The policy question is whether the current mix of more generous, encounter-based Medicaid rates, DSH payments, and grants from the Health Resources and Services Administration (HRSA) is the best way to pay safety-net providers. This mix of payment methods seems to lack the accountability of conventional claims-based payment systems.

Conclusion

Medicaid payment methods and rates differ widely among provider types and among states. The differences reflect the results of having distinct health care delivery systems and markets, distinct political processes, and distinct approaches to meeting the needs of the poor in a way that is consistent with voter preferences. Innovations in payment methods may help to create incentives for more cost-effective care, but the fundamental rate-setting issues for states are, first, to determine what level of payment is needed to ensure adequate access to services, and, second, to ensure that all types of providers are treated in a way that protects that access in all areas. As policy tools, appropriate payment methods and levels will do much to shape the Medicaid program's role in the financing system and help achieve program objectives.

13

Gaining Control of Provider Payment

Provider payment is a policy tool whose wielding is sure to engender controversy, and in many cases flat-out opposition. Providers are protective of any advantages they may receive, and vocal about any perceived payment inadequacy. How, then, are we to proceed to satisfy providers that they are being treated fairly, taxpayers that their funds are being used efficiently, and recipients that they have adequate access to care? In this chapter we provide our recommendations for payment policy. Steps can be taken at both state and federal levels to make provider payment more accountable and to help bring payment into line with what providers require to make needed services available to Medicaid recipients.

Provider Payment for Accountability

Our first set of recommendations relates to wresting control of certain aspects of payment determination from providers who, under current politics, have often been able to write their own tickets for higher payment than their peers. We focus on two areas mentioned in chapter 12, above: provider classification and the practice of using provider-based status to achieve higher payment by simply channeling bills through hospitals. In each case, changes are needed both in the way rates are set for various entities and in limits on the ability of providers to self-select the basis on which payment is made.

Provider Self-Classification and Rate-Setting. Medicaid and Medicare provider payment methods have evolved since the program began in the

1960s. Originally, procedures were simple: Most covered services were provided by hospitals (which then provided inpatient and emergency services)
and by physicians (who provided services in largely private practice offices or
in inpatient or ER hospital settings and nursing homes). Providers were classified as either institutional or professional providers, and two distinct payment
systems, Part A and Part B, were developed in Medicare to reflect that division.

Over time, the dominant payment methods have changed toward
approaches that provide the payer with better tools for cost control—from
cost reimbursement to prospective payment for hospitals, and from "reasonable charges" to fee schedules for professional providers. But the basic
methods for classifying providers have also changed in ways that can give
the providers more flexibility to maximize payment by choosing their own
classifications for payment purposes. Hospitals can choose to be classified
as urban or rural, for example, or as critical access or satellite hospitals, and
professional providers can choose to be classified as "provider-based," and
bill for their services through hospitals. This can reduce the ability of
Medicaid programs to control costs, and to make payment that corresponds
to what it costs to deliver a given service.

This situation has become more problematic over the years, as
providers have employed consultants to identify revenue opportunities in
complex payment regulations and have lobbied legislatures to create ever
more permissive provisions in Medicare and Medicaid payment laws. Such
provisions often begin as small, intentional loopholes created to assist one
or a few hospitals. Then other providers seek to be included, and over time
the legislature allows use of the favored classifications to grow in size and
importance. It is common for legislators, at both federal and state levels, to
pass laws with (often obscure) permissive provisions that effectively allow
some individual providers or groups of providers to obtain favorable payment rates. Such lobbying and organizing of provider business lines to
maximize Medicaid revenue have become important for outside consultants and, in some cases, for politically well-connected administrators hired
by providers in part to seek preferential payment provisions in law or regulation, or to help providers take advantage of such provisions once adopted.

Revenue-maximization opportunities exist whenever Medicaid and Medicare (to which Medicaid is linked for many provider classification and payment purposes) pay different rates for similar services produced by different

providers in different settings. Federal law allows, and often requires, such differential payments for essentially identical services. Hospital outpatient departments are paid more than independent physicians in offices to treat earaches and provide other such common, often primary care, services. Critical access hospitals are reimbursed for costs for inpatient services, while other hospitals may be paid fixed rates. Federally qualified health centers (FQHCs) receive higher payment than physicians for primary care services. Children's hospitals are exempt from Medicare's hospital prospective payment system (PPS). While Medicare is a comparatively minor payer for children's hospitals, they often receive very favorable payment rates under Medicaid. Outpatient surgery, including endoscopic procedures that are rapidly becoming more prevalent, is reimbursed at higher rates in hospital settings than in ambulatory surgery centers. Physician practices and other ambulatory care providers are paid more when they affiliate with hospitals and obtain "provider-based status" with permission to bill through the hospitals, often at higher payment rates. Community mental health centers receive higher payment rates than independent professionals for behavioral health services. The list goes on and on.

Congress has provided by law for Medicaid and Medicare to use preferred payment methods and rates that result in higher-than-average payments to a wide variety of providers that meet specific criteria. State Medicaid programs sometimes follow Medicare in these preferences and sometimes introduce preferences of their own for locally favored providers or groups of providers. These preferences have been accumulating in the laws and regulations for the more than forty years of the program's history. In some cases, they have resulted from excluding some providers from changes in payment policy that have occurred over time; in others, they have been introduced by Congress in an attempt to meet a perceived need of a specific group of providers. All the preferences represent products of the political process, as provider groups have found legislators responsive to plausible arguments for them.

Federal policymakers, then, need to restore integrity to the provider classification system used for setting rates in Medicare and Medicaid. A review should be made of all the various special provisions that exist for payment with rates or methods that differ from the standard—that is, any payments made outside the provisions of inpatient PPS or physician fee schedules. This would include any cost reimbursement, hospital outpatient rates for office-based services, differential rates by urban and rural location, or payment through other facilities, such as satellites of hospital facilities. A determination should be made as to whether such differential rates are still needed, and as to whether the privileged rates should be applied to all providers now classified for them. At a minimum, this review should include critical access hospitals, FQHCs, community mental health centers, children's hospitals, all office-based providers classified as provider-based, and hospitals that are classified as rural or rural referral centers or receiving rates based on such prior classifications.

Once this is done, the practice of self-classification of providers should end. Providers should be placed in categories that best reflect their services and local input costs and should not be given a choice of payment status. If federal policymakers are unwilling to undertake this task, states should be empowered to undertake their own reviews and reclassify providers as necessary for Medicaid payment purposes.

Public Program Payment Rates as a Commodity for Exchange. It is natural for markets to develop means to exchange items of value, especially where such assets can be used more advantageously by one party than another and where ways can be found to transfer them efficiently. In some sense, the different rates paid to different providers for the same services under the public programs Medicare and Medicaid are a resource for the higher-paid providers. This preferred access to higher payment has value, and if ways can be found to extend, share, or transfer such rights, then one might expect a market to develop for such a "commodity."

Whatever reasons there may have been historically for Medicare and many state Medicaid programs to pay more for services in hospitals than in physicians' offices and for some types of hospitals than others, these payment differentials now serve as incentives for creative providers to devise mutually advantageous exchanges. The opportunity to do so has been provided by Congress in laws that allow (as we have noted above) providers to self-classify and affiliate organizationally one with another. Examples of such classifications (some of which will be described below) are provider-based status, hospital within a hospital status, sole community hospital status, critical access hospital status, and FQHC and lookalike status, all of which, in the right circumstances, can be used to enhance Medicare and/or Medicaid payments. Providers that receive or can offer such status can sometimes find ways to provide other providers with access to their higher payment rates. While we do not know the details of particular financial arrangements, there is room for both sides in such transactions to benefit significantly.

The law provides many ways to facilitate such arrangements. A primary care provider can affiliate with a more highly paid hospital and be designated "provider-based" even if located off-campus up to thirty-five miles away, and the status can be granted in response to simple attestation by the provider that it meets the requirements.[1] Such attestations can require little more than adding a line to office signage and stationery to indicate the hospital affiliation and making professionals accountable to the hospital through some form of financial arrangement. Medicaid typically follows Medicare in granting this form of provider-based status, which allows higher reimbursements to providers who affiliate with their local hospitals, with minimal effort on their part and little or no change in the care provided in the local office settings.

Another such arrangement allows a hospital relatively easily to meet requirements to segregate and exclude a part of itself from prospective payment by making it a satellite of another hospital that is exempt from PPS based on costs.[2] We see children's hospitals offering to establish satellite facilities in other hospitals that will be eligible for higher payment rates, as well as widespread affiliation of primary care providers with their local hospitals. The reason for the growth in these affiliations is the ability to receive the higher cost-based payment rates of the hospitals who have access to them. A PPS-exempt children's hospital, for example, can contract with the satellite facility at higher payment rates than the affiliated hospital could otherwise receive and submit Medicaid claims for these services at the even higher preferential rates that Medicaid programs often pay to children's hospitals.

Aside from the equity issues of paying some providers more than others, the economic losses associated with such exchange behavior may become substantial over time if trends are not reversed. The costs are reflected in fees to consultants and lobbyists and salaries of executives, and in the inefficiencies of providers' choosing their affiliations simply to take advantage of Medicaid payment differentials. Other inefficiencies may come from reduced competition among providers affiliated with a dominant local hospital, and reduced competition with the hospital as it acquires provider-based relationships with the large majority of ambulatory care providers in its local market. We would expect the providers with access to the higher payment rates eventually to acquire or drive out the lower-paid providers. The net costs and benefits of the resulting hospital-centric delivery systems are unclear at this point. What is clear, however, is that it is not underlying efficiencies that have prompted the increasing prevalence of provider-based status; it is produced, rather, by the differential payments for similar services of the major third-party payers.

The ability to bill public programs at premium rates is thus a commodity that can be exchanged for a share of the higher revenue that will be received for services of the newly affiliated providers. We expect such a valuable commodity to be eagerly pursued and expanded where possible. In its more advanced form, the commodity-exchange behavior goes beyond the work of those consultants who help providers meet the technical requirements of existing Medicaid and Medicare laws and regulations to obtain favorable payment rates. It can manifest itself in the actions of consultants and lobbyists who work behind the scenes with legislators to build loopholes into pending legislation that will allow for later expanded use of special payment classifications and then market their services to hospitals to make use of the new provisions. It can also take the form of providers' marketing their access to higher payment to other providers, allowing the others to affiliate and bill through the better-paid providers' Medicaid numbers, as allowed by provider-based rules.

What we have, then, is a system that is shifting in response to revenue maximization behavior and is largely unaccountable to Medicaid program managers who are unable to control the provider classifications used for payment purposes—a system that is manipulated by savvy revenue-maximizing providers and their consultants and lobbyists. This system creates inequities among providers and favors particularly those who are able to market to other providers their access to higher payment rates.

Most disturbingly, we may be seeing just the thin edge of the wedge as these revenue-enhancing techniques become more widespread. In some geographic areas, the health care delivery system is being reshaped around hospitals, which can offer access to higher payment rates to a wide range of physician practices and other ambulatory care providers. Policymakers concerned with the long-run structure of the U.S. medical care industry should not overlook this emerging shift in provider relationships. In particular, they should be aware of the role of Medicaid (and Medicare) payment structures in determining the new order of provider affiliations. Provider self-classification provisions that well-intentioned lawmakers have built into Medicare and Medicaid to help constituent interests are altering the structure of the industry in ways that were probably not intended, but are nevertheless having very real effects on Medicaid costs and access to care. They tend to reduce states' ability to control costs, and they divert states' resources to a more limited number of higher-cost providers, increasing Medicaid costs and leaving fewer funds available to maintain access to providers who choose not to take advantage of these provisions.

Policymakers interested in reversing this trend need simply to focus on ways to ensure that Medicaid pays more nearly the same amount for a service, regardless of where or by whom it is rendered. This could include:

- Paying hospital outpatient departments the same as physicians for primary care services

- Paying equal rates for ambulatory surgery, whether it is provided in a hospital or ambulatory surgery center

- Paying federally qualified health centers and community mental health centers for professional services at rates equal to those paid other professional providers

- Eliminating cost-based reimbursement for critical access hospitals (CAHs)

Payment based on the service delivered, rather than on the provider or provider type, will do much to reduce the more blatant and inefficient revenue-maximizing behaviors and will lead to the delivery of services in the most efficient settings. Eliminating the hidden subsidies for the favored providers, especially provider-based ambulatory care, FQHCs and CMHCs, and other safety-net providers, may require recycling any savings into other program elements to serve the uninsured. We argue, however, as we do in greater detail below, that the hidden subsidies should be eliminated and replaced with more accountable systems that require providers to document what services are being delivered and to whom. Reducing the payment preferences is just one step toward a more efficient and accountable Medic-aid program.

Recommendations for Reforming Provider Payment Methods

Provider payment is an important Medicaid function that deserves careful attention by both state and federal policymakers. An understanding of the economics of local health care markets and clear policy goals are needed to develop an appropriate provider payment policy in an environment that otherwise might be driven by short-term budget considerations and the squeaky wheels of the most aggressive provider and advocacy groups.

Perhaps the most important lesson about Medicaid provider payment is that providers respond to incentives. When payment is adequate, the providers will be available and willing to serve Medicaid patients. Even safety-net providers are not an exception to this rule, as they often receive payment that is more favorable than what is available to other Medicaid providers, through classification for favorable rates or supplemental payments. Safety-net hospitals receive DSH and other supplemental payments for inpatient services, and payment rates for primary care provided through hospital outpatient departments (whether in the hospital proper or in an off-campus or even distant hospital-affiliated, provider-based group practice) are effectively higher than rates for other physician office visits.

Providers receiving these favored rates typically do not turn away Medicaid patients. Payment rates are the key determinant of access, and the desired level of access must be a key factor in developing payment rate policy. If a state wants Medicaid patients to be largely confined to safety-net providers, then only these providers need receive adequate payment rates. If it wants Medicaid patients to have services available more broadly, then it will have to offer adequate payment rates to all providers.

Medicaid programs should strive, then, to pay at rates that are adequate to ensure access to what the state regards as needed services, at what it regards as an appropriate level of quality, and they should be clear about what they are trying to achieve. If a state chooses to pursue a low-payment strategy, it should do so with the knowledge that, for better or worse, its strategy will reduce federal funds coming into the state, will reduce resources available to the local health care system, and may, possibly, have some effect on reducing quality and access to health care for all in the state. A tight, low-payment strategy can make sense if one's goal is to curb local health care spending (possibly to counter the moral hazard effect of insurance), and if one is willing to accept some reduced access to, or amenities in, the care provided to the poor. Setting low prices and then feigning surprise at the resulting low quality and limited access is neither transparent politics nor good long-run payment strategy.

In a tight budget environment, low provider payment rates can be viewed as a lesser evil compared with cuts in eligibility and benefits. If state taxpayers are unwilling to fund fully, even with federal matching, a Medicaid program that would provide for access for the poor equivalent to that in Medicare, the state may choose to meet any shortfall through informal rationing of provider access in competitive markets. Thus, the provider payment rate issue is inexorably tied to state decisions on how much to spend on Medicaid. Chronically low Medicaid payment rates relative to other payers may simply be a byproduct of the financing system and a way to implement rationing through limited accessibility or quality differences. To interpret the results of such decisions as reflecting defective choices by Medicaid or provider unwillingness to behave in a socially acceptable fashion is distracting. It is better to interpret them as a reflection of the idea that you get what you pay for, and of its corollary, that you should not expect more than what you pay for.

We have suggested that the objective of adequate and equitable payment may be best achieved if the state develops a clear, well-defined provider payment strategy. Such a strategy should specify the goals desired for each type of provider, use benchmarks to determine where the state currently stands relative to those goals, and adopt a payment methodology that can support achieving them. Target payment levels that will support the degree of access desired for each provider type should also be developed. We recommend that many states consider paying higher rates for services where access is perceived as a problem, especially as higher provider payment rates have the added benefit of bringing greater federal funds into the state. Such funds may be needed if, as we suggest, the federal government curtails use of supplemental payments and tightens accountability for services.

On the other hand, states should be free to choose a strategy that includes lower-than-average payment for some providers, if that is well considered and consistent with their objectives. Rates for hospitals that are below those of other payers are not a fundamental problem and may help control system-level costs. State and federal policymakers should consider whether it really makes sense to pay some providers more than others. Why pay an FQHC more than $100 for a visit for which a private practice physician would receive $40? Would not access be improved at no greater cost if private physicians were paid rates closer to those received by FQHCs and provider-based physicians for these professional services?

State-Level Provider Payment Policy Issues. We really have two sets of recommendations for states regarding provider payment. The first relates to having an overall strategy that is coherent and internally consistent and that reflects the state's particular objectives with respect to how it wants to treat its providers and how it intends to control cost and beneficiary access to services.

The process of developing such a strategy should give the state perspective on its own program. If it chooses to pay providers below-market rates, it should understand why it is doing so (to meet short-term budget requirements, for instance, or control access and utilization), whether the stated logic applies to all providers, and what the implications are (such as reduced access or forgone federal dollars). If it wants to use low payment to limit beneficiary access, it should say so, and not engage in posturing about "overcharging" and "excess profits." The state should also know whether or not it has set its payment rates (relative to benchmarks) consistently with its objectives, and if not, why not. It should have a long-term plan for bringing its payment structure into line with its long-term objectives.

Our second set of recommendations relates to the operational methods a state uses to set and maintain its provider payment rates. Most of these suggestions entail using benchmarks and regularly adjusting rates over time. States can maintain a payment system that includes both regulated fee schedules and rates for contracted services set by competition. As a standard practice, they should regularly benchmark their regulated payment rates against those of other payers. Some states are developing private payer databases of private market health insurance claims. While such databases can provide another source for rate benchmarking, the most useful benchmarks are probably national Medicare price-relative values, which avoid any local or provider-specific rates that reflect provider self-classification.

While the unfortunate political influences that have given Medicare providers the ability to self-classify for payment purposes should not be accepted by Medicaid programs as a basis for setting payments, Medicare rates do already apply to many services for dual-eligibles. Medicare, like Medicaid, is a large public payer with some market and regulatory power, and, for better or worse, it is subject to many of the same political influences.

The difficulty for some states, particularly the smaller ones, is that Medicare payment methods can be complex, and states with their own diverse payment methods may not always have staff familiar with Medicare rates and methods. In addition, Medicare payment levels are generally higher than those that lower-income or financially distressed states are able and willing to put into place for Medicaid. Tying Medicaid payment levels too closely to Medicare may increase the likelihood of challenges to low Medicaid levels. For technical issues, the federal government could provide valuable assistance to states in determining where their rates for all Medicaid services stand in relation to Medicare. CMS, for example, might annually provide each state Medicaid director with a report and associated rate files that show what Medicare is paying for all types of Medicare-covered services in the state. While much of this information is available piecemeal from the CMS website and published federal regulations, it does not make sense for each of fifty states to have to develop expertise in Medicare payment methods to pull it all together. A technical-assistance unit created to help states benchmark their rates against Medicare would have benefits at the federal level as well, as states are better able to meet requirements to keep Medicaid rates below Medicare upper payment limits.

State policymakers themselves should look generally to see where payment to providers may be higher than necessary to bring forth the level of Medicaid access they desire. Although most of the U.S. health care system has moved to prospectively set rates, pockets of cost reimbursement remain within the various state Medicaid programs. Such cost-based rates can, in some cases, lead Medicaid to pay more for services than is needed to serve recipients. Where the excess is used by nonprofit organizations to serve noneligibles, we can ask whether such services are in the public interest, and, if so, whether there are more direct and accountable ways to pay for them.

Both federal and state policymakers should also look closely at safety-net providers and work toward ensuring that Medicaid payment rates reflect

States Need Technical Assistance with Rate-Setting

Most states, particularly the smaller ones, do not have the resources necessary to develop and maintain sophisticated rate-setting methodologies. The federal government should provide technical assistance with rate-setting that includes at a minimum:

- A detailed report provided annually to each state on applicable Medicare payment rates within the state to use as benchmarks

- The extension of research on Medicare payment rates to include all Medicaid-covered services, so that valid Medicaid-specific pricing factors (for instance, relative values and DRG weights) can be computed for common Medicaid services that are currently not adequately measured or weighted by Medicare, such as prenatal care, neonatal care, and long-term care.

the cost of serving Medicaid patients and are not unduly inflated for other activities. Safety-net providers should be directly and adequately paid for the services they provide, but their roles may be reduced, expanded, or changed, with future programs providing for more universal coverage of those currently uninsured. The grants they receive may be replaced with claims paid by public and private insurance for newly covered individuals. Medicaid can play an important role in providing such coverage. But additional Medicaid costs will need to be paid in part with savings from reductions in other payments (for instance, grants, DSH, or cost-based reimbursement) to safety-net providers. Many of the reforms we suggest—including better federal financing for coverage of the lowest income groups and state options for expanded coverage of the working poor at an income-related federal match—may help enable this to happen. At the federal level, policy reform in this area should include a review of policy across agencies—CMS and the HRSA—to develop a more consistent and comprehensive policy for payment of safety-net providers.

Federal Policy Issues in Medicaid Provider Payments. While states find the flexibility of provider payment rates very useful—perhaps essential—to controlling their Medicaid spending and meeting their budget requirements, it is appropriate that the federal role not be prescriptive in this area. Nonetheless, in some areas a more active federal role could help promote more equitable distribution of federal funds to the states. We are not suggesting uniform national rates, nor are we particularly concerned about cross-state equity for providers; rates should vary with local market conditions and supply and demand. We are concerned, however, about unevenness in the extent to which states take advantage of supplemental payment provisions, and we are concerned when particular providers or groups of providers use local political influence to obtain favorable treatment from state policymakers so they can tap more federal and state Medicaid dollars than their fellow providers who are not as well connected. Some things can be done at the federal and state levels to prevent providers from taking undue advantage of the system this way.

Phase out DSH and Other Supplemental Payments. Disproportionate share hospital and other supplemental payments represent perhaps the least accountable and most differentially used parts of Medicaid. The differences among the states in use of federal DSH funds are wider and less related to need than other Medicaid payments.[3] While some have argued that tighter and more uniform standards for use of these funds might help ensure that states benefit more uniformly from these provisions, our view is that the DSH funding mechanism is inherently unaccountable and should be replaced with funding explicitly linked to specific services reported on claims for persons authorized to use them. Such substitute funding could come through the use of higher Medicaid provider payment rates, new programs to cover those currently uninsured, or claims-based access systems for users of safety-net providers.

States that wish to continue paying hospitals less than costs and providing supplemental payments to particularly affected hospitals could continue their own disproportionate share hospital programs with state funds. While the elimination of federal DSH payments may seem harsh or extreme to some who view the program as important, we see this as the best solution to its well-documented misuse as a vehicle for revenue maximization (for the states) that does little to achieve its original purposes.[4] Much preferable is substituting more accountable claims-based payment at adequate rates to get needed resources to hospitals delivering services to Medicaid recipients and to any others for whom coverage is authorized.

Extend and Enforce Upper Payment Limits. Upper payment limits (UPLs) should be applied at the individual provider level to ensure that no provider is paid with federal funds at more than Medicare-equivalent rates. Since most state Medicaid rates are well below the Medicare-based upper payment limit, enforcement of this is not going to bring about widespread changes. States that do exceed upper payment limits for individual providers (they are required to meet the UPL for each type of provider as a group) may be engaged in unjustified federal revenue enhancement or addressing the specific interests of locally favored providers. Some services do not have well-defined or meaningful upper payment limits. This is especially true of those types of services not heavily used by the Medicare population and those important Medicaid providers exempt from Medicare prospective payment methods, such as children's hospitals and critical access hospitals. Additional work to define meaningful upper payment limits for such services would provide better guidance to states on appropriate payment, as well as more uniformity across states in how Medicaid programs pay such providers.

Encourage Use of Medicare-Like Payment Methods and Price Relatives. Medicare provides the most thoroughly researched methodologies in existence for setting medical provider rates. They are, of course, not based on medical outcomes and effectiveness or the benefit derived from the services, as would be ideal, but rather on measures of inputs and their costs and sometimes relative charges. They provide objective and measurable methods for computing rates based on what it costs to produce services, if not their end value.

In many cases, Medicare payment methods have been adopted by other payers, including state Medicaid programs. But many states continue to operate with poorly constructed, outdated payment methods, or they do not follow the regular updating of the Medicare program. State Medicaid programs should be encouraged—perhaps with 90 percent federal matching or free technical-assistance services from a federal contractor—to invest in adopting Medicare-like payment methodologies across a wide range of services. They might be encouraged to set rates at state-specified percentages of Medicare payment relatives with variations in the percentages among services that reflect the degree of Medicaid dependence of providers, and perhaps well-considered local market factors.[5] More consistency and uniformity in this area would promote greater equity in payment rates among providers.

If Medicare payment methods are to be more widely used by Medicaid, the federal government should invest in extending them to all the Medicaid services and populations. For example, samples that determine inpatient DRGs for neonatal care will need to be representative of the Medicaid population, since, as we have noted, few such cases are represented in the Medicare data. For this purpose, additional research should be conducted to develop Medicaid-specific relative value schedules and parameters for services that differ from Medicare's in content or intensity. Doing so is an appropriate federal function that CMS, MedPAC, and their contractors should be well qualified to perform, and would provide a significant service to the states. It is certainly better than having fifty states all struggling to develop their own such methodologies. Nothing in this recommendation for rate *methodologies* implies that Medicaid payment *levels* must necessarily be brought up to the Medicare level, however.

Develop More Accurate, Research-Based Medicare Payment Levels for Specialty Providers. Medicare, which serves as a benchmark or foundation for Medicaid provider payment in many states, has, on occasion allowed exceptions from cost controls, such as prospective payment for certain types of specialty providers. For inpatient services, for example, these include critical access hospitals and children's hospitals exempted from Medicare's inpatient prospective payment system (PPS) and paid based on costs, rehabilitation hospitals and long-term care hospitals with their own PPSs, and hospital distinct part units (DPUs), particularly for rehabilitation and psychological conditions. While the distinct elements in their cost structures may somewhat justify treating these specialty provider types differently from other providers, these differences and exemptions from some common elements of cost accountability and control may create opportunities for unjustified revenue-maximization behavior on their parts. That is, higher, or even just different, rates and rules allow providers to obtain higher-than-standard Medicare payment rates for presumably sicker patients, who may yet not be so much sicker as to justify the higher rates. Rates might also be adjusted to better reflect patterns of care when patients transfer among such specialized facilities as they step down from one level of care to the next (for example, from acute care hospital, to rehabilitation hospital, to nursing home, to home health care), generating a prospective payment or the fully allowed length of stay for the case at each step.

The popularity and growth of specialty hospitals may well reflect exploitation of new revenue-maximization opportunities more than new-found efficiencies in service provision. Arguments made by advocates that specialty hospitals are more efficient imply, after all, that costs for the specialty providers ought to be lower, not higher, than for conventional providers such as community hospitals. But most of these institutions receive rates that are higher, and/or they serve less acutely ill patients than community hospitals. Because Medicare policies spill over to Medicaid—in provider certification, through references in state Medicaid plans, and in upper payment limits—it is important that Medicaid as well as Medicare have ways of setting rates that truly reflect the costs, adjusted for the complexity of case-mix of serving the patients who use specialty care providers.

Community hospitals, for their part, have been critical of specialty hospitals, accusing them of cream-skimming—that is, taking well-insured patients, for whom the better reimbursement is available. One can argue that specialty hospitals exist in large part not because of any inherent efficiency, but rather because of provisions for special payment rates their sponsors have been able to obtain, mostly from public programs, through legislative and administrative processes. Taxpayers may not be receiving full value for dollars spent on specialty hospitals if payment exceeds what is required to serve Medicaid patients in appropriate settings at their needed levels of care. Of course, measured costs at any given level of quality are only the starting point for setting prices; they are never definitive in themselves.

Pay for the Service, Not the Setting. One way to prevent providers from gaming the system to maximize reimbursement is to ensure that payment for Medicaid services is close to the costs incurred by efficient or low-cost providers in producing them.[6] Pricing by service will require states to base rates more closely on each patient's diagnosis and care needs rather than the setting in which the service is delivered. Payment for treating an earache should, for example, be the same whether the service is delivered in a doctor's office, a hospital outpatient department, an emergency room, or a community health clinic. This may entail increasing payments for services delivered in physicians' offices and reducing them for hospital outpatient services, particularly those of provider-based hospital affiliates who are paid as hospitals for office-based primary care even in locations remote from the hospital.

Encourage More Aggressive Pharmacy Benefit Management. Many states have been successful using pharmacy benefit management tools, and, with rebates, Medicaid pays less than most other payers for prescription drugs. But Medicaid programs lost some clout in the market when the benefit for dual-eligibles was transferred to Medicare Part D. To compensate, more attention might be paid to the methods used to encourage the use of generic and favorably priced brand-name drugs. This could include some form of reference pricing, as is used in Germany.[7] Unless a drug has demonstrated unique effects, Medicaid payment for a prescription would be made at the rate of the lowest drug in its therapeutic class. Some have even suggested that it would make sense to use reference prices based on an international index (say, of developed countries) rather than an average of U.S. prices. As other countries develop their economies and increase income per capita, we might hope that they will begin paying higher prices that will encourage more pharmaceutical development—if they truly desire new products. While the U.S. market has subsidized development of drugs for the benefit of the world, it is not clear that this is Medicaid's mission. In the meantime, it may not be in the taxpayers' interest to use limited Medicaid resources to subsidize development of similar new "me-too" drugs by paying more than the rest of the developed world pays for such products. Here is an instance in which Medicaid can decline to pay high prices for things that provide little or no additional value over cheaper alternatives; it will then forgo the potential (if small) benefit from such things, but it will not be paying for activities that do not contribute to its basic program goals.

Technical Assistance in Benchmarking. As we have noted, an important tool for helping states set provider payment rates at appropriate levels is benchmarking—particularly to Medicare and to Medicaid programs in other states.[8] For all states to develop benchmark rates independently is quite inefficient, how-ever, and many smaller states do not have the technical resources to deal with the complexities of Medicare rate-setting, much less the even more obscure methods of other states. National research studies currently avail-able that come out with two- or three-year-old data are of limited value in setting rates for the coming year or two and often seem to overlook some important limitation in data or idiosyncrasies of state methodologies. We would suggest that CMS or the Medicaid and CHIP Payment and Access Commission contract for a timely and thorough annual process to compile and report Medicare and state Medicaid benchmarks for current-year rates on all the major Medicaid services. Reporting levels of provider participation at those benchmark rates would also be useful, perhaps helping states decide where to set their rates to reflect their own tradeoffs and leading to greater uniformity among them. If payment methods become more Medicare-like over time, we may see more equitable schedules of payment rates across states, and across provider types within states.

Conclusion

Reforms to Medicaid rate-setting may be difficult in the face of recipient needs, provider demands, and political influences. The goal here, however, may be a limited one, focused more on uniformity in payment methods than on uniform levels of payment rates. The newly formed Medicaid and CHIP Payment and Access Commission (MACPAC) may provide the analytical support that Congress will need to provide the right kind of federal struc-ture, limits, and assistance to the states. Well-crafted efforts to promote these payment-reform goals should enjoy bipartisan support if they can be sepa-rated from the debate about the level of federal financial aid to the states. In recent years, we have seen the states sometimes successfully oppose federal efforts to curtail their use of questionable financing gimmicks to enhance their federal matching payments. To avoid state opposition based on concern about funding cuts, action to limit state use of questionable financing meth-ods should be accompanied by offsetting federal payment increases in other areas. Not every state would benefit, of course, but at least reasonable efforts to provide for greater equity in distribution of federal funds could not be opposed on the grounds that the federal government is unfairly cutting aid to the states. Payment reforms will require Congress to spend less time seeking to satisfy desires of particular constituent providers and more time supporting development of payment rate structures that are equitable and create the right incentives for provision of services.

Conclusion to Part IV:
Payment to Shape the Delivery System
of the Future

Provider payment is important for policy, and not just because it is used to meet short term goals of budgets and access to care. The health care delivery system we have today was, to a large degree, shaped by payment methods that have been employed by the major public and private payers. The expanded roles of doctors and inpatient hospital services surged with the advent of open-ended payment in the early years of Medicare and Medicaid. The growth in hospital outpatient services coincided with the shift to more restrictive prospective payment for inpatient services. In many states, the higher Medicaid primary care payment rates for community health centers, hospital outpatient services, and provider-based physicians have supported a system of access for the poor through a distinct set of providers who are paid more generously than their private physician counterparts. Medicaid managed care programs are successful in achieving access in part because they pay their providers more than Medicaid's traditionally low fee-for-service rates. There is no doubt that adequate payment is a key to achieving access to care, and that providers' responses will follow the structure of payment rates.

The methods of provider payment chosen today will undoubtedly shape the delivery system of the future. We can hope that those payment methods will be designed to guide providers toward delivery of cost-effective services and will reflect public priorities about access to, and cost and quality-of-care. While supportive Medicaid financing is needed, we do not see the program in a leadership role in conceptualizing and creating alternative care delivery models. That should be done by (private) providers themselves, and then offered to Medicaid (and to other insurers) at prices and with quality levels they may find attractive.

In part 4 we have developed a conceptual framework for thinking about rate-setting issues and suggested techniques that might be used to determine what rates should be and methodologies for implementing them. We have suggested a balancing of interests in making decisions about provider payment methods and rates to address both allocation and distribution issues. Promises to providers should not be made without considering the competing needs and interests of recipients and taxpayers—that is, the *allocation* part of the policy problem. For the *distribution* of payment resources among providers, we have suggested the need to consider carefully the reasons for any differential payment for similar services and to be wary of providers seeking special classifications or treatment for payment purposes.

Provider payment policy is a key to fulfilling the promises policymakers choose to make to Medicaid recipients, providers, and taxpayers. States would do well to think carefully about their allocation and distribution objectives for provider payments and to develop clear strategies for achieving them. The federal government can assist them in some important ways by providing technical assistance in the rate-setting functions. Extending the computation of Medicare-like price relatives to all major Medicaid services and enforcing an accountable framework for provider classification that cannot be manipulated will restore integrity to the rate-setting process.

In short, we recommend that states take the rate-setting function seriously, as a key to getting what is wanted out of the providers who deliver Medicaid services. Rate-setting is a complicated activity that can be subject to manipulation by those providers who complain the loudest or have the greatest political influence. States should approach this task with a clear set of goals and a determination to develop and implement a strategy that will achieve them. Support will be required at the federal level, including technical assistance for rate-setting functions and rationalizing the provider classification and payment methods that Medicaid shares with Medicare.

PART V

Promises to the Near Poor—
CHIP and Fiscal Federalism

The problem of uninsurance among those with incomes above Medicaid eligibility levels but without access to affordable employer-sponsored insurance has been a major element of the discussion regarding national health care reform. As we noted earlier, U.S. health care policy has avoided making explicit promises to the near poor. Assistance to this group has been provided through various safety-net programs, through Medicaid in some states with less restrictive income-eligibility requirements, and through the State Children's Health Insurance Program (CHIP). As a separate program that in some states covers children and, in certain cases, their families, CHIP provides perhaps our best real experience with public funding for health insurance for those who have not previously been able to obtain a subsidy for it either through tax exclusion for employer-sponsored insurance or through another publicly funded program. In this section we consider what can we learn from the CHIP experience to help guide the design and development of future programs that may move beyond assisting some lower-income children to serving the broader population of the near poor without insurance.

14

From SCHIP to CHIP—
Economics, Politics, and Policy

No bright line, either in theory or reality, separates the "poor" from the "not poor." The vehicle so far developed to attempt a graceful transition from the necessarily generously subsidized and carefully controlled Medicaid program for those with little means to an appropriate program for those who fall in the gap between genuinely poor and safely middle class is the State Children's Health Insurance Program. In the chapter that comprises the fifth and final part of our book before the conclusion, we look at SCHIP (now CHIP) both as a program for children and as an example of a possible transitional program for the rest of the population.

The State Children's Health Insurance Program is a small program compared to Medicaid, accounting for less than 3 percent of the combined total of Medicaid and CHIP spending in all states. It represents, however, a visible and continuing popular effort to extend medical insurance coverage to children in families with incomes above the poverty level and, in the view of many analysts, is a potential first step in extending Medicaid or something like it in the direction of universal coverage. CHIP has been a hotly contested political battleground in recent years in at least two ways. First, it has generated policy debates over the need for, and form of, an expanded public program for the uninsured who are not poor, the appropriate level of beneficiary cost-sharing, and the possibility of crowding out private insurance. Second, it has engendered disagreements between federal and state policymakers over the relative sizes of budgets for program costs—that is, whether one level of government should pay more of the cost than the other.[1]

Here we use the public choice ideas about governments' responses to matching and the concept of ideal (or inferior) matching as the basis for a

273

discussion of why these controversies have arisen and how CHIP might be appropriately integrated into a reformed Medicaid program. Although we must engage in some speculation about the objectives of voters and politicians, we try to stick as closely as possible to the idea that governments will, and should, do approximately what voter-taxpayers want.

Background

The controversy over the 2009 renewal of the CHIP legislation was largely framed in the press and on the campaign trail as a struggle between two polar-opposite evils: a plot of the left to "socialize" the provision of pediatric health insurance and health care on the one hand, and a valuable program opposed by those on the right who allegedly wanted to "stiff-arm children's health" on the other. What was generally forgotten in this debate was that CHIP (like Medicaid before it) is a joint federal–state program, with both its financing and control shared between the two levels of government. That these two levels might see things differently, especially (but not only) when they are controlled by different political parties, should come as no surprise; what should also, therefore, be no surprise is that the debate is at its core largely generated by conflicts associated with the program's current financing, rather than by closet socialism or any prejudice against children.[2]

In both Medicaid and CHIP, federal eligibility rules apply only to families whose insurance is to be financed in part by federal matching payments. Outside of federal programs, every state is completely free to offer insurance to children in better-off families or to able-bodied adults with no dependents at any income level it chooses; the only limit is that the state itself has to pay all of the cost of these add-ons. It is also free to choose to cover other medical services as long as it pays for them in full. It can be as generous as it likes, as long as it does so with its own money. Up to the time CHIP was passed, however, few states chose to provide any benefits that were fully state-funded, even to uninsured children at incomes above the Medicaid maxima, or to uninsured poverty-stricken adults. In fact, many states set Medicaid income eligibility limits below the federal maximum.

CHIP was created by a bipartisan bill that was passed in 1997, when the states were emerging from the fiscal distress of the economic slowdown of the early 1990s, and the federal budgetary picture had brightened considerably. This semi-recession simultaneously had lowered state tax collections and pushed more families into low income levels. A longstanding Republican desire to loosen federal limits on what states could do in Medicaid, combined with perennial Democratic aspirations to extend help to a shrinking, but still sizeable, fraction of uninsured children at higher income levels, led to the passage of CHIP.

CHIP was intended to help states finance insurance programs for children in lower-income families with incomes above the state-selected Medicaid limits, in a way that would give the states flexibility in providing or contracting for insurance functions and in setting cost-sharing and beneficiary premiums.[3] To induce financially strained states to go forward with the program when many were then trying to cut back on Medicaid, the CHIP federal matching rates in all states were "enhanced"—that is, increased across the board over the previous Medicaid levels. As a result, states could now spend new money while paying only 15–35 percent of the cost and having the remainder paid by the federal government.[4] But to make this program come close in format to a closed-end block grant, which was thought by Republicans to give better incentives and mutual independence to both levels of government, total spending was made subject to a cap.[5] A state that spent under the cap in one year could shift any unspent funds forward to subsequent years, and, at first, many states did not spend up to their cap. Except during the occasional episodes of panic that ensued when a state miscalculated and had funds it had either to spend right away or send back to the Treasury, CHIP was effectively a program with a predetermined federal spending contribution at the federal share of the capped level of spending, combined with a matching rule that all but guaranteed the state would want to come up with its share. It was approximately equivalent to a block grant.

The precise political reasons at the time for specifying the change in the amount of the share or the level of the cap are unclear; certainly, no bright-line standard told the writers of the law how much additional medical insurance spending on these next-in-line populations was just right, or what federal matching rate was needed to make the new program just attractive enough to states. Budgetary targets in the larger federal budget, not population need, were the crucial determinants. The most obvious

And then there was the issue of creating another entitlement. The Senate Finance Committee was crucial to the whole thing. Because the House had pretty much figured out what it was going to do . . . But the Finance Committee had this issue of the 20 members and Chafee and Hatch, on the Republican side, you know, voting with the Democrats and pretty much putting the Chairman in the position of voting out or having a bill voted out of committee that was going to have a new entitlement in it. And he wasn't going to do that.

—Julie James
Senate Finance Committee staffer in the 1990s

Source: Smith and Moore 2003, May 13 interview on the origin of SCHIP.

rationale for the cap was that it made administering this budget in the context of other health insurance budgets easier, and it was consistent with a vestigial Republican preference for some clear limits on open-ended spending to prevent CHIP from constituting a new entitlement program. The Democrats wanted the program to take the form of a Medicaid expansion; the Republicans wanted a separate, standalone insurance model. The final bill was a compromise: A state could choose to participate in CHIP either as a Medicaid expansion program, or as a separate child health program, or as both.[6]

What actually happened was also clearly predictable. The intrinsic challenge to states was having to set up programs, procedures, premiums, and patient cost-sharing without knowing exactly what the total cost of a given program with a given set of rules would be. They presumably wanted to choose a program whose cost (after phase-in) would not be appreciably under the cap on federal funds at the federal matching rate so as not to leave federal money on the table. The need to hit the maximum spending target grew more pressing as the possibility rose over time that unspent funding would expire.

But now the states were faced with what some might have perceived as an almost irresistible temptation. Up to the cap, it was sensible to expand programs, as long as the perceived benefit to the state exceeded the state's share; the state would, in effect, be spending fifteen- to thirty-five-cent dollars. But at the cap, the state's price per dollar of spending would suddenly rise up to sixfold, to a hundred cents on the dollar. Beyond the incremental CHIP programs that just fit under the cap, other programs on states' wish lists that might even be preferred if costs were comparable now became off limits. In addition, the higher federal matching rate for CHIP might have crowded out spending on other state programs for the truly poor, such as efforts to increase Medicaid enrollment. In any case, the new program provided a vehicle for states so inclined to obtain additional federal funds, which, as a result, were very unevenly distributed among the states.

Imprecision in forecasting, wishful thinking in policy, and a willingness to take risks arguably caused some states *ex ante* to select programs that were aimed in the general vicinity of the cap but might end up going somewhat over. The design of the program was virtually certain to leave state health policymakers with meritorious programs already planned and ready to go that ended up with no external funding at the margin; a more certain recipe for frustration is hard to imagine. The result was that states that overspent their allocations and ran "deficits" while adding children to the ranks of the insured petitioned for waivers of the limits and for (implicitly) generous federal funding of any overrun. Any sudden limit to this process was perceived to be arbitrary and hard-hearted.

Explaining the Unexplainable

To understand CHIP, one must go back and review what we know about the long-playing fiscal dance between the federal government and the states that Medicaid represents. Matching rates varied in the original Medicaid design because of the plausible expectation that policymakers in lower-income states would choose less generous plans or less generous programs than those in higher-income states, if matching were uniform. The rationale for income-varying rates was partly to base them on ability to pay and partly to provide an incentive for greater equality across states in programs for the poor. The plan also built on preexisting federal–state matching rates for preexisting, smaller federal–state health programs.

For the higher-income states that tended to have high Medicaid eligibility limits, CHIP potentially provided, at long last, a relaxation of the Medicaid spending restrictions for nonpoor children from lower-income families in two ways. First, income limits on beneficiaries of federal–state subsidies were abolished; states were free to make higher-income families eligible for subsidies. Second, the federal matching rate for rich states (as well as others) was increased, so their demand for child insurance was increased. The cap on federal spending was supposed to offset these stimuli, and apparently it did so. But it left state policymakers still frustrated, now not by federal recipient income limits, but by the spending cap.

The federal government could have used matching rates that varied more steeply with state income to achieve whatever spending targets it had in mind. Why it chose instead to offer incentives that sorely tempted higher-income states to spend more than a cap while at the same time imposing difficult and irritating spending limits is a puzzle. Perhaps the federal policymakers were just more comfortable with the clear spending limits of the cap, wanted to keep things simple, or needed the support of those states' congressional delegations. What principles might have helped them make the hard choices about how far up the income distribution government subsidy programs for children's insurance should go? We can list three:

- **Principle 1: Crowd-out should be limited.** We know that the proportion of children with private coverage rises fairly steeply as income rises above 125–150 percent or so of the federal poverty level. At money incomes above about 140 percent of poverty, most families obtain private insurance for their children, primarily through employer-sponsored plans.[7] Many low-wage and part-time jobs do not come with employer-sponsored health insurance, however, so some of these families remain uncovered. Even in the group at 200–300 percent of the poverty level, about 15 percent of pregnant women are without health insurance.[8] Furthermore, we have recently seen some smaller employers limiting growth in health insurance expenses by offering plans to fewer workers, with less coverage, or with greater employee cost-sharing. Insurance in the individual market is generally available only at high premiums that may be beyond the reasonable reach of many lower-income working families.

  This leaves many lower-income workers and their families facing what can be some rather stark choices, depending on the level of their income and assets, on their family situation, on whether health care programs such as safety-net providers or lower-income subsidy plans are locally available, on the cost of employer coverage, if it is available, and on the affordability of private plans. While the decision to be uninsured is a choice, for many lower-income persons it is a choice that must be made from among a very unattractive set of opportunities. One thing public programs for lower-income workers without employer-sponsored coverage could do is make some opportunities for insurance coverage more attractive and thereby encourage the worker to make the effort to arrange coverage and regularly pay premiums, which will need to be subsidized—probably on an income-based sliding scale—if the choice to be insured is to be feasible.

- **Principle 2: State and federal subsidies should be set appropriately.** We have already seen evidence in existing federal and state programs that many lower-income workers will take responsibility for enrolling in and making the premium payments for a plan if it is available and offered at well-subsidized rates. The mandatory Massachusetts Commonwealth Care program has been very successful in getting lower-income families and individuals to enroll and pay premiums in a subsidized plan, exceeding expectations (though also its budget). CHIP itself has been successful in enrolling children—and, in some cases, their parents—in plans requiring premium payments, though heavily subsidized. It has shown that an enhanced federal matching rate is sufficient for many states to offer a package, at least to children and, in some cases, parents, for which many lower-income families are willing to pay something.

But can an appropriate program model be found that can be made to work in many states across the country? The answer depends, in part, first on whether there is a range within which the subsidy level can be set so that it is high enough to induce consumers to choose public coverage, yet low enough so that state taxpayers are willing to pay it. While this range may not always be attainable, the available evidence strongly suggests it may exist in some situations *if there is substantial federal support*, and if public coverage can be easily substituted for private. Once the range is found, we can then turn back to the question of whether federal taxpayers are willing to pay enough to get states to move forward in this way. To get a state to offer more coverage, higher subsidies have to be offered. Both the Massachusetts and CHIP examples involved rather high federal subsidy levels in excess of those typically available through other programs for these lower-income, working-population groups—the Massachusetts plan through a waiver, and CHIP through enhanced federal matching. A key question is whether the benefits from these programs were worth this higher subsidy. The conclusion is that the CHIP debate is significantly about who shall pay for this insurance: state budgets, federal budgets, or family budgets. That part of the debate in turn is about value, and about payments by each group relative to their perception of value.

- **Principle 3: Private spending should be sustained.** Since all this depends on the behavior of families, their willingness to pay for coverage, and their choice of insurance, another potential design or evaluation issue is whether an expanded CHIP would displace private spending on private insurance (albeit with some tax subsidies). Many CHIP-eligible families will not have access to private health insurance through an employer, but some will. That significant crowd-out may occur for these households seems evident from research: Many families appear to prefer subsidized CHIP insurance to whatever insurance and whatever financing they might arrange in private settings.[9] From the viewpoint of economic efficiency, however, it is not crowd-out per se that is inefficient; the main attraction of the public coverage may be the subsidization, which may tempt people to choose insurance that is not ideal for them. While the public coverage may come with limits on provider choice or benefits or offer more generous benefits procured at a cost in excess of the value to the participant, it also comes with such a low premium price tag that it is hard to pass up.

  Alternatively, if the public coverage is similar to what people would have chosen privately, the main consequence of the CHIP program is then the subsidy itself. In effect, some lower-income families are given a transfer administered by the state, but paid for in part with a federal subsidy. The higher one goes up the income distribution, the less is the impact on coverage chosen and/or access to medical care, and the more the effect is simply a transfer. The value of such a program needs to be judged in the context of the appropriate state and federal tax burdens on lower-income earners, including the payroll taxes and sales taxes for which they often bear disproportionately higher shares. The question becomes one of deciding at what point such a transfer is no longer an appropriate use of federal matching funds. In effect, there is an increasing cost (of mismatched insurance and selective tax transfers) as CHIP moves up the income distribution, which must be set against the social and political gains from having the remaining small fractions of uninsured children obtain some insurance coverage.

What to Do and Why

Many voter-taxpayers support the proposition that reducing the number of uninsured children is a desirable goal and one toward which they would be willing to pay higher taxes if that were needed to achieve it. But, as we have seen in the past, how a health care program is financed can be a critical determinant of public support.[10] The CHIP allotments that limit the dollar amount of the federal contribution are not usually in sync with state spending desires, especially at the enhanced CHIP matching rates. CHIP allotments are determined for each state as a proportion of total funds allocated nationally. State proportions depend on the number of poor children in the state and a state cost factor, but are subject to limits designed to ensure that states' shares of available funds do not change greatly over time—something that tends to favor states with large programs in place prior to 1999. The formula makes no allowance for differences in taxpayer income or state fiscal capacity.[11] So, similar to the Medicaid FMAP formula, this method of allocating federal funds favors the higher-income states that can afford to take advantage of it.[12]

In the early years, most state programs operated well below the allotments, but as CHIP enrollments grew, more of them came up against the allotment cap. At an analytical level, it is clear that the flaw that led to federal–state conflict over CHIP in the years of the George W. Bush administration was the combination of a very low state sharing rate with a crisp upper limit. Had the federal matching rate been lower—closer to the standard Medicaid rate—more states might have kept spending below their caps. Had the limit on state spending been a softer cap (for example, one providing some matching for overspending but at a less favorable but declining rate), phasing out matching to zero at some point above the cap, state desires might have clashed less strongly with total resources.

While actual CHIP matching rates did lead states to select some relatively less cost-effective programs than they would have if matching had been higher, however, variation in the generosity or scope of the desired programs would still have occurred among those at roughly the same income per-capita level because the voter-taxpayers (or the political systems) in some states desired to do more than in others. That is, even if the matching had been precisely selected to get states to propose programs that just hit the federal target on average, the most desired programs of some would have been above or below the target. Indeed, another rationale for the cap might have been as a way to prevent states with tastes more expensive than average from overshooting the federal target. In practice, however, the states that overshot did not blame themselves, but rather looked for a way to get a pass on their exuberance.

Our fundamental premise here is that it is better to control states' decisions on federal–state matching programs by selecting a matching rate that will induce them to choose the ideal outcome, rather than to have a federal matching rate so high that their generosity must be heavily constrained by complex federal rules. Of course, there cannot be a program with no rules. But it is better to have incentives built into the matching process that generate state behavior in the neighborhood of ideal than to be in a situation where matching is so far off that heavy-handed and controversial rules must be put into place. Luring states with high matching rates to do things that rules must then forbid is a temptation to sin, not a path to a good outcome.

There are, then, mechanical fixes to the current problem: Lower the federal share, and develop a more coherent argument to explain the cap.

These steps might go a long way toward dissipating state pressure to expand subsidies for health insurance for children further up the income distribution. But this sort of analysis only helps if there is an identifiable "federal target" that makes sense and stays put. Because the federal government's policy will (and should) change as voters select representatives with different objectives, the idea of a given and unchanging federal demand overspreading the system and structuring it in a particular way is not realistic. It seems plausible that, relative to the pre-CHIP situation in 1997, state preferences for going beyond the initial caps at the federal level have strengthened, as has federal tolerance for allowing them to do so. To make sense out of this we need to go further and ask: When it comes to health insurance for children, who wants what, and why?

The debate over how generous is too generous can be framed analytically: Is a state's proposed plan similar to that which taxpayers in other, similar states would demand, given the prevailing federal matching rate? But what if taxpayers or their representatives at the federal level disagree over the value to be placed on expansion of coverage? All policymakers presumably value better access for children, but they have different priorities for this outcome compared to other types of federal spending or lower federal taxes. The value they place on health benefits for children determines the ideal federal matching rate, but where do we find the golden tablets on which that ideal value is specified?

The controversy over extending CHIP coverage to children in families with incomes greater than 200 percent of the federal poverty level exemplifies this problem. Clearly, some federal policymakers (primarily members of Congress) have felt that the nationwide benefit from such an expansion would be large, even at currently high CHIP federal matching rates, while others (especially in the Bush administration) have felt that the current level of benefits to this part of the nonpoor population is adequate.

In the future, better information on the likely effects of different combinations of matching rates and a better understanding of the impact of potential crowd-out of private insurance on beneficiary welfare might help to resolve this type of disagreement. Better information would come from the estimation of state demands (without caps or rules) at various federal matching rates, so that one could determine a pattern of such rates that would motivate the state to hit a limit of 200 percent of poverty,

300 percent, or any other specification of the generosity of state benefits in the dimensions of eligibility. In itself, this information would not tell us what is ideal, but it would display the opportunities and the tradeoffs among them.

Beyond this, however, how can we understand what is at stake from the expansion of eligibility for government-financed insurance programs further up the income distribution? Answering this question will require a richer specification of what subsidized insurance programs do.

Crowd-Out, Take-Up, and Efficiency

Will all families with uninsured children take up public insurance if they become eligible for it, and will no one who already has some form of private or public insurance for their children switch to the new subsidized option? The answer is probably negative on both counts. First, not everyone who can enroll actually does. For those families who are eligible for Medicaid or CHIP, the take-up rate (that is, the percentage of eligible children who enroll) is at about 70 percent—below the rate of participation in employer-sponsored insurance, which is at about 83 percent. The difference is largely associated with income; if one looks just at children in lower-income families, the rates are comparable, at 64 percent for employer-sponsored insurance and 66 percent for Medicaid/CHIP.[13]

We expect this may well be due in large part to the rational behavior of lower-income families, who may avoid getting insurance, both because of the hassle and because of any monetary cost, when they do not have or expect to have significant medical expenses. That they can wait to apply for the public insurance until such time as they need it also fosters procrastination. For Medicaid, at least, perhaps the greatest contributing factor relates to the difference between it, as a free entitlement program, and employer plans, as insurance that must be paid for. Unlike private insurance, Medicaid offers coverage to those entitled to it even on an as-needed or retroactive basis. Often lower-income families do not enroll in Medicaid until they have expenses, and then the provider helps them enroll to receive payment. At any given time, there are many unenrolled potential eligibles who thus effectively have Medicaid coverage.

The situation with CHIP is rather more complex, as premiums are required in advance; but some lower-income families may rationally decide not to enroll if premiums are viewed as unaffordable, if Medicaid or other programs are viewed as a backup, or if medical expenses they expect (rationally or not) are very low.[14] Also, some families with income very near the Medicaid/CHIP cutoff eligibility level cycle between the two programs, shifting from CHIP to Medicaid every March, when federal poverty guidelines get their annual increase, and back to CHIP later in the year, perhaps upon receipt of annual pay increases from employers. They may decline CHIP enrollment, which requires a premium payment, and but accept Medicaid for that part of the year in which they are eligible, especially if medical expenses are incurred. In any case, not everyone eligible to enroll in either program actually does.

Since the take-up rate for Medicaid is below 100 percent, even for poor families, and since the improvement in health that results from moving to being insured from being uninsured is presumably higher the lower the family's income, the Bush administration proposed that states be required to enroll a specified percentage of eligible children from families with incomes below 200 percent of the poverty level before they could use CHIP funding for higher-income families. Proponents of the proposal also pointed to the higher rate of crowd-out of private insurance for children that occurs as public coverage eligibility is extended to income levels at which most children already have private coverage. While the proposal was opposed largely because of the difficulties states would face in trying to enforce it, the proposal did have on its side the logic of providing coverage to lower-income groups first. The main point is that for any plan in which enrollment is voluntary, policymakers must account for the fact that not everyone will enroll and for the possibility that enrollees may be giving up other coverage when they do.

While taxpayers' desires to cover formerly uninsured children determine policymakers' choices, what more specific taxpayer views on eligibility and enrollment come from our public choice framework? There are actually two costs from enrolling a person in the CHIP program. The first component is the expected or average value of benefits, while the second is the administrative cost of the program. While some of the administrative cost goes to pay for claims of those already enrolled, part also goes to pay for enrolling and maintaining enrollment records for the population covered. In Medicaid and CHIP, as in private insurance, the largest item of administrative cost is not the expense of claims processing, but rather the cost of marketing and enrollment, billing, and administration. Traditional Medicaid can at least avoid billing for premiums because coverage is free; to the extent that positive premiums are charged for CHIP, there may well be an order-of-magnitude increase in administrative cost (compared to free insurance). In some cases, much of the CHIP premium goes to pay the cost of the enrollment process and of collecting the premium itself.

From a taxpayer's point of view, the benefit from enrolling an additional child in a public program is presumably related to the size of the expected or average improvement in health (compared to the child's having no insurance).[15] Since finding and enrolling poor families becomes more and more costly as the fraction of eligibles remaining uninsured shrinks, the full marginal cost of adding beneficiaries in the income stratum increases. Extending eligibility to families over 200 percent of the poverty level will at first carry a much lower administrative cost per newly insured child (as the families most eager to have insurance sign up), relative to the cost of finding and enrolling children for Medicaid at current participation levels. The health benefit from having insurance (compared to being uninsured) will, however, be smaller for these less-poor children.

The question, then, is whether the decrease in marginal benefit from covering the less needy uninsured as we move up the income scale is less than the fall in administrative cost per child from enrolling the more eager but not quite as needy families. The difference in administrative cost is a piece of the information needed to judge where the eligibility line should be placed, but so is the magnitude of the expected improvement in health and the value taxpayers place on that. Fairly good evidence is available on health improvements from insurance for poor children, but much less exists on impacts on families in the relevant population at 200 percent or more of the federal poverty level. The unavailability of this information has resulted in a controversy that cannot be resolved a priori.

Voter-taxpayers may discount the value of extending CHIP eligibility further up the income distribution if they become aware that the offering of a heavily subsidized CHIP plan could crowd out private insurance (when that subsidy exceeds the implicit tax subsidy of employer-sponsored insurance). When this happens, the perceived health improvement benefit (from reducing the uninsured population) per dollar of subsidy obviously falls. For those who would have been privately insured, however, the subsidy does not necessarily represent funds wasted; the expense per formerly insured beneficiary should lead to higher mean real income among participating families, in which case crowd-out is a transfer. The political economy issue is the value taxpayers might place on such tax cuts or transfers to some—but not nearly all—lower-income families with children who are not poor.

EBEB Matching and CHIP

Equal-burden-for-equal-benefit matching, which we discussed in chapter 8 in connection with Medicaid, may be even more important for programs such as CHIP, where ability to pay as well as ability to benefit would come into play. Children and mothers with infants would continue to receive favored matching rates. But the current CHIP-enhanced matching for persons far above the federal poverty level and other-state eligibility standards would be cut back. States could choose to continue with such programs, provided they raised the nonfederal share with some combination of state or local funds or recipient cost-sharing. Note that counting cost-sharing toward the state share would be a change from current practice that is consistent with our view that the federal government ought not be too concerned with the source of in-state funds.

The dilemma here is that the value to state taxpayers of extending benefits to households that are definitely not poor (even though they are not well off) is apparently low; that was part of the reason CHIP used a crudely enhanced matching rate. But the value of that additional spending to federal taxpayers is also lower than the value of spending for poorer people. The absolute value of marginal benefits, to both state and federal taxpayers, is lower than for more needy populations. The fact that enhanced federal matched rates were needed and provided for CHIP suggests the falloff is steeper for state taxpayers than for federal voter-taxpayers, who are apparently willing to take on a greater share of the cost to extend benefits to children. We see the enhanced CHIP match as illuminating federal voter-taxpayer willingness to contribute a greater share toward children over other categories of recipients, and not as an indication that they prefer the higher-income CHIP children over the lower-income Medicaid children.

CHIP Renewal and Expansion in 2009

After several failed attempts, Congress passed a bill to renew CHIP in early 2009. This renewal will modestly expand the number of children covered, by encouraging the states to enroll 1.6 million children who were formerly eligible for CHIP but either had not applied or were excluded because the state reached its block grant limit. It is estimated that only 700,000 newly eligible children will be covered; total coverage under CHIP is about 14 million children.[16]

In addition to renewal and modest expansion of the federal funding for CHIP, the most striking feature of the current program is its greater use of variations in the federal matching percentage, apparently in line with voter-taxpayer marginal values for covering different populations. To be specific, the enhanced matching (up to the limit of the block grant) will not apply to states that newly extend eligibility to children in families with incomes above 300 percent of the poverty line; instead, the matching will only be at the original Medicaid matching rate (and, of course, will be constrained by the total amount of the block grant). After fiscal year 2013, expenditures for parents who are newly enrolled will be matched at a rate between the original Medicaid rate and the enhanced rate—the paradoxically named "reduced enhanced Medicaid assistance percentage." Finally, spending on childless adults will only be matched at the original Medicaid matching rate.

These changes seem fully consistent with our public choice model, in which marginal evaluations decline with the incomes of beneficiaries and the degree of dependency of the population. They suggest that the political preferences in early 2009 did support CHIP coverage for the original target population, although the population of children in families with incomes just below or just above 300 percent of the poverty line seemed still to challenge development of a consistent long-term policy. Some major alterations in CHIP are envisioned by the health reform bills before Congress at the time of this writing.

Conclusion to Part V:
Implications of Subsidizing Coverage for the Near Poor

Here again with CHIP, as with Medicaid, the public value of providing care at public expense falls off as the subsidy recipients come from higher-income households. And so it is an economic efficiency rationale that leads to income limits on eligibility for these public programs. From a state perspective, the voter-taxpayers' resistance to covering higher-income persons at public expense falls off and is only overcome with higher federal subsidies. But at the federal level, too, policymakers must consider how the public value of subsidizing coverage relates to the incomes of those receiving the subsidy.

We do not have all the answers here. We can only note the importance of considering CHIP policy in the broader context of taxes of all kinds and subsidies on medical care of all kinds. Blaming, moralizing, questioning motives and ethics, invoking incipient doom, or ignoring constraints do not help with solutions. Solving these problems will require considering the consistency and equity effects of all taxes and subsidies available to the lower-income population and, for workers, their employers. Most importantly, getting the incentives right is the key to state behavior that satisfies federal voters and does not frustrate state voters. In a separate work, we suggest a plausible approach to meeting the needs of this group, which includes many of the nation's uninsured,[1] but this is an area that requires careful attention and much work to address as a program policy issue.

Conclusion

At the outset of this book, we introduced our public choice framework for thinking about Medicaid as a set of public promises or assurances made to the poor, to providers, and to taxpayers. We suggested that viewing the program from such a consistent and coherent perspective could help policymakers sort through the tough decisions it presents. Our discussion has ranged widely over the field of Medicaid topics. Nonetheless, our suggestions for change all arise from, and conform to, a public choice–based model that encourages policymakers to focus on the competing objectives, limited resources, and distinct interests of three broad stakeholder groups: the poor, the providers, and the taxpayers.

In all this, we have paid attention to issues of equity and the political balance of interests in a federal–state system. We have directed efforts toward making the program one on which the key stakeholders can rely to meet their basic program needs. The key to avoiding unfulfilled promises is to choose promises carefully, making sure they are backed by popular support and available financial resources. Policymakers, in Medicaid as elsewhere in the public sector, are prone to overpromise and underdeliver on public programs. But the usual political slippage between promise and delivery can have severe consequences for some affected by this program. Medicaid promises and their resource limits should be made clear to beneficiaries and providers; Medicaid promises and their associated costs should be made clear to voter-taxpayers.

To do this, policymakers must understand the implications of choices, not only for program rules and budgets, but for what each choice implies about the level of commitment by and to each of the Medicaid stakeholder groups. Policy made in an open public process will require tradeoffs, and no group will get everything it wants. In this conclusion we consider some

---

Program Choices to Consider

Choice 1: Will Medicaid accountability be strengthened by covering the costs of safety-net providers in a way that reaches states more equally, replacing current DSH payments with more accountable, preferably claims-based, payment methods?

Choice 2: How far will Medicaid eligibility be expanded to cover poor people who do not fit the traditional categories?

Choice 3: How far will Medicaid/CHIP eligibility be extended to children and families at somewhat higher income levels?

Choice 4: Will Medicaid's federal–state matching formula be revised to produce greater equality in benefits and taxpayer burden?

Choice 5: Will federal Medicaid policy be revised to help states support more uniformly adequate payment rates for providers? Will states respond by adopting more consistent and rational fee-setting methods?

Choice 6: Will ways be found to reduce the effects of the economic cycle on state Medicaid financing?

Choice 7: Will Medicaid become part of a national- or state-mandated system to extend health care coverage to all?

---

of the key choices facing policymakers in the years ahead and their implications for the public promises that may be made.

Key Policy Choices

Medicaid faces several key policy choices. Some of these issues are rather low in profile, while others have been included to some degree in the broader public debate on national health care reform. While much attention has been paid to consideration of more exciting new programs or program extensions to cover the uninsured, Medicaid itself is the foundation of our system of helping low-income persons to obtain needed medical care. Changes, adaptations, and expansions in Medicaid will need to be effectively implemented to support and mesh with new programs to reduce the number of uninsured. The key financial levers for directing and controlling these changes are federal financial incentives and provider payment. Effective use of these tools for Medicaid will be needed to contribute to the success of the national reform effort.

Federal–State Incentives. Perhaps the most important theme we have developed in these pages is that many of the problems with our current system of financing care for lower-income persons can be traced back to poorly constructed incentives inherent in the structure of the federal–state program. First, with respect to Medicaid, the program's current matching-rate system has provided inadequate financial incentives for lower-income states to meet the basic needs of their poor and near-poor populations, while stimulating some higher-income states to create programs that draw national resources into provision of benefits for many people well above the federal poverty level. As a result, Medicaid has failed to achieve anything near equality in treatment of the poor across states; by some measures, it even promotes redistribution of resources from lower-income to higher-income states. Second, rates of uninsurance are greatest among those persons who receive the least federal subsidy for coverage for lower-income people—those without access to public programs or employer-sponsored insurance.

We believe correcting federal financing incentives in these two areas—for Medicaid and for lower-income people not taking employer-sponsored insurance—would do much to promote broader health insurance coverage and a greater degree of equity in health care financing, from both the taxpayer and patient points of view. Reforms such as those we have suggested for basic Medicaid and an expanded subsidy program for the working poor provide a reasonable approach to altering the fundamental incentive structure of the current system, founded on principles of equity in the distribution of program costs and benefits. Efficiency of such programs would be further supported by the suggestions we have made for better management using, where appropriate, principles of competition.

These proposed changes would constitute a major reform of the Medicaid program. In the area of federal–state financing, they would entail a considerable shift in the distribution of federal funds and would require significant changes at the state level as well. In terms of covering the uninsured, they would build on Medicaid's existing federal–state structure to administer a program of neutral subsidies for employment-based insurance and individual coverage for the self-employed and those not currently taking group coverage. Additional adjustments would be needed in the federal tax code to provide for the more equitable application of federal subsidies for health insurance coverage.

Changing the matching-rate structure will be no easy thing. We are calling for a basic change in a formula that has been resistant to changes since the program began. The change will be complex, with subtle implications designed to achieve two goals simultaneously, each of which will have its opponents.

Medicaid has evolved over time to meet needs and an expanding awareness of obligations; we believe that both liberals and conservatives could find reason to support using the program as one vehicle toward more comprehensive or even universal coverage in the future, and toward a system that makes greater use of markets and competition to allocate resources. Most important, Medicaid's federal–state structure allows for resource allocation decisions that reflect voter preferences, ensuring that uniform universal coverage comes when—and only when—taxpayers see value in the program and are ready to pay for it.

The changes we recommend reflect growing recognition of the limitations of the current system. While they might lead to increases in public program budgets, costs would be reduced for the employers and workers who indirectly bear the costs of uncompensated care today. Such changes could provide increased federal assistance to lower-income states, primarily in the South and West, to be used for ensuring basic medical benefits to greater numbers of those in the lowest income groups. At the same time, they would provide some federal assistance to states that wish to work toward more universal coverage and would give them the freedom to pursue such efforts in ways consistent with local preferences.

Provider Payment. We have devoted a fair amount of space in this book to issues of provider payment. This reflects our view that the incentives inherent in provider payment methods and rates determine much of what any health care financing program (public or private) will accomplish in terms of getting medical services delivered to those it covers. For Medicaid, provider payment rests largely with the states, so we are dealing with more than fifty separate systems, each covering many types of providers and a wide diversity of payment methodologies. We have highlighted the importance for states of having a well-thought-out strategy that can be applied consistently across providers. We have noted the dangers of falling prey to aggressive providers with their persistent requests for special treatment in payment rates or methods. We have emphasized the need for broader use of more accountable payment methods, particularly noting the lack of accountability that exists with cost-based reimbursement, supplemental payments, such as DSH, and medical education payments. We have suggested the advantages of payment based on the specific services delivered regardless of the setting or provider type, rather than the current system, in which most states have different rates for nearly identical services, depending on whether they are delivered in a hospital-affiliated office, an independent physician's office, an ambulatory surgery center, or a community health center.

In all this, we suggest that Medicaid works best when it is used as it was designed: to provide specific covered services to specific eligible individuals. Accountability is lost when high payment rates or supplemental payments are used, even by well-intentioned policymakers, to try to direct resources to enable providers to do other things. While it is tempting to use Medicaid as a ready-made funding source, other more suitable, and separately accountable, vehicles should be used for these other purposes—whether they are helping hospitals with their uncompensated care, supporting academic medical centers, or enabling community health centers to serve the uninsured.

A powerful tool that can be used or misused, provider payment policy should not be neglected, only to be made piecemeal as providers come asking for their specific issues to be addressed. If it is, the likely results will be wasted public resources through unnecessarily high payment rates, provision of care in more costly settings, and the absence of incentives to reduce the provision of uncostworthy care. Payment policy should be developed with specific objectives in mind—for recipients and taxpayers, as well as for providers—and used to shape the provision of services in an efficient and equitable manner. Incentives can be the key to getting providers to meet these objectives.

Managing the Policymaking Process

Medicaid requires a balancing of interests among groups that have stakes in Medicaid and other health care programs for the poor. The public choice framework suggests a focus on fundamental underlying concerns, and it cautions policymakers not to go too far in meeting the needs of any one group, lest that lead to inefficient choices. It also acknowledges the ultimate accountability of the program to the voter-taxpayers, who provide the resources and must support any solution.

Going too far to meet the demands of, for instance, advocates for nonmedical personal care services for recipients, or to extend eligibility at public expense too far up the income scale, will lead to expenditures that are not highly valued either by those who receive them or by the taxpayers paying the bills—who in some cases may have incomes not too different from those of beneficiaries. Acknowledging this reality and taking it into account with appropriate income-related premiums or other cost-sharing will be important in any achieving and maintaining support for any publicly financed health insurance program.

Similarly, going too far to accommodate the short-term demands of some constituent groups for lower taxes or to meet state budget requirements in hard economic times can reduce benefits below what might be supported by the median voter as a reflection of his or her values of caring for the poor. This suggests a need to focus on long-run preferences and resources and find ways to adjust federal support cyclically, to ensure that needs are met in adverse times and not overextended when times are good.

Going too far to meet provider demands has two risks. One is to pay more than necessary to induce the supply of needed services, and thereby necessitate the shortchanging of recipients or the unnecessary burdening of taxpayers. The other is to respond to the more vocal and aggressive provider interests and neglect other providers who may simply reduce their supply of services—if not with respect to participation, then in the number of Medicaid patients seen.

In all these things, policymakers often hear the most vocal proponents of one or another interest group. They should be wary of the industry lawyers, lobbyists, and advocacy groups who make a business of helping these beneficiaries and providers get their fair shares, and sometimes more than their fair shares, of Medicaid benefits or provider payments. When budgets are tight, and all payment rates low, it is all too easy to give much or all of any feasible payment increase to those knocking at the door. We would encourage policymakers in both legislative and executive branches at both the state and federal levels to avoid the extremes and the specific interests and attend, rather, to balancing interests and meeting the fundamental goals of the program.

In other words, policymakers should focus on Medicaid basics: coverage of those unable to provide for themselves; payment of specific claims for covered services for eligible individuals; and payment at rates that just cover costs or are just sufficient to induce the provision of needed services at an acceptable level of access. We encourage policymakers to ask what the promises are that we as a society wish to make:

- To the poor: How far up the income scale are 100 percent subsidies to go, and how much subsidy is needed beyond that?

- To providers: How much payment is needed to induce the desired level of supply and access to services?

- To taxpayers: How much funding is really needed to meet program goals, and how can the program be managed to ensure that the maximum value is achieved for the amount spent?

Things to Keep and Things to Change. As we strive to implement a national health care reform agenda, one can ask: What is the role of Medicaid? How can it be made to work better? What elements should the program keep, and what elements should be changed? We can also ask what has been learned from the Medicaid experience that may say something about expanding coverage to those not currently eligible for Medicaid. The following list represents our suggestions for things to keep and things to change:

- **Keep a state role in funding decisions for the poor.** Among the things we think are worth retaining in Medicaid is the federal–state partnership, with states determining benefits for the poor at the local level. The local nature of preferences—for caring for those in one's own community—appears to be important and has apparently been a contributing factor to the resilience of the Medicaid program, as well as allowing for taxpayers in higher-income states to express their preferences for relatively generous benefits in their communities. We believe there is evidence of a local dimension in altruism that ought not to be ignored in planning for our national health care system. It should be allowed expression, along with some level of federal participation, to reflect the value that federal taxpayers attach to ensuring access to needed care for all. This will require accepting some variation in benefits and the mixture of services across states.

- **Change the matching-rate structure.** The federal matching-rate structure should be changed to ensure the provision of basic services in the lower-income states before providing more generous benefits in the higher-income states. We believe this can best be accomplished with a federal matching-rate structure based on the equal-burden-for-equal-benefit (EBEB) framework that we outlined in chapter 8. That structure would ensure the maintenance of equity in financing through the provision of a basic benefit but reduce the level of federal support for states that greatly exceed national spending norms. It would direct more resources to the lower-income states so that basic funding in other states is brought along before federal funds are poured into waiver program expansions that only the higher-income states are financially able to afford. It would allow policymakers to set federal assistance at any level desired, but would at any level provide for a division of resources that would better reflect relative state needs and fiscal capacities. And, in contrast to the current situation, it would enable each state to achieve a specified national level of benefits without devoting more than a specified share of taxpayer income to the state contribution.

- **Change federal assistance to make funds to states automatically countercyclical.** States have needs for medical (and other) federal assistance that depend on the business cycle and on abilities to raise revenue that are reduced when need is greatest. While we might hope for states to improve their planning for years of abundance and scarcity, it is really the federal government that has the fiscal capacity to adjust for business cycles, and increased federal assistance in lean years should be built in, not something that states should have to wait for Congress to grant. This could be accomplished with more timely or even prospective adjustments in matching to current or expected economic conditions and with funds set aside in trust, thereby making more efficient use of state fiscal capacity, when available, to support the long-term sustainability of the program.

- **Change federal requirements for Medicaid eligibility.** Medicaid mandatory coverage groups should be extended somewhat further up the income scale, with the expansion supported with enhanced matching for the lower income levels. The intention would be to make eligibility more uniform among the states but to leave benefits to be determined by them, and not to extend eligibility further in higher-income, higher-eligibility states. Some program other than Medicaid should then be used to effect insurance coverage for those above the maximum Medicaid income cutoff.

- **Change Medicaid's spend-down provisions.** While tighter monitoring of asset transfers and family obligations is warranted prior to making individuals eligible for long-term care under spend-down provisions, we also suggest developing equally strict standards governing retroactive Medicaid eligibility for persons and families with large one-time medical expenses.

- **Change the system of DSH and supplemental payments, as well as cost reimbursement and episode-based payments, to more accountable funding methods.** We have argued that it is inherently difficult to monitor use of funds spent on the supplemental payment components of Medicaid. The rationale for cost reimbursement is weak, and cost-based payment should be replaced by rates that reflect average costs of producing services in the most appropriate settings.

- **Change the rules to allow states to pursue a variety of cost containment and quality efforts.** These efforts should include tightening accountability in provider payment, implementing evidence-based payment, and enabling states to exclude providers determined not to be cost-effective—as private-sector preferred provider organizations can do now.

- **Change the structure of federal subsidies to account for the continuity of preferences.** Net federal subsidies (program benefits, premium subsidies, and tax deductibility) should decline continuously across the full range of the income distribution so they will be seamless and equitable for all. This should be accomplished by designing interfaces among Medicaid, CHIP, a premium subsidy program, and employer-based coverage so that each individual will receive very nearly the same subsidy as others at the same income level, regardless of his or her state of residence or individual access to employer-based coverage.

Lessons for Implementing National Health Care Reform. Experience from previous efforts at national health care reform, such as the 1988 Medicare Catastrophic Coverage Act and the Clinton health security plan proposed in 1993, suggests that for reform to be successful it must convince the public, or at least the politically active portion of the public, that it is not being asked to give up too much for the sake of health care for others. This has been one theme of this book. Our model implies that decisions to provide publicly funded benefits or subsidies for health insurance should follow voter preferences, with particular attention paid to the voter with median preferences on the issue.

Efforts toward national health reform are testing the limits of willingness to pay for public programs to help cover those now uninsured. There are some indications that voters may not be ready to provide publicly funded (particularly state-funded) benefits much further up the income distribution. We have seen that the federal government has had to induce states to extend CHIP programs with higher federal matching than provided by the basic Medicaid formula. We have seen lower-income states, in particular, unwilling to fund even basic Medicaid up to the level of higher-income states (a situation we have suggested is in part—if only in part—related to the currently skewed federal matching).

This general view has been confirmed over the years by taxpayer unwillingness to support much additional spending on national health insurance
or any more-than-incremental expansions of existing programs. Recent
research confirms this hesitation. Blendon and others, reporting in a 2008
article on polls taken at the time of the then-recent presidential election,
found voters to be favorably inclined toward a broad array of program initiatives that would help people get access to health care. But this support
seemed not to extend to programs that would require significant additional
public spending. Except in the case of medical care for veterans and programs to prevent disease and improve health, the survey on which the article was based found that only a minority of voters, when reminded of the
budget deficit and competing priorities, favored increases in spending on
various medical care programs. Medicaid (with 33 percent favoring
increased spending) ranked last among the medical programs, behind veterans (72 percent), programs to prevent disease and improve health (53 percent), Medicare (41 percent), programs to protect against bioterrorism (38
percent), and biomedical research (34 percent). Even among voters for
Barack Obama, only 42 percent supported increased Medicaid spending,
though only 12 percent of all voters and 7 percent of Obama voters indicated
a preference for decreased Medicaid spending. The poll suggested that most
voters (51 percent) supported keeping Medicaid spending about the same.

While nothing here shows that voters will support greatly extending publicly funded coverage to the uninsured if it is perceived to involve additional
spending, our model does offer some indications about how their resistance—and that of policymakers—might be overcome. First, we must recognize that preferences, as expressed in votes and polls, reflect assumptions
about medical costs and the nature of the financing and delivery systems that
would be employed to pay them. We may be able to change those assumptions by altering the financing and delivery systems so voters will be more
receptive to proposals for filling the coverage gaps.

A second lesson from Medicaid—one that comes from observing the
wide interstate variations—is that one can have a program that not everyone or every state can afford to use to full advantage. As the implications of
any new national program become apparent, it will be important to watch
for signs that some groups have been left out, in that the level of public subsidy available to them is insufficient to support participation in the program

or insurance option. There is a real risk that new program components and expanded roles for Medicaid may create options that are more fully used by many of the same higher-benefit states that we have seen account for a disproportionate share of benefits and federal funding. Policy adjustments can be made. As we have suggested, one solution is to get the subsidy levels right for both individuals and states. We have provided details on ways to set federal matching based on principles of equity for taxpayers and the poor.

Third, our work suggests that greater public support for programs may follow greater value. Achieving high value in these programs requires that the services go to those most in need and have a real impact on the recipients' health or well-being. We have seen evidence that policymakers respond to the lower prices that result from a higher federal CHIP match in a federal–state structure. They may similarly respond to lower costs of coverage or greater value in program services that are regarded as a public good. We have suggested a variety of possible reforms that would tend to enhance the value of Medicaid spending in this sense. Similar methods will be needed in any proposal for national health reform that asks voter-taxpayers to support spending on programs or subsidies to extend health insurance coverage to those groups now uninsured. These methods include the following:

- **Redirect federal funds toward lower-income states.** Our analysis suggests that the poor in lower-income states have gotten the short end of Medicaid benefits compared with their counterparts in higher-income states, which are better able to afford more extensive Medicaid programs. We suggest revising federal matching to direct a greater share of funding to the lower-income states, particularly those with higher-than-average poverty rates and with lower-than-average incomes among taxpayers. This could be done in any number of ways, but the equal-burden-for-equal-benefit approach we outline above provides a tool to help policymakers achieve equity in the distribution of federal funds at any desired budget level. We recognize the political difficulty of this task and the need for some combination of phase-in over time with additional federal funds to hold harmless (at least in the short run) those benefiting from the current system.

- **Reduce use of unaccountable payment methods.** We have noted a number of areas in which provider payment methods do not provide for accountability sufficient to ensure that resources are used for Medicaid-eligible persons or covered services, or in many cases even related groups and services. These areas include DSH and other supplemental payments, indirect medical education payments to hospitals, cost reimbursement of critical access and other hospitals, such as children's hospitals, and payment to FQHCs of a high flat rate for visits regardless of visit content or complexity. Many of these methods apply to safety-net providers, so it will be important to ensure that changes toward greater accountability do not impair the mission of these organizations.

- **Reduce special favorable payment rates.** In many states, specific providers receive atypical, differentiated, or otherwise favorable funding above what is paid to other providers for similar or equivalent services. These arrangements include favorable payment rates for public or captive providers or provider groups, such as public hospitals, school-based clinics, and community mental health centers. Such exceptions, which often produce rates unrelated to costs of care, have been used by states to tap federal revenue for state-supported service providers and to support providers who serve the uninsured, and they will be less needed when the number of uninsured is reduced.

- **Allow states to direct patients to the most cost-effective providers.** Among all the various managed care methods that have been tried through the years in the private sector, the most commonly used and longest-lasting approach has been the preferred provider organization (PPO). In the public sector, by contrast, all providers willing to accept Medicaid rates are generally allowed to participate, at least in fee-for-service Medicaid. The ability to direct patients to trusted cost-effective providers, as is common in private health plans, needs to be allowed in fee-for-service Medicaid. Methods that should be considered include competitive bidding and preferred provider arrangements.

- **Institute evidence-based payment.** To reduce use of (and/or payment for) services not proved to be effective or cost-effective, evidence-based coverage limitations or payment rate adjustments should be allowed where evidence that distinguishes the effectiveness of treatments is available. We have noted that reduced payment, rather than all-out prohibition, may reduce and discourage such services without impinging (except in a monetary way) on providers who, while persisting in some unproven practices, may be useful providers in other respects.

- **Redirect federal subsidies by income/coverage group.** More value from, and better continuity of, subsidies may be achieved by reducing employer-based tax subsidies above a capped value and using the funds to extend Medicaid or other susbsidies to lower-income groups. This would likely enhance value to taxpayers in two ways. First, it would save money from the subsidy of last-dollar coverage of the most generous employer-based plans and put more of the subsidy into the hands of lower-income groups (perhaps including workers), many previously uncovered, whose health may be expected to benefit most from the coverage. Second, the public value of the spending would be enhanced, and the expected private value reduced, for the median voter, as some voters would be beneficiaries of the subsidy for high-end employer coverage.

- **Maintain state flexibility.** This list should not preclude states from using existing controls on eligibility, benefits, provider payment, and contracting for managed care. Room should remain for state initiatives to control costs and redirect resources toward higher-value care in ways that are consistent with state priorities and local health care delivery systems.

The application of all these methods may produce more taxpayer support for, and acceptance of, additional spending on Medicaid and CHIP, with the increased funds available going toward expanding coverage. Our model suggests that lower costs of providing benefits will lead taxpayers to demand more of the public programs that provide them. We see these reforms of Medicaid and CHIP as going hand in hand with any program expansions or new programs that would extend or subsidize coverage to additional groups as part of a national health care reform initiative. Even if voters prove tolerant of additional spending (if not accompanied by additional taxes) in times of economic downturn, these or some other forms of significant and meaningful cost containment may be necessary to obtain their continuing support for such programs in the long run. Cost containment beyond what has been used in public programs to date may also be needed to ensure support for any broad-based expansion of the government's role in helping lower-income persons to obtain public or private health insurance coverage.

The changes we recommend for Medicaid are needed regardless of the direction and pace of national health care policy changes, and nearly all of them are crucial if we go on to new or expanded programs to reduce the number of uninsured. The cost containment strategies we propose will be needed to help free up resources for changes, and the lessons we have learned about balancing the needs of the poor, providers, and taxpayers will be very relevant as policymakers try to find the right program models and levels of spending, and assign appropriate state and federal roles in the administration of the new or expanded programs.

What We Can Expect from Medicaid Reform. The realignment of Medicaid spending that we propose will require some sacrifices from all stakeholder groups and will provide all of them with new benefits as well. The poor will find benefits to be more equal across states, with those in higher-benefit states perhaps seeing some reduction in the availability of the less costworthy services and those in lower-benefit states finding it easier to qualify and perhaps seeing improvements in access to care that really make a difference. Particularly in lower-income states, the poor should attain better access to primary care doctors and require less emergency room use. In all states, recipients may see better access to primary care physicians outside safety-net provider settings.

At the same time, taxpayers in lower-income states will find they can now afford to cover more of the poor uninsured in their states, and that they may have a mandate to do so. But they will have less incentive to provide extensive benefits to those at the upper end of Medicaid's income distribution and may have new and greater reasons to attend to care management and cost containment methods based on provider payment. They will find their tax dollars used to better advantage and directed to Medicaid's specific purposes, and will have greater confidence that each state is getting its full share of federal resources.

Providers would also see mixed results. Safety-net providers may see some of the greatest changes, especially if Medicaid reform is eventually combined with new programs to expand coverage of the uninsured. Public hospitals, FQHCs, and other safety-net providers would see a reduction in the use of fixed, but loosely monitored, funding sources such as grants, as well as in cost-based reimbursement, supplemental payments (for instance, DSH), medical education payments, and high preferential rates. Their funding would shift to payments more closely linked to services delivered to identifiable individuals and rates closer to what other providers receive for similar services. But with Medicaid coverage of more persons, especially in the lower-income states, they would see reductions in the amount of uncompensated and discounted care. If reforms include payment based on the service delivered rather than the type of provider or place of service, private physician practices would see increases in Medicaid payment rates relative to those of hospital outpatient departments. Freestanding ambulatory surgery centers and radiology providers would see Medicaid rates more nearly comparable to those paid to hospital outpatient departments for similar services. With evidence-based payment rates, providers would see enhanced payment for services of proven effectiveness and reduced payment for those failing to meet the criteria. While this would affect different providers differently, it would give all incentives to alter practice styles in favor of treatments supported by evidence of effectiveness.

In the end, we would expect to see considerable net gains for each of our three Medicaid stakeholder groups: the poor, taxpayers, and providers. The gains will come from a reformed Medicaid that does a better job of directing resources where they make the most difference in terms of health outcomes and of covering all lower-income persons who need assistance with the cost of medical care, and they should be reflected in national statistics. With more resources flowing to the lower-income states, where the rates of uninsurance are the highest, we should see the greatest drop in the number of uninsured. These changes in Medicaid would be directed

Principles for Reform

- **Principle of Interstate Equity:** Public programs should promote greater (if not complete) equality of treatment for beneficiaries and taxpayers across states.

- **Principle of Continuity of Subsidy:** The public subsidy for health insurance coverage should decrease in a continuous way with the income of the individual or family.

- **Principle of Equality of Payment across Settings:** Medicaid payment methods should be altered to provide for equality of payment for similar services for providers by type and setting.

- **Principle of Claims-Based Accountability:** Payment methods not based on claims should be eliminated and replaced with other systems to account for use of funds.

- **Principle of Provider Network Control:** Publicly funded health insurance programs should exercise a greater degree of control over their provider networks, similar to the control exercised by private managed care plans.

- **Principle of Economy in Production of Health:** Public funding should favor those services for which there is evidence of better health outcomes.

- **Principle of Objective, Nonpolitical Coverage and Rate-Setting Decisions:** Both coverage and rate-setting decisions should be made on a technical basis by objective decision-makers with the requisite expertise.

- **Principle of Value-Based Cost Containment:** Public programs should not pay more than necessary to obtain the supply of services needed by program beneficiaries.

- **Principle of Automatic Economic Adjustment:** Public programs for lower-income persons should provide for automatic adjustments to the economic cycle.

- **Principle of Partitioned Responsibility:** Any reform program should clearly partition the responsibility to provide for everyone to whom the plan applies.

toward equalizing coverage among the lowest-income populations. They are needed as enabling factors to support any broader reform efforts by building a foundation for programs to reduce the number of uninsured at somewhat higher income levels.

What Is Required of Policymakers

With this book we provide a framework for policymakers to look at Medicaid in a new way, a way that highlights the importance of public choices that balance the interests of those who may receive Medicaid benefits, those who pay for the program, and those who provide the services. This may, to some, appear to be a simple proposal that asks for what already happens in the political process. But it is really quite hard: We are calling upon policymakers to confront some of the forces that have frustrated health care reform efforts for years. We make the request based on the logic of equity and efficiency concerns, based on our understanding of the economics of the Medicaid program and the markets in which it procures services, and based on the public values embodied in the constitutionally empowered institutions from which the Medicaid program derives its support and financing.

Meeting the seemingly simple objective of balancing the interests of the poor, taxpayers, and providers in a way that enhances equity, efficiency, and democracy will require some complex thinking on the part of policymakers who face the problems of Medicaid reform. It will also require elected representatives to grapple with political tradeoffs and compromises based on a set of principles. We hope that the principles will provide a bit of common ground upon which workable compromises can be created, and a tool to address three significant barriers to health care reform: ideology, local self-interests, and provider interests.

With respect to ideology, both conservatives and liberals will need to quit looking at proposed Medicaid policies based almost exclusively on whether they increase or decrease spending on the program. Too often, liberals are willing to support programs without proper accountability to provide funds where needs are perceived. Too often, conservatives are willing to overlook opportunities for program changes that would add value to recipients and taxpayers but at some additional cost. Both groups will need to set aside their advocacy roles and focus instead on equity and efficiency. Some important goals for Medicaid can only be achieved by reducing uncostworthy care and making programs more accountable, to free up resources needed to help cover those in need and provide services that have a real impact on health and well-being. Future program reforms must do more than just offer the prospect of (uncertain) future savings if we only spend more (with certainty) on the latest approach to care management, or information systems, or medical homes, or whatever. They must actually limit and direct the flow of resources within the health care system—through changes in provider payment or federal financing—and do so in ways that create real budget constraints for programs and health plans, along with incentives for the provision of high-value care and the elimination of beneficial but uncostworthy care.

With respect to local self-interests, a major barrier to political agreement is the need of each state's representatives to achieve an agreement that provides at least as much in federal financing as the states received before. We have extensively highlighted the current unequal distribution of federal funds among the states and how it would need to be changed to be more consistent with program goals of equity for the poor and for taxpayers. The unwillingness of higher-income, higher-benefit states to give up their current shares of federal funds is a significant obstacle to both Medicaid reform and any broader reform that includes public assistance in some form to lower-income workers and their families.

It would be all too easy to allow previous patterns in the distribution of federal funds to continue, by means of new federal support through CHIP expansions or state-specific, Massachusetts-like waivers that can best be taken advantage of by states with relatively few poor persons, high incomes, and even better-than-average employer-based coverage. These states will want to continue open-ended federal funding at matching rates of 50 percent or higher. We have suggested equal-burden-for-equal-benefit (EBEB) matching as a standard for equitable distribution of funds, but equalizing burdens with such an approach will require either greater federal spending to raise the lagging states or, alternatively, a redistribution of federal assistance from higher-spending to currently lower-spending states. This leaves policymakers with the difficult choice of accepting current inequities, or obtaining new funds to support a greater federal role. It should be noted, however, that higher federal spending for this purpose would directly address the nation's problem of the uninsured and, if done through Medicaid with EBEB matching, would do so in a way that would fairly distribute the burden among state taxpayers across the nation. The difficulty with such an approach to national reform would be with the higher-income, higher-benefit states that are actively seeking additional federal support for their own program expansions.

With respect to the interests of providers, we have suggested that, to improve accountability and equalize payments among them, supplemental payments, cost reimbursement, and otherwise preferential payment rates should be ended for a number of provider types. Substitute payment sources will need to be found for these providers where they play a safety-net role. The most logical approach is to provide more adequate Medicaid payment and coverage of some form to the uninsured patients they serve. This part of Medicaid reform is then connected to broader health care reform, as one should not happen without the other.

Of these three barriers to meaningful Medicaid reform based on equity, efficiency, and democracy—and to meaningful health care reform in general—the local self-interests of the higher-income, higher-benefit states in protecting their current advantages are probably the most serious. Red states and greedy providers will not present the only opposition to a broad-based, national health care reform that includes greater equity in benefits. Self-interested representatives in some blue states, well positioned on health care committees on Capitol Hill, may also prefer more narrow reforms that do not disrupt the current distribution of federal health care dollars to their states.

The barriers of ideology, local self-interests, and provider interests are not insurmountable, but true reform that addresses the issues raised in this work will not be easy. It will require senators and representatives to vote for legislation that will close the loopholes their most favored providers are using to obtain better payment than their peers. It will require representatives from higher-benefit states to accept that the lower-income, lower-benefit states will receive the largest share of any new resources, at least until the interstate differences in spending per poor person are reduced or eliminated. To achieve more equal payment for similar services across settings, reform will require budget-conscious legislators to accept increases in provider payment rates for physicians and ambulatory surgery centers, for example, while at the same time requiring hospitals' outpatient departments and FQHCs to accept rates lower than they currently receive. It will require states to give up some control over eligibility in return for better protection against swings in economic activity.

Extending reform into these areas will require a willingness to restructure Medicaid's incentives for states and for providers, since those of the current system, while insufficient to encourage many lower-income states to cover more than basic benefits and eligibility, have yet been sufficient to lead many higher-income states to be more generous to recipients at higher income levels than those in the lower-income, lower-benefit states. It will also require more equal payment for similar services among provider types and settings to improve access for recipients in locations where access has been difficult.

Pursuing further Medicaid reform in such mundane areas as provider payment and federal financing could be a major step toward this type of reform. It would be particularly valuable in laying the groundwork for the cost containment and cost-effectiveness that will be needed to free resources for investment in broader eligibility and more effective care. Even if the backroom activities of economists and actuaries can provide the basis for the savings required to achieve the most important program and social goals, these must be translated into policy by federal policymakers with some willingness to compromise—to refrain from blindly pursuing their own states' self-interests, and instead reach agreements built on principles that will lead programs toward achieving broader national goals. To that end, we suggest that Congress must change its mindset and attend more directly to the issues of

- equity, in a program that treats both recipients and taxpayers fairly across states;

- efficiency, in a program that provides incentives for costworthy care and pays enough but no more than what is needed to bring forth the desired level of services; and

- democracy, in a program that reflects the desired level and type of spending that is supported by the voters.

For this to happen, Congress will need to be willing to distance Medicaid policy from traditional interests of well-represented provider and advocacy groups. The program will need to be reconstituted as one that reduces the flow of funds into low-value services and increases the availability of basic benefits. It must also integrate these principles and methods into any new national health reform plan. We believe that many of the ideas and suggestions in this book can help in that process.

Appendix 1:
State Tables

TABLE A1-1

MEDICAID ELIGIBILITY RATIOS BY STATE, 2004

States in order of median household income	Medicaid recipients to number of poor	Elderly recipients to elderly population	Disabled recipients to disabled population	Child recipients to children in poverty
District of Columbia	1.62	0.12	0.40	2.23
New Jersey	1.33	0.08	0.17	2.05
Maryland	1.59	0.09	0.18	2.74
Hawaii	1.69	0.11	0.16	2.88
New Hampshire	1.26	0.07	0.10	2.56
Connecticut	1.95	0.11	0.16	2.72
Alaska	2.27	0.15	0.15	2.73
Minnesota	1.69	0.10	0.18	2.59
Massachusetts	1.88	0.10	0.34	2.26
Utah	1.20	0.06	0.13	1.65
Virginia	1.07	0.09	0.14	1.74
Colorado	1.01	0.09	0.14	1.65
California	2.15	0.17	0.26	2.02
Washington	1.40	0.10	0.18	2.47
Delaware	1.97	0.08	0.16	2.59
Vermont	2.76	0.22	0.22	4.22
Rhode Island	1.57	0.11	0.25	2.11
Nevada	0.82	0.06	0.12	1.32
Illinois	1.38	0.18	0.21	1.79
New York	1.78	0.14	0.29	1.89
Nebraska	1.31	0.09	0.13	2.41
Wisconsin	1.57	0.16	0.21	1.89
Pennsylvania	1.32	0.10	0.23	1.82
Wyoming	1.34	0.07	0.11	2.54
Iowa	1.36	0.08	0.16	2.10
Arizona	1.34	0.06	0.15	1.75
Idaho	1.05	0.08	0.14	2.24
Michigan	1.49	0.07	0.21	1.96
Ohio	1.37	0.09	0.18	2.07
Georgia	1.52	0.12	0.23	2.08
Maine	1.88	0.14	0.21	2.85

Continued on the next page

Table A1-1, continued

States in order of median household income	Medicaid recipients to number of poor	Elderly recipients to elderly population	Disabled recipients to disabled population	Child recipients to children in poverty
Missouri	1.73	0.12	0.20	2.31
Oregon	1.13	0.09	0.13	1.58
Indiana	1.45	0.09	0.14	2.12
South Dakota	1.58	0.09	0.19	2.23
Florida	1.43	0.09	0.20	1.96
Kansas	1.31	0.08	0.15	1.71
Texas	0.99	0.12	0.14	1.60
North Carolina	1.20	0.14	0.20	1.87
North Dakota	1.07	0.09	0.11	1.78
South Carolina	1.35	0.19	0.20	1.92
New Mexico	1.32	0.09	0.19	2.47
Tennessee	1.99	0.16	0.38	2.39
Oklahoma	1.26	0.11	0.14	2.36
Alabama	1.14	0.10	0.24	1.73
Louisiana	1.31	0.16	0.25	2.03
Kentucky	1.23	0.11	0.27	1.80
Arkansas	1.49	0.14	0.19	2.25
Montana	0.89	0.07	0.13	1.43
West Virginia	1.19	0.10	0.23	1.87
Mississippi	1.20	0.23	0.27	1.61
United States	*1.48*	*0.12*	*0.21*	*1.96*
Income quintiles				
Top ten	1.59	0.10	0.17	2.39
Second ten	1.62	0.12	0.20	2.25
Third ten	1.42	0.10	0.19	2.13
Fourth ten	1.32	0.11	0.17	1.91
Bottom ten	1.30	0.13	0.23	2.00
DC	1.62	0.12	0.40	2.23
Ratio top ten to bottom ten	1.22	0.76	0.75	1.20

SOURCE: Computed by the authors from U.S. Department of Health and Human Services, Centers for Medicare and Medicaid Services (2007) and U.S. Census Bureau (2006).

TABLE A1-2

MEASURES OF OVERALL MEDICAID BENEFITS PER LOWER-INCOME PERSON
BY STATE, FY 2007

States in alphabetical order	Medicaid pay per person < FPL	Medicaid pay per person < 125% FPL	Medicaid pay per person < 125% FPL COL Adj. FPL	Real cost-adjusted Medicaid pay per person < 125% FPL COL Adj. FPL
United States	$8,576	$6,283	$6,283	$6,283
Alabama	$6,220	$4,913	$5,364	$5,901
Alaska	$18,706	$13,629	$8,845	$8,530
Arizona	$7,256	$5,656	$5,112	$5,270
Arkansas	$8,003	$5,922	$6,766	$7,577
California	$7,838	$5,332	$3,622	$3,344
Colorado	$6,126	$4,633	$4,381	$4,480
Connecticut	$14,081	$10,664	$7,665	$6,949
Delaware	$12,386	$8,542	$8,102	$7,975
District of Columbia	$13,342	$10,673	$8,221	$7,314
Florida	$6,037	$4,438	$4,234	$4,025
Georgia	$5,416	$4,023	$4,524	$4,659
Hawaii	$11,680	$8,645	$4,175	$3,942
Idaho	$7,359	$5,053	$5,666	$6,179
Illinois	$10,034	$7,138	$7,495	$7,578
Indiana	$6,919	$5,252	$5,750	$6,092
Iowa	$9,612	$7,313	$7,939	$8,763
Kansas	$6,700	$4,697	$5,390	$5,871
Kentucky	$7,033	$5,041	$5,667	$6,214
Louisiana	$7,998	$6,144	$6,571	$6,767
Maine	$14,024	$10,265	$8,427	$8,871
Maryland	$11,071	$8,985	$6,400	$6,324
Massachusetts	$14,562	$11,766	$9,184	$8,418
Michigan	$8,614	$6,327	$6,590	$6,448
Minnesota	$12,846	$9,954	$9,348	$9,718
Mississippi	$5,017	$4,008	$4,340	$4,769
Missouri	$8,885	$6,679	$7,594	$8,002
Montana	$6,005	$4,387	$4,213	$4,697

Continued on the next page

Table A1-2, continued

Nebraska	$8,831	$6,074	$7,224	$7,991
Nevada	$4,976	$3,616	$3,177	$3,120
New Hampshire	$15,332	$10,593	$8,392	$8,342
New Jersey	$12,018	$7,941	$5,992	$5,393
New Mexico	$9,720	$6,807	$6,731	$7,138
New York	$16,082	$11,749	$9,163	$8,500
North Carolina	$6,908	$5,120	$5,348	$5,683
North Dakota	$8,912	$6,048	$6,565	$7,434
Ohio	$9,029	$6,985	$7,549	$7,743
Oklahoma	$7,087	$4,792	$5,900	$6,534
Oregon	$6,018	$4,495	$3,829	$3,980
Pennsylvania	$12,514	$9,082	$8,838	$8,811
Rhode Island	$17,450	$13,187	$9,859	$9,408
South Carolina	$6,749	$4,770	$5,107	$5,509
South Dakota	$8,374	$5,252	$6,382	$7,171
Tennessee	$7,869	$5,722	$6,809	$7,345
Texas	$5,276	$3,988	$4,511	$4,589
Utah	$5,453	$3,631	$3,962	$4,170
Vermont	$14,825	$10,766	$7,943	$8,283
Virginia	$7,474	$5,154	$5,114	$5,053
Washington	$8,761	$6,558	$6,257	$6,232
West Virginia	$8,203	$6,607	$6,973	$7,531
Wisconsin	$8,215	$6,095	$6,444	$6,720
Wyoming	$7,736	$5,855	$5,626	$6,210
Maximum	$18,706	$13,629	$9,859	$9,718
Third quartile value	$11,849	$8,594	$7,629	$7,859
Median	$8,215	$6,074	$6,400	$6,534
First quartile value	$6,913	$4,977	$5,113	$5,332
Minimum	$4,976	$3,616	$3,177	$3,120
Ratio max to min	3.76	3.77	3.10	3.11
Ratio third to first quartile	1.71	1.73	1.49	1.47

SOURCES: Computed using data from U.S. Census Bureau (2008b) and Kaiser Family Foundation (2009, "Federal and State Share of Medicaid Spending, FY2006," http://www.statehealthfacts.org).
NOTES: Total federal and state medical payments include DSH, exclude administrative costs; payments deflated by average of physician practice cost index; number of poor estimated by adjusting 125 percent of FPL by ACCRA cost-of-living index.

TABLE A1-3

MEDICAID HAS HIGHER- AND LOWER-BENEFIT STATES
RELATIVE TO MEDICARE

States in alphabetical order	Ratio Medicaid payment per poor person/Medicare FFS payments per beneficiary	States in alphabetical order	Ratio Medicaid payment per poor person/Medicare FFS payments per beneficiary
Alabama	64%	New Jersey	64%
Alaska	114%	New Mexico	92%
Arizona	61%	New York	94%
Arkansas	83%	North Carolina	63%
California	38%	North Dakota	105%
Colorado	57%	Ohio	82%
Connecticut	80%	Oklahoma	58%
Delaware	101%	Oregon	63%
District of Columbia	101%	Pennsylvania	104%
Florida	42%	Rhode Island	112%
Georgia	56%	South Carolina	63%
Hawaii	78%	South Dakota	99%
Idaho	83%	Tennessee	70%
Illinois	70%	Texas	41%
Indiana	82%	Utah	60%
Iowa	121%	Vermont	114%
Kansas	70%	Virginia	69%
Kentucky	65%	Washington	84%
Louisiana	61%	West Virginia	85%
Maine	115%	Wisconsin	86%
Maryland	64%	Wyoming	82%
Massachusetts	91%		
Michigan	67%	Maximum	123%
Minnesota	123%	Third quartile value	97%
Mississippi	54%	Median	80%
Missouri	95%	First quartile value	63%
Montana	65%	Minimum	34%
Nebraska	102%		
Nevada	34%	Ratio max to min	3.56
New Hampshire	100%	Ratio third to first quartile	1.53

SOURCES: Computed by the authors using data from U.S. Boards of Trustees (2008) and Kaiser Family Foundation (2009, "Federal and State Share of Medicaid Spending, FY2006," http://www.statehealthfacts.org).

TABLE A1-4

MEDICAID AND CHIP PAYMENTS PER POOR PERSON BY STATE, FY 2007

States in alphabetical order	Medicaid payment per person below FPL				CHIP
	Acute care	Long-term care	Disproportionate share hospital payments	Total Medicaid	
United States	$5,225	$2,922	$429	$8,576	$233
Alabama	$3,597	$1,983	$640	$6,220	$184
Alaska	$11,415	$6,996	$295	$18,706	$452
Arizona	$5,341	$1,757	$157	$7,256	$168
Arkansas	$4,991	$2,892	$120	$8,003	$218
California	$4,964	$2,461	$414	$7,838	$335
Colorado	$3,378	$2,383	$364	$6,126	$212
Connecticut	$5,514	$7,551	$1,017	$14,081	$118
Delaware	$7,915	$4,411	$61	$12,386	$166
District of Columbia	$9,111	$3,514	$717	$13,342	$87
Florida	$4,055	$1,840	$142	$6,037	$164
Georgia	$3,934	$1,167	$316	$5,416	$345
Hawaii	$7,745	$3,934	$0	$11,680	$283
Idaho	$4,646	$2,586	$127	$7,359	$232
Illinois	$7,361	$2,516	$157	$10,034	$547
Indiana	$4,136	$2,335	$448	$6,919	$169
Iowa	$4,949	$4,505	$157	$9,612	$265
Kansas	$3,760	$2,801	$138	$6,700	$196
Kentucky	$4,675	$2,060	$298	$7,033	$158
Louisiana	$4,141	$2,469	$1,387	$7,998	$226
Maine	$8,787	$4,946	$291	$14,024	$296
Maryland	$6,905	$3,921	$244	$11,071	$433
Massachusetts	$10,570	$4,545	($554)	$14,562	$463
Michigan	$6,025	$2,166	$423	$8,614	$229
Minnesota	$6,863	$5,785	$198	$12,846	$206
Mississippi	$2,982	$1,743	$292	$5,017	$197
Missouri	$5,740	$2,178	$967	$8,885	$146
Montana	$3,381	$2,515	$109	$6,005	$191
Nebraska	$4,807	$3,868	$156	$8,831	$270

Continued on the next page

Table A1-4, continued

| States in alphabetical order | ————Medicaid payment per person below FPL———— | | | | CHIP |
	Acute care	Long-term care	Dispropor-tionate share hospital payments	Total Medicaid	
Nevada	$3,186	$1,467	$323	$4,976	$179
New Hampshire	$5,935	$6,707	$2,689	$15,332	$177
New Jersey	$5,417	$4,799	$1,802	$12,018	$581
New Mexico	$6,947	$2,701	$72	$9,720	$203
New York	$8,289	$6,909	$884	$16,082	$181
North Carolina	$4,547	$2,058	$302	$6,908	$156
North Dakota	$3,258	$5,626	$29	$8,912	$245
Ohio	$4,634	$3,575	$820	$9,029	$180
Oklahoma	$4,522	$2,478	$86	$7,087	$260
Oregon	$3,891	$2,012	$115	$6,018	$190
Pennsylvania	$6,944	$5,025	$544	$12,514	$219
Rhode Island	$11,623	$5,810	$16	$17,450	$723
South Carolina	$4,390	$1,640	$719	$6,749	$65
South Dakota	$4,850	$3,509	$16	$8,374	$180
Tennessee	$5,531	$2,244	$94	$7,869	$6
Texas	$3,644	$1,263	$368	$5,276	$136
Utah	$3,894	$1,471	$89	$5,453	$193
Vermont	$7,143	$6,900	$782	$14,825	$88
Virginia	$4,081	$3,123	$270	$7,474	$257
Washington	$5,457	$2,854	$450	$8,761	$60
West Virginia	$4,687	$3,233	$282	$8,203	$165
Wisconsin	$4,594	$3,526	$95	$8,215	$200
Wyoming	$3,798	$3,937	$2	$7,736	$208

SOURCES: Computed using data from Kaiser Family Foundation (2009, "Federal and State Share of Medicaid Spending, FY2006," http://www.statehealthfacts.org) and U.S. Census Bureau (2008b).

TABLE A1-5

COMPARISON OF MEDICAID MANAGED CARE SHARES
WITH HMO PENETRATION RATE, FY 2007

States in alphabetical order	Medicaid managed care as a percentage of payments	HMO penetration rates	Ratio
Alabama	24.8%	4.1%	6.05
Alaska	0.0%	0.2%	0.00
Arizona	81.9%	25.3%	3.24
Arkansas	0.7%	3.0%	0.23
California	24.2%	42.9%	0.56
Colorado	15.0%	19.6%	0.77
Connecticut	39.4%	21.5%	1.83
Delaware	58.9%	19.2%	3.07
District of Columbia	31.5%	52.9%	0.60
Florida	22.6%	19.4%	1.16
Georgia	40.9%	19.2%	2.13
Hawaii	44.6%	47.7%	0.94
Idaho	1.4%	4.6%	0.30
Illinois	1.6%	12.3%	0.13
Indiana	31.8%	17.0%	1.87
Iowa	8.7%	7.5%	1.16
Kansas	25.6%	14.7%	1.74
Kentucky	23.6%	8.0%	2.95
Louisiana	0.0%	7.5%	0.00
Maine	0.2%	9.4%	0.02
Maryland	49.6%	26.1%	1.90
Massachusetts	27.5%	34.3%	0.80
Michigan	51.6%	27.7%	1.86
Minnesota	50.5%	21.3%	2.37
Mississippi	0.0%	1.5%	0.00
Missouri	20.3%	13.2%	1.54
Montana	1.0%	5.9%	0.17
Nebraska	9.3%	4.6%	2.02
Nevada	21.4%	20.0%	1.07
New Hampshire	0.3%	11.3%	0.03

Continued on the next page

Table A1-5, continued

States in alphabetical order	Medicaid managed care percentage of payments	HMO penetration rates	Ratio
New Jersey	34.0%	20.8%	1.63
New Mexico	66.3%	26.6%	2.49
New York	28.5%	27.7%	1.03
North Carolina	1.5%	5.3%	0.28
North Dakota	0.4%	2.6%	0.15
Ohio	47.5%	17.9%	2.65
Oklahoma	7.6%	6.6%	1.15
Oregon	52.0%	27.1%	1.92
Pennsylvania	72.1%	28.0%	2.58
Rhode Island	20.1%	20.2%	1.00
South Carolina	6.3%	10.1%	0.62
South Dakota	2.7%	10.0%	0.27
Tennessee	64.2%	25.5%	2.52
Texas	21.6%	13.2%	1.64
Utah	16.9%	29.6%	0.57
Vermont	10.6%	8.8%	1.20
Virginia	44.0%	16.3%	2.70
Washington	36.4%	18.6%	1.96
West Virginia	19.6%	15.0%	1.31
Wisconsin	45.9%	24.8%	1.85
Wyoming	0.0%	4.2%	0.00

SOURCES: Kaiser Family Foundation 2009, "State HMO Penetration Rates," http://www.statehealthfacts.org/comparetable.jsp?ind=349&cat=7&sub=85&yr=71&typ=2&sort=a, and "State Medicaid Managed Care Enrollees as a Percent of Medicaid Enrollees," http://www.statehealthfacts.org/comparetable.jsp?ind=217&cat=4&sub=56&yr=1&typ=2&sort=a.

TABLE A1-6

REDISTRIBUTION EFFECT OF MEDICAID,
NET OF FEDERAL TAX, BY STATE, FY 2006

States in alphabetical order	Net transfer due to Medicaid, DSH, and CHIP	————Net transfer due to federal participation———— ($ millions)		
		Net transfer due to Medicaid	Net transfer due to DSH	Net transfer due to CHIP
Alabama	$1,359	$1,124	$195	$41
Alaska	$183	$176	$1	$6
Arizona	$1,619	$1,643	−$55	$31
Arkansas	$527	$566	−$54	$15
California	−$3,541	−$3,596	−$213	$268
Colorado	−$1,837	−$1,694	−$101	−$42
Connecticut	−$1,190	−$1,105	−$5	−$80
Delaware	−$484	−$417	−$45	−$22
District of Columbia	−$432	−$376	−$20	−$37
Florida	−$2,695	−$2,225	−$397	−$73
Georgia	−$537	−$663	−$36	$163
Hawaii	$86	$118	−$32	$1
Idaho	$78	$95	−$23	$6
Illinois	−$3,610	−$3,456	−$309	$156
Indiana	$731	$708	$29	−$6
Iowa	$393	$422	−$38	$9
Kansas	−$339	−$278	−$53	−$8
Kentucky	$1,456	$1,393	$38	$25
Louisiana	$1,624	$999	$588	$38
Maine	$864	$777	$72	$16
Maryland	−$1,432	−$1,284	−$156	$8
Massachusetts	−$222	−$240	−$19	$36
Michigan	−$108	−$78	−$37	$8
Minnesota	−$2,197	−$1,886	−$213	−$98
Mississippi	$1,904	$1,725	$98	$81
Missouri	$994	$775	$252	−$32

Continued on the next page

Table A1-6, continued

States in alphabetical order	Net transfer due to Medicaid, DSH, and CHIP	Net transfer due to Medicaid	Net transfer due to DSH	Net transfer due to CHIP
Montana	$185	$187	–$9	$7
Nebraska	–$100	–$67	–$32	–$1
Nevada	–$694	–$646	–$34	–$14
New Hampshire	–$13	–$112	$111	–$12
New Jersey	–$2,677	–$2,863	$161	$25
New Mexico	$1,181	$1,169	–$17	$29
New York	$7,846	$7,421	$615	–$189
North Carolina	$1,530	$1,493	$19	$18
North Dakota	$75	$79	–$6	$2
Ohio	$407	$485	–$29	–$49
Oklahoma	$345	$371	–$65	$40
Oregon	$146	$190	–$55	$11
Pennsylvania	$1,090	$1,077	$80	–$67
Rhode Island	$311	$265	$22	$25
South Carolina	$1,564	$1,362	$221	–$19
South Dakota	$39	$51	–$10	–$2
Tennessee	$385	$683	–$192	–$106
Texas	–$2,949	–$2,921	$64	–$93
Utah	–$46	–$4	–$44	$3
Vermont	$280	$279	$5	–$4
Virginia	–$1,956	–$1,763	–$163	–$30
Washington	–$934	–$805	–$42	–$87
West Virginia	$1,141	$1,084	$37	$20
Wisconsin	–$253	–$158	–$82	–$13
Wyoming	–$99	–$78	–$18	–$3

SOURCES: Computed using data from U.S. Internal Revenue Service (2007) and Kaiser Family Foundation (2009, "Federal and State Share of Medicaid Spending, FY2006," http://www.statehealthfacts.org).

TABLE A1-7

PER CAPITA REDISTRIBUTION EFFECT OF MEDICAID,
NET OF FEDERAL TAX, BY STATE, FY 2006

| D.C. and states in order of median household income | Net transfer due to Medicaid, DSH, and CHIP | —————————Net transfer per capita————————— | | |
		Net transfer due to Medicaid	Net transfer due to DSH	Net transfer due to CHIP
District of Columbia	−$738	−$641	−$34	−$63
New Jersey	−$309	−$330	$19	$3
Maryland	−$256	−$229	−$28	$1
Hawaii	$68	$92	−$25	$0
New Hampshire	−$10	−$86	$84	−$9
Connecticut	−$340	−$316	−$1	−$23
Alaska	$270	$260	$1	$8
Minnesota	−$426	−$366	−$41	−$19
Massachusetts	−$35	−$37	−$3	$6
Utah	−$18	−$2	−$17	$1
Virginia	−$256	−$231	−$21	−$4
Colorado	−$385	−$355	−$21	−$9
California	−$98	−$99	−$6	$7
Washington	−$147	−$126	−$7	−$14
Delaware	−$567	−$489	−$53	−$26
Vermont	$452	$450	$8	−$6
Rhode Island	$293	$249	$20	$24
Nevada	−$278	−$259	−$14	−$6
Illinois	−$283	−$271	−$24	$12
New York	$407	$385	$32	−$10
Nebraska	−$57	−$38	−$18	$0
Wisconsin	−$45	−$28	−$15	−$2
Pennsylvania	$88	$87	$6	−$5
Wyoming	−$193	−$152	−$36	−$5
Iowa	$132	$142	−$13	$3
Arizona	$263	$266	−$9	$5
Idaho	$53	$65	−$15	$4
Michigan	−$11	−$8	−$4	$1

Continued on the next page

Table A1-7, continued

D.C. and states in order of median household income	Net transfer due to Medicaid, DSH, and CHIP	Net transfer per capita		
		Net transfer due to Medicaid	Net transfer due to DSH	Net transfer due to CHIP
Ohio	$36	$42	−$3	−$4
Georgia	−$57	−$71	−$4	$17
Maine	$657	$591	$55	$12
Missouri	$170	$133	$43	−$5
Oregon	$39	$51	−$15	$3
Indiana	$116	$112	$5	−$1
South Dakota	$49	$65	−$13	−$3
Florida	−$149	−$123	−$22	−$4
Kansas	−$123	−$101	−$19	−$3
Texas	−$126	−$125	$3	−$4
North Carolina	$172	$168	$2	$2
North Dakota	$118	$124	−$10	$3
South Carolina	$361	$315	$51	−$4
New Mexico	$608	$602	−$9	$15
Tennessee	$63	$112	−$32	−$17
Oklahoma	$97	$104	−$18	$11
Alabama	$296	$245	$42	$9
Louisiana	$383	$235	$139	$9
Kentucky	$346	$331	$9	$6
Arkansas	$188	$201	−$19	$5
Montana	$196	$198	−$9	$7
West Virginia	$631	$600	$20	$11
Mississippi	$657	$595	$34	$28
United States	−$5	−$5	$0	$0

SOURCES: Computed using data from U.S. Internal Revenue Service (2007); Kaiser Family Foundation (2009, "Federal and State Share of Medicaid Spending, FY2006," http://www.statehealthfacts.org); and U.S. Census Bureau (2008a).

Appendix 2:
Equal-Burden-for-Equal-Benefit
Matching Rates

"Equal burden for equal benefit" (EBEB) is a method for computing Medicaid matching rates that are equitable for both taxpayers and the poor.[1] Ideally, such rates should enable each state to provide the same real level of benefits as each other state to its poor population by spending the same fraction of taxpayer income on its share of Medicaid.

We begin by defining some terms:

- **EBEBFMAP$_i$** is the equal-burden-for-equal-benefit matching rate in state i.

- **AggFiscalCap$_i$** is the measure of the state's aggregate fiscal capacity (such as adjusted gross income, as reported in individual tax returns).

- **FixedPct** is the fixed percentage of the fiscal capacity measure (for example, state taxpayer income) to be contributed by the state as its share of Medicaid costs. (This would be, by our estimates, 1.625 percent in the United States in 2006 if the standard benefit were set at the national average.)

- **Npoor$_i$** is the number of persons below the federal poverty level in the state.

- **StdBenPPP** is the standard benefit level, e.g., the dollar Medicaid benefit per poor person (by our estimates, an average of $7,692 in the United States in 2006).

329

- **MedPrice$_i$** is a state medical care relative cost index based so the U.S. level is 1.00 (our examples use the physician practice cost index).

We can then define EBEB matching rates by the formula for the federal medical assistance percentage (FMAP):

$$EBEBFMAP_i = 1 - (AggFiscal\ Cap_i * FixedPct) / (Npoor_i * StdBenPPP * MedPrice_i)$$

It is then a simple matter to demonstrate the EBEB equity property:

The state percentage is 1.0 minus the federal share or:

$$StatePercentage = (AggFiscal\ Cap_i * FixedPct) / (Npoor_i * StdBenPPP * MedPrice_i)$$

The state payments are then:

$$State\ Payments = [StatePercentage] \times [StateMedicaidPayments]$$

If the state provides the standard benefit per poor person to every poor person in the state and pays providers based on its local medical prices, its cost is:

$$State\ Payments = [(AggFiscal\ Cap_i * FixedPct) / (Npoori * StdBenPPP * MedPrice_i)] \times [(Npoor_i * StdBenPPP * MedPrice_i)]$$

$$= [AggFiscal\ Cap_i * FixedPct)]$$

The state payment as a percentage of state taxpayer income (or other measure of fiscal capacity) is:

$$[StatePayments / AggFiscal\ Cap_i] = FixedPct$$

which is the specified fixed percentage that would be the same for every state that provided the specified level of benefits (on average) to its poor population. In effect, these rates give each state the ability to achieve a specified real (cost-adjusted) benefit level at the same level of taxpayer effort or burden.

Examples Illustrating EBEB Possibilities

We indicate the structure such a revised matching-rate system might have and illustrate with some computed examples of the equal-burden-for-equal-benefit matching approach. Table A2-1 shows, for every state, the key elements that will be determining variables in the matching formula. It shows the wide interstate differences in poverty measures and in taxpayer income, as well as the current Medicaid benefits per poor person, which ranged in 2006 from $4,559 in Nevada to more than three times that in New York.

Case 1: Proportional EBEB. Rates are designed to move all states toward a national average benefit level. EBEB matching rates are computed in accordance with the formula above, using the U.S. averages for the taxpayer burden and standard benefit parameters. Matching rates illustrating this are shown in table A2-2, which shows a basic rate and enhanced rate computed with this formula. The basic rate uses the U.S. average benefit per poor person as a standard. The enhanced rate uses a standard benefit 30 percent higher (roughly equivalent to the current benefit level in Pennsylvania, Delaware, or New Hampshire). This shows how the formula could be used to compute matching rates that would support higher benefit levels at the same level of state taxpayer contribution.

Case 2: Progressive EBEB. Table A2-2 also shows progressive rates computed for the same two benefit levels. These progressive rates allow states to achieve the standard benefit by contributing as the state share an amount proportional to its taxpayers' obligations under federal personal income tax law. Relative to the proportional rates, this produces lower rates in states with higher-income taxpayers, such as New York, and higher rates in several of the southern and western states, without a thick upper tail of very high-income taxpayers on their income distributions. This is also shown with basic and enhanced rates.

Case 3: Proportional EBEB with Cost-of-Living Adjustment and Step-Down. Case 3 adds two key elements to the matching cost-of-living adjustment and step-down rates to apply to spending above the national average. The step down is used to reduce the incentive for a few states to provide benefits greatly in excess of the standard amount. Step-down is implemented through a tiered rate structure, as shown in table A2-3. A state's Medicaid spending per poor person would determine the applicable tier for each portion of state spending. In this example, a state gets the full EBEB matching for benefits up to 100 percent of the standard benefit times the number of poor persons in the state; 75 percent of EBEB matching for spending between 100 and 125 percent of the standard; 50 percent of EBEB matching for spending between 125 and 150 percent; and 25 percent of EBEB matching for spending between 150 and 175 percent of the standard. States do not receive federal assistance for payments in excess of 175 percent of the standard times the number of poor persons in the state. In this step-down example, federal taxpayers are not expected to support Medicaid benefits in a state that approach twice the national average. It is worth noting that even with the cost-of-living adjustment, we see several higher-income states with revised FMAPs below 50 percent. The formula does tend to provide higher rates for some states with many lower-income persons, such as California.

Case 4: Progressive EBEB with Cost-of-Living Adjustment and Step-Down. Our fourth example, with results shown in table A2-4, incorporates the elements of case 3, but with a progressive structure to the state contribution. It includes all of our key elements to promote greater equity in matching rates: EBEB rates to provide a base, a progressive structure for state contributions related to taxpayer income, and step-down to limit the extent to which lower-benefit states might subsidize higher-benefit states. The progressive structure tends to trim the federal matching in the highest benefit states, particularly with income distributions skewed to the right— that is, states with some very high-income industries or wealthy individuals, such as Connecticut and New York.

Case 5: Progressive EBEB with Cost-of-Living Adjustment, Step-Down, and 50 percent Minimum on Base Matching. The final case shown in table A2-5 is the same as case 4, but it scales the entire matching schedule upward by raising the standard benefit in the calculation and keeping state contribution the same to allow for a minimum of 50 percent matching on the base spending with other states higher, to ensure all states have at least that amount of federal support on state benefits up to 125 percent of the higher standard amount. To maintain the equity properties of the EBEB with even higher-income states receiving 50 percent matching, the standard benefit has to be increased substantially, to $9,351 per person below 125 percent of the federal poverty level. Bringing New Hampshire and Connecticut to 50 percent leads to a matching rate of 90 percent in Mississippi and over 80 percent in twelve other states.

TABLE A2-1
VALUES OF VARIABLES USED TO COMPUTE
EXAMPLE EBEB MATCHING RATES

States in alphabetical order	Number below FPL	Poverty Percentage poor	Percentage of U.S. poor
United States	38,757,253	13.3%	100.0%
Alabama	743,556	16.6	1.9%
Alaska	71,120	10.9	0.2%
Arizona	860,355	14.2	2.2%
Arkansas	471,161	17.3	1.2%
California	4,686,706	13.1	12.1%
Colorado	539,332	11.6	1.4%
Connecticut	281,079	8.3	0.7%
Delaware	88,749	10.7	0.2%
District of Columbia	99,671	18.1	0.3%
Florida	2,232,534	12.6	5.8%
Georgia	1,340,255	14.8	3.5%
Hawaii	117,811	9.4	0.3%
Idaho	182,933	12.8	0.5%
Illinois	1,536,133	12.3	4.0%
Indiana	768,642	12.5	2.0%
Iowa	315,973	11.0	0.8%
Kansas	327,103	12.2	0.8%
Kentucky	694,866	17.0	1.8%
Louisiana	808,319	19.4	2.1%
Maine	163,293	12.7	0.4%
Maryland	436,978	8.0	1.1%
Massachusetts	623,775	10.0	1.6%
Michigan	1,328,888	13.5	3.4%
Minnesota	487,044	9.7	1.3%
Mississippi	588,288	20.9	1.5%
Missouri	783,101	13.8	2.0%
Montana	132,537	14.4	0.3%
Nebraska	194,595	11.3	0.5%

――Cost――	――――Taxpayer income――――		―Benefit level―
Physician practice cost index average	Adjusted gross income (000)	PI Tax amount (000)	Medicaid payments per poor person 2006
1.000	$7,945,456,251	$1,023,644,566	$7,692
0.909	$96,623,613	$10,979,024	$5,191
1.037	$17,947,050	$2,262,567	$13,289
0.970	$147,978,344	$17,982,915	$7,194
0.893	$50,651,815	$5,432,649	$6,058
1.083	$1,035,151,862	$137,232,470	$7,220
0.978	$138,876,098	$18,062,971	$5,285
1.103	$141,719,454	$23,161,751	$14,474
1.016	$24,150,367	$3,008,775	$10,660
1.124	$21,406,242	$3,305,255	$12,891
1.052	$510,336,621	$71,125,036	$5,653
0.971	$216,331,873	$25,885,124	$4,835
1.059	$33,030,898	$3,769,398	$9,263
0.917	$31,708,725	$3,488,498	$5,613
0.989	$362,235,603	$48,970,055	$6,488
0.944	$142,501,220	$15,908,786	$7,333
0.906	$66,192,610	$7,105,899	$8,035
0.918	$66,432,725	$7,871,434	$6,290
0.912	$82,558,702	$8,772,812	$6,230
0.971	$91,887,850	$11,428,639	$5,800
0.950	$29,466,685	$3,090,195	$11,614
1.012	$181,096,029	$23,280,923	$11,249
1.091	$222,928,374	$31,883,724	$15,328
1.022	$233,372,609	$26,793,190	$6,198
0.962	$145,576,400	$17,874,175	$11,020
0.910	$49,860,479	$5,083,420	$5,507
0.949	$131,089,335	$15,084,043	$8,150
0.897	$20,404,746	$2,162,864	$5,430
0.904	$41,039,481	$4,654,025	$7,704

Continued on the next page

Table A2-1 continued

States in alphabetical order	Number below FPL	Poverty Percentage poor	Percentage of U.S. poor
Nevada	257,828	10.5%	0.7%
New Hampshire	101,872	8.0	0.3%
New Jersey	740,721	8.7	1.9%
New Mexico	350,120	18.3	0.9%
New York	2,670,773	14.2	6.9%
North Carolina	1,256,624	14.6	3.2%
North Dakota	71,059	11.7	0.2%
Ohio	1,475,788	13.2	3.8%
Oklahoma	576,689	16.7	1.5%
Oregon	487,358	13.4	1.3%
Pennsylvania	1,442,858	12.0	3.7%
Rhode Island	117,585	11.5	0.3%
South Carolina	657,405	15.7	1.7%
South Dakota	102,589	13.6	0.3%
Tennessee	947,105	16.1	2.4%
Texas	3,862,741	16.9	10.0%
Utah	269,611	10.7	0.7%
Vermont	61,694	10.2	0.2%
Virginia	713,181	9.6	1.8%
Washington	736,907	11.8	1.9%
West Virginia	310,842	17.6	0.8%
Wisconsin	589,377	10.9	1.5%
Wyoming	51,728	10.3	0.1%

SOURCES: U.S. Census Bureau 2008b; U.S. Internal Revenue Service 2007; and Kaiser Family Foundation 2009, "Federal and State Share of Medicaid Spending, FY2006," http://www.statehealthfacts.org.

—Cost—	—Taxpayer income—		—Benefit level—
Physician practice cost index average	Adjusted gross income (000)	PI Tax amount (000)	Medicaid payments per poor person 2006
1.018	$77,211,961	$10,427,538	$4,559
1.006	$40,176,027	$5,176,919	$10,663
1.111	$302,073,205	$43,577,647	$12,297
0.943	$39,282,794	$4,434,035	$6,982
1.078	$604,209,378	$89,771,971	$16,307
0.941	$203,102,967	$22,977,310	$6,940
0.883	$14,228,763	$1,575,940	$7,018
0.975	$266,209,812	$30,242,439	$7,974
0.903	$74,932,461	$9,029,858	$4,979
0.962	$88,482,771	$9,928,326	$5,950
1.003	$320,781,502	$39,844,090	$10,674
1.048	$28,128,464	$3,466,035	$14,235
0.927	$91,820,608	$9,923,162	$5,985
0.890	$17,667,783	$2,140,096	$5,868
0.927	$134,041,381	$16,328,905	$6,350
0.983	$562,874,768	$76,430,684	$4,578
0.950	$57,463,484	$6,254,166	$5,377
0.959	$15,779,630	$1,761,930	$15,349
1.012	$230,254,681	$29,554,772	$6,461
1.004	$186,216,128	$24,113,543	$7,496
0.926	$31,973,340	$3,251,470	$6,680
0.959	$141,048,306	$16,407,580	$7,776
0.906	$17,059,474	$2,536,350	$8,071

TABLE A2-2

ILLUSTRATION OF ALTERNATIVE FORMS OF EBEB
MATCHNG RATES BY STATE

	Current		Proportional		Progressive	
Fixed pct:	n/a	n/a	1.6252%	1.6252%	12.6157%	12.6157%
Standard benefit:	n/a	n/a	$7,692	$10,000	$7,692	$10,000

	Current FMAP 2009	Current Enhanced FMAP 2009	EBEB matching U.S. standard	Enhanced EBEB matching	EBEB matching U.S. standard	Enhanced EBEB matching
51 jurisdictions (mean)	59.98%	71.99%	53.22%	64.02%	55.01%	65.06%
51 jurisdictions (median)	60.27%	72.19%	55.66%	65.89%	58.81%	68.31%
States in alphabetical order						
Alabama	67.98%	77.59%	69.80%	76.77%	73.36%	79.51%
Alaska	50.53%	65.37%	48.58%	60.45%	49.68%	61.30%
Arizona	65.77%	76.04%	62.54%	71.18%	64.66%	72.81%
Arkansas	72.81%	80.97%	74.56%	80.43%	78.82%	83.71%
California	50.00%	65.00%	56.91%	66.85%	55.66%	65.89%
Colorado	50.00%	65.00%	44.37%	57.21%	43.83%	56.80%
Connecticut	50.00%	65.00%	3.42%	25.71%	0.00%	5.75%
Delaware	50.00%	65.00%	43.41%	56.47%	45.27%	57.90%
District of Columbia	70.00%	79.00%	59.63%	68.95%	51.61%	62.78%
Florida	55.40%	68.78%	54.09%	64.68%	50.33%	61.79%
Georgia	64.49%	75.14%	64.88%	72.98%	67.38%	74.91%
Hawaii	55.11%	68.58%	44.06%	56.97%	50.45%	61.88%
Idaho	69.77%	78.84%	60.06%	69.28%	65.89%	73.76%
Illinois	50.32%	65.22%	49.62%	61.25%	47.13%	59.33%
Indiana	64.26%	74.98%	58.51%	68.08%	64.04%	72.34%
Iowa	62.62%	73.83%	51.15%	62.42%	59.29%	68.68%
Kansas	60.08%	72.06%	53.26%	64.04%	57.01%	66.93%
Kentucky	70.13%	79.09%	72.47%	78.83%	77.30%	82.53%
Louisiana	71.31%	79.92%	75.26%	80.97%	76.12%	81.63%
Maine	64.41%	75.09%	59.87%	69.13%	67.33%	74.87%
Maryland	50.00%	65.00%	13.48%	33.44%	13.66%	33.58%

Continued on the next page

Table A2-2 continued

	Current FMAP 2009	Current Enhanced FMAP 2009	EBEB matching U.S. standard	Enhanced EBEB matching	EBEB matching U.S. standard	Enhanced EBEB matching
Massachusetts	50.00%	65.00%	30.79%	46.76%	23.16%	40.89%
Michigan	60.27%	72.19%	63.69%	72.07%	67.64%	75.11%
Minnesota	50.00%	65.00%	34.35%	49.50%	37.43%	51.87%
Mississippi	75.84%	83.09%	80.32%	84.86%	84.43%	88.02%
Missouri	63.19%	74.23%	62.73%	71.33%	66.71%	74.39%
Montana	68.04%	77.63%	63.74%	72.11%	70.16%	77.05%
Nebraska	59.54%	71.68%	50.71%	62.08%	56.61%	66.62%
Nevada	50.00%	65.00%	37.85%	52.19%	34.84%	49.88%
New Hampshire	50.00%	65.00%	17.17%	36.29%	17.15%	36.27%
New Jersey	50.00%	65.00%	22.44%	40.34%	13.15%	33.19%
New Mexico	70.88%	79.62%	74.86%	80.66%	77.97%	83.06%
New York	50.00%	65.00%	55.66%	65.89%	48.86%	60.66%
North Carolina	64.60%	75.22%	63.71%	72.08%	68.13%	75.48%
North Dakota	63.15%	74.21%	52.09%	63.14%	58.81%	68.31%
Ohio	62.14%	73.50%	60.91%	69.93%	65.53%	73.48%
Oklahoma	65.90%	76.13%	69.60%	76.61%	71.56%	78.12%
Oregon	62.45%	73.72%	60.12%	69.33%	65.27%	73.28%
Pennsylvania	54.52%	68.16%	53.17%	63.97%	54.84%	65.26%
Rhode Island	52.59%	66.81%	51.77%	62.90%	53.87%	64.51%
South Carolina	70.07%	79.05%	68.17%	75.51%	73.29%	79.46%
South Dakota	62.55%	73.79%	59.12%	68.55%	61.56%	70.43%
Tennessee	64.28%	75.00%	67.74%	75.19%	69.50%	76.54%
Texas	59.44%	71.61%	68.68%	75.91%	66.99%	74.60%
Utah	70.71%	79.50%	52.60%	63.54%	59.95%	69.19%
Vermont	59.45%	71.62%	43.65%	56.65%	51.16%	62.43%
Virginia	50.00%	65.00%	32.59%	48.15%	32.84%	48.34%
Washington	50.94%	65.66%	46.82%	59.09%	46.55%	58.88%
West Virginia	73.73%	81.61%	76.53%	81.95%	81.47%	85.75%
Wisconsin	59.38%	71.57%	47.27%	59.44%	52.39%	63.38%
Wyoming	50.00%	65.00%	23.09%	40.84%	11.24%	31.72%

SOURCES: U.S. Department of Health and Human Services 2009 and EBEB matching rates computed by the authors.

TABLE A2-3

ILLUSTRATION OF PROPORTIONAL EBEB
COST-OF-LIVING–ADJUSTED MATCHING RATES WITH STEP-DOWN TIERS

	Proportional EBEB matching U.S. standard			
Fixed pct:	1.6252% of taxpayer income			
Standard benefit:	$5,877 per person < 125% FPL			

States in alphabetical order	Tier 1 up to standard benefit per poor person	Tier 2 up to 125% of standard benefit per poor person	Tier 3 up to 150% of standard benefit per poor person	Tier 4 up to 175% of standard benefit per poor person
Alabama	61.71%	46.28%	30.85%	15.43%
Alaska	55.63%	41.72%	27.81%	13.91%
Arizona	67.41%	50.56%	33.70%	16.85%
Arkansas	65.73%	49.30%	32.87%	16.43%
California	73.38%	55.04%	36.69%	18.35%
Colorado	41.25%	30.93%	20.62%	10.31%
Connecticut	37.41%	28.06%	18.70%	9.35%
Delaware	46.25%	34.69%	23.13%	11.56%
District of Columbia	68.80%	51.60%	34.40%	17.20%
Florida	58.18%	43.64%	29.09%	14.55%
Georgia	60.24%	45.18%	30.12%	15.06%
Hawaii	67.20%	50.40%	33.60%	16.80%
Idaho	50.59%	37.94%	25.30%	12.65%
Illinois	40.05%	30.04%	20.03%	10.01%
Indiana	53.12%	39.84%	26.56%	13.28%
Iowa	36.79%	27.59%	18.39%	9.20%
Kansas	49.53%	37.15%	24.77%	12.38%
Kentucky	69.11%	51.83%	34.55%	17.28%
Louisiana	68.05%	51.04%	34.03%	17.01%
Maine	63.70%	47.78%	31.85%	15.93%
Maryland	41.74%	31.30%	20.87%	10.43%
Massachusetts	49.59%	37.19%	24.80%	12.40%
Michigan	55.11%	41.33%	27.55%	13.78%
Minnesota	36.82%	27.61%	18.41%	9.20%

Continued on the next page

Table A2-3 continued

States in alphabetical order	Tier 1 up to standard benefit per poor person	Tier 2 up to 125% of standard benefit per poor person	Tier 3 up to 150% of standard benefit per poor person	Tier 4 up to 175% of standard benefit per poor person
Mississippi	79.99%	59.99%	40.00%	20.00%
Missouri	56.00%	42.00%	28.00%	14.00%
Montana	63.82%	47.87%	31.91%	15.96%
Nebraska	40.98%	30.74%	20.49%	10.25%
Nevada	46.44%	34.83%	23.22%	11.61%
New Hampshire	20.46%	15.35%	10.23%	5.12%
New Jersey	49.48%	37.11%	24.74%	12.37%
New Mexico	70.57%	52.92%	35.28%	17.64%
New York	67.97%	50.98%	33.98%	16.99%
North Carolina	67.53%	50.64%	33.76%	16.88%
North Dakota	42.42%	31.81%	21.21%	10.60%
Ohio	56.34%	42.26%	28.17%	14.09%
Oklahoma	59.87%	44.90%	29.93%	14.97%
Oregon	66.36%	49.77%	33.18%	16.59%
Pennsylvania	50.93%	38.20%	25.47%	12.73%
Rhode Island	57.64%	43.23%	28.82%	14.41%
South Carolina	66.41%	49.81%	33.20%	16.60%
South Dakota	43.46%	32.60%	21.73%	10.87%
Tennessee	61.81%	46.36%	30.91%	15.45%
Texas	65.31%	48.98%	32.65%	16.33%
Utah	52.34%	39.26%	26.17%	13.09%
Vermont	60.03%	45.03%	30.02%	15.01%
Virginia	35.17%	26.38%	17.58%	8.79%
Washington	44.58%	33.44%	22.29%	11.15%
West Virginia	69.37%	52.03%	34.68%	17.34%
Wisconsin	46.91%	35.18%	23.46%	11.73%
Wyoming	32.38%	24.28%	16.19%	8.09%

SOURCE: Computed by the authors.

TABLE A2-4

PROGRESSIVE EBEB COST-OF-LIVING–ADJUSTED MATCHING
WITH STEP-DOWN TIERS

Progressive EBEB matching U.S. standard			
Fixed pct:	12.62% of federal taxes		
Standard benefit:	$9,351 per person < 125% FPL		

States in alphabetical order	Tier 1 up to standard benefit per poor person	Tier 2 up to 125% of standard benefit per poor person	Tier 3 up to 150% of standard benefit per poor person	Tier 4 up to 175% of standard benefit per poor person
Alabama	66.22%	49.67%	33.11%	16.56%
Alaska	56.57%	42.43%	28.29%	14.14%
Arizona	69.26%	51.94%	34.63%	17.31%
Arkansas	71.47%	53.60%	35.73%	17.87%
California	72.61%	54.46%	36.30%	18.15%
Colorado	40.68%	30.51%	20.34%	10.17%
Connecticut	20.59%	15.45%	10.30%	5.15%
Delaware	48.02%	36.02%	24.01%	12.01%
District of Columbia	62.60%	46.95%	31.30%	15.65%
Florida	54.76%	41.07%	27.38%	13.69%
Georgia	63.07%	47.30%	31.53%	15.77%
Hawaii	70.95%	53.21%	35.47%	17.74%
Idaho	57.81%	43.35%	28.90%	14.45%
Illinois	37.09%	27.82%	18.54%	9.27%
Indiana	59.37%	44.53%	29.69%	14.84%
Iowa	47.32%	35.49%	23.66%	11.83%
Kansas	53.58%	40.19%	26.79%	13.40%
Kentucky	74.52%	55.89%	37.26%	18.63%
Louisiana	69.16%	51.87%	34.58%	17.29%
Maine	70.45%	52.84%	35.23%	17.61%
Maryland	41.86%	31.39%	20.93%	10.46%
Massachusetts	44.03%	33.03%	22.02%	11.01%
Michigan	59.99%	44.99%	30.00%	15.00%
Minnesota	39.78%	29.83%	19.89%	9.94%

Continued on the next page

Table A2-4 continued

States in alphabetical order	Tier 1 up to standard benefit per poor person	Tier 2 up to 125% of standard benefit per poor person	Tier 3 up to 150% of standard benefit per poor person	Tier 4 up to 175% of standard benefit per poor person
Mississippi	84.17%	63.12%	42.08%	21.04%
Missouri	60.70%	45.52%	30.35%	15.17%
Montana	70.23%	52.67%	35.12%	17.56%
Nebraska	48.04%	36.03%	24.02%	12.01%
Nevada	43.85%	32.89%	21.93%	10.96%
New Hampshire	20.44%	15.33%	10.22%	5.11%
New Jersey	43.43%	32.57%	21.71%	10.86%
New Mexico	74.21%	55.66%	37.11%	18.55%
New York	63.06%	47.29%	31.53%	15.76%
North Carolina	71.48%	53.61%	35.74%	17.87%
North Dakota	50.49%	37.87%	25.25%	12.62%
Ohio	61.50%	46.12%	30.75%	15.37%
Oklahoma	62.46%	46.84%	31.23%	15.61%
Oregon	70.70%	53.02%	35.35%	17.67%
Pennsylvania	52.69%	39.52%	26.35%	13.17%
Rhode Island	59.48%	44.61%	29.74%	14.87%
South Carolina	71.82%	53.86%	35.91%	17.95%
South Dakota	46.84%	35.13%	23.42%	11.71%
Tennessee	63.89%	47.92%	31.94%	15.97%
Texas	63.43%	47.58%	31.72%	15.86%
Utah	59.74%	44.80%	29.87%	14.93%
Vermont	65.36%	49.02%	32.68%	16.34%
Virginia	35.40%	26.55%	17.70%	8.85%
Washington	44.29%	33.22%	22.15%	11.07%
West Virginia	75.82%	56.86%	37.91%	18.95%
Wisconsin	52.06%	39.05%	26.03%	13.02%
Wyoming	21.95%	16.47%	10.98%	5.49%

SOURCE: Computed by the authors.

TABLE A2-5

PROGRESSIVE EBEB COST-OF-LIVING–ADJUSTED 50 PERCENT
MINIMUM BASIC MATCHING WITH STEP-DOWN TIERS

Progressive EBEB matching U.S. standard			
Fixed pct:	12.62% of federal taxes		
Standard benefit:	$5,877 per person < 125% FPL		

States in alphabetical order	Tier 1 up to standard benefit per poor person	Tier 2 up to 125% of standard benefit per poor person	Tier 3 up to 150% of standard benefit per poor person	Tier 4 up to 175% of standard benefit per poor person
Alabama	78.77%	59.08%	39.39%	19.69%
Alaska	72.71%	54.53%	36.35%	18.18%
Arizona	80.68%	60.51%	40.34%	20.17%
Arkansas	82.07%	61.55%	41.03%	20.52%
California	82.78%	62.09%	41.39%	20.70%
Colorado	62.72%	47.04%	31.36%	15.68%
Connecticut	50.09%	37.57%	25.05%	12.52%
Delaware	67.33%	50.50%	33.67%	16.83%
District of Columbia	76.49%	57.37%	38.25%	19.12%
Florida	71.57%	53.68%	35.78%	17.89%
Georgia	76.79%	57.59%	38.39%	19.20%
Hawaii	81.74%	61.31%	40.87%	20.44%
Idaho	73.48%	55.11%	36.74%	18.37%
Illinois	60.46%	45.35%	30.23%	15.12%
Indiana	74.47%	55.85%	37.23%	18.62%
Iowa	66.89%	50.17%	33.45%	16.72%
Kansas	70.83%	53.12%	35.41%	17.71%
Kentucky	83.99%	62.99%	41.99%	21.00%
Louisiana	80.62%	60.46%	40.31%	20.15%
Maine	81.43%	61.07%	40.71%	20.36%
Maryland	63.46%	47.59%	31.73%	15.86%
Massachusetts	64.83%	48.62%	32.41%	16.21%
Michigan	74.86%	56.14%	37.43%	18.71%
Minnesota	62.15%	46.61%	31.08%	15.54%
Mississippi	90.05%	67.54%	45.02%	22.51%

Continued on the next page

Table A2-5 continued

States in alphabetical order	Tier 1 up to standard benefit per poor person	Tier 2 up to 125% of standard benefit per poor person	Tier 3 up to 150% of standard benefit per poor person	Tier 4 up to 175% of standard benefit per poor person
Missouri	75.30%	56.47%	37.65%	18.82%
Montana	81.29%	60.97%	40.65%	20.32%
Nebraska	67.35%	50.51%	33.67%	16.84%
Nevada	64.71%	48.53%	32.36%	16.18%
New Hampshire	50.00%	37.50%	25.00%	12.50%
New Jersey	64.44%	48.33%	32.22%	16.11%
New Mexico	83.79%	62.84%	41.90%	20.95%
New York	76.78%	57.59%	38.39%	19.20%
North Carolina	82.08%	61.56%	41.04%	20.52%
North Dakota	68.88%	51.66%	34.44%	17.22%
Ohio	75.80%	56.85%	37.90%	18.95%
Oklahoma	76.40%	57.30%	38.20%	19.10%
Oregon	81.58%	61.19%	40.79%	20.40%
Pennsylvania	70.27%	52.70%	35.13%	17.57%
Rhode Island	74.53%	55.90%	37.27%	18.63%
South Carolina	82.29%	61.72%	41.14%	20.57%
South Dakota	66.59%	49.94%	33.29%	16.65%
Tennessee	77.30%	57.98%	38.65%	19.33%
Texas	77.02%	57.76%	38.51%	19.25%
Utah	74.70%	56.02%	37.35%	18.67%
Vermont	78.23%	58.67%	39.11%	19.56%
Virginia	59.40%	44.55%	29.70%	14.85%
Washington	64.99%	48.74%	32.49%	16.25%
West Virginia	84.80%	63.60%	42.40%	21.20%
Wisconsin	69.87%	52.40%	34.94%	17.47%
Wyoming	50.95%	38.21%	25.47%	12.74%

SOURCE: Computed by the authors.

Notes

Introduction

1. See chapter 14, note 1 for the controversy concerning the SCHIP/CHIP acronym.

Chapter 1: Financing Care for the Poor in a Democracy

1. Meulen et al. 2001, 2, 1.
2. Arts and Verburg 2001.
3. Ibid.
4. Johnson and Cullen 2001.
5. Smith and Moore 2008, 4–8.
6. See Stevens and Stevens (2003). Michael Sparer (1996) describes the growth of the two largest state programs, in New York and California; Jonathan Engel (2006) takes the Medicaid historical narrative through the Clinton years.
7. Smith and Moore 2008, 14–15.
8. Of course, in reality, many continental European systems, especially those modeled on the German system, allow the very best-off to exit the social insurance system and have private insurance and better-perceived access to care than is available to others.
9. Wilson 1980, chapter 5; Dawkins 1989, chapter 6; Madsen et al. 2006. This view of an inherent genetic predisposition toward altruism would suggest that this motivation for providing medical care to the needy might be stronger in local areas and in ethnically homogeneous communities where the taxpayer is more likely to be related to the recipient. This might explain the weaker support for uniform national health insurance in a country such as the United States with a large, ethnically diverse, and geographically mobile population, compared with the experience of smaller, more ethnically homogenous European countries. It is also consistent with the view that voters may be more willing to pay for medical care for the poor who are located nearby, in their own states and communities.
10. The law establishing Medicaid is found in Title XIX of the Social Security Act.
11. Capitated managed care programs, in which HMOs or other health plans are paid on a per-capita basis rather than for each service, began for Medicaid in the early 1980s (Hurley and Zuckerman 2003).

12. We will use "Medicaid spending per poor person" as a convenient metric representing an average level of spending made available to the poor and near-poor population; not all poor persons are eligible for Medicaid, and some benefits go to individuals and families above the poverty level.

Chapter 2: Medicaid's Roles in Our Health Care System

1. See Kotter (2008) for a recent view of the need to create a sense of urgency to bring about change in organizations.

2. U.S. Department of Health and Human Services, Centers for Medicare and Medicaid Services, Office of the Actuary 2008.

3. Vernon Smith et al. 2008, 15.

4. U.S. Department of Health and Human Services, Centers for Medicare and Medicaid Services, Office of the Actuary 2008, 15.

5. Ibid., 20.

6. Computed from U.S. Boards of Trustees (2008, 173).

7. See chapters 7 and 8.

8. Grannemann and Pauly 1983.

9. The origins of Medicaid financing through the financing of its predecessor, the Kerr-Mills Program, are described by Stevens and Stevens (2003), Moore and Smith (2005), Engel (2006), and Smith and Moore (2008).

10. U.S. Department of Health and Human Services, Centers for Medicare and Medicaid Services, Office of the Actuary 2009.

11. Throughout this work we will often use the term "adults" to refer to persons in the eligibility category of adults in families with dependent children, who are distinct from the adults in separate eligibility groups for elderly and disabled persons. When used to refer to an eligibility group, "adults" does not include the elderly and disabled.

12. U.S. Department of Health and Human Services, Centers for Medicare and Medicaid Services, Office of the Actuary 2008.

13. J. A. Buck 2003.

14. This is consistent with a finding reported by David Mechanic (2006, 68) that two-fifths of the growth in mental health expenditures in the 1991–2001 period was due to the prescription of drugs.

15. The smaller share of capitated services in payment than in recipients reflects the fact that managed care plans tend to serve the less costly segment of the Medicaid population—for example, families enrolled in the Temporary Assistance for Needy Families (TANF) program—and do not include long-term care services.

16. Phased-down state contributions, or "clawback" payments, are payments made by states to the federal government as a contribution toward the drug costs of dual-eligibles as a result of the transition to Medicare Part D drug coverage. See *Code of Federal Regulations*, 42 CFR §423.908.

17. Medicaid eligibility is limited by law to persons who fall in specific categories and meet income and asset tests. The group definitions can be complex, but they include the elderly, the blind and disabled, children, pregnant women, and adults in families with dependent children. We will sometimes refer to the last four of these eligibility groups as "TANF adults" or "TANF children" as they are often eligible as a result of receiving Temporary Assistance for Needed Families (or TANF) or in some cases simply as adults or children. Notably absent, at least to 2009, are able-bodied adults without children. See Kaiser Commission on Medicaid and the Uninsured (2009b) for basics on who is eligible.

18. Fox 2006.

Chapter 3: Ensuring Access for the Poor Population

1. Schneider et al. 2002; or see the *Code of Federal Regulations*, 42 CFR Part 435, for details.

2. U.S. Department of Health and Human Services, Centers for Medicare and Medicaid Services, Office of the Actuary 2008.

3. *Code of Federal Regulations*, 42 CFR §435.225, or see Schneider (2002, 22–23).

4. There are a number of such program components with less than full coverage, such as the "medically needy," who spend down to eligibility by contributing to the cost of their care, and other groups, including Qualified Medicare Beneficiaries (QMB), for whom Medicaid pays Medicare premiums and cost sharing, and Specified Low-Income Medicare Beneficiaries (SLMB), for whom Medicaid pays only Medicare Part B premiums. Additionally, Qualified Disabled Working Individuals (QDWI) participate in a program component known as "ticket to work" that allows limited Medicaid coverage for some working disabled people who meet certain requirements. See, for example, Thornton et al. (2007).

5. John Holahan (2003) discusses variation in employer-sponsored insurance and Medicaid spending and concludes, as we do, that states need to be given incentives to provide more health coverage for their low-income residents.

6. See, for instance, the Dartmouth Health Atlas Project at www.dartmouthatlas.org.

7. Spending per poor person, as distinct from spending per recipient, reflects eligibility standards as well as benefit levels.

8. Ross et al. 2008, 9.

9. We examined two measures of state income—personal income per capita, which is used in the federal medical assistance percentage (FMAP) formula (see chapter 7), and median household income, which may best represent median voter income—and adjusted gross income per return from federal personal income tax. These are all highly correlated, but we use the AGI per return measure in this analysis, as it is more closely related to fiscal capacity, which is our focus here.

10. In 2003, Maine began its unusual Dirigo health care reforms; see Lipson et al. (2007).

11. This is comparing the states in the left column of table 3-2 with those in the right column.

12. This entails comparing the states in the top row of table 3-2 with those in bottom row.

13. This is comparing the states in the upper left cell of table 3-2 with those in the lower-right cell.

14. Epstein and Newhouse 1998.

15. Dave et al. 2008.

16. Brown and Finkelstein 2008.

Chapter 4: Medicaid and Care Management

1. We use the term "costworthy," as suggested by Menzel (1983, 17), to signify "care which brings patients and other affected parties benefits whose value is at least as great as that which would be obtained by using the same money to satisfy other needs and desires instead." Defining "value" is the challenge.

2. Grannemann 1979, 1980.

3. Winnett 2008.

4. McKie and Richardson 2003.

5. Newman 2008; Fuchs 1974.

6. Jacobs et al. 1999; Grannemann 1991.

7. Premiums are strictly limited by federal regulations; see *Code of Federal Regulations*, 42 CFR §447.51.

8. Artiga and O'Malley 2005.

9. Vermont Joint Fiscal Office 2004.

10. See *Code of Federal Regulations*, 42 CFR §447.54.

11. In a nationally representative sample of 18,462 Medicaid-eligible children ages zero to seventeen in the 1994 and 1995 National Health Interview Survey, 56 percent were enrolled in Medicaid, 27 percent had private insurance, and 17 percent were uninsured (U.S. Department of Health and Human Services, Centers for Disease Control and Prevention, National Center for Health Statistics 2008).

12. 42 USC §1395dd.

13. See, for example, Fredrickson et al. (2004) and De Alteriis (1991).

14. Williams 1996; Thompson et al. 1999.

15. Many primary care providers are finding ways to accomplish this on their own, but in a way that increases physician payments without lowering hospital payments. By affiliating with local hospitals and seeking "provider-based status," they are allowed to submit their bills through the hospitals, so that the physicians and their hospital partners receive much higher payments in total.

16. New Hampshire Department of Health and Human Services, Office of Medicaid Business and Policy 2005.

17. See, for example, Esposito et al. (2008).

18. See Hurley et al. (1993), Davidson and Somers (1998), and Hurley and Somers (2003) on expectations and early experiences of Medicaid managed care.

19. See, for example, Draper and Gold (2003).

20. See McCall et al. (1985).

21. Kaye 2005.

22. Ibid.

23. The correlation coefficient is 0.63.

24. Hurley and Zuckerman 2003, 237; Zuckerman et al. 2002.

25. Brown et al. 2001.

26. See Hurley and Zuckerman (2003) and Bailit et al. (2004) for review and assessment of state experiences.

27. Smith et al. 2000; Lewin Group 2004.

28. Hurley and Zuckerman 2003.

29. Brown et al. 2001, 71.

30. See, for example, one of many popular books, *How to Protect Your Family's Assets from Devastating Nursing Home Costs: Medicaid Secrets*, by K. Gabriel Heiser (2008).

31. Coates et al. 2003.

32. Weissert 1985.

33. Kemper et al. 1987, 98.

34. The National Long Term Care Demonstration was designed to channel services to elderly participants in their homes in the community. The demonstration program was implemented in ten sites in the early 1980s.

35. Kemper 1988, 172.

36. Thornton et al. 1988, 141.

37. Fox et al. 2000, 87.

38. Brown et al. 2007.

39. Grabowski 2006, 3.

Chapter 5: Achieving High-Value Care for the Poor

1. As indicated in chapter 3, above, we use three measures of state income in this work: personal income per capita, currently used to compute federal matching rates; median household income, which reflects median income of residents and can represent the income of the typical (median) voter; and adjusted gross income per personal income tax return filed, which provides a better indicator of state fiscal capacity. These measures at the state level are all highly correlated.

2. Mandatory services in all states include hospital inpatient and outpatient services, physician services, lab and x-ray, FQHCs and rural health centers, nurse midwives, pediatric or family nurse practitioners, nursing facilities, and home health services. See *Code of Federal Regulations*, 42 CFR §440.210–20.

3. Optional services include, among others, prescription drugs, intermediate care facilities for the mentally retarded, dental services, physical therapy, prosthetic devices, and eyeglasses.

4. Economists would treat the crowd-out portion as a transfer of value rather than an addition to value.

5. Hillman et al. 1999.

6. Pauly and Blavin 2008.

7. Wang and Pauly 2005.

8. Cutler 2004.

9. U.S. Government Accountability Office 2008a.

10. Grannemann and Pauly 2009.

11. See Lischko, Bachman, and Vangeli 2009 for a description of the Massachusetts program.

12. See the discussion on national altruism in chapter 1, above.

13. This impediment might be avoided if the states were left to develop their own Massachusetts-style or health insurance exchanges to facilitate access to affordable care in approved health plans, as has been proposed in federal legislation considered as part of health care reform in 2009. But such an approach would do little to reduce interstate inequalities, as the more urban, higher-income states with greater employer-based insurance can better afford to close the smaller gaps in coverage, leaving much the same interstate inequities we see in Medicaid today.

14. Granemann and Pauly 2009.

Part III: Making and Meeting Promises to Voter-Taxpayers

1. In a number of states this includes lower levels of government (counties and cities) that have had delegated to them funding and/or administrative responsibilities.

Chapter 6: Medicaid Financing as a Product of Democracy

1. Some might argue that Medicaid's obligation to use funds wisely is an obligation to taxpayers as distinguished from voters (and even that the obligation is perhaps greater to those who pay more taxes). While nearly everyone directly or indirectly pays some form of taxes, not everyone votes. In our democracy, however, it is the voters who are entitled to a voice in the public decision-making process. For purposes of this discussion, we will accept the median voter model as reflective of voter-taxpayer interests and one that approximates how public decisions ought to be made if decision-makers respond to voters rather than special interests. In this sense, it is our standard for appropriate public decisions. For more information on the theory of the median voter, see Borcherding and Deacon (1971), Bergstrom and Goodman (1973), Stiglitz (1974), Tresch (1974, 1975), Lovell (1978), and Congleton (2003).

2. Kaiser Commission on Medicaid and the Uninsured 2006.

3. Coughlin and Zuckerman 2008, 209.

4. National Association of State Medicaid Directors and Health Management Associates 2007.

5. See, for example, Grogan and Gusmano (2007), who provide a view of state-level health advocacy focusing on Medicaid in Connecticut.

6. Smith et al. 2008.

Chapter 7: Medicaid Financing for Taxpayer Equity

1. Grannemann and Pauly 1983, 42–67.

2. Section 1905 (b) of the Social Security Act states that the "federal medical assistance percentage [FMAP] shall be 100 per centum less the State percentage; and the State percentage shall be that percentage which bears the same ratio to 45 per centum as the square of the per capita income of the United States (including Alaska and Hawaii); except that (1) the Federal medical assistance percentage shall in no case be less than 50 per centum or more than 83 per centum, (2) the Federal medical assistance percentage for Puerto Rico, the Virgin Islands, Guam, the Northern Mariana Islands and American Samoa shall be 50 per centum."

3. See note 16 in chapter 2 on "clawback."

4. A review of Medicare Part D is beyond our scope here, but it is useful to note that dual-eligibles receive a low-income subsidy (LIS) for Medicare Part D and can select from a more limited set of lower-cost drug plans than is available to other Medicare beneficiaries.

5. *Code of Federal Regulations*, 42 CFR §423.910.

Chapter 8: Recommendations for Revising Federal Financing

1. This is similar to the "declining matching rates" (rates that decline with recipient income) that we discussed in our previous book (Grannemann and Pauly 1983).

2. One possible explanation for the situation is, of course, that voters value more highly benefits they are likely to receive themselves. This could explain the popularity of tax exclusions for employer-sponsored insurance and deductions for mortgage interest. But we will leave it to others to resolve whether benefits directed toward the median-range voter to the exclusion of others provides a sound basis for public policy.

3. See Grannemann (1979), Grannemann and Pauly (1983), U.S. General Accounting Office (1983, 1997), and Miller and Schneider (2004).

4. This follows an approach originally suggested by Grannemann (1980, 118–20).

5. More detailed state-specific results are provided in appendix 2.

6. We use the average physician practice cost index for all localities in the state as a deflator.

7. Our simulation suggests this would raise Connecticut's EBEB federal matching rate to 49 percent, and most other states would have rates greater than 75 percent.

8. In previous work we explain why it is not possible with simple matching rates alone to achieve the goals of equal benefits, equal tax burdens, and satisfaction of voter demand for Medicaid; see Grannemann and Pauly (1983, appendix A).

9. The current system, which favors higher-income, higher-benefit states, also presents a potentially important barrier to any national health care reform, if it would redirect resources through benefits or subsidies to states where the lower-income uninsured are located and finance them with taxes from where the higher-income taxpayers are located. The higher-income states may find it in their self interest to oppose national efforts for uniform benefits at lower levels and instead pursue state efforts with enhanced federal subsidies to protect their favored status in obtaining federal financing.

10. We distinguish cyclical economic activity from sectorial trends, such as declining industries (in some states or regions), although they are an issue as well and may not always be entirely distinguishable from the cycles.

11. U.S. Census Bureau (2007) provides figures for state tax collection by source.

Chapter 9: Medicaid Financing for Accountability

1. See Rousseau and Schneider (2004).

2. U.S. General Accountability Office 2008b.

3. Coughlin et al. 2007.

4. U.S. Government Accountability Office 2007c, 7.

5. See Smith and Moore (2008, 207–11).

6. Coughlin et al. 2007.

7. Social Security Act Section 1923(b); see also Ku and Coughlin (1995).

8. U.S. Government Accountability Office 2007c.

9. See U.S. Government Accountability Office 2007b and 2008b.

10. Ku and Coughlin 1995.

11. See table A1-3 for DSH figures for 2007 in comparison with Medicaid and CHIP measures.

12. There is clear evidence from the Massachusetts experience that expanding coverage reduces uncompensated care (Massachusetts Hospital Association 2008).

13. Sherman 1973; see Jesilow et al. (1993) for a review with a historical perspective and Sparrow (2000) for other examples.

14. Levy and Luo 2005.

15. Florida Agency for Health Care Administration 2008, 20–21.

16. Ibid., 18.

17. See, for example, U.S. General Accounting Office (2000) and U.S. Department of Health and Human Services, Office of Inspector General (2006).

18. Requirements for states are described in *Code of Federal Regulations*, 42 CFR part 455.

19. See for example, New York's list of unacceptable practices under medical assistance programs, *New York Codes Rules and Regulations*, 18 NYCRR §515.2; the list of thousands of excluded persons and entities on the website of the New York State Office of the Medicaid Inspector General, www.omig.state.ny.us; and the criteria for termination at 18 NYCRR §504.7.

20. See U.S. Government Accountability Office (2006) and U.S. Department of Health and Human Services, Centers for Medicare and Medicaid Services, Center for Medicaid and State Operations, Medicaid Integrity Group (2006).

21. U.S. Department of Health and Human Services 2008.

22. U.S. Department of Health and Human Services, Centers for Medicare and Medicaid Services, Center for Medicaid and State Operations, Medicaid Integrity Group 2008.

Part IV: Promises to Providers—Payment Policies and Strategies

1. Public Law 111-3—February 4, 2009, §506 and Title XIX (42 U.S.C. 1396 §1900).

Chapter 10: Provider Payment in a Democracy

1. Medicaid programs typically have less ability to set prices for managed care plans and may need to pay market rates for Medicaid managed care plan services.

2. *Code of Federal Regulations*, 42 CFR §447.200.

3. Ibid., §447.253 (b) (1).

4. *Wilder v. Virginia Hospital Association*, 496 U.S. 498 (1990).

5. See Coughlin and Zuckerman (2008).

6. *Code of Federal Regulations*, 42 CFR § 438.6 (c) (3).

7. Hurley and Somers 2003, 84.

8. Bailit et al. 2004.

9. Martinez and Closter 1998.

10. *District of Columbia Hospital Association v. District of Columbia*, U.S. Court of Appeals for the District of Columbia, July 21, 2000.

11. Table 2-6 shows managed care (capitation payments) accounting for only 21.6 percent of provider payments.

Chapter 11: Medicaid Payment for Provider Equity

1. Dobson et al. 2006, 31.

2. Ibid.

3. We note that diminished quality evenly spread among payers may slightly reduce what private payers are willing to pay—but only if they are able to perceive the difference in quality, which in medical care can be quite difficult to judge for small changes.

4. Zwanziger and Bameizi 2006; Zwanziger et al. 2000.

5. Vernon K. Smith (in a review of an early draft of this work) commented that he once inquired about an HMO's refusal to participate in Medicaid and found the refusal to be based on the resistance of the medical staff. He was told, "You have to understand a doctor's status depends on the status of his patients. You will never get them to accept Medicaid." Fortunately, this is not the attitude of all doctors, but it surely applies to many.

6. On physician cost-shifting and its very small magnitude, see Gruber and Rodriguez (2007).

7. This is a more reasonable assumption than one may at first perceive, as providers will tend to develop a practice style in use of resources that is supportable by the largest payment source (typically Medicare), and community standards of acceptable care may evolve to reflect this level, as well. In the long run, practice style and quality are constrained by available payment.

Chapter 12: Implementing Payment Policy

1. *Code of Federal Regulations*, 42 CFR 413.65.

2. See Paringer and McCall (1991) and Salmon et al. (1988).

3. Limited forms of competitive bidding have been tried on a demonstration basis by Medicare for durable medical equipment, but Congress seems to have grown more negative toward this approach to procuring services for Medicare beneficiaries. In July 2008, it overrode a presidential veto to pass the Medicare Improvement for Patients and Providers Act, which delayed a previously authorized implementation of competitive bidding for durable medical equipment.

4. See chapter 4.

5. Grannemann (1991) points out that direct restrictions on physician choices are largely avoided when the priority list is used to establish budgets for managed care plans rather than to make coverage rules at the procedure level.

6. Quinn (2007) provides a somewhat different perspective on evidence-based payment.

7. Kuhmerker and Hartman 2007.

8. National Health Expenditures data from U.S. Department of Health and Human Services, Centers for Medicare and Medicaid Services, Office of the Actuary 2009.

9. *Code of Federal Regulations*, 42 CFR §423.908.

10. U.S. Department of Health and Human Services, Centers for Medicare and Medicaid Services, Office of the Actuary 2009.

11. National Association of State Medicaid Directors 2006.

12. See Sparer (1998) for a discussion of federalism and safety-net providers.

Chapter 13: Gaining Control of Provider Payment

1. See *Code of Federal Regulations*, 42 CFR §413.65.

2. *Code of Federal Regulations*, 42 CFR §412.22 (h).

3. Of Medicaid, CHIP, and DSH, only DSH net transfers are not significantly correlated (negatively) with per-capita or household income, and DSH net transfers are least correlated with the poverty rate.

4. See Coughlin and Zuckerman (2003) and Coughlin and Liska (1998).

5. We focus on Medicare price relatives, not rates, particularly for hospital services, because, as noted above, providers have some ability to reclassify to obtain a higher payment based on hospital wage indexes of another (usually adjacent or nearby) geographic area.

6. A provider can be low-cost either because it is technically efficient or because it has had a comparative advantage from a productivity advantage or access to inputs at low prices or wages.

7. Cheng and Reinhardt 2008, w211.

8. See chapter 12, above.

Chapter 14: From SCHIP to CHIP—Economics, Politics, and Policy

1. Even the program's name has been a topic for debate among those with different views of the relative state and federal responsibilities for it. Although the official name remains the State Children's Health Insurance Program, the Children's Health Insurance Reauthorization Act of 2009 officially changed the program acronym from SCHIP to CHIP. This CHIP/SCHIP controversy goes back to the days of the pending original legislation in 1997, when all the Senate bills specified "CHIP" (see Judith Moore and David Smith's interview with former Senate Finance Committee staffer Julie James in Smith and Moore 2003–6), but the program became "SCHIP" in the final law after the House weighed in. Complicating things further, each state sets the name for its own program. It is CHIP in several states and SCHIP in a few, and many state programs have their own state-created names, such as PeachCare in Georgia and Dr. Dynasaur in Vermont. Kaiser Family Foundation (2007) provides a list of state program names and types.

2. See U.S. Government Accountability Office (2007a) for background on CHIP reauthorization and U.S. Congressional Research Service (2006) for description of CHIP allotments.

3. See Weil and Hill (2003) for a discussion of CHIP in the context of federal–state financing.

4. The CHIP federal matching rate for federal financial participation (FFP) is either 70 percent of the regular FFP plus thirty percentage points, or 85 percent— whichever is lower. CHIP matching rates are specified by *Code of Federal Regulations*, 42 CFR subpart F §457.622, and state allotments by §457.608. These were temporarily increased by the American Recovery and Reinvestment Act (ARRA); see Kaiser Commission on Medicaid and the Uninsured (2009c).

5. Other reasons for the cap will be discussed below.

6. *Code of Federal Regulations*, 42 CFR 457.70.

7. Pauly 2004.

8. Thorpe et al. 2001.

9. Gruber and Simon 2007.

10. The repealed Medicare Catastrophic Coverage Bill of 1988 is one notable example. See Rice, Desmond, and Gabel 1990.

11. For the allotment calculation method, see *Code of Federal Regulations*, 42 CFR 457.608, and U.S. Congressional Research Service (2006).

12. See chapter 8, above.

13. Cunningham 2003.

14. See Zuckerman and Perry (2007).

15. There might also be some taxpayer satisfaction in providing financial protection to poor people, but there are better ways to do that than with health insurance.

16. Kaiser Commission on Medicaid and the Uninsured 2009a.

Conclusion to Part V:
Implications of Subsidizing Coverage for the Near Poor

1. Grannemann and Pauly 2009.

Appendix 2: Equal-Burden-for-Equal-Benefit
Matching Rates

1. This follows an approach originally suggested in Grannemann (1980), 118–20.

References

Artiga, Samantha, and Molly O'Malley. 2005. Increasing Premiums and Cost Sharing in Medicaid and SCHIP: Recent State Experiences. Kaiser Commission on Medicaid and the Uninsured. May. http://www.kff.org/medicaid/loader.cfm?url=/commonspot/security/getfile.cfm&PageID=53261 (accessed June 24, 2009).

Arts, Wil, and Rudi Verburg. 2001. Modernisation, Solidarity and Care in Europe: The Sociologist's Tale. In *Solidarity in Health and Social Care in Europe*, ed. Ruud ter Meulen, Wil Arts, and Ruud Muffels. *P&M Philosophy and Medicine* 69:15–39. Norwell, Mass.: Kluwer Academic Publishers.

Bailit, Michael, Laurie Burgess, and Tricia Roddy. 2004. *State Budget Cuts and Medicaid Managed Care: Case Studies of Four States.* National Academy for State Health Policy. June. http://www.nashp.org/Files/MMC63_budget_cuts_in_four_states.pdf (accessed June 24, 2009).

Bergstrom, Theodore C., and Robert P. Goodman. 1973. Private Demand for Public Goods. *American Economic Review* 63 (3): 280–96.

Blendon, Robert J., Drew E. Altman, John M. Benson, Mollyann Brodie, Tami Buhr, Claudia Deane, and Sasha Buscho. Voters and Health Care Reform in the 2008 Presidential Election. *New England Journal of Medicine* 359 (19): 2050–61. http://content.nejm.org/cgi/content/full/359/19/2050. Supplementary material at http://content.nejm.org/cgi/data/NEJMsr0807717/DC1/1 (accessed April 29, 2009).

Borcherding, T., and R. Deacon. 1972. The Demand for Services of Non-Federal Governments. *American Economic Review* 62 (December): 891–901.

Brown, Jeffrey R., and Amy Finkelstein. 2008. The Interaction of Public and Private Insurance: Medicaid and the Long-Term Care Insurance Market. *American Economic Review* 98 (3): 1083–1102.

Brown, Randall S., B. L. Carlson, S. Dale, L. Foster, B. Phillips, and J. Schore. 2007. *Cash and Counseling: Improving the Lives of Medicaid Beneficiaries Who Need Personal Care or Home and Community-Based Services.* Mathematica Policy Research. August. http://www.rwjf.org/pr/product.jsp?id=37718 (accessed June 24, 2009).

——, Judith Wooldridge, Sheila Hoag, and Lorenzo Moreno. 2001. *Reforming Medicaid: The Experiences of Five Pioneering States with Mandatory Managed Care and Eligibility Expansions.* Mathematica Policy Research. April 30. http://www.mathematica-mpr.com/publications/pdfs/reformmed.pdf (accessed June 24, 2009).

Buck, Jeffrey A. 2003. Medicaid, Health Care Financing Trends, and the Future of State-Based Public Mental Health Services. *Psychiatric Services* 54 (7): 969–75.

Cheng, Tsung-Mei, and Uwe Reinhardt. 2008. Shepherding Major Health System Reforms: A Conversation with German Health Minister Ulla Schmidt. *Health Affairs Web Exclusives* 27 (3): w204–13.

Coates, Andrew, Michael Deily, Fred Elig, George Hoover, Kathy Plant, Dennis Priest, Betty Rice, and Meredith Van Pelt. 2003. *The Role of Annuities in Medicaid Financial Planning: A Survey of State Medicaid Agencies.* Washington, D.C.: American Public Human Services Association, National Association of State Medicaid Directors.

Congleton, Roger D. 2003. The Median Voter Model. In *The Encyclopedia of Public Choice*, ed. C. K. Rowley and F. Schneider. New York: Springer.

Coughlin, Teresa A., and David Liska. 1998. Changing State and Federal Payment Policies for Medicaid Disproportionate Share Hospitals. *Health Affairs* 17 (3): 118–36.

———, and Stephen Zuckerman. 2003. States' Strategies for Tapping Federal Revenues: Implications and Consequences of Medicaid Maximization. In *Federalism and State Health Policy*, ed. John Holahan, Alan Weil, and Joshua M. Wiener. Washington, D.C.: Urban Institute Press.

———. 2008. State Response to New Flexibility in Medicaid. *Milbank Quarterly* 86 (2): 209–40.

———, and Joshua McFeeters. 2007. Restoring Fiscal Integrity to Medicaid Financing. *Health Affairs* 26 (5): 1469–80.

Cunningham, Peter. 2003. SCHIP Making Progress: Increase Take-Up Contributes to Coverage Gains. *Health Affairs* 22 (4): 163–72.

Cutler, David M. 2004. *Your Money or Your Life: Strong Medicine for America's Healthcare System.* New York: Oxford University Press.

Dave, Dhaval, Sandra Decker, Robert Kaestner, and Kosali Simon. 2008. Re-examining the Effects of Medicaid Expansions for Pregnant Women. National Bureau of Economic Research. NBER Working Paper No. 14591. December.

Davidson, Stephen M., and Stephen Somers, eds. 1998. *Remaking Medicaid: Managed Care for the Public Good.* San Francisco: Jossey Bass Publishers.

Dawkins, Richard. 1989. *The Selfish Gene.* New York: Oxford University Press.

De Alteriis, Martin. 1991. A Public Health Model of Medicaid Emergency Room Use. *Health Care Financing Review* 12 (3): 15–20.

Dobson, Allen, Joan DaVanzo, and Namrata Sen. 2006. The Cost-Shift Payment "Hydraulic": Foundation, History, and Implications. *Health Affairs* 25 (1): 22–33.

Draper, Debra A., and Marsha R. Gold. 2003. Provider Risk Sharing in Medicaid Managed Care Plans. *Health Affairs* 22 (3): 159–67.

Engel, Jonathan. 2006. *Poor People's Medicine: Medicaid and American Charity Care since 1965.* Durham, N.C.: Duke University Press.

Epstein, Arnold M., and Joseph P. Newhouse. 1998. Impact of Medicaid Expansion on Early Prenatal Care and Health Outcomes. *Health Care Financing Review* 19 (4): 85–99.

Esposito, Dominick, Randall Brown, Arnold Chen, Jennifer Schore, and Rachel Shapiro. 2008. Impacts of a Disease Management Program for Dually Eligible Beneficiaries. *Health Care Financing Review* 30 (1): 27–46.

Florida Agency for Health Care Administration. 2008. *Annual Report on the State's Efforts to Control Medicaid Fraud and Abuse FY 2007–08.* December. http://ahca.myflorida.com/docs/2008_Fraud_and_%20Abuse%20Binder_signed.pdf (accessed June 25, 2009).

Fox, Patrick, Robert Newcomer, Cathleen Yordi, and Pamela Arnsberger. 2000. Lessons Learned from the Medicare Alzheimer Disease Demonstration. *Alzheimer Disease and Associated Disorders* 14 (2): 87–93.

Fredrickson, Doren D., Craig A. Molgaard, S. Edwards Dismuke, Jay S. Schukman, and Anne Walling. 2004. Understanding Frequent Emergency Room Use by Medicaid-Insured Children with Asthma: A Combined Quantitative and Qualitative Study. *Journal of the American Board of Family Practice* 17: 96–100.

Fuchs, Victor R. 1974. *Who Shall Live? Health, Economics and Social Choice.* Hackensack, N.J.: World Scientific Publishing Company.

Grabowski, David C. 2006. The Cost-Effectiveness of Noninstitutional Long-Term Care Services: Review and Synthesis of the Most Recent Evidence. *Medical Research and Review* 63 (1): 3–28.

Grannemann, Thomas W. 1979. *The Demand for Publicly Financed Medical Care: The Role of Interdependent Preferences.* Ann Arbor: University Microfilms.

———. 1980. Reforming National Health Programs for the Poor. In *National Health Insurance: What Now, What Later, What Never,* ed. Mark V. Pauly. Washington, D.C.: American Enterprise Institute.

———. 1991. Priority Setting: A Sensible Approach to Medicaid Policy? *Inquiry* 28: 300–305.

———, and Mark V. Pauly. 1983. *Controlling Medicaid Costs: Federalism, Competition, and Choice.* Washington, D.C.: American Enterprise Institute.

———, and Mark V. Pauly. 2009. *Reform Medicaid First: The Logical Initial Step of Any National Health Reform Plan.* Washington, D.C.: American Enterprise Institute.

Grogan, Colleen M., and Michael K. Gusmano. 2007. *Healthy Voices, Unhealthy Silence: Advocacy and Health Policy for the Poor.* Washington, D.C.: Georgetown University Press.

Gruber, Jonathan, and David Rodriguez. 2007. How Much Uncompensated Care Do Doctors Provide? National Bureau of Economic Research. NBER Working Paper No. 13585. November.

———, and Kosali Simon. 2007. Crowd Out Ten Years Later: Have Recent Public Insurance Expansions Crowded Out Private Insurance? National Bureau of Economic Research. NBER Working Paper No. 12858. January.

Heiser, K. Gabriel. 2008. *How to Protect Your Family's Assets from Devastating Nursing Home Costs: Medicaid Secrets.* Superior, Colo.: Phylius Press.

Hillman, A. L., M. V. Pauly, J. J. Escarce, K. Ripley, M. Gaynor, J. Clouse, and R. Ross. 1999. Financial Incentives and Drug Spending in Managed Care. *Health Affairs* 18 (2): 189–200.

Holahan, John. 2003. Variation in Health Insurance Coverage and Medical Expenditures: How Much Is Too Much? In *Federalism and State Health Policy*, ed. John Holahan, Alan Weil, and Joshua M. Wiener, 111–43. Washington, D.C.: Urban Institute Press.

———, Alan Weil, and Joshua M. Weiner, eds. 2003. *Federalism and State Health Policy*. Washington, D.C.: Urban Institute Press.

Hurley, Robert E., Deborah A. Freund, John E. Paul. 1993. *Managed Care in Medicaid: Lessons for Policy and Program Design*. Chicago: Health Administration Press.

———, and Stephen A. Somers. 2003. Medicaid and Managed Care: A Lasting Relationship? *Health Affairs* 22 (1): 77–88.

———, and Stephen Zuckerman. 2003. Medicaid Managed Care: State Flexibility in Action. In *Federalism and State Health Policy*, ed. John Holahan, Alan Weil, and Joshua M. Wiener. Washington, D.C.: Urban Institute Press.

Jacobs, Lawrence, Theodore Marmor, and Jonathan Oberlander. 1999. The Oregon Health Plan and the Political Paradox of Rationing: What Advocates and Critics Have Claimed and What Oregon Did. *Journal of Health Politics, Policy and Law* 24 (1): 161–80.

Jesilow, Paul, Henry N. Pontell, and Gilbert Geis. 1993. *Prescription for Profit: How Doctors Defraud Medicaid*. Berkeley, Calif.: University of California Press.

Johnson, Malcolm, and Lesley Cullen. 2001. Solidarity and Care in the United Kingdom. In *Solidarity in Health and Social Care in Europe*, ed. Ruud ter Meulen, Wil Arts, and Ruud Muffels, 107–31. Norwell, Mass.: Kluwer Academic Publishers.

Kaiser Commission on Medicaid and the Uninsured. 2006. *Deficit Reduction Act of 2005: Implications for Medicaid*. February. http://www.kff.org/medicaid/upload/7465.pdf (accessed July 9, 2009).

———. 2009a. Children's Health Insurance Program Reauthorization Act of 2009 (CHIPRA). *Key Facts*, publication no. 7863. February. http://www.kff.org/medicaid/upload/7863.pdf (accessed October 4, 2009).

———. 2009b. *Medicaid: A Primer, 2009: Key Information on the Nation's Health Program for Low-Income People*. January. http://www.kff.org/medicaid/upload/7334-03.pdf (accessed July 9, 2009).

———. 2009c. *American Recovery and Reinvestment Act (ARRA): Medicaid and Health Care Provisions*. http://www.kff.org/medicaid/upload/7872.pdf (accessed October 5, 2009).

Kaiser Family Foundation. 2007. CHIP Program Name and Type, 2007. statehealthfacts.org. http://www.statehealthfacts.org/comparetable.jsp?cat=4&ind=238 (accessed October 1, 2009).

———. 2009. State Health Facts searchable database. http://www.statehealthfacts.org/index.jsp (accessed October 28, 2009).

Kaye, Neva. 2005. Medicaid Managed Care: Looking Forward, Looking Backward. National Academy for State Health Policy. June. http://www.nashp.org/Files/mmc_guide_final_draft_6-16.pdf (accessed July 9, 2009).

Kemper, Peter. 1988. The Evaluation of the National Long Term Care Demonstration: Overview of the Findings. *Health Services Research* 23 (1): 161–74.

————, Robert Applebaum, and Margaret Harrigan. 1987. Community Care Demonstrations: What Have We Learned? *Health Care Financing Review* 8 (4): 87–100.

Kotter, John P. 2008. *A Sense of Urgency*. Watertown, Mass.: Harvard Business Press.

Ku, Leighton, and Teresa Coughlin. 1995. Medicaid Disproportionate Share and Other Special Financing Programs. *Health Care Financing Review* 16 (3): 27–54.

Kuhmerker, Katheryn, and Thomas Hartman. 2007. *Pay-For-Performance in State Medicaid Programs: A Survey of State Medicaid Directors and Programs.* Commonwealth Fund. April. http://www.commonwealthfund.org/Content/Publications/Fund-Reports/2007/Apr/Pay-for-Performance-in-State-Medicaid-Programs—A-Survey-of-State-Medicaid-Directors-and-Programs.aspx (accessed July 9, 2009).

Levy, Clifford J., and Michael Luo. 2005. New York Medicaid Fraud May Reach into Billions. *New York Times.* July 18.

Lewin Group. 2004. Medicaid Managed Care Cost Savings—A Synthesis of Fourteen Studies. July. http://www.ahipresearch.org/pdfs/MedicaidCostSavings.pdf (accessed September 29, 2009).

Lipson, Debra, James M. Verdier, and Lynn Quincy. 2007. *Leading the Way? Maine's Initial Experience in Expanding Coverage through Dirigo Health Reforms.* Mathematica Policy Research Inc. December. http://www.hcfo.net/DirigoReport.pdf (accessed July 9, 2009).

Lischko, Amy M., Sara S. Bachman, and Alyssa Vangeli. 2009. The Massachusetts Commonwealth Health Insurance Connector: Structure and Functions. Commonwealth Fund issue brief. May. http://www.commonwealthfund.org/~/media/Files/Publications/Issue%20Brief/2009/May/Issue%20Brief.pdf (accessed October 27, 2009).

Lovell, Michael C. 1978. Spending for Education: The Exercise of Public Choice. *Review of Economics and Statistics* 60 (4): 487–95.

Madsen, Elaine A., Richard J. Tunney, George Fieldman, Henry C. Plotkin, Robin I. Dunbar, Jean-Marie Richardson, and David McFarland. 2006. Kinship and Altruism: A Cross Cultural Experimental Study. *British Journal of Psychology* 98 (2): 339–59.

Martinez, Marie, and Elizabeth Closter. 1998. Public Health Departments Adapt to Medicaid Managed Care. Issue Brief No. 16. Center for Studying Health System Change. November. http://www.hschange.com/CONTENT/65/ (accessed July 9, 2009).

Massachusetts Hospital Association. 2008. Hospital Uncompensated Care Trends and Health Care Reform. February 13.

McCall, Nelda, D. Henton, M. Crane, S. Haber, D. Freund, and W. Wrightson. 1985. Evaluation of the Arizona Health Care Cost Containment System (AHCCCS): The First Eighteen Months. *Health Care Financing Review* 7 (2): 77–88.

McKie, John, and Jeff Richardson. 2003. The Rule of Rescue. *Social Science and Medicine* 56 (12): 2407–19.

Mechanic, David. 2006. *The Truth about Health Care Reform: Why Reform Is Not Working in America.* New Brunswick, N.J.: Rutgers University Press.

Menzel, Paul T. 1983. *Medical Costs, Moral Choices: A Philosophy of Health Care Economics in America.* New Haven, Conn.: Yale University Press.

Meulen, Ruud ter, Wil Arts, and Ruud Muffels, eds. 2001. *Solidarity in Health and Social Care in Europe*, 1–11. Norwell, Mass.: Kluwer Academic Publishers.

Miller, Vic, and Andy Schneider. 2004. *The Medicaid Matching Formula: Policy Considerations and Options for Modification.* AARP. No. 2004-09. September. http://assets.aarp.org/rgcenter/health/2004_09_formula.pdf (accessed July 9, 2009).

Moore, Judith, and David G. Smith. 2005. Legislating Medicaid: Considering its Origins. *Health Care Financing Review* 27 (2): 45–52. http://www.cms.hhs.gov/HealthCareFinancingReview/downloads/05-06Winpg45.pdf (July 9, 2009).

National Association of State Medicaid Directors and Health Management Associates. 2007. *2007 State Perspectives: Medicaid Pharmacy Policies and Practices.* http://www.nasmd.org/resources/docs/PharmacyRpt1107.pdf (accessed October 27, 2009).

———, and Avalere Health LLC. 2006. State Perspectives on Emerging Medicaid Pharmacy Policies and Practices. November. http://www.nasmd.org/resources/docs/State_Perspectives-Emerging_Medicaid_Pharmacy_PP.pdf (accessed September 29, 2009).

New Hampshire Department of Health and Human Services. Office of Medicaid Business and Policy. 2005. Avoidable Hospital Costs in New Hampshire Medicaid: Emergency Department and Inpatient Services. Working paper by Thomas W. Grannemann. March 3.

Newman, David H. 2008. *Hippocrates' Shadow.* New York: Scribner.

Paringer, Lynn, and Nelda McCall. 1991. How Competitive Is Competitive Bidding? *Health Affairs.* Winter. http://content.healthaffairs.org/cgi/reprint/10/4/220.pdf (accessed July 9, 2009).

Pauly, Mark V. 2004. Compromises and Tradeoffs in Universal Health Insurance Plans. *Journal of Law, Medicine, and Ethics* 32 (3): 465–73.

———, and Blavin, Frederick, 2008. Moral Hazard in Insurance, Value-Based Cost Sharing, and the Benefits of Blissful Ignorance. *Journal of Health Economics* 27 (6): 1407–17.

Quinn, Kevin. 2007. How Much is Enough? An Evidence-Based Framework for Setting Medicaid Payment Rates. *Inquiry* 44 (7): 247–56.

Rice, Thomas, Katherine Desmond, and Jon Gabel. 1990. The Medicare Catastrophic Coverage Act: A Post-Mortem. *Health Affairs.* Fall. http://content.healthaffairs.org/cgi/reprint/9/3/75.pdf (July 9, 2009).

Ross, Donna Cohen, Aleya Horn, Robin Rudowitz, and Caryn Marks. 2008. *Determining Income Eligibility in Children's Health Coverage Programs: How States Use Disregards in Children's Medicaid and SCHIP.* Kaiser Commission on Medicaid and the Uninsured. May. http://www.kff.org/medicaid/upload/7776.pdf (July 9, 2009).

Rousseau, David, and Andy Schneider. 2004. *Current Issues in Medicaid Financing: An Overview of IGTs, UPLs, and DSH.* Kaiser Commission on Medicaid and the Uninsured. April. http://www.kff.org/medicaid/upload/Current-Issues-in-Medicaid-Financing-An-Overview-of-IGTs-UPLs-and-DSH.pdf.

Salmon, J. Warren, Mary C. Ayesse, and H. Stephen Lieber. 1988. Reducing Inpatient Hospital Costs: An Attempt at Medicaid Reform in Illinois. *Journal of Health Politics, Policy and Law* 13 (1): 103–27.

Schneider, Andy, with Risa Elias, Rachel Garfield, David Rousseau, and Victoria Wachino. 2002. *The Medicaid Resource Book.* Kaiser Commission on Medicaid and the Uninsured. July. http://www.kff.org/medicaid/loader.cfm?url=/commonspot/security/getfile.cfm&PageID=14266 (accessed July 9, 2009).

Sherman, William. 1973. Medicaid Probe: A Cold? Take Three Doctors Every Hour. *New York Daily News.* January 23, 7, 35.

Smith, David G., and Judith D. Moore. 2006. CMS Oral History Project, Centers for Medicare and Medicaid Services. http://www.cms.hhs.gov/History/Downloads/cmsoralhistory.pdf (accessed September 30, 2009).

———. 2008. *Medicaid Politics and Policy 1965–2007.* New Piscataway, N.J.: Transaction Publishers.

Smith, Vernon K., Terrisca Des Jardins, and Karin A. Peterson. 2000. Exemplary Practices in Primary Care Case Management: A Review of State Medicaid PCCM Programs. Princeton, N.J.: Center for Health Care Strategies.

———, Kathleen Gifford, Eileen Ellis, Robin Rudowitz, Molly O'Malley, and Caryn Marks. 2008. *Headed for a Crunch: An Update on Medicaid Spending, Coverage and Policy Heading into an Economic Downturn—Results from a 50-State Medicaid Budget Survey for State Fiscal Years 2008 and 2009.* Kaiser Commission on Medicaid and the Uninsured. September. http://www.kff.org/medicaid/upload/7815.pdf (accessed July 9, 2009).

Sparer, Michael S. 1996. *Medicaid and the Limits of State Health Reform.* Philadelphia: Temple University Press.

———. 1998. Safety Net Providers and the New Medicaid: Choices and Challenges. In *Medicaid and Devolution: A View from the States*, ed. Frank J. Thompson and John J. Dilulio. Washington, D.C.: Brookings Institution.

Sparrow, Malcolm K. 2000. *License to Steal: How Fraud Bleeds America's Health Care System.* Boulder, Colo.: Westview Press.

Stevens, Robert, and Rosemary Stevens. 2003. *Welfare Medicine in America: A Case Study of Medicaid.* Piscataway, N.J.: Transaction Publishers.

Stiglitz, J. E. 1974. The Demand for Education in Public and Private Schools. *Journal of Public Economics* 3 (4): 349–85.

Thompson, Karen MacDonald, and Doris F. Glick. 1999. Cost Analysis of Emergency Room Use by Low-Income Patients. *Nursing Economics* 42 (8): 142–48, 155.

Thornton, Craig, Shari Miller Dunstan, and Peter Kemper. 1988. The Effect of Channeling on Health and Long Term Care Costs. *Health Services Research* 23 (1): 129–42.

———, Gina Livermore, Thomas Fraker, David Stapleton, Bonnie O'Day, David Wittenburg, Robert Weathers, Nanette Goodman, Tim Silva, Emily Sama Martin, Jesse Gregory, Debra Wright, and Arif Mamun. 2007. *Evaluation of the Ticket to Work Program: Assessment of Post-Rollout Implementation and Early Impacts.* Mathematica Policy Research. May. http://www.mathematica-mpr.com/publications/PDFs/TTWpostrolloutvol1.pdf (July 9, 2009).

Thorpe, Kenneth E., Jennifer Flome, and Peter Joski. 2001. The Distribution of Health Insurance Coverage among Pregnant Women, 1999. Paper prepared for the March of Dimes. April. http://www.marchofdimes.com/files/2001FinalThorpeReport.pdf (accessed July 9, 2009).

Tresch, Richard. 1974. Estimating State Expenditure Functions: An Empirical Test of Time Series Informational Content of Cross Section Estimates. *Public Finance* 29 (3–4): 370–85.

———. 1975 "State Governments and the Welfare System: An Econometric Analysis." *Southern Economic Journal* 42 (1): 33–43.

U.S. Boards of Trustees of the Federal Hospital Insurance and Federal Supplementary Medical Insurance Trust Funds. 2008. *2008 Annual Report.* March 25. http://www.cms.hhs.gov/ReportsTrustFunds/downloads/tr2008.pdf (accessed July 20, 2009).

U.S. Census Bureau. 2006. Annual Demographic Survey March Supplement. POV 46 Poverty Status by State. http://pubdb3.census.gov/macro/032005/pov/new46_001_100125.htm (accessed October 28, 2009).

———. 2007. 2007 Annual Survey of State Government Tax Collections. http://www.census.gov/govs/statetax/historical_data_2007.html (accessed October 18, 2009).

———. 2008a. *Current Population Survey.* 2008. Annual Social and Economic Supplement. State Median Income. http://www.census.gov/hhes/www/income/statemedfaminc.html (accessed October 4, 2009).

———. 2008b. *Current Population Survey.* 2008. Annual Social and Economic Supplement. Table POV 46: Poverty Status by State: 2007. http://www.census.gov/hhes/www/macro/032008/pov/new46_100125_01.htm (accessed October 4, 2009).

U.S. Congressional Research Service. 2006. *SCHIP Original Allotments: Description and Analysis.* By Chris L. Peterson. October 31. Order code RL 33666. http://www.ahipresearch.org/PDFs/RL33366.pdf (accessed September 30, 2009).

U.S. Department of Commerce. Bureau of Economic Analysis. 2009. Interactive Access To National Income and Product Accounts Tables. http://www.bea.gov/national/nipaweb/Index.asp (accessed October 20, 2009).

U.S. Department of Health and Human Services. 2009. Federal Medical Assistance Percentages or Federal Financial Participation in State Assistance Expenditures FMAP. http://aspe.hhs.gov/health/fmap.htm (accessed November 29, 2009).

————. 2008. *Report to Congress on the Medicaid Integrity Program for Fiscal Year 2007.* By Michael O. Leavitt. http://www.cms.hhs.gov/DeficitReductionAct/Downloads/fy07reporttocongress.pdf (accessed September 30, 2009).

————. Centers for Disease Control and Prevention. National Center for Health Statistics. 2008. State, Regional, and National Estimates of Health Insurance Coverage for People under 65 Years of Age: National Health Interview Survey, 2004–2006. By Robin A. Cohen and Diane M. Makuc. In *National Health Statistics Reports.* June 19. http://www.cdc.gov/nchs/data/nhsr/nhsr001.pdf (accessed September 30, 2009).

————. Centers for Medicare and Medicaid Services. 2007. Medicaid Statistical Information System State Summary FY2004. Fiscal Year 2004 National MSIS Tables. http://www.cms.hhs.gov/MedicaidDataSourcesGenInfo/downloads/MSISTables2004.pdf (accessed October 28, 2009).

————. Centers for Medicare and Medicaid Services. Center for Medicaid and State Operations. Medicaid Integrity Group. 2006. *Comprehensive Medicaid Integrity Plan of the Medicaid Integrity Program, FY 2006–2010.* July. http://www.cms.hhs.gov/DeficitReductionAct/Downloads/CMIP%20Initial%20July%202006.pdf (accessed July 9, 2009).

————. Centers for Medicare and Medicaid Services. Center for Medicaid and State Operations. Medicaid Integrity Group. 2008. *Comprehensive Medicaid Integrity Plan of the Medicaid Integrity Program, FY 2008–2012.* June. http://www.cms.hhs.gov/DeficitReductionAct/Downloads/fy08cmip.pdf (accessed July 9, 2009).

————. Centers for Medicare and Medicaid Services. 2008. CMS Data Compendium, 2008. http://www.cms.hhs.gov/DataCompendium/16_2008_Data_Compendium.asp (accessed October 4, 2009).

————. Centers for Medicare and Medicaid Services. Office of the Actuary. 2008. *2008 Actuarial Report on the Financial Outlook for Medicaid.* October. http://www.cms.hhs.gov/ActuarialStudies/downloads/MedicaidReport2008.pdf (accessed September 29, 2009).

————. Centers for Medicare and Medicaid Services. Office of the Actuary. 2009. *National Health Expenditures by Type of Service and Source of Funds, Calendar Year 1960–2007.* http://www.cms.hhs.gov/NationalHealthExpendData/02_NationalHealthAccountsHistorical.asp (accessed September 29, 2009).

————. Office of Inspector General. 2006. *Review of School-Based Administrative Costs in Minnesota from July 1, 2003 through June 30, 2004.* Report no. A-05-05-00040. September. http://oig.hhs.gov/oas/reports/region5/50500040.pdf (accessed September 29, 2009).

U.S. General Accounting Office. 1983. *Changing Medicaid Formula Can Improve Distribution of Funds to States.* GAO/GGD-83-27. March 9. http://archive.gao.gov/ f0102/120787.pdf (accessed September 30, 2009).

———. 1997. *Medicaid Matching Formula: Effects of Need Indicators on New York's Funding.* GAO/HEHS-97-152R. June 9. http://archive.gao.gov/paprpdf1/158827.pdf (accessed September 30, 2009).

———. 2000. *Medicaid in Schools: Improper Payments Demand Improvements in HCFA Oversight.* GAO/HEHS/OSI-00-69. April. http://www.gao.gov/archive/2000/ h600069.pdf (accessed September 30, 2009).

———. 2004. *Medicaid: Intergovernmental Transfers Have Facilitated State Financing Schemes.* GAO-04-574T. March 18. http://www.gao.gov/new.items/d04574t.pdf (accessed September 30, 2009).

U.S. Government Accountability Office. 2006. *Medicaid Integrity: Implementation of New Program Provides Opportunities for Federal Leadership to Combat Fraud, Waste, and Abuse.* GAO-06-578T. March 28. http://www.gao.gov/new.items/d06578t.pdf (accessed September 30, 2009).

———. 2007a. *Children's Health Insurance: States' SCHIP Enrollment and Spending Experiences and Considerations for Reauthorization.* GAO-07-558T. March 1. http://www.gao.gov/new.items/d07558t.pdf (accessed September 30, 2009).

———. 2007b. *Medicaid Financing: Federal Oversight Initiative Is Consistent with Medicaid Payment Principles but Needs Greater Transparency.* GAO-07-214. March. http://www.gao.gov/new.items/d07214.pdf (accessed September 30, 2009).

———. 2007c. *Medicaid Financing: Long-Standing Concerns about Inappropriate State Arrangements Support Need for Improved Federal Oversight.* Statement of Dr. Marjorie Kanof. GAO-08-255T. November 1. http://www.gao.gov/new.items/d08255t.pdf (accessed September 30, 2009).

———. 2008a. *Medicaid Demonstration Waivers: Recent HHS Approvals Continue to Raise Cost and Oversight Concerns.* GAO-08-87. January. http://www.gao.gov/new. items/d0887.pdf (accessed September 30, 2009).

———. 2008b. *Medicaid Financing: Long-Standing Concerns about Inappropriate State Arrangements Support Need for Improved Federal Oversight.* Statement of James Cosgrove. GAO-08-650T. April 3. http://www.gao.gov/new.items/d08255t.pdf (accessed September 30, 2009).

U.S. Internal Revenue Service. Statistics of Income Division. 2007. SOI Tax Stats Historic Table 2. http://www.irs.gov/taxstats/article/0,,id=171535,00.html (accessed October 18, 2009).

U.S. Office of Management and Budget. 2008. *Budget of the United States Government, Fiscal Year 2009.* http://www.gpoaccess.gov/usbudget (October 9, 2009).

Vermont Joint Fiscal Office. 2004. Effects of Medicaid Premiums on Program Enrollment: Preliminary Analysis. By Steve Kappel. April 8.

Wang, Yize, and Mark Pauly. 2005. Spillover Effects of Restrictive Drug Formularies and Physician Prescribing Behavior. *Journal of Economics and Management Strategy* 14 (3): 755–73.

Weil, Alan. 2003. There's Something about Medicaid. *Health Affairs* 22 (1): 13–30.

———, and Ian Hill. 2003. The State Children's Health Insurance Program: A New Approach to Federalism. In *Federalism and State Health Policy*, ed. John Holahan, Alan Weil, and Joshua M. Wiener, 293–323. Washington, D.C.: Urban Institute Press.

Weissert, William G. 1985. Seven Reasons Why It Is So Difficult to Make Home and Community Based Long-Term Care Cost-Effective. *Health Services Research* 20 (4): 423–33.

Williams, Robert M. 1996. The Costs of Visits to Emergency Departments. *New England Journal of Medicine* 334 (10): 642–46.

Wilson, Edward O. 1980. *Sociobiology: The Abridged Edition*. Cambridge, Mass.: Belknap Press of Harvard University Press.

Winnett, Robert. 2008. Patients "Should Not Expect NHS to Save Their Life If It Costs Too Much." *Telegraph.co.uk*. August 13. http://www.telegraph.co.uk/news/2547393/Patients-should-not-expect-NHS-to-save-their-life-if-it-costs-too-much.html (accessed July 9, 2009).

Zuckerman, Stephen, Niall Brennan, and Alshadye Yemane. 2002. Has Medicaid Managed Care Affected Beneficiary Access and Use? *Inquiry* 39 (3): 221–42.

———, and Cynthia Perry. 2007. Concerns about Parents Dropping Employer Coverage to Enroll in SCHIP Overlook Issues of Affordability. Urban Institute. September. http://www.urban.org/UploadedPDF/411555_schip_overlook.pdf (accessed July 9, 2009).

Zwanziger, Jack, and Anil Bamezai. 2006. Evidence of Cost Shifting in California Hospitals. *Health Affairs* 25 (1): 197–203.

———, Glenn Melnick, and Anil Bamezai. 2000. Can Cost Shifting Continue in a Price Competitive Environment? *Health Economics* 9 (3): 211–226.

Index

About the Authors

Thomas W. Grannemann is Associate Regional Administrator for Medicare Financial Management and Fee for Service Operations in the Boston Regional Office of the U.S. Centers for Medicare and Medicaid Services. His work has included research on Medicaid financing, hospital costs, long-term care, physician productivity, provider payment methods, and workers' compensation. Previously, Dr. Grannemann served as chief of the Bureau of Economic Analysis and Rate Setting Policy with the State of New Hampshire Office of Medicaid Business and Policy. Dr. Grannemann taught health economics, health policy, and public finance at the University of Colorado's Graduate School of Public Affairs and managed his own research and consulting business, Andover Economic Evaluation. For several years he was a senior economist at Mathematica Policy Research Inc., where his work involved design and analysis of major national Medicare and Medicaid demonstration projects. He is the author of numerous publications on Medicaid, Medicare, and health care reform topics. Thomas Grannemann holds a PhD in economics from Northwestern University. His e-mail address is TGrannemann@AndoverEcon.com.

Mark V. Pauly is Bendheim Professor in the Department of Health Care Management, professor of health care management, insurance and risk management, and business and public policy at the Wharton School, and professor of economics in the School of Arts and Sciences at the University of Pennsylvania. He is also an adjunct scholar of the American Enterprise Institute. Dr. Pauly is an active member of the Institute of Medicine and serves on the national advisory committees for the National Institutes of Health National Center for Research Resources and the National Academy of Sciences' Committee to Study the Veterinary Workforce. He is a coeditor in chief of the *International Journal of Health Care Finance and Economics* and an associate editor of the *Journal of Risk and Uncertainty*. A former commissioner on the Physician Payment Review Commission, Dr. Pauly has also served on the advisory committee to the Agency for Health Care Research and Quality and the Medicare Technical Advisory Panel.